The Sons of
Westwood

SPORT AND SOCIETY

Series Editors
Randy Roberts
Aram Goudsouzian

Founding Editors
Benjamin G. Rader
Randy Roberts

A list of books in the series
appears at the end of this book.

The Sons of
Westwood

John Wooden, UCLA, and the Dynasty
That Changed College Basketball

JOHN MATTHEW SMITH

UNIVERSITY OF ILLINOIS PRESS

Urbana, Chicago, and Springfield

All photos, unless otherwise noted, are from the Los Angeles
Times Photographic Archive, Department of Special
Collections, Charles E. Young Research Library, UCLA.

Library of Congress Cataloging-in-Publication Data
Smith, John Matthew.
The sons of Westwood : John Wooden, UCLA,
and the dynasty that changed college basketball /
John Matthew Smith.
    pages   cm
Includes bibliographical references and index.
ISBN 978-0-252-03777-1 (hardcover : alk. paper) —
ISBN 978-0-252-07973-3 (paperback : alk. paper) —
ISBN 978-0-252-09505-4 (e-book)
1. UCLA Bruins (Basketball team)—History.
2. University of California, Los Angeles—Basketball—History.
3. Wooden, John, 1910–2010.
4. Basketball coaches—United States. I. Title.
GV885.43.U423S58   2013
796.323'630979494—dc23   2012045100

To my parents, Jay and Kim

Contents

Illustrations follow page 152

Preface

Time was running out. The old man everyone called "Coach" was dying. John Wooden had lived for nearly a century, spending most of his life teaching basketball and life lessons. As he approached his one-hundredth birthday, people often asked the shrinking little man in a wheelchair if he feared dying. "I am not afraid of death," he answered barely above a whisper. "I am very much at peace with myself." He had lived a blessed life, touched by his children, grandchildren, great-grandchildren, and the players whom he had coached at the University of California–Los Angeles (UCLA). Wooden's peace of mind derived from his faith, a belief that he would be reunited with his beloved wife, Nell, who had passed away in 1985 after fifty-three years of marriage. The memory of Nell, his first and only true love, inspired him to recite a poem penned by Swen Nater, one of his former players:

> Once I was afraid of dying.
> Terrified of ever-lying.
> Petrified of leaving family, home, and friends.
> Thoughts of absence from my dear ones,
> Drew a melancholy tear once.
> And a lonely, dreadful fear of when life ends.
> But those days are long behind me;
> Fear of leaving does not bind me.
> And departure does not host a single care.
> Peace does comfort as I ponder,
> A reunion in the Yonder,
> With my dearest who is waiting for me there.[1]

When Kareem Abdul-Jabbar learned that Wooden was fatally ill and had checked into the Ronald Reagan UCLA Medical Center, he immediately canceled his travel plans in Europe and rushed home to Los Angeles. On the long plane ride home, he thought about how much Wooden meant to him and how so much had changed since they first met in 1965 during Abdul-Jabbar's recruiting trip at UCLA. The two men came to California from completely different worlds. Wooden, a bespectacled, middle-aged white man, grew up in small-town rural Indiana. He looked liked the former English teacher or Protestant church deacon he was. At the time, Abdul-Jabbar was still known as Lew Alcindor, the most famous high school recruit in the nation. The skinny, seven-foot-one black teenager came of age on the politically charged streets of Harlem. Despite their differences in age, race, and social experiences, basketball helped bridge the cultural divide between them. Together, the most dominant player in history and the most successful coach in the country would redefine college basketball's import in American culture.[2]

After an anxious flight home, Abdul-Jabbar drove directly from the airport to the hospital, hoping to see his old coach one last time. Standing near the hospital bed, he could see that Wooden was heavily sedated, frail and weak. He was not even sure if Wooden knew that he was there. Abdul-Jabbar paused for a moment, struggling to accept that his coach, his teacher, would not be alive much longer. Shortly thereafter, he said his final good-bye. About three hours later, on June 4, 2010, Wooden took his final breath.[3]

Three weeks after he passed away, more than four thousand people attended a public memorial in his honor at Pauley Pavilion, an arena that Wooden had built into a monument of unprecedented basketball glory. Looking up at the rafters, the audience could see multiple royal-blue national championship banners. In twelve seasons, from 1964 to 1975, Wooden's teams won ten national titles, including seven consecutively. In that period, UCLA finished four seasons undefeated, setting numerous records. During one three-year stretch, the Bruins won eighty-eight consecutive games. What is most impressive about UCLA's championship run, perhaps, is that Wooden's teams never lost a national title game. For more than a decade, the UCLA dynasty defined college basketball.

Fans, friends, and family paid tribute to Wooden for nearly two hours. Everyone had a story to tell. Former players shared their favorite memories of Coach, laughing and shedding tears. Dudley Rutherford, senior pastor of Shepherd of the Hills Church in San Fernando Valley, gave a moving speech. Rutherford spoke of Wooden's religious faith, kindness, and his passion for teaching. "Every person in attendance," he said, "you are a testament to his ability to influence lives."[4]

During his twenty-seven seasons at UCLA, Wooden influenced the lives of hundreds of players. The very best players in school history gathered at Pauley Pavilion for the memorial. Walt Hazzard, Gail Goodrich, Keith Erickson, Lynn Shackelford, Mike Warren, Henry Bibby, Keith (Jamaal) Wilkes, Sidney Wicks, Dave Meyers, Marques Johnson, Bill Walton, Abdul-Jabbar, and many others appeared courtside. These men, whom Wooden once called "his boys," had aged considerably since their playing days. Their bodies once lean, lithe, and active had become softer and heavier. Back pain and aching joints slowed many of them. Most of the former players mentioned how their relationship with Coach Wooden had changed after they graduated. "The real relationship began after we left basketball," said Shackelford, a starter on three national title teams. "He was always our coach but he became our friend, a person we could trust and rely on to be there."[5]

Looking back on their time at UCLA, the players commented that they did not always appreciate what Wooden had tried to teach them. There was no question that the players respected him when they were younger, but they were not always interested in his lectures on discipline, sacrifice, and hard work. For these young men in their late teens and early twenties, Wooden appeared quaint, from a generation that did not understand them. One player described him as "kind of a square." In an age of political unrest and youthful liberation, when college students questioned American institutions and established authorities, Wooden's message often fell on deaf ears. Andy Hill, a reserve on three national championship teams, admitted, "I just tuned him out. I wasn't listening. *No one,*" he said emphatically, "was listening."[6]

O

The Sons of Westwood: John Wooden, UCLA, and the Dynasty That Changed College Basketball is a narrative history of the most significant college basketball program at a pivotal moment in American history. On one level, it tells the story of how UCLA dominated college basketball during the 1960s and 1970s, when the sport became deeply inscribed into our national culture. On another level, it weaves together a story of sports and politics in an era of social and cultural upheaval, a time when college students and college athletes joined the civil rights movement, demonstrated against the Vietnam War, and rejected the dominant Cold War culture. This is the story of America's culture wars played out on the basketball court by college basketball's most famous coach and some of its greatest players.[7]

The UCLA dynasty transformed college basketball from a regional pastime into a national spectacle, ushering the sport into its modern age. The Bruins' racially integrated teams played exciting basketball, emphasizing a dynamic up-tempo offense and a gambling pressing defense—a style of play that revolutionized the sport. In the 1960s, when Los Angeles emerged as a national media center, UCLA basketball evolved into a highly commercialized brand of entertainment for television networks, the National Collegiate Athletic Association (NCAA), and the university. As a cultural attraction, the dynasty shaped the national identity of UCLA—a university that many considered nothing more than a provincial college when Wooden arrived in Westwood in 1948.

The Sons of Westwood captures the momentous changes in sports and in California. In the aftermath of World War II, California represented a microcosm of America's postwar culture. Like much of the rest of the country, the state invested some of the surplus wealth from a wartime economy into building and expanding its universities in order to admit thousands of new students. The result was more than a cohort; rather, it engendered an entire generation that not only redefined the social and political landscape of America's campuses but also shaped the popularity of college basketball. As millions of baby boomers attended and graduated from universities all across country, the audience for college basketball swelled. With rising student enrollments, the construction of bigger arenas on campus, and more games broadcast on television, college basketball became a salient feature of the American experience.

In the 1960s and 1970s, California was a politically schizophrenic state, a battleground between Reagan Republicans on the Right and Berkeley beatniks on the Left. On California's campuses, students, faculty, and administrators argued over free speech, civil rights, and political demonstrations. As the war in Vietnam escalated, student protests, sit-ins, and confrontations with authorities occurred with increasing regularity in Westwood. Some UCLA basketball players responded to the social turmoil by rejecting the values prescribed by the dominant sports culture. College athletes were supposed to respect authority, honor old traditions, and conform to conservative political boundaries. Suddenly, for the first time in American history, the critics of this culture included a substantial number of college athletes, including UCLA basketball players.

When Lew Alcindor and Bill Walton, the most famous college basketball players of their generation, spoke out against racism, poverty, and the Vietnam War, they carved out a new role for athletes, compelling the public to view their actions on and off the court through a political lens. This Athletic Revolution represented a significant period in American history not only because college athletes enjoyed a platform from which they could make political statements, but also because conservative coaches like Wooden, as well as administrators, journalists, alumni, and fans, resisted the social and cultural changes taking place on the court and around the country. These contests mark the politicization of college sport in America.[8]

While students and college athletes rebelled against authority, John Wooden emerged as a cultural icon, a symbol of moral leadership during America's moral crisis. At the height of his success, he possessed a reputation and influence unequaled by any other coaching figure in America. His supporters glorified him as a champion of discipline, character, and traditional values. For many people, he represented an ideal leader whose unquestioned authority reminded the public of a nostalgic past when America was a winner, strong, unified, and committed to order.

O

During the Wooden memorial, UCLA players, alumni, and fans sat beneath the dimmed lights of Pauley Pavilion. A spotlight shining over a blue-cushioned seat behind the team bench drew everyone's attention.

The empty chair, section 103B, row 2, seat 1, was Wooden's. For years he sat there watching UCLA games as a fan. The vacant seat symbolized the end of an era and served as a reminder that Wooden's legacy lives on. Every March, during the NCAA Tournament, when fans and writers discuss the greatest teams and coaches in history, the conversation always begins with UCLA and Wooden. When alumni, students, and tourists walk through the Westwood campus, few ever leave without visiting the John Wooden exhibit at the UCLA Athletics Hall of Fame. There they see trophies, plaques, jerseys, and photographs commemorating the dynasty. Throughout the country, motivational speakers, corporate executives, and teachers distribute copies of his Pyramid of Success, a blueprint for achievement that many have applied to life beyond the court. Aspiring to be more like Wooden, high school basketball coaches study his teaching philosophy and quote him during practice. And whenever UCLA sells out Pauley Pavilion, one chair in section 103B, row 2, will forever remain unoccupied. No one will ever sit in Wooden's seat again because no one could ever take his place.

Acknowledgments

This book, and my career as a historian, has been shaped and influenced by great teachers. Looking back, my interest in John Wooden began when I was an undergraduate, studying to become a teacher myself. As a lifelong basketball fan and aspiring teacher, I turned to Coach Wooden's little blue book of wisdom, *Wooden: A Lifetime of Observations and Reflections On and Off the Court.* I took copious notes on everything Wooden wrote about teaching, coaching, and self-improvement. I did not know it at the time, but reading Wooden's maxims stuck with me; they became part of how I saw myself as a student and as a teacher. I never had the chance to meet Coach Wooden, but I hope that my book tells his life story in a way that he would appreciate.

I did not know that I would become a historian until I met Pero Dagbovie at Michigan State University. He showed me that I could write about the two subjects I love most: history and sports. I will never forget how he encouraged me to always do my best. Lucky for me, he was the best professor I ever had at MSU. At Western Michigan University, Mitch Kachun's mentorship helped me develop into a professional historian. Mitch always showed great enthusiasm for my work and took a genuine interest in me as a student and as a person. Thanks, Mitch.

I owe a special debt of thanks to Randy Roberts, my major professor at Purdue University. In every way, Randy has influenced how I see myself as a historian. More than anyone else, Randy helped me conceptualize the book, shape its outline, and refine the writing. My name may be on the cover of the book, but Randy's imprint is on every page. I am forever grateful for what Randy taught me, but most of all, I am thankful for his friendship and the generosity he and his wife, Marjie, have shown me.

I am especially grateful to Aram Goudsouzian. In addition to advising about a dozen graduate students of his own at the University of Memphis, Aram became a mentor to me as well. His outstanding biography of Bill Russell influenced my entire vision of this project. Aram pushed me to become a better writer and a more thoughtful historian. Thanks for your encouragement and friendship, Aram.

My professors and fellow graduate students in the Department of History at Purdue University offered tremendous professional and personal support. Professors Darren Dochuk, Nancy Gabin, and Jim Farr challenged me in graduate seminars and in the writing of my dissertation. Ron Johnson and I set numerous records for three-hour lunches discussing our projects. Ron's genuine enthusiasm for my work energized me throughout the writing process. Eric Hall read every chapter of the dissertation, offering suggestions that helped me clarify my ideas and improve the writing. In the process of revising the dissertation into a manuscript, Andrew Smith provided constructive criticisms of many chapters. In support of my project, a Woodman Travel Grant from the Purdue Department of History helped finance a research trip to UCLA. The Purdue Research Foundation funded me for a summer, and the Purdue Graduate School generously provided financial support for an entire year with the Winifred Beatrice Bilsland Dissertation Fellowship.

Throughout the research process, many people offered their time and assistance. At UCLA, archivists Charlotte Brown and Monique Sugimoto helped me locate critical documents and answered numerous questions about the history of UCLA. At the UCLA Special Collections, Simon Elliott worked with me to select many of the photographs for the book. The UCLA Special Collections also provided copies of oral histories. Anyone who writes about the history of American sports should visit the University of Notre Dame's Special Collections. Curator George Rugg offered invaluable assistance there, helping me find old basketball magazines, game programs, and media guides. Indiana State University archivist Susan Davis sent me a stack of news clippings related to John Wooden's early coaching career. Kevin Walker, the son of Indiana State player Clarence Walker, generously shared his father's diary with me. Lisa Greer Douglass and Ellen Summers were especially helpful at the National Collegiate Athletic Association in Indianapolis. The Interlibrary Loan Department at Purdue University handled my requests with incredible efficiency and kindness.

The most enjoyable aspect of writing this book was conducting interviews with former UCLA players. Deep thanks to everyone who agreed to talk with me, especially Kenny Booker, Dwight Chapin, Denny Crum, John Ecker, Eddie Einhorn, Keith Erickson, Larry Farmer, Ronald Gallimore, Gail Goodrich, Larry Gower, John Green, Jaleesa Hazzard, Ken Heitz, Andy Hill, Les Hunter, Ronald Lawson Jr., Swen Nater, Lynn Shackelford, Bill Sweek, John Vallely, Perry Wallace, and Charles Young.

I am thankful for the incredible support of my editor, Willis G. Regier, Tad Ringo, and the entire staff at the University of Illinois Press. Sam Walker and David Wiggins read the manuscript for UIP and offered insightful suggestions that helped me revise the book. I also want to thank my copy editor, Annette Wenda, whose attention to detail and care for the language helped me make the book considerably better.

I am fortunate to have a wonderful group of friends whose endless encouragement helped me succeed. I am especially grateful for my friendship with Ryan Doyle, who is looking forward to the day when I write a book about his life. Brandon Fleming's friendship has rewarded me with countless memories of good times. Brandon made my first trip to UCLA a memorable one. Sorry about the Angels game, Brandon. For all of my friends who listened to me talk about John Wooden and UCLA and pledged to read my book, I thank you.

The love and support of my entire family have sustained me throughout my academic journey and the completion of this book. I am especially thankful for Ed Arriola's endless encouragement and support throughout the writing process. When my brother, Paul Smith, learned I was writing a book, he asked me if there would be pictures. Yes, Paul, there are pictures. I hope you like them. I am especially thankful for my sister, McKenna St. Onge, who always listened to my latest idea and let me read passages to her over the phone. Thanks for everything, McKenna.

My parents deserve more credit than anyone else for what I have accomplished. My father, Jay Smith, is the greatest man I know. When it comes to work ethic, kindness, and generosity, my dad is the gold standard. My mother, Kim St. Onge, made me believe that I had something important to say. Thanks for listening, Mom. You continue to inspire me.

1

Goodness! Gracious! Sakes Alive!

John Wooden wanted to turn around, but it was too late. Indiana was long gone in his rearview mirror. In the summer of 1948, Wooden and his family packed their car and headed west on Route 66. Over the course of two weeks, they crossed the Mississippi River, traversed the Great Plains of Missouri, and continued through the flatlands of Oklahoma and Texas. Along the scenic route, they saw diners, motels, and ghost towns. They visited Carlsbad Caverns and the Grand Canyon and toured the Mojave Desert. From there, they snaked up and down the mountains and valleys of California. The Golden State welcomed them with roadside fruit stands, billboards, palm trees, and plenty of sunshine. When Wooden steered onto the Pasadena Freeway, cars zoomed passed him, ignoring the posted speed limits. Other drivers carelessly wove in and out of lanes. It was no wonder that California led the country in auto accidents. This was nothing like the small-town country roads that he was used to driving. There were no stoplights or police with whistles directing the boundless traffic. It felt unsafe to the father of two children. He nervously gripped the steering wheel a little tighter, his knuckles white. His voice reverberated off the car ceiling as he shouted, "What are we doing here anyway?"[1]

It was a good question. For a long time, he asked himself why he left Indiana. The moment he stepped on campus, Wooden realized that building a basketball program at UCLA would not be easy. The only basketball tradition UCLA fans knew was losing. From the time UCLA joined the Pacific Coast Conference (PCC) in 1928 until Wooden took over as head coach twenty years later, the Bruins had only three winning seasons, and they had never captured the conference title. For two decades, the Bruins were considered the doormat of the PCC. The best high school players in the Los Angeles area ignored UCLA and played for their crosstown rival, the University of Southern California (USC). From 1932 to 1943, the Bruins lost thirty-nine consecutive games to the despised Trojans. Thirty-nine straight. It was humiliating.

Before Wooden's first season, local writers predicted that UCLA would finish dead last in the conference, just as they had the year before. After evaluating the ragtag group, the new coach could not disagree with their assessment. All five of the starting players from the previous season were gone, including All-American Don Barksdale. Wooden's first team had less talent than the men he taught in physical education at Indiana State Teachers College. Without a doubt, he thought, his Indiana State varsity team "could have named the score" against UCLA. He was shocked that few of the Bruins had learned the game's fundamentals. When he evaluated the team's equipment, it was clear that the athletic department spent next to nothing on the basketball program. Wooden discovered lopsided basketballs that did not bounce, worn-out sneakers, and frayed uniforms.[2]

Worse yet, the Men's Gymnasium, where the team practiced and played their games, was nothing like the basketball gyms in Indiana. With pullout bleachers, it barely seated two thousand fans, less than half the size of Wooden's hometown high school gym. His team shared the crowded facility with the wrestling team and the gymnastics squad; both left the basketball court caked with rosin dust for Wooden to sweep every day before practice. Amid all the commotion, his players had a difficult time hearing his instructions. With only one window, the poorly ventilated, malodorous third-floor gym earned the nickname the "B.O. Barn." Without private showers or a locker room to wash up, the stench followed the players home. UCLA basketball literally stunk.[3]

Wooden's journey from Indiana to California is more than a story about how one man went from coaching at a small-town teachers college to leading a national dynasty. His life reveals UCLA's ascent as a preeminent academic and athletic institution. From the time Wooden arrived at UCLA in 1948 until the Bruins' first national championship in 1964, Southern California experienced momentous change and economic development, rapidly transforming UCLA from a provincial normal school into a distinguished research university. At the same time, Wooden redefined the importance of college basketball at UCLA by building a respectable program on fundamentals and traditional values—values he learned in Indiana.

○

For as long as John Wooden could remember, his life centered on the trinity of family, God, and basketball. The son of a tenant farmer, Wooden was born in 1910 in South Central, Indiana. His parents, Joshua Hugh and Roxie Anna, lived a hardscrabble life on a sixty-acre farm in Centerton, a whistle-stop with nothing more than two general stores, a church, and a three-room grade school. Without electricity, running water, and indoor plumbing, the Woodens raised their four sons in a meager two-bedroom farmhouse. Twice, they suffered devastating losses: one daughter died at birth, and another passed away from diphtheria at age three. In the face of tragedy and hardship, Joshua and Roxie Anna drew strength from family and their faith in God.[4]

Daily life was difficult for the Woodens, but they found a way to survive by relying on each other. Growing up on the farm, John learned the importance of hard work. Without it, his father often said, there was no harvest. Every morning before sunrise, the family rose to do their chores. John milked the cows, picked tomatoes and fruit, and fed the chickens. His mother spent the day attending to domestic duties: ironing and sewing clothes, baking, canning food, and washing dishes; his father cut hay, hunted for food, and plowed the fields with stubborn mules, not a modern-day tractor.[5]

At the end of the workday, the family enjoyed the fruits of their labor with a home-cooked meal of roasted chicken, corn, sweet potatoes, warm bread covered with strawberry jam, and pumpkin pie for dessert. When the family gathered around the kitchen table for dessert, Joshua said grace. He was a man of few words, uninterested in small talk or lectures. When he spoke, his boys listened. At the dinner table, Joshua often articulated his "two sets of threes," a moral code that he tried to live by. The first set were principles of integrity: "Never lie. Never cheat. Never steal." The second set served as a reminder of how to handle adversity: "Don't whine. Don't complain. Don't make excuses." What mattered most to Joshua Wooden was character—doing the right thing.[6]

After everyone cleared their plates, the boys gathered around him as he read out loud next to a burning potbelly stove. Shakespeare, Poe, Longfellow, and James Whitcomb Riley were among young John's favorite authors. On most nights, Joshua read from the Bible, instilling a devout religious faith in his sons. When John graduated from high school, his father did not have enough money to buy him a present, but he found a way to give him a gift that lasted a lifetime. After the graduation ceremony, he handed his son a crisp white three-by-five index card. On one side, he inscribed a poem written by Reverend Henry Van Dyke:

> Four things a man must learn to do
> If he would make his life more true:
> To think without confusion clearly,
> To love his fellow man sincerely,
> To act from honest motives purely,
> To trust in God and Heaven securely.

On the other side of the card, Joshua outlined a six-point creed that reflected his simple moral values: be true to yourself; make each day your masterpiece; help others; drink deeply from good books, especially the Bible; make friendship a fine art; and build a shelter against a rainy day. This last point did not mean that his son should build a home or save money for an emergency. John understood that his father "was talking about faith. Specifically he wanted me to put trust in God to prepare a home for me after this life is over." After reading the card, he tucked it into his wallet and kept it with him at all times for the rest of his life. It served as his moral compass, a standard of values, and the center of his teaching philosophy.[7]

As a teenager, it was not always easy for John to live up to his father's moral code. At times, his temper got the best of him. On one occasion when he and his brother Maurice were cleaning out the horse stalls, Maurice thought it would be funny to flip a pitchfork of manure at John's face. Covered in dung, John dropped his shovel, cursed his brother, and wrestled him to the ground. Joshua immediately separated them and sternly admonished his sons for fighting. He made it clear that he would not tolerate profanity. Losing self-control was unacceptable, he said. Then he punished each boy with an unforgettable whipping. Supposedly, John never swore again.[8]

More than anyone else, John Wooden aspired to be like his father, a man who embodied masculine ideals of the mid– to late nineteenth century. Notions of "manhood" and "masculinity" are socially constructed, dynamic and fluid, shaped and reshaped over time. Joshua Wooden personified the virtues of "a good man"—the self-made man who supported his family with his own labor. He believed that hard work, more than talent, and strong moral habits defined a man's success in life. Whether he cultivated his fields or improved his moral character, the good man was dedicated to self-improvement. "Never cease trying to be the best you can be," Wooden often told his sons. Like all good men, Wooden never fought, never got too excited, and never lost his temper. He was, according to John, "strong enough to bend a thick iron bar with his hands, but he was also a very gentle man who read poetry to his four sons at night." In the Wooden home, Joshua was the authority figure and chief disciplinarian, responsible for teaching his boys industry, ambition, perseverance, and virtue—valuable lessons John later taught as a father and coach.[9]

○

Like so many Indiana kids, John Wooden learned how to play basketball on the farm. His father made a makeshift basketball hoop out of an old tomato basket and nailed it to the hayloft where his sons spent countless hours playing with a ball made of rags stuffed into cotton hose. Nothing, except their farm duties and homework, kept them from playing. Basketball, a game that revolved around the rhythms of farm life, was made for Indiana. It was the perfect indoor activity for Hoosiers seeking recreational entertainment during the harsh winter months between harvest and planting. In the early twentieth century, most towns were too small to field a football or baseball team, or too poor to afford all of the equipment. But basketball required nothing more than a ball and a hoop. It could be played on a dirt-covered driveway or inside a church with ten kids or one. Not even nightfall kept boys and girls from bouncing a basketball. Sometimes they checked the *Farmer's Almanac* to determine when a full moon would appear. A full moon meant that they could see the basket clearly and shoot well into the night, ignoring a farmer's hours.[10]

In the early twentieth century, basketball evolved as a high school sport and as a popular pastime in Indiana. When the boys state tournament began in 1911, the games were played in makeshift venues, school auditoriums, Masonic halls, theaters, settlement houses, churches, and barns—any place with high ceilings. By the 1920s, "Hoosier Hysteria" permeated Indiana popular culture, inspiring a growing demand for the construction of larger gyms throughout the state. Rival communities competed with each other by building bigger and better gyms. In 1924 Martinsville built a massive redbrick gym with fifty-two hundred seats—four hundred more seats than the entire town population. In Indiana high school basketball was more than a sport—it was a way of life.[11]

That same year, the Woodens' hogs caught cholera and died, making it impossible for Joshua to pay the mortgage. The bank repossessed the farm, and the family moved to Martinsville, where Wooden played for the high school team. In Martinsville the townspeople followed high school basketball religiously. On Friday nights, every town shop and restaurant put up signs in the front window that read, "Sorry, we're closed. Gone to the game." Indiana's most famous thief, John Dillinger, would have had no problem robbing a Martinsville bank. Everyone in Martinsville had a ticket to the game, and everyone had an opinion about the team. On the courthouse steps, at the lunch counter at Riley's Café, at the Blackstone pool hall, and at the barbershop, people debated the team's chances of winning the state title. Even on the most bitter cold winter nights, a long line of headlights motored along icy country roads following the team bus wherever it went.[12]

Wooden was the pride of Martinsville, considered by many as the best player in the state's history. For three consecutive seasons, from 1926 to 1928, he led Martinsville to the state championship, winning once during his junior year. After graduation Wooden enrolled at Purdue University in West Lafayette, where he earned a reputation as the most intense competitor in the Midwest. Strong, skilled, and quick, there was nothing he could not do on the court. A writer from the *Lafayette Journal and Courier* observed that his speed and sensational dribbling allowed him "to do things with a basketball that few players ever did unless they carried the leather sphere under their arm." Athletically built at five-foot-ten and 183 pounds, Wooden had broad shoulders, thick wrists, and springs for legs. He played relentlessly, banging into other players and bouncing off the floor. Sometimes he drove so hard toward the basket that his momentum carried him into the stands, where Purdue officials stationed two men to catch him. At the end of each game, his body was covered with bruises, bumps, and floor burns. But the pain was worth it. In 1932 Wooden shattered the single-season scoring record in the Big Ten Conference and was named a consensus All-American for the third consecutive year. Many writers, including one from the *Chicago Daily Tribune,* praised him as "the greatest player of the decade." That season, before there were any national rankings or postseason tournaments, most scribes viewed Purdue as the best team in the country.[13]

When Wooden enrolled at Purdue, he dreamed of becoming a civil engineer, not a basketball coach. Unfortunately, he could not afford an engineering degree. Long before the days of athletic scholarships, Wooden had to pay his own way through school. Purdue required all engineering students to attend summer school, but Wooden needed the summertime to earn a living. So he pursued his passion for literature and became an English major. With encouragement from his coach, Ward "Piggy" Lambert, Wooden began taking physical education electives, planning a career as an educator and high school coach.[14]

More than anyone else, Piggy Lambert shaped Wooden's coaching philosophy—a philosophy centered on fundamentals, team unity, and conditioning. Lambert believed that if his players were in better condition than the opposition, then his team would have an advantage at the end of the game when most players fatigued. Like many coaches of his time, he not only addressed his players' physical conditioning but also expressed concern for their mental and moral conditioning. In the early 1900s, Lambert learned the game at the Crawfordsville Young Men's Christian Association. At the YMCA, ministers and educators taught basketball to develop "the whole man": the physical and spiritual well-being of male youth. These "muscular Christians" used basketball to promote Victorian values, religious faith, health, and manliness. As a coach, Lambert conformed to the muscular Christian tradition and prescribed "right rules for living," a strict code of behavior that required players to refrain from using tobacco and alcohol, overeating, and staying out late. For Lambert, basketball served a larger moral purpose of teaching young men self-control, order, and character.[15]

His practices were meticulously organized around learning fundamentals. He drilled the team on the proper techniques of shooting, passing, dribbling, rebounding, and defense. Controlled and intense, the short, stocky coach paced throughout practice, barking out instructions to his team. During every drill and scrimmage, Lambert demanded precision, enthusiasm, and speed. At a time when most teams played a slow, methodically choreographed, start-and-stop style of basketball, his teams employed a furious fast-break offense. With only a few diagrammed plays, his players exercised freedom within structure, an approach that Wooden later adopted. Lambert's offensive plan was simple: get the ball, run and shoot; then do it again.[16]

As a young coach at Dayton High School in Kentucky, Wooden adopted Lambert's practice methods. In 1932, after graduating from Purdue, he accepted his first job teaching English; coaching basketball, baseball, football, and track; and serving as the school athletic director. His eighteen-hundred-dollar salary was barely enough to support him and his new bride, Nellie Riley, so he played semiprofessional basketball on the weekends for the Kautsky Athletic Club. He quickly learned that playing basketball was much easier than coaching. In his first season as a coach, Wooden's team lost eleven games and won only six. He often lost his patience, disgusted at the sight of errant shots, sloppy passes, and careless mistakes. The following season, with a little more tolerance for error, Wooden focused more on teaching the basics, drilling the players over and over again until they got things right. The Dayton Green Devils showed great improvement, finishing the season 15-3, but it was not enough to keep him in Kentucky.[17]

In the summer of 1934, Wooden moved back to Indiana. At South Bend Central, he coached in one of the toughest conferences in the state. When he was not teaching English or in the gym, he spent considerable time studying the pedagogy of coaching. He talked to some of the most successful coaches he knew, pored over their instructional books, and maintained copious notes on every aspect of the profession. Although he never won a state title, Wooden earned an outstanding coaching reputation. In 1942, shortly after Japan attacked Pearl Harbor, Wooden enlisted in the navy, interrupting his coaching duties for more than three years. During the war, Lieutenant Wooden served as a physical trainer, helping combat pilots get into shape. When he returned to South Bend in January 1946, he immediately took over his old coaching duties, but other coaches who had served in the war were not offered their old jobs. He strongly believed that veterans deserved their old coaching jobs, and when they were not rehired, Wooden decided to leave South Bend for Terre Haute, where he took over as head basketball coach and athletic director at Indiana State Teachers College, a school with about twenty-five hundred students.[18]

In just two seasons, after building an impressive record, including an appearance in the National Association of Intercollegiate Basketball championship game, Wooden moved to the top of the hiring list of college athletic directors. In April 1948, after the Sycamores lost the NAIB title game to Louisville, he turned down a number of offers because there was really only one job that he actually wanted. In his eyes, there was no better conference than the Big Ten, so when the University of Minnesota contacted him, he never really thought of coaching anywhere else. But when UCLA athletic director Wilbur Johns invited him to California, he agreed to visit the school out of respect to Los Angeles Rams radio announcer Bob Kelly, an old friend from Indiana who had recommended him.[19]

When Wooden returned from his West Coast trip, he told Nellie that he preferred to move the family to Minnesota. Compared to Minnesota, coaching at UCLA was like directing a "B movie." A Big Ten job meant greater prestige, playing in a large field house, and a bigger paycheck. He knew numerous high school coaches in the Midwest, which could prove beneficial during recruiting. But there was a catch to the Minnesota offer: the athletic board wanted him to retain the former head coach as his assistant, which meant that he could not bring his right-hand man, Eddie Powell, with him from Terre Haute. Wooden refused to accept the job unless he could choose his own assistant. After a few phone calls, Minnesota athletic director Frank McCormick said he would talk to the athletic board about hiring Powell. Wooden told McCormick and Wilbur Johns that he would make his final decision on Saturday, April 17. If Minnesota allowed him to bring Powell, he would take the job, but if they did not, he would go to UCLA.

Saturday evening had arrived. Wooden and his wife sat in their Terre Haute living room, waiting anxiously for the phone to ring. They expected McCormick to call promptly at six. As the time passed, they became increasingly concerned. Finally, the phone rang at seven. When Wooden picked up the receiver, he heard Wilbur Johns's voice on the end of the line, not McCormick's. Wooden told Johns that McCormick never called and reluctantly accepted UCLA's offer. Wooden did not know that McCormick had tried to call him earlier, but a blizzard had knocked out the Twin Cities' telephone lines. Finally, at seven thirty, the phone lines had been restored, and McCormick called with good news. The athletic board had approved Powell as his assistant coach. But it was too late. McCormick could not convince Wooden to change his mind. He had given Johns his word, and where he came from, a man's word meant everything.[20]

O

When John Wooden arrived in Los Angeles, he never imagined UCLA basketball would become a program of national significance. He had no idea that Southern California was on the verge of an incredible transformation, one that would dramatically alter the rise of the university. The ascendance of UCLA began during World War II, when a three-decade population and economic boom spurred an incredible transformation in Southern California. Regional defense production created hundreds of thousands of new jobs in shipbuilding, aircraft manufacturing, oil refining, tank assembly, and food processing. The federal government invested billions of dollars in California and set up military bases throughout the coast. In Los Angeles, the "arsenal of democracy" created new factories, service industries, science centers, and the country's largest urban military-industrial complex. According to the *Los Angeles Times,* the state's postwar economic promise had spread "like the story of the discovery of gold . . . luring hopeful men whose dreams are spun of golden opportunity." From 1940 to 1960, the city's population grew from 1.5 million to 2.5 million, and by 1962 California had become the most populous state in the country. Los Angeles's swelling population and its surrounding mass suburbanization transformed the city into a "regional metropolis."[21]

The development of Los Angeles helped shape UCLA's rapid maturation. In 1919, when UCLA was founded as a two-year school, it was known as the "Southern Branch" of the University of California (UC). By World War II, UCLA had become a fully accredited four-year institution offering under-graduate and graduate courses, but it was still a commuter college lacking autonomy from Berkeley. After the war, an influx of veterans moved their families to Southern California, where they took advantage of government loans and the GI Bill to fund their education at UCLA. With Uncle Sam paying for tuition and books, the GI Bill created new opportunities for Americans to attend college, regardless of background. From 1944 to 1950, UCLA's enrollment nearly tripled, and the number of faculty and staff grew as well. Over the next decade, the Westwood campus, like much of Southern California, witnessed an unprecedented construction boom. "I have never taught a class which was not interrupted by the insistent chatter of a jackhammer or the roar of giant bulldozers," one professor told *Newsweek.* By the end of the 1950s, UCLA had constructed fifty-three new permanent buildings. The university magazine boasted, "No college or university in the United States is ahead of UCLA in the number of new buildings being erected, total floor space added or total value of construction." At the end of the decade, UCLA had become "America's fastest growing major university."[22]

Even with all of the distracting noise of clattering cement mixers, jackhammers drilling through concrete, and bulldozers uprooting trees, the campus appealed to prospective students. Situated on four hundred acres of gently rolling land off of Sunset Boulevard between Santa Monica and Beverly Hills, UCLA was the perfect setting for a Hollywood movie. On a clear, sunny day, the vista reveals chaparral-covered hills, lush greenery, oak trees, and palms. Walking through campus, students enjoyed the scent of eucalyptus, jasmine, and fresh-cut grass and the peaceful sounds of chirping birds and bubbling water fountains. The school's terra-cotta brick buildings, warm weather, and close proximity to Los Angeles encouraged many teenagers to attend UCLA. The official university catalog promoted UCLA's ideal location "for varied recreation and entertainment. The beaches and mountain resorts are within easy driving distance. Hollywood is close by. And the community is served by a number of fine restaurants." It seemed UCLA had everything—except maybe a decent basketball team.[23]

○

John Wooden's first practices at UCLA were almost too painful for him to watch. The sight of missed layups, careless passes, and lazy defense made Wooden sigh, shake his head, blow his whistle, and sternly shout, "Goodness! Gracious! Sakes alive!" Everyone froze whenever they heard those four words. Wooden did not swear, but when he said *goodness-gracious-sakes-alive* his players knew that he was angry. That first season, his team heard those four words more times than they cared to remember. It was clear that Wooden did not have any great players. The majority of the roster was filled with junior varsity scrubs and community college transfers who had not been recruited to play "big-time" college basketball. None of them executed the fundamentals to his standards, and worse yet, many of them were out of shape. The new coach would fix that.

When the season began, he had two objectives: improve the team's conditioning and teach the players proper fundamentals. The Bruins did not have much talent, but they would become the best-conditioned team in the conference. In the first few weeks, his players ran more than they had the entire previous season. Wooden did not build up the players' endurance by running laps or climbing steps. Instead, he followed Piggy Lambert's methods, demanding that the players run hard during every drill. Wooden paced the sidelines, urging his players to move quickly. "Be quick, but don't hurry!" he exclaimed. For several minutes, his players ran and jumped without a break. No one, and he meant *no one,* could stop moving until he blew the whistle. A local writer called him "a remorseless slave driver in practice, keeping his protégés constantly on the move—up and down the floor." When he finally gave them a break, the whole team hunched over, gasping for air. Some players wanted to choke the new coach so he knew exactly how they felt.[24]

Practice revealed his obsession with details. Every two-hour practice was planned to the exact minute. When Wooden coached in South Bend, he often visited Notre Dame football coach Frank Leahy, whose practices ran like clockwork. Observing Leahy at work convinced Wooden to run practice like a drill sergeant. He spent as much time preparing for practices as he did conducting them. Most coaches agreed that "proper team organization" was "a prerequisite for success." Each morning, the coaching staff met for two hours, outlining blocks of time for the day's practice. During these planning sessions, Wooden instructed his secretary that he wanted no interruptions, phone calls, or visitors. Preparing for practice was the most important part of his day.[25]

Wooden's practices reflected his faith in order and efficiency. With every single minute accounted for, the players never had to wait for the coaching staff to decide what to do next. When one drill ended, Wooden read his three-by-five index cards and instructed his players to move to the next station. Every drill ran for five to ten minutes, never any longer. The shorter the drill, the longer his players could sustain high intensity and focus. He kept his demonstrations and criticisms concise and punctuated, never lecturing. He taught them the proper way to execute the fundamentals in crisp, short commands: "Pass from the chest!" "Move your feet; don't reach." "Keep your hands up when free throws are shot!" "You're too slow! Hustle!" If a player made a mistake, he quickly corrected him, pointing out specific details. His team had to understand what they were doing and how to do it correctly.[26]

For Wooden, there was a right way to do everything. He instructed the players on good manners, grooming, dress, and diet. Hair was cut short; clothes were clean. He insisted that they act like "gentlemen in all ways at all times." He did not tolerate smoking, drinking, gambling, or profanity. He even spent time planning the pregame meal, which consisted of "a ten-to-twelve ounce steak broiled over medium or an equivalent portion of lean roast beef, a small baked potato, a green vegetable, three pieces of celery, four small slices of melba toast, some honey, hot tea, and a dish of fruit cocktail." "Occasionally," Wooden said, "I let a player eat as he thinks best."[27]

He even demonstrated how he wanted them to put on their socks. Sure, the players could dress themselves, but he had to make sure that they did it properly, his way. First he rolled the sock over the toe, sliding it up the ball of the foot, arch, and around the heel. Second, he snuggly pulled the sock up so that there were no wrinkles—wrinkles were unacceptable because they caused blisters, and blisters interfered with performance. Next, he checked the socks for any folds or creases. Then he slid his hand over the side and bottom of the foot to smooth out any wrinkles. Be sure to check the heel, he told them, because that is where most wrinkles develop. Finally, he had them show him that they could do it properly. If they did it correctly, he gave his approval, and his approval was all that mattered. Wooden's obsessive concern for details revealed his desire for control. His paternalistic methods served a larger purpose: every rule and regulation was designed to instill order, discipline, and character.[28]

Following his rules was a lot easier than learning the fast-break offense. It was a completely new concept on the West Coast, where most teams played a slow, methodical system. Wooden realized that if he could teach his team the fast break, they would have an advantage against opponents who were not used to defending it. Gradually, the Bruins improved their conditioning, but sprinting up and down the court and executing the fast break were not the same thing. The players had to learn how to run the break under control, and too many times they played sloppily, out of control. Wooden demanded perfection, and when the team failed to meet his expectations, he often became frustrated and irritated. Sometimes the thirty-eight-year-old coach removed his blue warm-up coat, handed his whistle to an assistant, and showed his players how the game was supposed to be played. For his players, practice was a constant challenge to eliminate mistakes. For Wooden, it was a test in patience.[29]

When not barking out instructions or demonstrating fundamentals, he scribbled various observations on the back of his index cards. After practice ended, he reviewed the cards to help him identify which players repeated the same mistakes. His copious notes helped him evaluate the progress of the team and learn which drills deserved further repetition. His meticulous records of every practice were filed away as a reference for future planning. "They're useful to me as a precise record of ways not to waste time," he said. Success required detailed self-analysis in which every minute, every impulse, and every motive were considered with improvement in mind. Details, Wooden argued, were the difference between winning and losing, success and failure.[30]

In his first season, UCLA had more success than Wooden ever imagined. The Bruins won twenty-two games, the most in school history, good for first place in the PCC Southern Division. The fast break kept the Bruins' opponents on their heels, backpedaling against constant offensive pressure. In 1950, Wooden's second season, the Bruins repeated as Southern Division champions and captured the PCC championship playoff, which sent them to the NCAA Tournament for the first time in UCLA history. Although UCLA lost to Bradley in their first game of the tournament, the Bruins finished seventh in the Associated Press (AP) national rankings. After two successful seasons, Los Angeles basketball fans began calling Wooden the "Miracle Man." Rumors swirled that Purdue, Minnesota, and Notre Dame wanted to lure him back to the Midwest. In March the UCLA varsity club organized a petition for a new basketball gym. Without a bigger, better arena, they argued, "there was no hope of keeping Wooden."[31]

Although Wooden had greater success in his first two seasons than he anticipated, he desperately wanted to return to the Midwest. At the end of his second season, his alma mater called, offering him the head coaching position. It made sense to leave California and return to Purdue. He was convinced that he could attract more elite high school prospects in Indiana, where basketball was more popular. "The better basketball players in the Midwest are no better than our better players in the Far West," he said. "But," he added, "there are many more of the better class players in the Midwest than we have out here." He noted that enthusiasm for basketball was far greater in Indiana, where more than eight hundred teams competed in the state high school tournament, in gyms two to four times the size of UCLA's gym. "You can see what that means," he explained. "Spectator interest adds to the interest and enthusiasm of the boys for the game. Therefore, more boys go out for basketball there than here and they start to work at the game earlier." Wooden was right: spectator interest in California lagged behind the rest of the country. But in the 1950s, there were important changes on the horizon.

In 1958 professional baseball finally came to California when the Brooklyn Dodgers uprooted for Los Angeles and the New York Giants moved to San Francisco. In 1959 the fourteen-thousand-seat Los Angeles Sports Arena opened, an important development that helped bring the Lakers basketball team from Minneapolis and provided a venue for UCLA and USC to play in front of large audiences. Of course, when Purdue offered Wooden the job, he had no idea that the popularity of sports in California would grow so quickly. He did know that when he came to UCLA, the administration informed that him that they intended to build a bigger gym. But after two years on campus, he was convinced that he would never see it built.[32]

It seemed like Purdue had offered him the world: a bigger gym, a new car each year, a country club membership, a home on campus, a rich life insurance policy, and a perpetual five-year contract with built-in pay raises at a salary nearly twice what he was making at UCLA. If he took the Purdue position, he could quit his part-time job at a local dairy farm and become a full-time basketball coach in the best conference in the country. Most important, he could go home. Wooden was uneasy living on the West Coast, especially at banquets where he had to socialize with sportswriters, alumni, and other coaches. Nothing made the shy, self-conscious Hoosier more uncomfortable than being in a room full of backslapping, drinking men who made crude jokes and questioned his coaching methods. To avoid such anxious encounters, he often retreated to a corner with a Coke in hand, hoping no one would notice him. The man had left the small town, but the small town had not left the man.[33]

Wooden prepared to leave Los Angeles. He informed Wilbur Johns and William Ackerman, the graduate manager of the Associated Students of UCLA, that he wanted his release from the third and final year of his contract. He resented the idea that ASUCLA ran the athletic department, which basically meant that the student body president was his boss. Johns and Ackerman did not want to lose the popular coach and denied his request. They reminded him that he was the one who had originally turned down a two-year deal and requested a three-year contract. Wooden left the meeting determined that he would finish his last year at UCLA and leave for Purdue the minute that his contract expired. But Purdue never made an offer. Neither did Minnesota, Notre Dame, or anyone else for that matter. When the phones stopped ringing, he signed a new contract. He was stuck at UCLA.[34]

○

On April 28, 1948, when John Wooden first met UCLA supporters and alumni at the annual team banquet, he announced, "I like to win—but I like to win the right way." It was a defining statement, one that revealed his core values and endeared him to local fans and sportswriters. They considered him a "grand guy—soft-spoken, pleasant, [and] intelligent." On the court, Wooden "radiated confidence, ability, integrity. And underneath his mild exterior was a controlled fire—a contagious enthusiasm and spirit which soon affected his entire team." Off the court, he was known as "the gentleman from Indiana," "a sincere, clean cut type of man," devoted husband and father, and upstanding citizen. He was, in the eyes of the UCLA community, the ideal coach—a coach who "turned out winning basketball combinations and at the same time developed men of outstanding character."[35]

Wooden's popularity can be attributed in part to cultural geography. Historically, transplanted Southern Californians migrated from the heartland: the Midwest, the border states, and the near South. In a region built by Evangelical preachers, small farmers and large ranchers, defense-plant workers, property developers, and middle-class townspeople, Wooden embodied the conservative values and religious beliefs that shaped the political culture of post–World War II Southern California. In Wooden California migrants saw a man who reminded them of where they came from. He was "the man on Main Street in a small town" who shared their belief in God, family, and country.[36]

When he was not coaching or spending time with his family, Wooden delivered public lectures on the "Pyramid of Success," a self-created blueprint for achievement. The pyramid evolved out of his experiences as a young high school teacher and coach in Dayton, Kentucky. He believed that some parents imposed unrealistic standards for success on their children. Too many adults were disappointed when their children earned anything less than an A grade. As a coach, he could not understand why a father would belittle his son for not making the starting lineup. "What's wrong with the boy?" the father asked. There was nothing wrong with the teenager, Wooden thought, but there was something wrong with his father's standard of success.[37]

Wooden recalled that one of his high school teachers, Lawrence Scheidler, had asked him and his fellow students to write an essay defining success. Most of them measured success by material things—money, fancy cars, and fame. Scheidler pointed out that success was not necessarily based on the accumulation of material possessions or prestige. For Wooden, a boy who had grown up poor on a meager farm, it was empowering to know that he could define success beyond cultural norms. As a teacher, he wanted to share that same lesson with his students, but he did not know how. Sitting in the Dayton barbershop in the winter of 1934, he read an inspiring poem.

> At God's footstool to confess,
> A poor soul knelt and bowed his head
> "I failed," he cried. The Master said,
> "Thou didst thy best, that is success."

He had found his answer. After a few drafts, he penned his own definition of success that he would teach his students and players for the rest of his life. "Success," he wrote, "is peace of mind which is a direct result of self-satisfaction in knowing you did your best to become the best that you are capable of becoming." It was a simple philosophy. But it was not enough simply to define success. He needed to give it shape and meaning and find a way to personify his own standard.[38]

His high school coach, Glenn Curtis, had used a "Ladder of Achievement," but he wanted something more complex, so he conceptualized a five-tier pyramid with blocks. Just before he left for UCLA in 1948, he completed the pyramid with fifteen blocks. The cornerstones of the pyramid reflected his father's values: "industriousness" and "enthusiasm." In his eyes, no one embodied industriousness more than his father. Enthusiasm, the coach reminded his pupils, comes from the Greek word *entheos,* which means "the god within." One's enthusiasm, according to Wooden, had "an almost divine quality on its impact on others," the same way his father's values had shaped him. In many ways, the values of the pyramid represented more than the ideal coach: it was the ideal man—his father.[39]

The pyramid included other blocks that reflected Wooden's Victorian sensibilities: self-control, initiative, and intentness. At the heart of the pyramid are three blocks: "team spirit," "skill," and "condition." Conditioning may have been the most important block in the pyramid. Like Piggy Lambert, Wooden firmly believed that the team in the best condition usually won the game. But it was not enough to be in top physical condition. His muscular Christian philosophy required mental and moral conditioning. The pyramid read like a Bible for the whole man: "Moderation must be practiced. Dissipation must be eliminated." He added in his autobiography, "You cannot attain and maintain physical condition unless you are morally and mentally conditioned. And it is impossible to be in moral condition unless you are spiritually conditioned."[40]

The top block in the pyramid is "competitive greatness," a generic slogan for reaching success. Wooden later added two blocks to the apex: "patience" and "faith through prayer." Success in any endeavor, he claimed, could not be separated from religion. Wooden echoed the muscular Christian creed: a coach "who is committed to the Christlike life will be helping youngsters under his supervision to develop wholesome disciplines of body, mind, and spirit that will build character worthy of his Master's calling." The pyramid functioned as a tool that helped Wooden "set the proper example by work and by deed."[41]

Wooden's pyramid reflects America's long history of success literature. Since the Puritans arrived in America, ministers, educators, and reformers have promised to teach people how to become successful. The idea of achieving success has appeared and reappeared in the writings of Benjamin Franklin, in Horatio Alger's "rags to riches" stories, and in the inspirational works of Norman Vincent Peale. For well over a century, these success writers have propagated the myth that all men can shape their lives exclusively by their own effort, regardless of birthplace, class, education, ethnicity, or race. Similarly, Wooden espoused his faith in this idea: "We are all equal as far as having the same opportunity to make the most of what we have."[42]

Undoubtedly, the pyramid has inspired people. One Los Angeles sportswriter pointed to it as an excellent teaching device that could be applied "to any game played, whether on the athletic field or the game of competitive business in life." Although the blocks represent admirable qualities, they fail to provide a methodology for achieving success. A close examination of the pyramid reveals that none of the building blocks logically builds upon one another. More important, the pyramid shaped the foundation of a Wooden mythology. Throughout and after the dynasty years, commentators, fans, and Wooden himself have credited the values of the pyramid as integral to winning ten national championships. Yet for sixteen seasons, while teaching the pyramid, he never won a championship. It would take more than the blocks of the pyramid—and wrinkle-free socks—to build a dynasty.[43]

○

In the 1950s, success did not come easily for John Wooden. By middecade, Wooden had assembled one of the best programs on the West Coast. Yet the Bruins' chances of making a run at the national championship were greatly diminished, thanks to one man: Bill Russell. Before him the most dominating centers were strong, slow-moving whites who played in stationary, plodding offenses. On defense coaches taught them never to leave their feet and discouraged jumping. Yet Russell had different ideas of how to play the game. At the University of San Francisco (USF), he redefined the center's role, relying on his quickness and leaping ability to block, swat, and catch shots in midair. When Russell blocked a shot, he deflected it toward his team's own basket, igniting fast-break scoring opportunities.[44]

In many ways, USF and UCLA represented the future of college basketball: integrated teams that relied on quickness, agility, and athleticism. USF and UCLA were two of the most integrated athletic programs in the country. From the start of the 1954–55 season, Wooden started all three of his black players: Willie Naulls, Morris Taft, and John Moore. Later that season, USF's Phil Woolpert did the same, starting Russell, K. C. Jones, and Hal Perry. At the time, only about 10 percent of college basketball teams at predominantly white schools recruited black players, let alone started one. Most teams, even outside the South, looked much more like Kentucky than UCLA. Wooden's integrated team was not simply a case of California's relative racial liberalism. In 1955 USC, Cal, and Stanford had no black basketball players on their varsity teams. For decades USC's segregated basketball teams convinced many black Californians that the Trojan basketball program operated by the color line. *California Eagle* writer Johnny Morris wondered if "maybe by 1965, USC as well as Mississippi will be able to see Negroes as people."[45]

Long before Wooden arrived, UCLA athletics had ignored the color line. Ralph Bunche started at guard for the Bruins' varsity basketball team from 1925 to 1927. From 1938 to 1941, five blacks played for the Bruins on the gridiron, making UCLA's squad the most racially integrated college football team in America. Three of those players—Woody Strode, Kenny Washington, and Jackie Robinson—made up the best backfield in the country. The "Gold Dust Trio" defied previous norms of token integration. Never before had a *group* of black players carried a college football team the way that Strode, Washington, and Robinson did. *Pasadena Star-News* writer Charles Paddock observed, "Take away the Negro stars from the UCLA team and you would not have a team." To many fans, UCLA football symbolized the great myth that sports were defined by equal opportunity, ignoring the fact that the Bruins were the exception, not the rule.[46]

For many black athletes recruited by UCLA, the Westwood campus appeared as a racial utopia. When assistant basketball coach Eddie Powell visited John Moore in his Gary, Indiana, home, Moore's mother was shocked to see a picture in the student yearbook of a black student body officer. In the 1950 yearbook, there is a picture of Sherrill Luke, a handsome, light-skinned black man who had come to UCLA inspired by the achievements of Washington, Robinson, and Strode. Below his photo, bold block letters make clear who he was: PRESIDENT. Shocked, Moore's mother asked Powell, "You mean they got a Negro holding office where there are fifteen thousand white folks?" In the fall of 1954, Rafer Johnson made his decision to attend UCLA the same way that Moore did. When he walked into the Student Union and saw a picture of Luke, he knew that he wanted to attend UCLA. Johnson played basketball for Wooden and became a national hero when he won a gold medal in the decathlon at the 1960 Rome Olympics. All across the country, writers applauded his athletic achievements and noted that he was extremely popular on campus, where he had become UCLA's third black student body president of the decade. The visible roles of black athletes and black student body presidents shaped an image of UCLA as an ideal place for African Americans, absent of racial prejudice.[47]

Despite UCLA's liberal reputation in race relations, black athletes learned that the school's integrated athletic history had done nothing to erase discrimination in student housing. Restrictive covenants in Westwood barred "any person not of the white or Caucasian race" from buying, renting, or leasing property; some of these deeds also excluded Jews. These prohibitions, and the fact that UCLA had only one dormitory until 1959, provided limited housing space for blacks. Private Greek fraternities also excluded blacks, and many non-Protestants, from membership as well. The *Daily Bruin* lamented that discrimination in the Greek system contradicted UCLA's tradition of integrated sports teams. Wooden was well aware of such bigotry and found housing for Moore and Naulls in two Jewish fraternity houses. Moore, Naulls, and their Jewish brothers found a common bond, forged by a shared empathy and commitment toward ending discrimination in Westwood. Wooden's quiet action and his black players' willingness to suffer second-class treatment protected UCLA's image as a good place for black athletes.[48]

Few people knew about the problems black athletes faced in Westwood. What basketball fans did know was that UCLA had an exciting team with a fully integrated starting lineup. In 1954–55, Wooden started three black players because Moore, Naulls, and Taft gave the team the best chance to win. Well before the majority of his colleagues embraced integration, Wooden challenged the status quo. But most coaches were not like him. Instead, they adhered to strict quotas based on racist assumptions that a basketball team might fall apart on the court without intelligent white leadership. Around the same time, in 1954, UCLA won the college football national championship with one of the most integrated teams in the country. In 1955 the local National Association for the Advancement of Colored People (NAACP) recognized the UCLA athletic department "for consistently fielding teams without regard to race or color." For many African Americans, UCLA represented the California Dream of racial equality.[49]

During the 1955–56 season, Wooden built his best team yet. Although John Moore had graduated, Willie Naulls emerged as an All-American, a fierce rebounder, and one of the finest scorers in the country, averaging more than twenty-three points per game. Speedy guard Morris Taft complemented Naulls's strong interior play with sharp outside shooting. With his quickness and deft ball handling, Taft easily blew past opponents and could elevate beyond their reach with his hanging jump shot. "Thanks to its two brilliant Negro performers," for the first time in four years, UCLA made the NCAA Tournament. Still, UCLA faced a nearly impossible task: to advance beyond the first round, they would have to beat USF, which had won fifty-one straight games. Worse yet, Taft had injured his back a few days before the game. With Taft hobbling around the court and missing seventeen of his twenty-three shots, the Bruins never had a chance. Bill Russell scored twenty-one points and snagged twenty-three rebounds. USF whipped UCLA, 72–61. The Dons ended the season on a fifty-five-game winning streak and claimed their second-consecutive NCAA Championship. For more than a decade, USF stood as the standard by which all great college basketball teams were measured.[50]

O

In early March 1956, two weeks before UCLA fell to USF in the NCAA basketball tournament, reporters documented how boosters at four schools in the PCC—UCLA, USC, Cal, and the University of Washington—illegally paid college football players for their athletic services. Investigations revealed that at UCLA, "all members of the football coaching staff had, for several years, known of the unsanctioned payments to student athletes and had cooperated with the booster club members or officers." With ASUCLA running the athletic department, there was a lack of administrative supervision over athletes' campus jobs. Many football players never actually worked or were paid more than the NCAA allowed. Before the scandals broke, UCLA's business manager had repeatedly alerted the chancellor and the dean of students of the suspicious relationship between boosters and athletes. Those warnings were ignored.[51]

The PCC football scandals had devastating consequences for UCLA athletics and the PCC. In May UCLA chancellor Raymond B. Allen imposed harsh penalties on the athletic department, including three years' probation for all sports, which meant that the football team could not play in the Rose Bowl and the basketball team could not participate in the NCAA Tournament. With no chance of playing in the tournament, Wooden struggled to recruit the most talented players. By 1957 the conference began falling apart, as UCLA, USC, and Cal withdrew their conference membership. Two years later, the PCC completely dissolved, and a new conference was created, the Athletic Association of Western Universities (AAWU), which included UCLA, Cal, USC, Stanford, and Washington. In 1960 the UCLA administration revoked control of the athletic department from ASUCLA, creating an official Department of Intercollegiate Athletics with the intent of cleaning up financial abuses. UCLA was no longer one of the most respected athletic programs in the country.[52]

O

When Franklin Murphy became UCLA chancellor in 1960, his primary goal for the university was "major scholarly distinction in worldwide terms." He realized that might prove difficult to accomplish since the university suffered from an image crisis. UCLA lacked its own institutional identity, separate from the more prestigious University of California at Berkeley. When Murphy called his office, the telephone operators answered, "University of California, *Los Angeles Branch.*" It greatly upset him. He was the chancellor of UCLA, *not* the University of California. One day he finally had enough, so he instructed the campus operators to answer, "Thank you for calling UCLA." From that point forward, he made it clear to his staff, "everything around here is UCLA. We will make those four letters as visible and indelible as MIT." Gradually, those four block letters appeared everywhere—on stationery, sweaters, signs, and championship basketball banners.[53]

Murphy recognized that building UCLA's national reputation required a successful athletic program. He had come from the University of Kansas, which had one of the most outstanding basketball programs in the country. When he arrived in Westwood, Murphy realized that the state of UCLA athletics was far from prosperous. He wanted to increase student participation in varsity sports and build facilities for track, baseball, and basketball, projects that cost millions of dollars. In 1962 the *Daily Bruin* reported that in a period of two years, the athletic department had accumulated financial losses of more than one hundred thousand dollars. At that time, the basketball program provided almost no income from gate receipts. Since 1955, when the fire department declared the Men's Gym unsafe unless crowds were limited to one thousand, the Bruins had been playing their "home" games anywhere they could find two baskets: Venice Beach High School, the Pan-Pacific Auditorium, Long Beach City College, Santa Monica City College, and the Los Angeles Sports Arena. Playing in off-campus gyms meant that UCLA had to pay rental fees and sometimes split ticket revenues with three other teams after a doubleheader.[54]

Raising money for the athletic department necessitated constructing a multipurpose arena. Before those plans could be made, Murphy needed to determine whether Wilbur Johns could effectively manage the athletic department. He asked his top aide, Charles Young, to speak with the coaching staff about Johns. According to Young, Johns had a serious drinking problem and sometimes showed up to meetings drunk. Murphy determined that Johns's leadership in the athletic department was "really most inadequate" and that he needed to find a replacement.[55]

In J. D. Morgan, Murphy found the perfect man for the job. Morgan grew up in a Presbyterian family on the flatlands of Cordell, Oklahoma. In 1937 the Okie migrant came to UCLA to play football. A back injury shortened his football career, so he decided to focus on tennis, a decision that UCLA would not regret. Like Wooden, Lieutenant Morgan was a navy man, serving as a PT boat commander during World War II. After the war, he returned to UCLA as assistant tennis coach and accountant for ASUCLA. In 1950 Morgan became head tennis coach and business manager for the athletic department. Five years later, he assumed important financial duties for the university as the associate business manager. In that role, he helped direct important on-campus developments, including the expanding residence hall program, securing a multimillion-dollar loan for the new Student Union, and planning for the new multipurpose center. By the time he became athletic director in 1963, Morgan had also made tennis a major sport at UCLA, coaching six national championship teams.[56]

Morgan was a workaholic. Working two full-time jobs, he usually skipped lunch and often did not retire to bed until two or three in the morning.

He treated his new position as a dictatorship, micromanaging those around him. His desk was usually covered with piles of paperwork—paperwork that could have easily been handled by his secretary or assistant coaches. He also took over all basketball-related business. No longer would Wooden deal with budgets, equipment, or scheduling. Thanks to Morgan, for the first time in his career, all Wooden had to do was recruit and coach.

At the same time, Morgan earned a reputation for pomposity and arrogance, a know-it-all, lecturing anyone who would listen. At forty-three years old, Morgan had a stout frame, oval face, cleft chin, and large nose. He slicked back his short brown hair. Most people recognized J. D. for his booming baritone voice. He could easily be heard conducting business behind closed office doors. Whenever his colleagues heard him roaming the hallways, they would say, "The lion's loose."[57]

Morgan had big plans for the athletic department. When he took over, Morgan immediately implemented budget procedures to prevent the athletic department from spending money based on the upcoming year's projected revenues. He had a "calculator for a mind" and understood that the key to reducing the athletic department's deficit meant increasing revenues, not cutting programs. Building a new basketball arena was integral to his plan. Filling that arena, he argued, required expanding the recruitment program beyond California. Signing star athletes, regardless of their hometown, would create interest in UCLA sports. "We feel we can sell our program by talking about athletes," he said. "People know your school if they know your athletes."[58]

Morgan and Murphy worked closely on planning the new arena. To cover the costs of the five-million-dollar, thirteen-thousand-seat pavilion, the state provided two million dollars, and student fees contributed another million. Financing the remaining two million dollars required donations from alumni and "friends" of the university. Murphy turned to an important friend, Edwin W. Pauley, an oil magnate, ardent anticommunist, leading figure in the Democratic Party, and influential member of the University of California Board of Regents. Murphy, a registered Republican, wisely steered his conversations with the Democrat toward their common interest in UCLA sports.

Frequently, the chancellor sent Pauley free football and basketball tickets. In April 1963, talking over dinner and drinks, Murphy persuaded Pauley to donate one million dollars, matching the total amount pledged by alumni. The chancellor convinced him that the new arena would be "the finest indoor pavilion in Southern California, maybe one of the best in the United States." And the best part was, Murphy said, "it will be called PAULEY PAVILION." Edwin Pauley could toast to that.[59]

2

The Wizard of Westwood

W alt Hazzard had never heard of John Wooden. John Wooden had never heard of Walt Hazzard, either. The UCLA coach disliked recruiting and paid little attention to high school players outside of Southern California. Hazzard grew up in Philadelphia, twenty-seven hundred miles from Westwood. In Philadelphia every high school and college coach knew about him. During his sophomore and junior years at Overbrook High, he played alongside future NBA players Wally Jones and Wayne Hightower, winning back-to-back city championships. In 1960, as a senior, Hazzard became a local star and was named Philadelphia high school player of the year.[1]

He may not have known much about Wooden, but Hazzard knew all about Ralph Bunche, Jackie Robinson, Woody Strode, Kenny Washington, Rafer Johnson, and Willie Naulls, heroes in the African American community. Naulls, UCLA's greatest black basketball star of the 1950s, played a pivotal role in persuading Wooden to give Hazzard an opportunity to play at UCLA. In March 1960, Naulls, then playing for the New York Knicks, went to Philadelphia to watch a playoff game between the Syracuse Nationals and the Philadelphia Warriors. His good friend and Hazzard's distant cousin Woody Sauldsberry played for the Warriors. Before the playoff game, Hazzard impressed Naulls by scoring thirty-six points in an Amateur Athletic Union game. Afterward, Sauldsberry introduced him to Naulls. Convinced that he had seen a special player, Naulls contacted Wooden about giving

Hazzard a scholarship. Knowing that Wooden counted character as much as talent, Naulls told him that Hazzard not only had great ability, but also came from a good family, raised by a strict Methodist minister, and was student body president. Finally, Naulls added, "Well, if he can't make your team then I'll pay for his scholarship."[2]

More than anyone else, Hazzard transformed UCLA into a championship basketball program. With his exceptional quickness, superb ball handling, and whirlwind speed, he made everyone around him better. Hazzard brought an exciting style of play never before seen on the West Coast. He could dribble behind his back and between his legs, thread "passes through holes where you couldn't throw a golf ball," and contort his body in midair as he laid the ball off the backboard. His creative no-look passes confused defenders and created open layups for teammates. "He was," said UCLA teammate Larry Gower, "a point guard before there was such a position. He got you the ball. He passed to a spot where you were supposed to be, not where you were. He made you think differently."[3]

Without Hazzard, without Naulls, and without Jackie Robinson, the UCLA dynasty would not have been possible. The foundation of the dynasty, therefore, was built on an infusion of black talent. Hazzard represented the key link in UCLA's athletic history; he was inspired by UCLA's black heroes of the past and paved a path for UCLA's black stars of the future. But Hazzard was more than a symbol of racial integration. He changed the way the game was played. Hazzard drove UCLA's explosive fast break, a style of play that compelled a more furious pace. The Bruins' fast break created greater possibilities on offense and stretched the defense horizontally, forcing opposing teams to cover more passing lanes than they ever had before. Hazzard left a distinct imprint on the sport, creating a faster, more fluid, creative game.

In 1962, with Hazzard leading the way, the Bruins reached the national semifinals, but most critics thought that UCLA's fantastic run was a fluke, since they had nine losses during the regular season. The Bruins were a Cinderella story, not a dynasty in the making. Before the 1964 season began, *Sports Illustrated* made its annual predictions, excluding UCLA from its top twenty teams. The magazine's editors included the Bruins in a group of "surprise packages," teams that had an outside chance to emerge as contenders.

UCLA's success, they argued, depended on one player: Walt Hazzard. The "flashy" point guard was "one of the best offensive players in the nation and one of the worst defensive players on the coast." "As he goes," the magazine forecast, "so go the team's chances."[4]

○

A week after the 1960 season ended, a reporter visited the home of John and Nell Wooden. In his worst year at UCLA, the Bruins finished 14-12 and missed the NCAA Tournament for the fourth consecutive season. He was tired of losing, weary of falling short of his own expectations, and fatigued from all of the sleepless nights. He often lay awake, replaying the games over and over again, wondering what he could have done differently to help his team win. The writer assumed that the coach had taken a break from basketball and asked if the family had plans to travel. "Vacation? Ha," Nell laughed at the suggestion. "Do you know what that husband of mine did last night to relax?" she asked. "Sat here all evening drawing court plays for NEXT year!" Although Wooden never talked to his players about winning, he desperately wanted to win. He spent the entire off-season reviewing every facet of his coaching philosophy, searching for clues, studying his notebooks, poring over his three-by-five index cards, and analyzing all practice and game statistics.

It appeared that no single factor had held the program back, but Wooden realized that he pushed the players harder in practice late in the season, leaving them fatigued during conference races and the NCAA Tournament. At the same time, he added new wrinkles to the playbook, which created confusion and untimely mistakes. In the future, he would simplify his instructions and relax conditioning down the stretch. Wooden also made another important change. He noticed that the reserves often played poorly with the starters. So he decided to split the squad in half, creating a seven- to eight-man rotation for games. This strategy would encourage more cohesive play between the starting players and the first two or three men off the bench. These were small but important changes that would shape the way he coached during the dynasty years.[5]

More than any philosophical changes, what he really needed to win were better players. In 1961 UCLA returned essentially the same team as the year before, with one important newcomer: Ron Lawson. At the time, the wiry six-foot-four sophomore guard was the most talented player Wooden had coached since Willie Naulls. The son of a physics professor, Lawson grew up in segregated Nashville, Tennessee, where he attended Pearl High, the city's most respected black high school. At Pearl he helped the Tigers win the national Negro championship two straight years. Lawson idolized Rafer Johnson and decided that he wanted to follow in his footsteps at UCLA. In 1960 the "jumping jack from Tennessee" broke every freshman scoring record, averaging nearly twenty-five points per game. The *Los Angeles Times* announced that "one of the best basketball players UCLA has ever had" was "on the verge of greatness."[6]

The following year, Lawson led the varsity team in scoring, and UCLA finished the season 18-8, second in the conference. Confident and assertive, Lawson played with "a chip on his shoulder." He loved to shoot, sometimes too much, according to his coach. At times they clashed in practice. Wooden said that Lawson had to learn how to play within the team structure. Lawson claimed that his grueling practices had taken the fun out of the game and made basketball seem "like a job." On one occasion, when Wooden criticized him during practice, Lawson stormed off the court. Wooden warned him not to walk out the door, or he would not be allowed to come back. Lawson ignored him. About a week later, Lawson apologized to the whole team, and they voted to let him return. Lawson's behavior frustrated Wooden, who complained that in all his years of coaching, "I've never had a boy who resented instruction and correction as much as Lawson did. He would have preferred to be completely on his own—even practice on his own, and not with the team. He's a boy who was always looking for excuses."[7]

Two months after the season ended, the *Los Angeles Times* printed the kind of headline that every college basketball coach feared: "UCLA Cager Lawson Admits Bribe Offer, Quits School." A decade after New York district attorney Frank Hogan first discovered that college basketball players had accepted bribes from gamblers, Hogan revealed that once again players had "shaved points" for money. Shaving points off the point spread was easy enough to do. Gamblers made bets based on the point spread, an estimated margin of victory for a favored team. This system made it easy for a player to shave points and control the margin of victory. All a player had to do was occasionally miss a free throw, fumble the ball out of bounds, or let his man score an easy basket. No one could tell he was shaving points as long as he made it look like he was trying to win.[8]

At the end of Hogan's investigation, he found thirty-seven players at twenty-two colleges who had fixed forty-four games. Lawson testified before a New York grand jury that a stranger had contacted him and asked if he would be interested in playing basketball in a Catskills summer league, a central recruiting site for fixers. The stranger also offered him "good money" to shave points. Lawson claimed that he turned down the offer and kept it a secret. After the FBI informed UCLA about Lawson's contact with gamblers, administrators asked him to leave school, citing his failure to report the bribe offer.[9]

Supposedly, Lawson took no money and committed no crime. "My only sin," he said, "was my failure to report the bribe." Still, a cloud of suspicion followed him. His uncertain relationship with gamblers threatened the reputation of UCLA's athletic program—a program that only five years earlier had left a trail of dirty money during the PCC football scandals. The last thing UCLA needed was another investigation of its athletic department. Facing another potential crisis, UCLA administrators were committed to protecting an image of athletic purity. More important than Lawson's innocence was the appearance of an innocent athletic program.[10]

In the early 1960s, point shaving, forged transcripts, and illegal payments became synonymous with college basketball. Syndicated columnist Jimmy Cannon called college basketball "the slot machine of sports." Sportswriters, coaches, and educators lamented that it had become morally bankrupt and a national disgrace. Critics complained that college athletes needed coaches who did "more than merely teach a kid to shoot, block, bat, or jump"; they needed coaches who taught the basic virtues of loyalty, honesty, and character—a coach like John Wooden.[11]

O

When John Wooden and his assistant coaches first reviewed Walt Hazzard's high school game films, they were amazed by what they saw. No one on the West Coast played like he did. He had exceptional peripheral vision and explosive quickness. One assistant coach said, "He's a little fancier on that court than we like." Another assistant suggested, "He might be a problem—might not fit in with our style of play." Wooden nodded in agreement. "But," he asked rhetorically, "he's some ball player isn't he?" He grinned, wondering about the possibilities. Finally, he said, "Maybe we can mold him to our way of thinking."[12]

After watching Hazzard practice at UCLA, Wooden thought that he lacked consistency and discipline. Hazzard's game, Wooden thought, suffered from excessive dribbling, careless passes, and a lack of control. Nothing upset him more than when Hazzard threw a pass from behind his back. Wooden said that not even the Boston Celtics' legendary guard Bob Cousy could "handle the ball as well behind his back as he can out front. Besides, if you let one guy get fancy other boys who don't have that ability will start getting cute, too. Then you're in trouble." Hazzard believed that he could make plays that Cousy could not. He liked to drive to the basket, rise up as if he was going to shoot, and then fire a pass to an unsuspecting teammate. Countless times his stinging passes bounced off his teammates' stomachs, faces, and feet. Sometimes he drilled them in that most vulnerable place. Frequently, Wooden yelled at him, "Quit trying to show how good you are!"[13]

The tension between Wooden and Hazzard revealed a clash of cultures. The Hoosier coach held steadfast to the fundamentals of the game, a philosophy founded on simplicity and structure. The Philadelphian brought an urban East Coast ethos to the West Coast, a style shaped by his experiences competing in playground pickup games. Writers stereotypically described Hazzard as "a product of the Asphalt Jungle," a "showboat" imitating the Harlem Globetrotters' dribbling genius Marques Haynes. They said that he played "schoolyard ball," implying that Hazzard, like other blacks, was undisciplined and selfish on the court. Essentially, these commentators described a game without rules—an allegedly inferior game that needed coaching. In reality, Hazzard's play was governed by a set of rules different from Wooden's. Playground basketball did not have coaches, referees, or timekeepers regulating games. Without these authority figures, creativity, improvisation, and freedom defined "the city game." In this environment, Hazzard learned a game that valued tempo control, individual performance, and "intimidation through improvisation." In a country where few blacks gained any recognition, playground basketball provided a space for them to distinguish themselves and earn respect among their peers.[14]

In the first few games of the 1961–62 season, Hazzard had distinguished himself as the team's leading source of turnovers and unhappy fans. Spectators rose to their feet cheering him whenever he flashed a spectacular pass. More often, they sat in their seats, sighing in disgust, watching his passes whiz out of bounds. Wooden yelled at his point guard, exhorting him to make better decisions. The Bruins lost their first two games of the season to Brigham Young University (BYU). In the second game, Hazzard was ejected for fighting. After winning their next two games, UCLA dropped three straight, including a devastating 91–65 loss to Houston. Once again, the referees forced Hazzard to leave the game early, only this time, it had nothing to do with unsportsmanlike conduct.[15]

Before UCLA arrived in Houston, writers and students debated whether the basketball team should play in a segregated southern city. Lloyd Wells, the sports editor of Houston's black newspaper, the *Informer*, wrote to the *Daily Bruin*, explaining that the Sam Houston Coliseum had segregated seating. He warned *Bruin* readers that if UCLA came to Houston and played under such conditions, Hazzard and his black teammates, Fred Slaughter and Larry Gower, would be subjected to racial discrimination and that the NAACP might picket the arena. Wells encouraged UCLA students to protest racial inequality as they had earlier in the fall, when it appeared that the football team might play lily-white Alabama in the Rose Bowl. A group of UCLA students proposed a boycott of the most prestigious bowl game in the country and gained the support of a number of players who agreed to join the protest. Consequently, Alabama and its football coach, Paul "Bear" Bryant, faced heavy criticism for refusing to integrate their program. The public pressure and the proposed boycott forced Alabama president Frank Rose to withdraw the team from Rose Bowl consideration. To UCLA students, Alabama football represented southern white bigotry. In their refusal to tolerate segregated competition, these students made clear that fighting for racial equality on the playing field was an important part of the civil rights movement.[16]

By 1961 student activism at UCLA had moved in a new direction. In the spring, James Farmer, the national director of the Congress of Racial Equality (CORE) spoke on campus about the group's plans to board buses and test federal laws that protected integrated interstate travel. CORE was committed to nonviolence, but Farmer believed that confrontation in the Deep South, even if it became violent, was necessary because it would provoke a crisis, forcing the federal government to protect their rights. A year earlier, the sit-ins had inspired unprecedented numbers of college students, black and white, from the North and the South, to join the civil rights movement. The sit-ins led to the successful desegregation of lunch counters across the South and proved that college students could successfully challenge Jim Crow. And now Farmer called on UCLA students to put their bodies on the line and join the "freedom rides."[17]

More than a dozen UCLA students participated in the freedom rides. One group traveled to Jackson, Mississippi, while the other group went to Houston. In Houston an integrated group of riders sat at the U-shaped lunch counter at the Union Station coffee shop. They were refused service, and the police arrested them for unlawful assembly, packing them like sardines in the back of a paddy wagon. Steve McNichols, a white UCLA student, felt relieved that he had been arrested. He thought that they had evaded a violent attack from angry onlookers and that they would be safe in jail. He was wrong. McNichols and three other California activists found themselves in "the tank" with what he described as "a small band of hardened criminals who shared common homosexual and sadomasochistic bonds." For the next forty-eight hours, a group of inmates brutally terrorized the four riders until they were bloodied and black and blue. When McNichols returned to campus, he shared his story with students. The riders' experiences made students aware of the life-threatening violence civil rights activists faced in the South and provided "the moral impetus" for them to confront segregation. It also made students question whether the basketball team should play in Houston.[18]

More than anyone on campus, McNichols understood that if the team went to Houston, UCLA's black players could face malicious racism. Concerned, he met with Wooden and asked him what he would do if any of his players refused to cross picket lines. Wooden replied, "I would never make a boy do anything against his moral convictions." McNichols had no idea that Wooden had once taken a moral stand against segregation when he coached at Indiana State. In 1947 Wooden's team received an invitation to play in the NAIB Tournament. When he learned that African Americans were barred from the tournament, he quietly turned down the playoff opportunity, knowing that if he accepted, Clarence Walker, a seldom-used guard, would have to stay behind.[19]

Looking back, Wooden's decision is truly remarkable, considering that he grew up in segregated Indiana, a state inhabited predominantly by WASPs—white Anglo-Saxon Protestants—who lived on farms and in small towns. Throughout the state, whites segregated blacks from lunch counters, theaters, hotels, schools, and athletic teams. Basketball reflected and reinforced patterns of segregation. When Wooden came of age during the 1920s, blacks and whites did not play high school or college basketball together. Perspiring white and black bodies touching skin to skin on the court would have violated the social order and invited notions of equality between the races. In 1948, when the NAIB again invited Indiana State to its postseason tournament in Kansas City, Wooden was the only coach in the state with a black player on his varsity team; Indiana, Purdue, Notre Dame, and Butler all fielded segregated squads.[20]

Excluding Clarence Walker from the tournament would have violated Wooden's ethical values and his belief in the importance of team unity. His father taught him that no one was better than anybody else, regardless of race. After Manhattan College turned down an invitation in protest of the NAIB's racist rules and the Olympic Basketball Committee pressured the NAIB to desegregate the tournament, the NAIB finally lifted its ban against black players. Now, NAIB officials said that Clarence Walker could play in the tournament, but only if he stayed in a separate hotel. Wooden refused to accept this Hobson's choice until the NAACP asked him to reconsider. The NAACP reminded him that if Walker played, he would break the color line of a national basketball tournament, opening the door for other black athletes. After Wooden discussed the matter with Walker and his parents, he agreed that his team would play in Kansas City. Walker admired Wooden for his willingness to do what he believed was right. "If all people were in mind as he is in character," Walker wrote to his diary, "I *think* Mr. [Jim Crow] would be trivial."[21]

Given his own experiences with segregation, Wooden clearly understood why UCLA students thought that the basketball team should not play in Jim Crow Texas. With growing concern about the welfare of the team, the Student Legislative Council (SLC) voted unanimously in support of canceling the Houston trip if the stands remained segregated. Student discontent and threats of civil rights protests persuaded the University of Houston administration to integrate the basketball arena. Still, there was no guarantee that the team would not face racial discrimination. Steve McNichols spoke with Wooden again, hoping that the coach would promise to pull the team out of Houston if they were confronted with any form of racism. Wooden told him that he could not commit to anything beyond his coaching duties. Curiously, he now said that any player who traveled with the team would "have to play regardless, picket line or no picket line."[22]

When the UCLA basketball team arrived in Houston for the four-team tournament, Wooden and his players tried to check into a downtown hotel, but the attendant at the front desk told him that "negroes" were not allowed. Wooden never swore, but "that was the closest I've ever seen Coach to swearing," starting guard John Green recalled. "I've never seen him that upset." Wooden learned that when Cincinnati and Bradley came to Houston, the black players from both teams were barred from staying in the city's downtown hotels. In this case, not only were UCLA's black players discriminated against, but the entire team had been segregated, providing Wooden with the impetus to remove the team from the tournament. Faced with the choice of playing in a segregated environment or returning to California, Wooden chose the former.[23]

From the opening tip-off, it was clear that UCLA's two black starters—Walt Hazzard and Fred Slaughter—were not welcome at the Coliseum, either. White fans yelled virulent racial epithets. Houston's players pushed, elbowed, and hip-checked Hazzard and Slaughter without penalty. The officials blatantly called phantom fouls on Hazzard and Slaughter the moment they made the slightest contact with a white player. The whistle-blowers were not simply officiating a basketball game; they were enforcing Jim Crow on the basketball court. "It was quite clear that you weren't going to come into Houston and play against the white Houston ball club with your black guys and compete," recalled UCLA forward Pete Blackman. Hazzard became so frustrated that he nearly came to blows with a white player. When Slaughter was called for his fourth foul, Wooden immediately pulled him from the game, fearing that the next foul might lead to real violence. Throughout the game, Wooden jumped out of his seat, pleading with the officials to call the contest fairly. They told him to "sit down and shut up." When that did not work, they silenced him by calling a technical foul on the UCLA bench. Long before the game had ended, Hazzard and Slaughter sat on the sidelines, and there was nothing that Wooden could do about it.[24]

The next night, UCLA beat Texas A&M by ten points, only this time the Bruins played without Hazzard and Slaughter. Afterward, Wooden tried to avoid writers' questions about what had happened, saying that the decision to sit them "was hard to explain." "There was no segregated seating, no picket lines, no cat calls," he claimed. But several UCLA players told the *Daily Bruin* that their black teammates had endured unjust treatment from fans, players, and the officials. Hazzard told the *Los Angeles Sentinel*, an African American newspaper, that Wooden "did the right thing" by sitting them, but refused to add anything more. In 1961 most college athletes kept their political views to themselves, and writers rarely asked them what they thought about civil rights or racism. Black college athletes were expected to perform on the field, appreciate their educational opportunity, ignore racial insults and humiliations, and behave like "good Negroes."[25]

Many concerned students and faculty wanted to know what had really happened during the Houston trip. The SLC asked Chancellor Franklin Murphy to create an official policy that prohibited UCLA athletic teams from participating in events that allowed segregated housing or any form of racial discrimination. The SLC also recommended that in future UCLA athletic contests, coaches should withdraw their teams when confronted with any form of racial discrimination. Murphy approved an investigation and reported to the Academic Senate that Wooden did not play Hazzard and Slaughter against Texas A&M "because they had played badly the first night—not because they were" black, an unjust condemnation against Hazzard and

Slaughter. The investigation convinced Murphy that Wooden's actions in Houston were "beyond criticism." He also announced a university policy that generally followed the SLC's recommendations—a policy that had actually existed since 1960 but was never made public. However, the "new" policy did not prevent UCLA from competing against lily-white schools. The administration's position was designed to protect its own athletes, not confront segregation at other schools. Equally important, the administration exonerated Wooden's decisions. However, had he adhered to the school's policy in the first place, UCLA would have taken a step closer to realizing the university's democratic ideals, and the team's black players could have avoided such a humiliating experience.[26]

John Wooden was not a crusader or an activist; he was a basketball coach who wanted to avoid any racial or political conflict. He accepted integration on his teams, but pulling the team out of Houston in protest would have violated the conservative political culture of college athletics. To some observers, it appeared that benching Hazzard and Slaughter accommodated segregation. When a writer from the *Los Angeles Sentinel* asked Wooden why he did not pull the team out of Houston after the first game, the coach vaguely replied that "his first duty was to the team." In his own way, he made a subtle gesture of protest: Wooden vowed that when he left Houston, "he would never return" as long as the city remained segregated.[27]

○

After the Houston trip, life did not get much easier for Walt Hazzard. Before the Bruins played Army, Hazzard was late for the team meal, so Wooden did not start him for the next two games. Hazzard had grown frustrated with Wooden, who seemed to constantly criticize him for not playing the game his way. At one point, he contemplated quitting the team and returning to Philadelphia, but his father refused to let him come home. UCLA easily beat Army, but the next game proved a greater challenge when they played Ohio State, the number-one team in the country. All-American center Jerry Lucas dominated the undersized Bruins with thirty points and thirty rebounds in a lopsided 105–84 loss. In the next game, UCLA fell to Utah, the Bruins' seventh loss in eleven games, the worst start in Wooden's career.

Sports Illustrated described the Bruins as a team with "no height, no center, no muscle, no poise, no experience, no substitutes, and no chance." With a number of quality teams left on the remaining schedule, *Daily Bruin* writer Arnold Lester pessimistically commented, "It may take a small John Wooden miracle for UCLA to have a winning record this basketball season."[28]

Still, the UCLA coach saw something in his team that no one else did. He noticed that the loss to Ohio State was not as bad as the score indicated. The Bruins showed great promise and resilience against the best team in the country, down only three points with seven minutes left in the second half. Gradually, over the next month, the Bruins improved, winning twelve of their last fourteen regular-season games and their first conference title in six years. The turnaround resulted from many factors: Fred Slaughter lost nearly thirty pounds and now could leap for rebounds instead of waiting for them to fall into his lap. On defense Wooden switched forward Pete Blackman to the frontcourt and placed the more physical guard John Green on the interior, giving Gary Cunningham help on the boards. But the most important change was the way the rest of the starters adjusted to Hazzard's style of play. They stopped watching him dribble and started catching his passes. Eventually, Green learned that Hazzard could get him the ball even in the tightest spaces, making him an even better scorer, as he averaged nearly twenty points per game. "If we got open, [Hazzard] would get the ball to us somehow, whether it was behind the back or a bounce pass," Green recalled.[29]

Few writers expected the Bruins to do much of anything in the NCAA Tournament. It seemed that this team had come out of nowhere. Surely, their luck would run out, critics thought. But the Bruins' fast break never slowed down. With a first-round bye and victories over Utah State and Oregon State, UCLA found itself in the semifinals against the defending national champion Cincinnati Bearcats, a team built on size, strength, and speed. With a large front line, led by muscular six-foot-eight center Paul Hogue and towering six-foot-eight forward George Wilson, the defending champs opened an 18–4 lead in five minutes. After switching to a 2-3 zone, the Bruins climbed back and tied the game at halftime.[30]

With 1:34 left on the clock and the game tied, 70–70, Walt Hazzard drove the lane and reversed his dribble as two defenders collapsed on him. He heard a whistle and was called for an offensive foul; Cincinnati now had the ball. Hazzard could not believe it. With no shot clock, Cincinnati held the ball for the last shot, tossing it around as time wound down. With ten seconds left, their coach, Ed Jucker, called time-out and drew up a play for Hogue to take the final shot. Hogue's teammate Tom Thacker, who had missed all six of his shots, could not get him the ball. With time running out, Thacker dribbled to the right corner and miraculously sank a twenty-five-foot jump shot with one second left. UCLA attempted a full-court inbounds pass that was broken up as time expired. Cincinnati won, 72–70. Afterward, Wooden wore the pain of the loss on his face. With tears welling up and his head down, he took off his glasses and said that he was proud of his boys. Unfortunately, he murmured, their effort "wasn't quite enough, I guess. But those boys never quit. I knew they wouldn't. They never have."[31]

○

In 1963, after seniors John Green, Pete Blackman, and Gary Cunningham graduated, Wooden had to figure out how to integrate three new players into the starting lineup. Two junior-college transfers, Jack Hirsch and Keith Erickson, won the two positions at forward. Wooden was unsure if he should start Fred Goss or Gail Goodrich in the backcourt, opposite Hazzard. Goodrich, a sharpshooter who had led the freshmen in scoring the previous year, expected not only that he would start, but that he would be one of the premier players on the team, but Wooden had different ideas about his role. For most of the season, Goodrich competed for playing time with Goss. He had never sat on the bench like this. When Goodrich did play, he had to share the ball and shoot less than he desired. Sometimes Wooden's incisive criticisms made it difficult for him to play his best. He recalled that the worst thing he could do in practice was allow another player to gain position near the basket. "Goodness gracious sakes alive!" Wooden yelled at him. "You do not let him do that. You never let *anyone* do that." On a few occasions, when Goodrich made intolerable errors, the coach kicked him out of practice. Frustrated, he contemplated giving up basketball to play baseball instead. Gradually, Wooden realized that what his young player needed was more pep talks and fewer critiques. Fortunately for the Bruins coach, Goodrich decided to stay.[32]

Goodrich was not the only player Wooden kicked out of practice. Jack Hirsch was a poker-playing misfit, a loner who often had trouble accepting the coach's authority. Raised in an affluent Jewish family, Hirsch grew up in Brooklyn, where his father made a fortune owning a chain of successful bowling alleys. He attended a predominantly black school and stayed out of trouble playing basketball on the blacktop courts of Bedford-Stuyvesant. When he was fourteen years old, his family moved to Van Nuys, California. As a senior, he was named All-City Co-Player of the Year. After high school, he played two seasons at Valley Junior College in the San Fernando Valley. He played at UCLA as a favor to his father, who told him that if he went there, he would quit smoking. At first Hirsch was not interested in going to UCLA. He preferred to ride around in his red Pontiac Grand Prix and "screw around" with his friends. Without his father's urging, he said, "I would never have gone there." But he wanted his father to quit smoking, so he went to UCLA. His father kept smoking anyway.[33]

It took a while for the independent youth and his disciplinarian coach to warm up to one another. Hirsch was not used to following rules or doing much of anything. "At first," he said, "I didn't like Wooden. He kind of rubbed me the wrong way." Hirsch hated practice and often found ways to entertain himself. Wooden, who would not put up with any form of "clowning around," dealt with Hirsch's shenanigans on an almost daily basis. When he grew tired of practice, Hirsch had no problem telling Wooden, "That's enough JW." He was the only player who addressed the coach informally. Sometimes he called him John. Other times he called him "Woody." Woody tolerated it as long as Hirsch said it with a smile.[34]

Like Hirsch, Keith Erickson transferred to UCLA after playing junior-college basketball. Ever since Wooden came to Westwood, California's junior-college system had always provided him with solid players. Throughout the dynasty years, Wooden built his teams on elite talent and role players from junior colleges.[35] Like most transfer players, Erickson was not highly recruited. His coach at El Camino Junior College, George Stanich, had played for Wooden and suggested to him that Erickson could be a decent player, if he could get his emotions under control. Erickson was not a great basketball player, but he was an incredible athlete. He was quick and agile and could jump high off the floor. He developed his explosiveness on the beach playing sand volleyball. UCLA offered him a scholarship—half for baseball and half for basketball. His teammates referred to him as the "Beach Bum" because he loved the sand, the sun, and the surf. Sometimes, the California kid made it known to Wooden that he would much rather hang out at the beach than practice.[36]

With this new group of players, returning to the national semifinals would not be easy, especially since the team had little experience playing together. "People have to realize," Wooden said, "that we're a very young team, having lost three three-year letterman from last year's squad." Adjusting for the roster turnover, Wooden asked Hazzard to lead the team and shoot more often. But too many times, his star player wanted to make the "fancy play" instead of a more simple, efficient one. Early in the season, Wooden sat him twice for "showboating." Frequently, he paced the sideline, intentionally scolding Hazzard in full view of his teammates and fans. Like many coaches, he acted as an armchair psychologist, yelling at Hazzard, believing it made him play better. The Bruins star often became angry, an emotion that fueled his focus and competitiveness. Sometimes during a stop in action, Wooden would wave Hazzard over to the bench for a brief lecture. When it was over, Hazzard furrowed his brow, ready to play, while Wooden turned the other way, grinning.[37]

Wooden had more to worry about than Hazzard's performance. He struggled to find an effective starting lineup. Wooden pulled Goodrich in and out of games and sometimes played him at forward, a position he did not relish. In late December, Erickson sprained his ankle and had to sit out for a while. Without him, the undersized, undermanned Bruins were hurt on the boards. Through it all, the talented team showed potential, finishing the year with a 20-9 record. Wooden was convinced that his team could reach the NCAA Tournament and make a run at the national championship, but not this year.[38]

Looking back on the games they lost, the Bruins almost always kept it close. Five of their seven regular-season losses came down to a difference of four points or less. At the end of the regular season, UCLA and Stanford were tied for the conference lead, but the Bruins found a way to beat the Indians by six points in a playoff game that sent them to the NCAA Tournament. After a season of close games, the third-ranked Arizona State Sun Devils easily defeated the Bruins in a 93–79 blowout. It was, the *Los Angeles Times* said, "the most thorough beating ever administered" against a John Wooden–coached team.[39]

When the season ended, Wooden and his top assistant, Jerry Norman, reviewed what had gone wrong. They knew that they had the talent to win, but something was holding them back. They pressed Stanford, but scored only fifty-one points. UCLA pressed Arizona State, but the Sun Devils were faster than the Bruins and simply sprinted past them. The coaches realized that their full-court man-to-man press against Stanford encouraged too much dribbling. In both games, the opposing team controlled the tempo by dribbling—Stanford slowed it down and Arizona State sped it up. Clearly, the man-to-man press did not work.

Norman had an idea. He always had ideas. The ambitious, opinionated thirty-four-year-old assistant frequently challenged Wooden over strategy. Wooden always listened, but usually he declined his assistants' suggestions. For years the two had disagreements. Playing for the Bruins in the 1950s, Norman was known for his quick temper. In one game, he became incensed at a referee's call and slammed the basketball so hard it nearly got lost in the rafters. Another time, Norman's hot fuse led Wooden to kick him off the team for a few games. But beneath Norman's temper, Wooden saw a leader. During Norman's senior year, Wooden named him co-captain, and in 1957, he brought him back as the freshmen coach. Three years later, Wooden promoted him to head assistant varsity coach.[40]

Norman remembered something Cal head coach Pete Newell had said: "The team that controls the tempo controls the game." He proposed that they use a full-court zone press. What they wanted to do was create more situations where Hazzard had the ball out in the open, running on the break where he could make plays. They wanted to exploit the team's quickness, using the entire court, from end line to end line. But how could they get Hazzard the ball more often? Norman wanted opposing teams to advance the ball faster by passing. A zone press positioned each defensive player in a specific area of the court, which meant that a dribbler would constantly run into defenders, forcing him to pass the ball. After the Bruins scored, the players would immediately fall into position, ready to attack. Once the opposing team had the ball, the Bruins would double-team and trap the ball handler, forcing him to stop, pick up his dribble with four arms waving in his face, panic, and hurry a poor cross-court pass. When the ball hung in the air, UCLA would intercept it, get it to Hazzard, and away they went.[41]

Initially, Wooden did not like the idea. He had tried similar versions of the zone press before, but he felt that college players were too talented to make mistakes facing such a harassing defense. Norman persisted, convincing Wooden to adapt and spend more time coaching defense. Finally, Wooden agreed to install the zone press. It was one of the best decisions he ever made.[42]

○

For Gail Goodrich, November 22, 1963, began like any other day. Usually, he slept late. At about twenty minutes before noon, he emerged from his bedroom at Beta Theta Pi, rubbing the sleep from his eyes, when he heard one of his fraternity brothers yell, "The president's been shot!" News of John F. Kennedy's assassination spread quickly. For a moment, it seemed like everything in America had stopped. At UCLA administrators canceled classes and postponed the football game against USC for a week. Students gathered in their dorm rooms and consoled one another. In the union, people sat in disbelief. Some blankly stared at the television screen, while others picked at their food. The president's sudden death had a lasting impact on America's youth. Kennedy had inspired them with his energy, idealism, and a new commitment to social change. It was an abrupt ending to a promising future. After three years of optimistic rhetoric and speeches filled with the hopeful message that America could achieve peace and prosperity and reach "new frontiers," Kennedy's assassination killed the hopes that he represented. It marked the end of innocence and foreshadowed a more turbulent, violent time to come.[43]

After Kennedy's funeral, Wooden resumed basketball practice. The Bruins worked on the zone press every single day, sharpening their defensive instincts. If Wooden had any doubts about using the zone press, they quickly disappeared when his team scored a school record 113 points in the opening game against Brigham Young. In a 42-point victory, the Bruins stunned the Cougars with pressure defense and seamless offense. After a string of impressive victories, UCLA climbed to number four in the Associated Press poll. During the L.A. Classic, UCLA squared off against Michigan, the best team in the Big Ten Conference, and the second-ranked team in the AP poll. The Wolverines were a physically imposing group that included athletic center Bill Buntin, wide-bodied forward Oliver Darden, and dynamic scoring guard Cazzie Russell. UCLA's relentless press neutralized Michigan's size. The inexhaustible Bruins, without a single starter taller than six foot five, proved that a small, quick team could beat a strong, big team. After UCLA's 98–80 victory, Bruins fans filed out of the L.A. Sports Arena, chanting, "We're No. 1!"[44]

By early January, the Bruins were ranked number one in both the Associated Press and the United Press International polls, a first in school history. No coach could figure out how to break the UCLA zone press. The "Bruin Blitz" was like a ticking time bomb that could detonate at any moment. When it did, the other team imploded. In the blink of an eye, UCLA would go on a scoring spurt, "like a string of exploding fire crackers." After about five minutes against Washington State, UCLA trailed by one point. Following a made basket, Wooden instructed his team to set up the press. Washington State crumbled under the pressure, throwing the ball right into UCLA hands. Hazzard raced down the court, with Goodrich, Hirsch, and Erickson filling the lanes, and before Washington State knew it, UCLA made the game look like a layup drill. UCLA's seven-point lead snowballed to 61–28 at halftime. It happened like that all season long. Sometimes the games were closer, but the press always created opportunities for UCLA to go on a run. "Somehow, some time," Hazzard confidently explained, "we know our pressure will get to 'em."[45]

In Los Angeles, UCLA's entertaining style generated greater interest in college basketball than ever before. Previously, no team from Southern California had been ranked number one. After UCLA convincingly beat Michigan, the Bruins became "the sports talk of the town." "Los Angeles' enthusiasm for college basketball is higher than anytime I've known," J. D. Morgan noted. For years local newspapers gave basketball scant coverage, and very few games were televised. But after the Los Angeles Lakers became the NBA's first West

Coast team in 1960, basketball became more popular in California. With the Bruins' newfound success, Los Angelenos increasingly followed the college game, and local writers filled their columns with stories about UCLA. Suddenly, larger crowds showed up to watch the Bruins at the Los Angeles Sports Arena, shattering attendance records. Throughout Southern California, basketball fans began asking the same question: would UCLA ever lose?[46]

It seemed impossible that such a small team could win every game. Most coaches believed that winning required big players. Wooden belied this theory with his quick, undersized team and his "run and shoot" offense. With his exceptional peripheral vision and pinpoint passes, Walt Hazzard made his teammates better players, especially Gail Goodrich, who emerged as a lethal shooter and a star in his own right. Together, they were the highest-scoring backcourt in the country, averaging an impressive forty points per game without the advantage of the three-point shot.[47]

Hazzard could single-handedly dictate the pace of the game with his speed dribble and imaginative passes. Initially, Wooden viewed Hazzard's improvisational no-look passes as selfish plays that only satisfied the guard's desire to "show off," a frequent criticism of black players. Wooden had misread the purpose behind those moves. Within black culture, improvisation, whether on the basketball court or in a jazz band, is a purely relational expression, intended to "isolate or draw attention to parts of the ensemble." Hazzard's head-turning moves drew attention to him, but at the benefit of his teammates, who were left unnoticed by the defense, open for easy shots. In essence, Hazzard redefined Wooden's playing rules, forcing the coach to adapt beyond his own limited vision. UCLA's success, then, was based on synergy between Hazzard's playing style and Wooden's coaching philosophy, a fusion of black expression and basketball tradition.[48]

O

As UCLA racked up win after win, John Wooden became a national icon, hailed by the press as a coach who "places emphasis on mental and moral conditioning, along with the physical." A *New York Times* headline suggested that UCLA's rise to the top was based not only on the fast break, but also on Wooden's philosophy of "clean living." One writer proposed that the UCLA coach's secret to success was "his handling of men." *Sports Illustrated* called his Pyramid of Success "a must for every player's locker." What was "most impressive" about Wooden, a *Daily Bruin* writer believed, "is not his winning record or his unique coaching ability but the man himself. He handles every task with firmness but dignity. He commands the respect of all who come in contact with him. He is a molder of men; winning for him is secondary."[49]

Sportswriters who visited his office could not help but think that they knew John Wooden. Pictures of his family, past teams, and the men he admired most—Piggy Lambert and his father—decorated his office walls. Much of his office looked like any other coach's, with trophies and plaques, tin canisters of game film, and practice notebooks. It also featured items that were undoubtedly his. He tacked the walls with the Pyramid of Success, a loyalty code, and his favorite epigrams and poems. Writers frequently noted that the "seraphic gentleman who appreciates Kipling and Keats as much as a good hook shot" loved to read. His shelves were lined with books that had nothing to do with sports: James Allen's *As a Man Thinketh*, Lloyd Gray's *Magnificent Obsession, Wise Sayings of the Orient*, and volumes of Victorian poetry. The most important book in the room sat on his desk: a small thumb-worn copy of the New Testament. Occasionally, his players picked it up as they waited for him to finish a telephone call. Nothing pleased him more.[50]

Sportswriters usually enjoyed their conversations with Wooden. He was friendly, intelligent, and articulate. At fifty-four years old, the veteran coach began to show his age: a few more wrinkles lined his face, and his brown hair had grayed near the temples. He had an austere countenance, pale skin, a long and narrow nose, oversize ears, thin lips, and piercing blue eyes. In a way, he resembled the pitchfork-wielding farmer in Grant Wood's painting *American Gothic*. But his clean, pressed suits and black tortoiseshell glasses made him look more like a preacher or a college English professor than an ordinary farmer. He simultaneously appeared both authoritative and accessible. He was the everyman.[51]

During Wooden's unprecedented winning streak, sportswriters began calling him the "Wizard of Westwood," a nickname he detested. Like Frank Baum's Wizard in *The Wonderful Wizard of Oz*, Wooden's image was shaped by populist ideals. Baum's character appeared to be an inventor who could solve any problem, though he was really nothing more than a common man from Omaha, Nebraska. Like Baum's Wizard, the Wizard of Westwood represented mythical purity, a celebration of traditional themes and images: an ordinary man from Middle America, a product of yeoman farm life, and a teacher who embodied exceptional moral values.[52]

Before the Wizard of Westwood became the most recognizable basketball coach in America, the point-shaving scandals stained college basketball with an image of corruption. Critics complained that coaches—especially those on the East Coast—had failed to teach young men the virtues of character, integrity, and loyalty, all of the things that Wooden seemed to represent. Restoring college basketball's reputation required a new face of the sport, a coach who not only won, but also won the right way. That coach was John Wooden. In the aftermath of the scandals, he emerged as a symbol of moral authority, an antidote to corruption in college basketball.

During UCLA's championship run, rebounds did not come cheap. Somehow, the undersized team led the conference in rebounding. Timing and quickness had a lot to do with it, though a group of boosters offered the players an extra incentive: bonus money. After each game, the players received envelopes filled with cash from alumni as a reward for pulling down rebounds. The players and the boosters worked out a system: each player received five dollars for each rebound up to ten rebounds and ten dollars for each rebound past ten. "It was a helluva great feeling to pick up one hundred bucks for a night's work," Jack Hirsch said. "Believe me, we really went all out for rebounds."[53]

Not everybody was happy with the payment plan. Gail Goodrich knew that accepting cash from boosters violated NCAA rules. He also knew that he had fewer chances to pull down rebounds than his taller teammates who played closer to the basket. For some reason, Goodrich complained to Jerry Norman that this cash-for-rebounds system was "very unfair" to him and the other guards. Norman then told Wooden what was going on, and Wooden immediately ended the pay-for-play system. Subsidizing college athletes went against everything Wooden stood for. He believed that a coach had a moral obligation to teach players right from wrong, to uphold college basketball's amateur ideals. But college basketball was no longer the amateur game that he once played. In the coming years, UCLA basketball would rapidly become a more commercialized program, a business driven by an entrepreneurial athletic director, television executives, boosters, and athletes who dreamed of cashing in on their athletic fame.[54]

○

As the season wore on, writers asked Wooden if he felt pressure to maintain an undefeated record. Initially, he denied the stress, but the increased attention from the media, the demands for more interviews, and heightened fan expectations made his job more difficult. In early February, after UCLA beat Cal by just two points, he admitted, "Yes, yes, it would be ridiculous to say that we're not feeling it." He confessed that after the close game at Berkeley, he became ill and vomited. The building pressure climaxed during the NCAA Tournament. The Bruins had finished the regular season 26-0, and now they had a chance to become only the third team in history to finish with a perfect record. In 1964 the NCAA Tournament field had twenty-five teams, which meant that with a first-round bye, UCLA had to win four games to become the national champion.[55]

UCLA's first three NCAA Tournament games went wire to wire, and each time the Bruins staged a remarkable comeback. They could have easily lost their first two games against Seattle and San Francisco, but Walt Hazzard, like a cool "pool hustler," made clutch shots when it mattered most. After beating Seattle by five points and San Francisco by only four, critics predicted UCLA's demise. Detractors charged the Bruins with overconfidence from beating too many weak teams; the Bruins, they said, were too reliant on their guards. The players looked emotionally exhausted, and Hazzard admitted as much. In the semifinal game, UCLA played anxiously against Kansas State, a team that the Bruins had beaten in December, 78–75. With a little more than seven minutes left, Kansas State led by five points. In one minute, in classic Bruin fashion, UCLA tied the score, and in less than another minute, they had a four-point lead. Late in the game, Hazzard split the Kansas State zone defense and fed the ball to Keith Erickson, who scored a season-high twenty-eight points on open layups and transition jump shots. The moment

Hazzard decided to take over and drive the lane, he ended Kansas State's dream of an upset. UCLA 90, Kansas State 84.[56]

On March 21, 1964, minutes before UCLA took the court against Duke for the national championship, the Bruins gathered in front of their coach to hear his final instructions. Wooden was not like Vince Lombardi. He did not give fiery motivational speeches. But on this night, he managed to deliver a short speech that his players would never forget. "You got here playing a certain way," he said. "We've rebounded, we've run, we've pressed, and we've made this a 94-foot game." Then he looked into the eyes of every player and asked, "How many of you remember who finished second last year?" No one raised a hand. "They don't remember who finishes second," Wooden said. "Now go out there and play."[57]

Prior to tip-off, UCLA players in shiny white uniforms warmed up in single-file layup lines as trumpets blared in the background and the fans clapped in unison to the school fight song, "Sons of Westwood." Wooden walked onto the court dressed in a simple suit and tie, rolled-up program in hand, and a little silver cross hidden in his left pocket. During a game's most anxious moments, he would clench the crucifix, a helpful reminder that a leader of men should maintain his faith. In his other pocket, he kept a lucky rubbing stone, a lucky penny, and a four-leaf clover (one leaf had fallen off). He followed an odd pregame ritual: First, he placed a stick of gum in Hazzard's mouth; when he made his way over to the bench, he tugged on his socks, lightly spit on the floor, and rubbed it out with his shoe. Then, he tapped assistant coach Jerry Norman on the arm and leg with his program. Finally, he turned toward the stands, winked at his wife, Nell, and gave her the "okay" sign.[58]

Before the semifinals, most writers had picked Michigan or Duke to win it all, though only one of them could advance, since they would play each other. Both teams had great size and rebounding prowess. Duke's best player was All-American Jeff Mullins, a fierce competitor and dangerous shooter. Against Michigan, Duke's two six-foot-ten post players, Jay Buckley and Hack Tison, controlled the glass, and Mullins efficiently scored twenty-one points in an eleven-point victory. In the opinion of *Kansas City Star* columnist Dick Wade and many other skeptics, there was "no way for UCLA to beat Duke." Anticipating a great game, a boisterous record crowd filled the

Kansas City Municipal Auditorium. Outside the arena, scalpers sold tickets for three times their face value. Early on, it looked like fans would get their money's worth, as Duke deftly handled the UCLA press. Fred Slaughter struggled in the first half, and Wooden replaced him with sophomore Doug McIntosh, a hustling center from Lily, Kentucky. McIntosh played well, but Duke controlled the tempo, and the lead, 30–27. Then Wooden inserted Kenny Washington for rebounding help. It was the most important move of the game.[59]

Washington was an unlikely hero who would not have even played at UCLA if it were not for Walt Hazzard. Washington grew up in segregated Beaufort, South Carolina, the sixth of seven children. He was not a prize recruit; the only school that offered him a basketball scholarship was South Carolina State, an all-black college. During the summertime, he visited his sister in Philadelphia. There, on the Haddington Park basketball court, he met Hazzard, who recommended him to Jerry Norman. In the backseat of a Greyhound bus, Washington rode 2,440 miles from Beaufort to Westwood. When he arrived, his teammates noticed that he was extremely shy and nervous around whites. In South Carolina, he had learned to walk with his head down and avoid any eye contact with white people; when a black man looked a white a man in the eye, it invited all kinds of trouble. But on this night, playing against Duke, a segregated team that he never could have played for, he had every reason to hold his head up high.[60]

Washington breathed new life into the press. The skinny six-foot-three guard was an extraordinary leaper with quick hands and fast feet. The press struck Duke like a lightning bolt, igniting a game-changing scoring surge. UCLA forced Duke into a faster tempo and costly turnovers. The ball changed hands, and the Bruins scored eight straight points. Duke coach Vic Bubas called time-out to rest his panting players. When play resumed, Hirsch stole the ball and hit Washington for two more quick points. Then, Jeff Mullins missed an uncontested fifteen-foot jump shot and grabbed his own rebound, only to have Hirsch strip the ball and pass it to Hazzard. On a two-on-one fast break with Goodrich on his right, Walt raced down the court, veered toward the middle of the floor, and without looking flipped the ball backward to Washington, who confidently sank an eight-foot shot. The Bruin Blitz continued until UCLA had scored sixteen unanswered points in a matter of two and a half minutes. Duke never recovered. UCLA's quickness pressed them into twenty-nine turnovers. In the highest-scoring championship game in history, Kenny Washington scored a career-best twenty-six points, while Goodrich poured in twenty-seven points of his own. UCLA 98, Duke 83.[61]

For Hazzard and Washington, two young blacks who lived with the scars of segregation, beating Duke was especially rewarding. For them, this win was a small triumph over racial bigotry. When the final buzzer sounded, Hazzard hurried over to Washington, smiling as the two slapped hands. Hazzard shouted above the noisy crowd, "Send Duke back to Dixie!" Beaming with pride, Washington sat back on the bench. "This is sweet, boys," he said. "This is sweet. We're No. 1, baby. We're No. 1."[62]

After the team finished cutting down the nets, Gail Goodrich turned to Jerry Norman and said, "Jerry, we'll be back in this same spot next year."[63]

3

The Promised Land

"I came here," Gail Goodrich declared, "to play basketball." It was his singular focus. His entire world centered on practice and games. As a boy, he dreamed of playing big-time college basketball, though he imagined that he would play for USC since his father had played there in the late 1930s. Unfortunately for him, few college coaches shared his dream. They said he was too small. During Goodrich's junior year, John Wooden came to the Los Angeles city high school tournament to scout other players, but something Goodrich did caught his attention. The scrawny, five-foot-eight, 120-pound guard showed incredible quickness and determination, caring little that there were bigger, taller players standing between him and the basket. He displayed a unique ability to drive toward the hoop, take off near the foul line, and levitate in the air. As he floated near the basket, Goodrich contorted his body to avoid the defense, switched the ball from one hand to the other, double-pumped, and then gently dropped it into the hoop. Wooden had never seen anyone make *that* move before.[1]

Goodrich came to UCLA fiercely determined to succeed. Despite leading Poly High to the city title as a senior and making Scholastic All-American, an honor given to the top thirty preps in the country, and growing to six-foot-one, only two colleges—UCLA and USC—offered him a scholarship. But Goodrich refused to believe the doubters. He was intensely driven, competitive, and confident. "He's not afraid of anything," a friend said.

"He would drive on King Kong if he had to." Dedication and hard work, sportswriters explained, transformed him into one of the best players in the country. More than anything, Goodrich loved to practice shooting. It was all he thought about. He once told a group of admiring high school players, "If your girl asks you to walk her home, tell her, 'I'm sorry, I gotta go shoot baskets.'"[2]

In 1964–65, Goodrich emerged as a national star, a symbol of the All-American athlete and "the All-American boy." He was "a winner," "a dedicated and complete college player" who probably "ate Wheaties for breakfast every morning." He looked like the male lead in a beach-party movie. Goodrich sported the latest "Ivy League look"—slacks, button-down shirts, and alpaca sweaters—though he sometimes wore his letterman jacket on cool, breezy days. He cut a lean, muscular figure with a handsome "baby face," bright white smile, "twinkling" brown eyes, and short brown hair, but people "remember it as blond," *Sports Illustrated* noted, "because all these kids in southern California are blond and this one is the embodiment of southern California."[3]

Goodrich's greatest ambition, outside of playing professional basketball, was to earn enough money "to live comfortably," an attitude he shared with the "the cool generation"—a generation more interested in "letting the good times roll" than campus protests. In the mid-1960s, when student protests erupted at Berkeley, the state's flagship campus, UCLA students—those "beautiful loafers"—showed little interest in political demonstrations. Looking back, Jack Hirsch recalled, "It was so carefree then. Remember? The dissenters, the war, all that hadn't come along yet. I was just having some fun and playing basketball. Life was fun."[4]

UCLA basketball embodied the pleasure ethic, a celebration of fun, innocence, and youthful exuberance. The Bruins' playing style, with its furious offensive pace and gambling defense, not only was an effective strategy, but also made college basketball a more thrilling pastime. "Our style," John Wooden declared, "is entertaining." It sounded like a business slogan, fit to print on UCLA T-shirts, pennants, buttons, and bumper stickers. Wooden was not just coaching a basketball team at UCLA; he was selling entertainment in America's entertainment capital. "We have an obligation not only to try to win," he said, "but to entertain the customers, especially here in Los Angeles. When people cease to be entertained, they'll go elsewhere."[5]

O

It was the year of the baby boomer. In 1964 the babies of World War II came of age, enrolling in college. Since the end of the war, unprecedented numbers of young couples had moved to California, married, and had children. By the time the first boomers went off to college, they accounted for nearly one-third of the state population. Education administrators predicted that over the next ten years, enrollment at the University of California system would increase from sixty-two to one hundred thousand students. In 1960 the state expanded its higher education system to accommodate the growing numbers of students, passing the Master Plan for Higher Education. Under the plan, the University of California admitted the top tier of high school students, providing undergraduate, doctoral, and law degrees. The California State University (CSU) system served the second tier of high school graduates, while two-year community colleges offered vocational training and course work transferable to either the UC or the CSU campus. Essentially, the state provided tuition-free college education to all high school graduates and a democratic model for higher education.[6]

The rapid increase of young people attending college in California reflected the swelling enrollments occurring across the country. In 1960 three million American youths went to college; a decade later, ten million young men and women attended institutions of higher learning. Before World War II, not a single university enrolled more than fifteen thousand students. By 1970 fifty schools had at least that many students, and eight universities enrolled more than thirty thousand students. Fewer young people began working full-time immediately after high school; instead, they spent at least four more years learning about the world around them, asking questions, and participating in social action groups. Consequently, the growing number of youths on college campuses helped create the social base for student activism.[7]

Few Americans pictured California as a place of student unrest. In the 1950s and early 1960s, popular culture portrayed the state as an idyllic "promised land." In California a *Look* writer claimed, "a man is limited only by the strength of his ambition, the dimension of his concern and the depth of his courage." Popular magazines portrayed California as the "best state" and an "ideal place to live." In the early sixties, when California became the most populous state in the country, the Golden State received more media attention than ever before. Television, movies, music, and magazines promoted the dream life in California, a life filled with sunshine and swimming pools, convertibles and drive-ins, beach parties and backyard barbecues, Hollywood and Disneyland. It also had plenty of traffic, smog, crime, and pockets of poverty, but those issues did not help sell the California Dream.[8]

The dream was shaped in part by popular images of a youthful ideal. According to Hollywood, television, and the record industry, life for California teens was one big beach party. It was a safe place, where white middle-class kids grew up in the suburbs and spent their free time at the beach, tanning, surfing, and playing volleyball. In California *Cosmopolitan* found "boys and girls grow bigger and more beautiful. They are longer of leg, deeper of chest, better muscled than other American youngsters." The kids in California were "happy-go-lucky, big, bronzed, and beautiful." Part of what made these teens so attractive was their surrounding environment, a place that resembled an upscale resort, with plenty of healthy food and year-round swimming, surfing, skiing, and sports. Supposedly, playing in the sun created carefree, well-behaved, "anxiety free youngsters." On the beaches, young men could find the "prettiest, biggest, lithest, tannest, most luscious girls this side of the international date line." Some of the most popular songs of the sixties shaped these fantastic images, including the Beach Boys' "California Girls" and "Surfin' U.S.A." and the Mamas and the Papas' "California Dreamin'."[9]

It appeared that California youth were content living a worry-free life, too busy having fun in the sun to have any real social or political concerns. A *New York Times Magazine* writer claimed that California was "so sunny, euphoric, and pleasant that it seems subversive to worry about the future. In this sense, California has very few subversives." Most Americans simply could not believe that California youths had anything to worry about, anything that would make them so angry that they would defy their parents, challenge university authorities, risk expulsion, and get arrested during a campus demonstration. University of California president Clark Kerr echoed this sentiment, claiming, "Employers will love this generation." Students in the 1960s, he predicted, "are going to be easy to handle. There aren't going to be any riots."[10]

In the fall of 1964, administrators at Berkeley informed students that they were no longer allowed to promote "off campus" causes on Sproul Plaza, an area where they traditionally organized political activities, passed out literature, recruited new members, and raised money. Many students viewed the ban as an attack on civil rights groups and a violation of freedom of speech. Throughout September twenty-two different groups protested the ruling, while the university deans suspended numerous students for violating the ban on political activities. On October 1, university officials ordered the arrest of a white civil rights worker who had set up a table on Sproul Plaza. When a police car arrived, several hundred students surrounded it, preventing the arrest. For the next thirty-two hours, students sat down, sang civil rights songs, and refused to move. From this spontaneous demonstration, leaders of various student action groups created the Free Speech Movement (FSM), organized to guarantee students the right to voice their political views on campus.[11]

The FSM continued throughout the fall, as several hundred student activists continued to demand an end to regulations on campus political activity. Frustrated with their subordinate position in the in loco parentis system, students determined that they would no longer be treated as children. In December the confrontation between the student activists and the administration climaxed with the largest mass arrest in California history. For many Americans, and Californians too, it was a shocking, unimagined sight: helmeted police officers dragging and carrying limp-bodied students from one of the most prestigious campuses in the country into police buses. In the aftermath of the arrests, the university finally relented, passing a motion that allowed for political activity on Sproul Plaza.[12]

Few UCLA students identified with the FSM at Berkeley. In fact, many in Westwood were shocked at the behavior of the Cal students. The *Daily Bruin* criticized the FSM for its "juvenile tantrum" and its militant and uncompromising tactics, which harmed the larger "cause of student rights, student responsibility, and the ideal university campus." Students at UCLA never organized an FSM of their own for a few reasons. First, UCLA was a commuter school. Most students still lived at home or away from campus. When classes were over, they went home to Santa Monica, or Venice, or the Valley; they did not stick around to organize rallies. Equally important, Chancellor Franklin Murphy tolerated free-speech activities as long as they remained peaceful, which helped create a democratic university climate. At UCLA, a graduate student from England observed, "parking was by far the most controversial issue on the campus, ranking a long way ahead of fallout shelters, the Vietnam crisis, and state and national elections."[13]

In the aftermath of the FSM demonstrations, many Americans conceived of the Berkeley campus as "a haven for eccentrics and malcontents." News outlets, television producers, and magazine editors shaped an image of the Berkeley student "as a sort of scrofulous beatnik affecting sandals and a moth-eaten beard and bearing a sign denouncing the American Way of Life." A writer for *Sports Illustrated* commented, "Not since Dink Stover strutted his turtleneck sweater with the big Y on the front has a college type been so clearly engraved on the public mind as the shaggy student of protest at Berkeley."[14]

Although the majority of protesters looked nothing like the stereotypical communist beatnik, many Berkeley alumni worried that the demonstrators had damaged the reputation of "our *best* California youth, which includes football players, who wouldn't be caught dead playing for a 'pinko' school." Most Americans believed that college athletes would never join a picket line. A sportswriter for the *Berkeley Gazette* argued that academic standards should be lowered to allow more clean-cut athletes into the university, implying that "jocks" were all the same—unintelligent, apolitical, and unquestioning of authority. The typical athlete, *New York Times* columnist Robert Lipsyte explained, "will do anything to win" and "will do nothing to rock the boat. . . . He will conform. He will not disrupt the team."[15]

In an age of student unrest, many Americans believed that the ideal college student was the All-American athlete. *Los Angeles Times* columnist Jim Murray longed for the days of Frank Merriwell, the fictional All-American sports hero who was wholesome, honest, humble in victory, and gracious in defeat—if he ever actually lost. "There was a time in this country when it was possible to believe in Frank Merriwell," Murray wrote. "But we are in the age of the 'non-hero' now. The bully rules the street, the state, the nation, the world. And, especially the campus." But at UCLA, Gail Goodrich ruled the campus. According to Murray, Goodrich was the modern-day Frank Merriwell: handsome, clean-cut, incredibly talented, and modest. In 1964–65, when most Americans identified Berkeley students as dissident bohemians, Goodrich emerged as the face of UCLA, an idealized California youth.[16]

○

Frank Merriwell never drank beer, but Gail Goodrich did, if only occasionally. On Friday, October 30, 1965, two weeks after UCLA's first basketball practice, Goodrich and his teammate John Galbraith made plans to drive to Berkeley for the annual All-Cal Weekend. John Wooden did not want his players carousing all weekend at late-night parties, so he ran practice for three hours, one hour longer than usual. Galbraith was on to Wooden's plan and suggested to Goodrich that they could still make it to Berkeley if they bought cheap airline tickets. It turned out to be a great idea. Goodrich had a blast that weekend, but when he returned home to the Beta Theta Pi fraternity house Sunday evening, there was a message waiting for him: Coach Wooden wanted to see him in his office on Monday at 9:00 a.m.[17]

The next morning, Goodrich went to see Coach Wooden. "Come in and close the door," Wooden said. "Did you have a good time over the weekend?" he asked. Goodrich grinned, "Yeah." "Well, I've heard some reports that you were drinking," Wooden said. "I don't know if they're true or not, but they're reports." Goodrich did not know what to say. Wooden reminded him that he was a captain, a leader on the team who needed to set a proper example. "You know my rules about drinking. If I catch you drinking," Wooden admonished, "you're off the team. And I *will* do it." Goodrich told him that he understood. "Okay," Wooden said. "I'll see you today at 3:30 practice."[18]

Goodrich knew that Wooden was serious about his rules, but he also knew that the starters sometimes caught breaks that other players did not. "Coach always said, 'If I catch you drinking, you're off the team,'" he remembered. "Now, he was also smart enough not to put himself in a position to catch us." Goodrich revealed a paradox of Wooden's leadership: the coach enforced the rules as long as they helped the team succeed. A good coach, Wooden believed, acted *in loco parentis*, insisting that his players follow the same rules he enforced in the home. He required the players to follow a strict curfew, and they were not allowed to have "visitors" (that is, women) in their hotel rooms. For Wooden, the young men who played for him were not just athletes; they were "his boys." The devout Protestant believed that he had a moral obligation to develop his boys into whole men, a task that required coaching with "fatherly concern" and "fatherly discipline."[19]

In the world of college sports, John Wooden filled a cultural void of moral authority and parental supervision. At a time when more and more college-aged sons and daughters no longer listened to their parents, Wooden maintained a strong commitment to teaching traditional moral values. In California many adults feared that they were losing youth to a culture of moral permissiveness, the sexual revolution, drug use, and rebellion. But in the mid-1960s, there was no doubt that Wooden's players respected his authority. "He was pretty much on a pedestal," Goodrich recalled. "He was certainly in charge. You did it his way and if you didn't, he pulled you out and sat you on the bench until you figured out that his way was the best."[20]

O

The season had barely started, and UCLA's thirty-game winning streak was already over. Most preseason polls picked Michigan number one, with UCLA a close second, but after a devastating 110–83 opening-game loss to Illinois, it appeared that the Bruins had no business being ranked in the top ten, let alone the top two. UCLA fans panicked after the crushing loss, forgetting that the team had lost three starting seniors in Walt Hazzard, Jack Hirsch, and Fred Slaughter. Wooden suggested that he might scrap the press because it might not match the talents of the current roster. Without Hazzard, writers wondered, who would run the fast-break offense? Could Gail Goodrich play point guard? Was this team built to win it all?[21]

Wooden told his players to forget about the winning streak and just focus on the fundamentals. Without the added pressure of maintaining the winning streak, the Bruins scored more than one hundred points in three of their next five games. Against Arizona State, UCLA maintained a modest eight-point lead for much of the first half. With about four and a half minutes left in the half, the Bruins clamped down on defense and blitzed the Sun Devils in a 19–4 spurt. At point guard, Goodrich played like a master craftsman, carving up the defense and creating open looks for his teammates without neglecting his own scoring duties. UCLA stunned Arizona State, 107–76. Suddenly, the Bruins looked like the team that had won the national championship. After watching UCLA's fine performance from the stands, esteemed Oklahoma State head coach Henry Iba commented, "My goodness, I believe they're faster than last year." It was clear, the *Los Angeles Times* declared, that the "Bruins are back to business."[22]

After losing to Illinois, UCLA won thirteen straight games and finished the regular season 24-2. Before the year began, Wooden had made an adjustment to his pressing defense to accommodate the roster changes. The previous season, the Bruins used a 2-2-1 alignment, but now he employed a 1-2-1-1 press. Wooden felt that the added wrinkle would better suit this team and might surprise opposing coaches who had spent the off-season preparing for the 2-2-1 version. The principles were the same, but the players attacked from different positions on the court. Against Illinois the players simply did not execute the new press effectively, but with more practice time and corrections from Wooden and Jerry Norman, the players learned from their mistakes and became more comfortable playing in the new system.[23]

Even if an opposing player broke the press with his dribble, he still had to get past Keith Erickson, who was considered by many coaches the best defensive player in the country. Cal coach Rene Herrerias called Erickson a "6-5 Bill Russell" for his ability to rebound, jump, and block shots. As the safetyman in the press, he frequently had to stop the other team's two-on-one breaks. Minnesota coach John Kundla thought that UCLA could afford to gamble for steals with the press and "let you break through now and then," because "Erickson's going to block your shot anyhow." "Mr. Defense" seemed to be everywhere on the court, intercepting passes, erasing shots, and "catapulting into the air under the backboards as if the floor were a trampoline." Time and time again, the Olympic volleyball player dared the other team to score in the paint, waiting for just the right moment to slide into position, leave his feet, elevate, and slap a shot back toward a teammate, igniting the fast break. Utah coach Jack Gardiner lamented that a play like that "destroys you—physically, mentally, and morally."[24]

With Erickson anchoring the defense and Goodrich leading the offense, the Bruins made another run at the NCAA Championship. After beating BYU and San Francisco in their first two playoff games, UCLA advanced to the semifinals against Wichita State. During the week before the game, Keith Erickson pulled a leg muscle hitting golf balls at the driving range. When Erickson hobbled onto the court against Wichita State, it was clear that he would not be able to perform at a high level. It did not matter that he managed only two points because the rest of the team ran Wichita State off the court. UCLA's furious speed made Wichita State look like they were running with ankle weights. Edgar Lacey, considered by many observers as the most talented sophomore forward in the country, scored twenty-four points and grabbed thirteen rebounds. By halftime the game was over, the Bruins leading 65–38. With more than twelve minutes left in the second half, Wooden benched Gail Goodrich, who had already scored twenty-eight points. UCLA's flawless 108–89 victory set up "everybody's dream game": number-one Michigan versus number-two UCLA.[25]

For nearly a year, long before anyone knew UCLA and Michigan would play in the biggest game of the season, every national championship ticket had been sold, a testament to the growing interest in college basketball. Ticket holders would not be disappointed watching Michigan, a deeply talented team that included two All-Americans, center Bill Buntin and guard Cazzie Russell, the best one-two scoring combination in the country. With Buntin, Russell, and forward Oliver Darden, Michigan relied on muscle, physically punishing other teams by pounding the ball in the paint. Buntin's fierce rebounding and intimidating presence around the basket made Michigan one of the best defensive teams in the country. Cazzie Russell was built like a linebacker, standing six-foot-five, 220 pounds of strength and speed. Michigan coach Dave Strack designed the entire offense around him because he could play anywhere on the court—in the post, in the backcourt, and on the wings. Smooth, quick, and deceptive with the ball, Russell played like a pro among college boys.[26]

When Michigan's players stepped onto the court at the Portland Memorial Coliseum, it was clear that they were much bigger than the team from Westwood. Before the game, Wooden told a group of writers, "We'll not try to beat them physically. We'll try to run them. If we can keep them from dominating the boards, we can beat them." Early in the game, Russell took advantage of Erickson's gimpy leg, easily scoring from close range. Michigan utilized its size, controlled the rebounds, and took a commanding 20–13 lead after eight minutes. Wooden pulled Erickson and inserted Kenny Washington, who had earned a reputation as the best "sixth man" in college basketball. For the rest of the game, Washington's job was to prevent Russell from receiving the ball inside and force him far away from the basket, a task easier said than done. From the moment he entered the game, the tempo changed in UCLA's favor. Suddenly, the Bruins went on one of their patented runs. Washington lit the fuse, blanketing Russell on defense and hitting back-to-back jump shots. UCLA pressed Michigan into hurried shots and panicked passes. The noise from UCLA fans grew louder and louder, reverberating down to the court, energizing the Bruins' play. In a matter of two and a half minutes, UCLA had taken a 24–22 lead.[27]

After the Bruins' 11–2 blitz, Michigan responded, rattling off baskets by Buntin and Russell. With a little less than six minutes left in the half, Michigan trailed by only one point. Then UCLA went on another burst. UCLA's press dismantled Michigan's offense and spurred a 15–3 scoring run. The Bruins' quickness drained the Wolverines physically and mentally. When a basketball player tires, his legs weaken and his concentration fades. With a minute left in the half, Edgar Lacey fouled Bill Buntin while he was shooting. The Michigan center toed the free-throw line, focused his eyes on the basket, and released the ball over his head. He missed. On his second shot, the ball did not even touch the basket. At that moment, Wooden turned to Jerry Norman and said, "I think we have them now."[28]

At halftime with UCLA leading 47–34, Wooden instructed Goodrich to take charge. For the rest of the game, Goodrich put on a virtuoso performance. Michigan spent the entire night chasing him all over the court. The UCLA All-American played in perpetual motion, darting through the lane, dribbling down the baseline, cutting back and forth, breaking left, and breaking right. The only person who knew what Gail Goodrich would do next was Gail Goodrich, and sometimes he had no idea what he would do with the ball. What made him so difficult to guard, a Michigan player explained, was that he never used the same move twice. He displayed an arsenal of moves: a series of shoulder dips, head nods, ball fakes, jab steps, pivots, reverse pivots, short shots, and long shots. When he did not have the ball in his hands, he disappeared in the traffic of players, lost his man, and then reappeared, ready to catch and shoot the ball in one quick motion. Toward the end of the game, Goodrich controlled the tempo with his dribble, forcing three Michigan players to foul out as they tried to stop him. Goodrich scored twenty-seven points in the second half and set a championship game record with forty-two total points. When the final buzzer sounded, the scoreboard read UCLA 91, Michigan 80. When it was over, Wooden found Goodrich, put his arm around him, and said, "You were the best." Goodrich smiled and replied, "Coach, we did it. We did it again."[29]

UCLA became the fifth team in history to win consecutive national titles. By 1965 John Wooden had built the most successful college basketball program in the country, "a dynasty" in the words of one colleague. He was considered one of the best coaches in the sport, "an unexciting intellectual whose teams play wildly exciting basketball." In two years, the Bruins had transformed the tempo of the game, proving that a team could win without a tall center. UCLA's success encouraged numerous coaches to employ a full-court press as their main defense, though no team did it as well as UCLA. Still, not everyone was convinced that the Wizard had a magic formula for success. "All I am asked about is the UCLA press," Michigan head coach Dave Strack said. "But anybody can press. To make it work you need personnel. The UCLA press is mostly the UCLA players."[30]

By 1965, when most Americans identified the University of California "as Berkeley," the Bruins' national championship teams made UCLA synonymous with basketball. The Bruins' basketball success, Chancellor Franklin Murphy later observed, "did more to catapult UCLA into becoming an entity unto itself than anything that happened during my time." After winning two national championships, UCLA basketball entered the national consciousness, attracting wider interest in the team and the school. Suddenly,

Westwood became a prized destination for top recruits all over the country. UCLA offered the California Dream: a beautiful campus filled with stunning coeds, year-round sunshine, a legitimate shot at the national championship, and the chance to play in a brand-new basketball arena for the greatest coach in the country. UCLA had become more than a great basketball program. It was an "Athlete's Promised Land."[31]

O

Jerry Norman nervously looked at his watch as he waited for the plane to arrive. It had rained all day in Los Angeles, two inches to be exact, and he worried that his guest would be disappointed that Southern California's typically clear blue sky had turned gray. He knew that good weather was an important part of selling UCLA to prized recruits, especially to a player from New York. Norman had waited for more than two years to meet him, and now his plane, TWA Flight 11 out of Kennedy International Airport, was running late. Finally, on Friday, April 2, at 7:16 p.m., the Boeing 707 landed. After the jet finished taxiing, a rail-thin, seven-foot-one black teenager emerged from Gate 35. His legs were so long that during the flight, he stretched across three seats, with his size 16D shoes hanging in the aisle. A stewardess asked him if he was a professional basketball player. "No. No, not yet," he answered in a gentle voice. Norman immediately recognized the most publicized high school basketball player since Wilt Chamberlain. The assistant coach walked up to him, tilted his head back, extended his right hand, and said, "Welcome to L.A." Then the famous teenager exchanged pleasantries with Edgar Lacey and Mike Warren, two of UCLA's finest black basketball players. After retrieving his luggage, the four men crammed into a university-owned station wagon, with the lengthy prep star sitting uncomfortably in the front passenger seat, his knees touching the dashboard. Excited, Norman pressed his right foot on the gas pedal and drove north to Westwood.[32]

For weeks the local papers speculated that Lew Alcindor was coming to UCLA. Basketball fans living far away in California knew all about the teenage phenom from New York, a player the *Sporting News* called "quite possibly the greatest schoolboy basketball prospect in history." His incredible combination of size, quickness, agility, and coordination made him the subject of unprecedented national media coverage for a high school athlete. Since he was fifteen years old, Alcindor had been the focus of numerous magazine features in *Sports Illustrated, Sport,* the *Sporting News, Time, Life, Look,* and the *Saturday Evening Post.* His dominating play on the court commanded attention from writers, college coaches, scouts, and the public at large. Thrust into the spotlight, he became more than a high school basketball player—he was a commodity, a star who could sell game tickets, encourage alumni donations, and bring publicity to a university. He dealt with interview and photo requests, letters and phone calls from college coaches and recruiters, and the constant rumors of where he would play college basketball and what kinds of "gifts" he would receive in return. People recognized him everywhere he went—at the movies, on the subway, on the sidewalk, and sitting in the stands at Madison Square Garden. He could feel their eyes fixed on him, staring, pointing, and gossiping. Were they staring because he was so tall? Were they staring because he was black? Were they staring because he was the one that they saw in the paper? All of it made him uncomfortable, but he had little choice in forfeiting his privacy. "It's not important to me, all this fame," he told one writer. "I don't need it."[33]

At Power Memorial Academy, a private Catholic school on Manhattan's West Side, Alcindor dominated the competition, leading his team to an astounding seventy-one-game winning streak and three straight New York City Catholic-league titles. The game was too easy for him. With his huge hands, he could "manipulate the ball like a grapefruit." He blocked so many shots that he made the basketball court look like "a huge Ping-Pong table." Alcindor was powerful, yet graceful, exhibiting a soft shooting touch near the basket, though he could dunk the ball whenever he wanted. College coaches expected that if they signed him to a scholarship, they were *guaranteed* to win a national championship. Writers reported that he had more than one hundred scholarship offers, but he would turn them all down, play one year for the Harlem Globetrotters, and then join an NBA team. No one knew for sure what he would do, but by the spring of 1965, there was no question that Lew Alcindor was "the most wanted basketball property in the nation."[34]

Alcindor faced enormous pressure to select a school, so John Wooden planned a low-profile visit for his guest. He usually lectured recruits on the "spiritual and educational advantages of UCLA," with little discussion of the athletic program. A *Los Angeles Times* writer noted that although Wooden was not interested in criticizing other programs, if an athlete had to choose between UCLA and another California school, "an extensive degrading of the other schools will almost inevitably take place—although not by the coach." The journalist explained how the athletic department sold UCLA: "If the boy is reserved and wants to go to Berkeley, he'll be reminded of the Free Speech Movement riots. If he's Jewish and interested in Stanford, he'll be told there are no national Jewish fraternities on the Palo Alto farm. . . . If he's a Negro and thinking of USC, he'll be informed of the Trojan varsity coach who reportedly underplayed a star because he was colored."[35]

Alcindor learned from Edgar Lacey and Mike Warren that UCLA treated black athletes relatively well. All weekend long, his hosts told him that UCLA was the best place to play basketball; it was like "heaven on earth." He strolled across the lush campus, relaxed at a dorm, attended a rock concert, and ate hamburgers at a local diner. He had demonstrated an interest in journalism, so Jerry Norman arranged for him to visit the offices of the *Daily Bruin*. Wooden gave him a tour of Pauley Pavilion, which would be finished in time for his freshman year. Just imagine, they told him; you could play in front of nearly thirteen thousand people, under the bright lights of the finest basketball arena in the country. He also watched the only campus athletic event that was not rained out—a tennis match with Arthur Ashe, a symbol of UCLA's progressive race relations. How many other schools had a black tennis player? Before he flew home on Sunday, he attended mass at Bel Air's St. Martin of Tours Church, "with Norman presumably praying that they would be able to worship together for the next four seasons."[36]

Wooden was confident that Lew would sign with UCLA if he could get his parents' approval, a challenging task, since there was no way that the Alcindors would send their only child twenty-four hundred miles across the country without meeting the coach. For years Wooden invested little time recruiting local players. He believed that the team's success would attract good athletes from Southern California and that a player could learn all he needed to know about the school on his own, without the coaches pressuring him or his parents. When Jerry Norman became the head assistant coach, he encouraged J. D. Morgan to expand the recruiting budget. From a business standpoint, Morgan agreed that a national recruiting strategy would attract the very best athletes to UCLA, even if it meant spending more money sending coaches on long trips out of state. He understood that Alcindor was a star who represented tremendous commercial value to the athletic department, and he was willing to do whatever was necessary to get him to play for UCLA.

Morgan told Wooden that he should make the trip to New York and take Jerry Norman with him, because Alcindor's parents, like Norman, were Catholic and Wooden was not. The coaches arranged to visit the Alcindors at one in the morning, after Lew's father finished his midnight shift working as a police officer for the New York Transit Authority. His parents were impressed that Wooden and Norman were the only coaches who visited their apartment. His mother instantly felt comfortable with Wooden, who acted "more like a minister than a coach." For nearly an hour and a half, Lew sat quietly as his parents and the coaches talked mostly about academics. Ferdinand Lewis Alcindor Sr. and his wife, Cora, had always stressed the importance of education to their son, and whether he played basketball or not, they said, he would graduate from an outstanding university. Wooden assured them that their son would receive a fine education and excellent supervision at UCLA. Three days after the two coaches visited his parents, Lew Alcindor would announce where he planned to go to school.[37]

The press had no idea where he was headed, but it did not stop the New York newspapers from publishing what seemed like "hourly bulletins with the odds on his final choice." His decision, a *Los Angeles Times* writer commented, "was awaited with more mystery and fanfare than the word on the first trip to the moon." Alcindor had offers from all over the country, including the Ivy League, the Big Ten, and segregated schools that were willing to ignore Jim Crow custom. Civil rights groups wanted him to shatter the color line at a school in the Deep South, a proposition that did not interest Alcindor. President Lyndon Johnson sent Alcindor a letter encouraging him to play at Houston. Countless universities above the Mason-Dixon line emphasized that they had successful black athletes. No school made this point better than UCLA, where famous black alumni, including Ralph Bunche, Jackie Robinson, and Willie Naulls, contacted him. Bunche, a distinguished United Nations diplomat, wrote to the prized recruit, "UCLA has an exceptionally fine record with regard to thorough and relaxed integration." When Alcindor watched the 1964 national championship game on television, he was impressed by the team's fast-break playing style, and he recognized the importance of racial cooperation to the Bruins' success. But it was another televised event that had the greatest influence on his choice. He remembered watching the *Ed Sullivan Show* as a young boy and seeing a handsome, well-built black man onstage who was a star decathlete and student body president at UCLA. Knowing that Rafer Johnson was accepted as more than an athlete proved to Alcindor that "UCLA was a place where a black man could succeed not only on the court, but off it as well."[38]

In late March, Power Memorial head coach Jack Donohue told the press that Alcindor had narrowed his list of schools to five finalists: St. John's, New York University, Boston College, Michigan, and UCLA. In mid-April, writers predicted that Alcindor would turn down the offers from these schools and follow Donohue to Holy Cross, where he had recently been named as its next head coach. "Although Lew has many offers, I definitely feel we have as good a chance at Holy Cross as anybody else, perhaps a better one," Donohue declared confidently. For the past four years, Alcindor's parents entrusted him to handle every letter, phone call, and visit from college coaches and scouts interested in their son. Any envelope addressed to Lew from a university was forwarded, unopened, to Donohue. He told the press that Lew was not allowed to speak to anyone without his permission, insisting it was for the young man's own good, to protect him from pestering reporters, harassing scouts, and seedy boosters.[39]

Alcindor's parents sent him to Power Memorial because it offered their son an excellent education and because Donohue was a strict yet likable Irish Catholic. Taught by the Christian Brothers of Ireland, the all-boys school was founded on the pillars of unquestionable authority, rigorous teaching, and holy virtue. The brothers expected that the students would respect the institution's hierarchical order, accept firm discipline, and dutifully attend mass. The boys dressed formally in uniform, suit coats and ties, and if Brother McLaughlin caught them with their shirts untucked, or without a belt, or if their hair was too long, he would certainly keep them after school for one hour of detention. The hallways were filled mostly with white kids, the majority from Irish and Italian families, and there were very few blacks, an environment similar to his grade school at St. Jude's.[40]

The more time Jack Donohue spent with Lew, the more he realized that the young man was smart, quiet, and sensitive about his height and his race. Donohue saw countless people walk up to Alcindor and make rude, idiotic comments about his height: "How's the weather up there?" "Watch your head." "Boy, and I thought *I* was tall." Lew responded with a cool glower, trying to ignore the patronizing strangers. Donohue seemed genuinely concerned about Alcindor's welfare and occasionally picked him up in his black Falcon sedan on the way to school. During the drive, the two often talked about his classes, their upcoming games, and the New York Knicks. When they talked about racism, Donohue told him that the word "nigger . . . should never be used. There's no excuse for it." He explained to Lew that it was important for him "to find pride in himself, because in everything he was in a minority. He was 7 feet. And a Negro. And a Catholic. And he went to a private school. A 7-foot Negro Catholic at a private school. That must be the smallest minority in the world." "Lewie," Donohue said, "let's face it. You're just a minority of one."[41]

As a teenager, Alcindor had become increasingly aware of the civil rights movement. He followed the actions of the freedom riders on television, horrified by black-and-white images of burning buses and bloodied faces. In support of the movement, Alcindor carried a CORE placard and pinned a Student Nonviolent Coordinating Committee (SNCC) button to his school uniform that read "Freedom Now." When he injected discussions about civil rights into the classroom, his classmates and teachers responded with resistance and uninterest. His religion teacher, Brother D'Adamo, contemptuously informed him, "Black people want too much too soon."[42]

Alcindor refused to accept his teacher's obtuse views on race relations, especially after he had witnessed firsthand what separate but equal meant in the South. In April 1962, his mother sent him to Goldsboro, North Carolina, about fifty miles outside of Raleigh, to attend the graduation of her friend's daughter. While the freedom riders continued their fight, Alcindor too boarded a Greyhound bus, crammed his wiry seven-foot frame into an aisle seat, and headed south. As the bus entered Washington, D.C., he saw Jim Crow signs that read "Johnson's White Grocery Store" and "Corley's White Luncheonette." For the first time in his life, Alcindor could not drink from the same water fountain, use the same bathroom, or eat at the same lunch counter as whites. Startled by these strict segregation codes, he wondered if he could even walk on the same side of the street as white people.[43]

His trip to the South could not prepare him for an unexpected racist attack so close to home. In early 1964, with a forty-six-game winning streak on the line, Power Memorial entered a game against a weak St. Helena's of the Bronx. Leading by only six points at halftime, Jack Donohue tore into every player for the team's poor performance. According to Alcindor, his coach pointed at him and ranted, "And you! You go out there and you don't hustle. You don't move. You don't do any of the things you're supposed to do. You're acting just like a nigger!" Stunned, he did not hear another word out of Donohue's mouth. All he "could think of was how the instant you do something wrong in front of the white race you're not only a misdoer, but you're a nigger too. They hold that word back until you slip up, and then they lay it on you like a crowbar." For a moment, Alcindor debated whether he should return to the court or go home to tell his parents. Ultimately, he decided against the advice of his two black teammates and played. After the game, Donohue called the star center into his office and said, "See? It worked! My strategy worked. I knew if I used that word it'd shock you into a good second half and it did." Donohue's animalistic view of Alcindor reflected the racial stereotype that black athletes' aggression could be provoked. In 1969, after Alcindor revealed this story in a three-part autobiography for *Sports Illustrated*, Donohue denied his racist diatribe, suggesting that Alcindor's "memory may be at fault or maybe he misunderstood what I said." In the end, Power Memorial won the game, but Donohue lost Alcindor's trust.[44]

Alcindor wanted nothing to do with Donohue, but his coach expected him to spend part of the summer at his basketball camp in upstate New York. Alcindor hated working at the camp. It was a place where everybody knew of him, but nobody really knew him. He informed Donohue that he did not want to go and that he preferred to spend his summer in Harlem. Shocked, Donohue explained that he had advertised the camp using Alcindor's name, and for the first time he had paying campers. Unpaid for his work, Alcindor felt exploited, and he noticed that the more games they won, the more "authoritarian [Donohue] became with me." "I seemed to become more of a property and less of a person to him," he later wrote. Donohue advised him to stay out of Harlem; it was a dangerous place, he said, and he did not want Alcindor getting mixed up with the "wrong people." Alcindor resented such paternalism, but he felt obligated to appear at the camp after Donohue had promised people that he would be there. If he did not go, the campers would be disappointed, and he would take the blame. Finally, he agreed to spend a few weeks at the camp in August. Until then, he would escape to Harlem.[45]

In the summer of 1964, Alcindor worked in the heart of Harlem at HARYOU-ACT, a youth education program that called for social action from within the black community to solve neighborhood problems. HARYOU-ACT embodied Black Power sentiment, a political and cultural movement defined by black unity, self-determination, and community control. For Alcindor, HARYOU-ACT fostered political, cultural, and social awareness. Writing for the organization's newspaper, he spent a great deal of time at the Schomburg Center for Research in Black Culture. The Schomburg Center introduced him to history that he had not learned at Power Memorial. Historian John Henrik Clarke encouraged him to learn about African American history, the Harlem Renaissance, Black Nationalist Marcus Garvey, and scholar-activist W. E. B. DuBois. He pored over the works of great black writers like Langston Hughes, Richard Wright, Zora Neale Hurston, and Ralph Ellison. He read the Nation of Islam's newspaper, *Muhammad Speaks.* Page after page, Alcindor discovered a whole new world, a world where black people had a history and a culture that filled him with racial pride.[46]

Outside the Schomburg Center, the busy streets of Harlem hummed with energy. People were "dancing in the street" to Martha and the Vandellas' new hit song. Merchants encouraged shoppers to "buy black." African Americans lined up outside the Apollo Theatre to hear their favorite soul artists. On the West Side, black men tested their basketball skills on the asphalt courts. On busy street corners, Black Nationalists stood on stepladders preaching that "the devil is the white man." Methodists, Baptists, Episcopalians, and Catholics congregated in "storefront churches." CORE activists protested discriminatory hiring practices by white-owned businesses, segregated housing, and poorly funded schools. Harlem was the center of New York's black culture and black activism.[47]

Beneath Harlem's diverse political culture, racial tensions simmered to a boil. On July 16, 1964, a white off-duty policeman shot and killed a fifteen-year-old African American. Conflicting reports grayed a story that many saw in black-and-white. Lieutenant Thomas Gilligan claimed that James Powell charged at him with a knife; other witnesses said Powell was unarmed. Two nights later, CORE organized a rally to protest the murders of civil rights workers in Mississippi. For many blacks, there was little difference between the killings in Mississippi and Powell's death in Harlem. Black activists set up an old blue kitchen chair and a miniature American flag at the intersection of 125th Street and Seventh Avenue. One after another, angry speakers climbed the chair and vented before an audience of black citizens and white police officers: "James Powell was killed because he was black. . . . It is time to let The Man know that if he does something to us, we are going to do something back." Later, more than two hundred people marched to the 123rd Street police station, where they demanded Gilligan's arrest for murder. When the police tried to turn the crowd away, the demonstrators sang the civil rights anthem "We Shall Not Be Moved."[48]

Almost immediately, Harlem turned into a war zone. When the police attempted to barricade the station, a scuffle broke out between officers and the protesters. Bottles rained down on helmeted police officers from tenement rooftops. Policemen charged back, taking over Harlem like it was enemy territory. Some of the demonstrators were arrested, others ordered to disburse. In a matter of minutes, violence spread like a kitchen fire in a tightly packed tenement. Rioters pelted police with rocks, bricks, and garbage-can lids. Others hurled Molotov cocktails through store windows. Looters grabbed radios, jewelry, and food. Police fought back with bullets and blood-soaked billy clubs. When twenty-four-year-old Melvin Drummond emerged from the subway, police immediately clubbed him, handcuffed him, and clubbed him again. When Lew Alcindor stepped off the subway, he could smell the smoke from the burning buildings. He could hear gunshots ringing in the alley. Men, women, and children cried for their lives. Fearing for his own life, Alcindor ran home to safety. For six days, Harlem and Bedford-Stuyvesant burned. When the smoke cleared, the riots left 1 dead, 141 seriously injured, 519 arrested, and hundreds of thousands of dollars in damage. None of these statistics measures the psychological damage on the people of Harlem.[49]

In the aftermath of the riot, Alcindor interviewed local residents who survived the wreckage. Listening to their stories, he identified with their suffering and frustration; he felt their pain and powerlessness. When Martin Luther King visited Harlem to talk with local civil rights leaders, the aspiring journalist covered the press conference for the HARYOU-ACT newspaper, listening to King advocate nonviolence. But King's strategy had little appeal for Alcindor and other young black activists who began to question the direction of the civil rights movement. For Alcindor, urban rebellion shaped his radicalization. It encouraged him to question nonviolence and embrace a more militant position. His experiences in Harlem fueled his anger toward whites and identification with Black Power. He later wrote, "I decided that in my personification of Black Power and black pride, I was no longer going to pussyfoot around the whites. I was going to speak my mind."[50]

O

It was decision day, Tuesday, May 4, 1965. After nearly four years of silence, the public would hear Lew Alcindor speak for the first time. His morning began like every other, boarding the subway train at Dyckman Street and riding it for twenty minutes until he reached downtown. He sat with his head down, reading a book, trying to ignore the strangers' stares and avoid their questions. Earlier that morning, someone had asked him, "Hey Lewie, Where ya gonna go ta college?" Like everyone else, the man would have to wait five hours for his announcement at a press conference, an unprecedented event for a high school athlete. A press conference was supposed to be held for important public figures, presidents, politicians, and police commissioners, not an eighteen-year-old basketball player. Several hundred people gathered in the Power Memorial Gym, including photographers, television crews, radio broadcasters, columnists, and students. The young star kept the people waiting while he ate lunch in the cafeteria. Finally, at 12:33 p.m., the gangly black teenager wearing a thin tie and an olive-green sport coat ducked his head through the doorway and walked slowly to the microphone, while photographers nudged each other, angling for the best shot. Poised with a serious look on his face, he declared, "I have always been captivated by California."[51]

The culture of California, UCLA's back-to-back national championships, the construction of Pauley Pavilion, and the presence of John Wooden strongly influenced his decision. What set Wooden apart from other coaches was that he never pressured him into coming to UCLA. Everywhere Alcindor went, people told him that they cared about him, but he knew that Wooden actually meant it. When they first met, Wooden said little about basketball and stressed the importance of hard work and disciplined study habits. Alcindor liked that Wooden called him "Lewis," not "Lewie," like Donohue did. It was a sign of respect, a sign that Wooden would treat him like a man, not like a child.[52]

For years Alcindor had dreamed of going to school in Southern California, the place of seemingly unlimited possibilities. UCLA's reputation as a good school for black athletes and the myth that California was a "racial paradise" helped lure him westward. After witnessing the violence of the Harlem race riots, he figured that "maybe it was better to get away from all that for a while and go out to California, where people were color-blind and a man could live his life without reference to color or race." From a distance, California appeared, in the words of Governor Pat Brown, as "a state where there is no racial discrimination." The idealization of California magnetized Alcindor, who envisioned UCLA as "an idyllic place where" he "could play basketball, study, go to an occasional beer bust, stroll arm in arm on the campus with the chicks, enjoy long bull sessions in the dorm," and, "in general, live the collegiate life that" he had "read about and been promised by" everyone he met in California. It sounded so good—too good to be true.[53]

4

Alone in a Crowd

"Freshmen are not allowed to talk to reporters." Every time a writer approached Lew Alcindor with a tape recorder, pencil, and paper, he replied with this standard line. During his freshman year, the UCLA athletic department received more than one hundred requests to interview him, an unmatched volume for any player nationwide. His high school coach had refused to allow the press anywhere near him, and now journalists would have to patiently wait another year to talk with him. J. D. Morgan maintained that UCLA "always" had a policy that prohibited freshman interviews, a rule that no writer seemed to remember. John Wooden claimed that the policy was not made up, but that there had never been any requests to interview a freshman. UCLA sports information director Vic Kelley explained that Morgan and Wooden were simply complying with the wishes of Lew's parents, an accusation that Alcindor later denied. Whatever the truth, the origins of the "gag" rule mattered less than its consequences. Alcindor's silence generated greater curiosity and anticipation over his first game and his first interview. Despite his notoriety as a high school phenom, the public wanted more from him. They knew that he was going to be a great basketball player, maybe the best ever, but they really wanted to know what he was thinking.[1]

No player in the history of college basketball created more media interest and public controversy than Lew Alcindor. As the best player on the best team, he was expected, not predicted, to lead UCLA to an undefeated season and win the national championship. Anything short of perfection would have been considered a failure. Under intense pressure, "the most publicized player of the decade" endured overwhelming attention and constant scrutiny. Photographers, writers, and autograph seekers hounded him everywhere he went. Public fascination with Alcindor persuaded newspaper and magazine editors to expand their coverage of college basketball. For UCLA he was a valuable commodity, responsible for endless ticket lines, attendance records, and lucrative gates at numerous arenas. Public interest in him also added stress to John Wooden's life. He had experience dealing with standouts like Walt Hazzard and Gail Goodrich, but now he had to handle the increasing demands of coaching college basketball's biggest celebrity.[2]

College athletes rarely defied the sports establishment, but Alcindor's developing racial consciousness inspired him to challenge preconceived notions about how a black athlete was supposed to act. When he came to UCLA, most writers described him as sweet, respectful, and humble. One *Los Angeles Times* writer noted that he had been warmly received by basketball fans because "they can see his manner on the court—polite, casual, and emotionless." Beneath the veil of his perceived nonchalance and youthful innocence was "a certain sensitivity and introspection not common in athletes," a seriousness and an anger over racial inequality. He echoed the rhetoric of Malcolm X, exhibited racial pride, and questioned the myth of an integrated American Dream. For some whites, it was very unsettling.[3]

Most people were shocked when he said that California was not the racial paradise that the public had imagined. "What everyone hears about California isn't true," he told *Ebony* magazine. "I expected to see a lot of aware people and there aren't. California runs a game on the rest of the country. It pretends to be liberal but it really isn't." He realized that the virulent racism that most Americans associated with the South was not a regional problem. "The South is in Montgomery, Alabama," he said. "But the South is also in Cicero, Illinois. The South is in Great Neck, Long Island. The South is in Orange County, California. It's everywhere." He could have added that the South was in Westwood, California, too. Although strangers exalted him for his athletic accomplishments, Alcindor rejected whites' acceptance solely on the basis of his talent, knowing that without basketball, he would have been treated, in his words, as just another "jive nigger."[4]

○

Watts was burning. On a hot and sticky August night, a white California highway patrolman stopped a swerving car on suspicion of drunk driving. When he confronted the black suspect, a group of black residents gathered in the street, eyeing the officer with contempt. The police had a reputation for stopping black motorists without cause and whacking them with their batons, or "nigger knockers," as some callously called them. As the crowd swelled to more than 250, more police arrived on the scene to maintain order, but their presence only made things worse. When a woman spat on an officer, he struck her and placed her under arrest. The crowd mistakenly thought that she was pregnant, and immediately rumors spread that a white cop had kicked a black pregnant woman in the stomach. Incensed by a history of police brutality, the crowd began throwing rocks at police cruisers. Soon the police lost control of the crowd and the entire section of Watts. For nearly a week, live television cameras captured the carnage as the California Dream went up in flames. Thousands of blacks directed their anger at the few whites who ever ventured into Watts: the shopkeeper, the landlord, and the policeman. Rioters hurled bricks and Molotov cocktails in every direction; smashed store windows; stole food, furniture, and appliances; flipped cars upside down; and shot at policemen and firemen. Armed with machine guns and gas masks, thousands of National Guardsmen marched on the city streets behind armored tanks, while police snipers rattled off rounds of ammunition from tenement rooftops. Watts had become, in the words of the *Los Angeles Times,* "a holocaust of rubble and ruins not unlike the aftermath in London when the Nazis struck, or Berlin after Allied armies finished their demolition."[5]

The news from Watts read like an attrition report from Vietnam: at least 34 people dead, more than 1,000 injured, and 4,000 arrested. More than 16,000 National Guardsmen, members of the L.A. Police Department (LAPD) and California Highway Patrol, and other law enforcement officers descended on Watts to restore "law and order." News reports estimated more than two hundred million dollars in property damages. Rioters destroyed whole blocks, mostly white-owned buildings and businesses, but few homes, churches, or libraries were damaged, evidence that the looters targeted those institutions that they felt exploited them. It was Harlem all over again, only worse.[6]

California was supposed to be America's racial promised land. "Why then," *Ebony* magazine wondered, "in God's name, was there a riot in Los Angeles, California?" The Watts uprising sprang from anger over pervasive discrimination, persistent unemployment, grinding poverty, merciless slumlords, and police brutality. The civil rights movement had raised black Americans' expectations for equality, but few African Americans found equality in California. One rioter explained his disillusionment with the California Dream: "Everywhere they say, 'Go to California! California's the great pot o' gold at the end of the rainbow.' Well now we're here in California, and there ain't no place else to go, and the only pot [is] the kind they peddle at Sixtieth and Avalon."[7]

The only thing about the Watts riots that surprised novelist Chester Himes was that it took "so long to happen." Himes came to California during World War II, when thousands of blacks flocked to California's defense plants. When the war ended and white G.I.s returned home, many blacks were forced to give up their jobs and accept menial labor as janitors, servants, doormen, shoe shiners, grave diggers, and sharecroppers. Himes later wrote, "Los Angeles hurt me racially as much as any city I have ever known—much more than any city I remember from the South. It was the lying hypocrisy that hurt me. Black people were treated much the same way as they were in any industrial city of the South. The difference was the white people of Los Angeles seemed to be saying, 'Nigger, ain't we good to you?'"[8]

In many ways, California looked a lot like the Jim Crow South. Until 1948 the state barred interracial marriage. Well into the 1950s, numerous hotels, restaurants, and swimming pools prohibited black patrons. The *California Eagle* claimed that more black children in Los Angeles attended segregated schools than in Little Rock, Arkansas. The 1960 census revealed that the City of Angels was more segregated than any city in Dixie. Four years later, Californians reinforced segregated neighborhoods by passing Proposition 14, the "segregation amendment," which rescinded a law that prevented property owners from discriminating against purchasers or renters on the basis of race.

Three out of four white voters supported the statewide referendum, sending a clear message: blacks were not welcome in most California neighborhoods. In the aftermath of the Watts uprising, a local community activist explained, "A person coming out of the south with a vision of the Promised Land . . . finds that Los Angeles is not the Promised Land that he expected."[9]

When Lew Alcindor arrived at UCLA in the fall of 1966, he was disappointed to find that this man was right. While walking on campus, people stared at him like he was an object, often making insensitive and inane comments about his height, or worse. He recalled one incident when a couple of white students spotted him. One of them asked his friend, "Hey, is that Lew Alcindor?" The friend replied, "Yeah, that's him. He's nothing but a big [nigger]." On another occasion, when Lew and a group of black friends disputed the bill at a Westwood diner, a police officer assumed that he was the transgressor. These incidents paled in comparison to the way white students reacted to his relationship with a white woman. The couple had been discreet, rarely strolling the campus, holding hands, or eating in the cafeteria. Bigots made crank calls, ostracizing her as a "nigger lover." When her friends found out that she was dating a black man, they reacted as if she had contaminated the purity of the white race. They asked her, "How can you do something like that?"[10]

It was not the first time that black athletes were discouraged from dating white women at UCLA. When a white assistant football coach caught Walt Hazzard walking on campus with a white coed, he informed him, "We don't do that here." Although John Wooden never said anything to Hazzard, he later had a conversation with Alcindor's teammate Mike Warren. Wooden had received death threats addressed to Warren concerning his dating preferences. The conservative coach discouraged interracial dating, tacitly accepting the racial order. "I think mixed dating is unwise in our society," he explained. "It can bring grief. I would advise against it, for the player's *own* sake. I'm not saying the situation is right, but that mixed dating presents too many problems." "But," he added, "I've never told a player who he could or couldn't date." Warren said that Wooden did not stop him from dating white women. "But, man, how about telling me my life is in danger? How's that for a hint?"[11]

Other black athletes at UCLA recounted similar experiences, but none of those stories came up during Alcindor's recruiting visit. The racial epithets, the threatening calls, and the glares from whites made it impossible for him to date a white woman. For years UCLA had been known nationally as a "paradise" for black athletes, but integrated basketball and football teams did not eliminate racial prejudice. In Westwood black athletes and students encountered whites who supported Proposition 14. When the *Daily Bruin* investigated housing discrimination, one landlady told a reporter, "I never rent to Negroes because they have oil on their skin that gets into the walls and never, never comes out." Although there were many white students who were appalled at such injustice, Alcindor believed that few of them were genuinely committed to social equality. He thought that most students at UCLA did not see the poor, hungry people in Watts because "they didn't care to know." Surrounded by a sea of white faces, he found few people who could relate to him. The more time he spent on campus, the more he felt disillusioned, alienated, and "alone in a crowd." He was filled with anger over the constant reminders of racism and made no more attempts to integrate himself on a predominantly white campus. He became "consumed and obsessed by" his "interest in the black man, in Black Power, black pride, black courage."[12]

If few UCLA students expressed concern for the plight of Watts's residents, many grew increasingly worried about the war in Vietnam. By 1965 it was clear to President Lyndon Johnson that he needed more troops to defeat the Vietcong. Few Americans could locate Vietnam on a map, let alone explain the United States' military involvement there, but when General Lewis B. Hershey, the director of the nation's Selective Service System, announced that universities had to provide draft boards with class ranks, students suddenly wanted to know exactly where Vietnam was. Full-time students in good academic standing could obtain a deferment, while students with poor grades faced the draft. Some students avoided service by attending graduate school, while others benefited from liberal professors who supported the antiwar movement by awarding generous grades.[13]

At the time, few Americans questioned President Johnson's Vietnam policy. Much of the public supported the military's position in Vietnam, fully trusting the government's claim that it would end in a quick victory. In the fall of

1965, after a series of "teach-ins" on the war, UCLA students rejected antiwar proposals in a campuswide referendum, with 57 percent voting in favor of maintaining the government's current policy on military escalation. Still, there was considerable debate over the war at UCLA. In a roundtable discussion for the *UCLA Alumni Magazine,* free-speech activist Jim Berland said, "Most students don't understand this war well enough to support it. And in the jungles of Vietnam, I think it's very clear that you would be putting *your* life on the line." Another young man agreed, admitting that he had a "lack of knowledge about what's really going on in Vietnam." He explained, "You watch the right wing and then the left wing, going around with placards, and they tell you one extreme and then the other, and somebody tells you to go and blow up the country and get the boys home. You don't really know *who* to believe."[14]

Although the antiwar movement did not escalate as quickly as the war itself, there were many students at UCLA who wanted the U.S. military to leave Vietnam. Leftist organizations such as the Students for a Democratic Society (SDS), the Vietnam Day Committee, and the DuBois Club held peaceful demonstrations in opposition to what they believed was an immoral war. Early in the war, most television reports were positive, but the *Daily Bruin* published images of innocent Vietnamese civilians suffering under relentless napalm bombings and reckless gunfire, igniting outrage among some students. At the same time, a strong presence of conservative groups, including the Young Americans for Freedom and the John Birch Society, claimed that the United States had a responsibility to defeat communism in Southeast Asia. Republicans and most Democrats maintained that if the United States did not prevent a communist takeover in South Vietnam, the red menace would spread throughout the region, like a row of falling dominoes. Student activism at both ends of the political spectrum revealed a growing crack in the consensus.[15]

O

When the gates at Pauley Pavilion opened at 6:00 p.m. on November 27, 1965, UCLA students forgot all about the war, Watts, and upcoming exams. For months, students, alumni, and local fans eagerly anticipated UCLA's freshmen-varsity game, an event that included Lew Alcindor's debut, a tribute to John Wooden, and the grand opening of the new basketball arena. In October nearly two thousand students lined up outside Pauley Pavilion, waiting for hours to buy season tickets. A few hundred students camped overnight in sleeping bags and sweatshirts, passing the time reading, listening to the radio, and playing cards.[16]

With Alcindor and three other prep All-Americans, many writers and coaches considered the "Brubabes" the best freshman class in college basketball history, a group that guaranteed UCLA sellouts for years to come. Ken Heitz and Lynn Shackelford were two of the best high school players in Southern California, outstanding shooters who would benefit when defenses double-teamed Alcindor. Lucius Allen, a smooth, ultraquick guard with pickpocket-fast hands, had nearly seventy-five scholarship offers from all over the country. At Wyandotte High in Kansas City, he earned national recognition as the most talented guard prospect in the country, leading his team to two consecutive state championships. Lucius's widowed mother raised him and his eight siblings in the Baptist church and sent him to the Fellowship of Christian Athletes' (FCA) summer camp, where he met his future coach.[17]

The Fellowship of Christian Athletes organized a ministry of Christian coaches and athletes who offered religious guidance to impressionable high school and college athletes. During the Cold War, the FCA evolved out of the Evangelical revival, a time when Americans "added sport to religious faith and patriotism to create an idealized 'American way of life' as an antidote to 'godless Communism.'" In 1954 Don McClanen, a Presbyterian, small-college basketball coach in Oklahoma, founded the organization and began recruiting prominent athletes and coaches to share their spiritual message. McClanen recognized the importance of hero worship among American youths and thought that sports could be used to bring young people closer to God. Every summer young athletes attended the FCA's camp in Estes Park, Colorado, listening in awe as Doak Walker, Otto Graham, Bob Pettit, Cazzie Russell, Bill Bradley, and Rafer Johnson testified how their faith made them better athletes. The most successful coaches in the country—Paul "Bear" Bryant, Paul Dietzel, Tom Landry, and John Wooden—discussed the importance of discipline, mental attitude, and faith. In the late sixties, an age of student rebellion, sexual permissiveness, and drug experimentation, the editors of *Christianity Today* claimed that college sports were "one of the last bastions of discipline on many campuses today." In this period of perceived moral crisis, Evangelical athletes and coaches served an important role on campus, inspiring Christian values and directing "sports admirers to the Master Coach of life."[18]

After winning two national championships, few coaches commanded more respect from FCA campers than John Wooden, who served as a trustee of the muscular Christian organization. Although he did not preach to his own players and rarely talked publicly about his faith, the FCA presented an opportunity for him to openly share his religious beliefs. "Virtue cannot be learned from a playbook or from chalk talks by the coach," he said. "It comes from example." When coaches inquired about his teaching philosophy, he emphasized the importance of moral conditioning. He added "faith" to the apex of the Pyramid of Success because he wanted his players to understand that "faith includes praying. If they are not willing to do that, they are not willing to pay the price." During a speech to a boys club, he sounded more like a minister than a coach, evoking the muscular Christian ethos: "It is a great experience to be an athlete, to test your skills against the best, to achieve records." He told his young admirers, "But there is One who is not very much impressed by all this. . . . We are on an aimless course which goes around in circles and ends nowhere until we win the real victory. And the life that wins the real victory is the one which places itself totally in the hands of the Lord Jesus Christ."[19]

Some of Wooden's colleagues resented his pious, impeccable image. They grew tired of reading articles that described him as the closest "embodiment of Jesus Christ as anyone on the current sporting scene." Some felt that "St. John" was a "sanctimonious hypocrite." One West Coast coach commented, "He's the sort of guy who goes to the conventions with his wife and they sit in the lobby and watch *you* come rolling in." A former coaching rival explained, "Wooden is a completely different person than what he appears. . . . And most of the coaches don't like him because he's never really been one of the guys." According to this coach, Wooden distanced himself from his colleagues, "acting one way sometimes, another way other times. He doesn't smoke, drink, or swear. He just eats candy bars behind garage doors." Other coaches believed that Wooden's saintly image hurt them on the recruiting trail. One colleague complained, "We thought we had the kid sewed up. But then Jesus Christ walked in." Despite the tensions between Wooden and some members of the coaching fraternity, his image as an "inspiring leader" earned the trust and respect of many parents and high school players. After Lucius Allen met Wooden at the FCA summer camp, his mother packed a Bible in his suitcase and told him that he was going to play basketball for "the finest coach in the United States."[20]

Before Lucius Allen, Alcindor, and the rest of the Brubabes took the court against the number-one varsity team in the country, many journalists predicted that UCLA would win another national championship. Wooden had lost his two best players from the 1965 championship team—Gail Goodrich and Keith Erickson—but Kenny Washington, Edgar Lacey, Doug McIntosh, Mike Lynn, and Fred Goss returned. And with the addition of sophomore point guard Mike Warren, many scouts thought that the UCLA press would be just as effective as it had been the previous two seasons.[21]

On the cover of *Sports Illustrated*'s annual college basketball preview, a bold headline read: "THE UCLA PRESS: HOW TO BEAT IT." In a lengthy feature article, the magazine dissected UCLA's full-court pressure defense, a strategy that every coach in the country planned to employ or worried about beating. *Sports Illustrated* could have saved a lot of ink with a much simpler explanation of how to beat the UCLA varsity: pass the ball to Lew Alcindor. His freshmen teammates handled the press with poise, lofting the ball up to Alcindor's outstretched arms as he stood at the middle of the free-throw circle. After he caught the ball, he displayed remarkable agility for such a tall player, dribbling and firing the ball up-court to streaking teammates. He performed better than expected, easily dunking the ball over two and three men at a time, his arm dangling halfway through the basket. His stat line—thirty-one points, twenty-one rebounds, and seven blocked shots—convinced many observers that he was going to be the best center in the history of college basketball, a combination of Wilt Chamberlain and Bill Russell. After watching Alcindor dominate the varsity in a shocking 75–60 victory, Sid Ziff of the *Los Angeles Times* claimed that if freshmen were allowed to play varsity basketball, "they could cancel the 1966 NCAA tournament. It would be no contest."[22]

Unfortunately for John Wooden, freshmen could not play varsity basketball. UCLA fans would have to wait another year for Alcindor to lead the Bruins. Frustration and disappointment defined the 1966 season. Starting guard Freddie Goss, an outstanding scorer expected to replace Gail Goodrich as the team leader, was diagnosed with a blood disorder that forced him to miss numerous games. After losing more than twenty pounds, his energy sapped, Goss returned midseason, a step slower. In February forward Edgar Lacey, considered the most talented all-around varsity player, suffered a knee injury that knocked him out for the rest of the season. Kenny Washington missed time with a pulled leg muscle, and late in the year starters Mike Lynn and Doug McIntosh fell to illness and injury. Wooden jumbled together a patchwork starting lineup that failed to make the NCAA Tournament. The Bruins watched the championship on television.[23]

O

In 1966 most journalists gave Texas Western, a small mining college, no chance of defeating Kentucky in the national championship. Like UCLA's championship teams, Kentucky had small, quick players who ran and pressed from end line to end line. To match Kentucky's quickness, Texas Western coach Don Haskins decided to start his three best guards, which meant starting five black players, a first in championship-game history. Contemporary popular culture has portrayed Haskins as a trailblazing racial pioneer, a coach who intentionally and exclusively played his seven black players against lily-white Kentucky. But Haskins was not trying to make a political statement or become, in his words, "some damn hero." He was simply trying to win the most important game of his career. He had started five blacks for most of the season and did not think twice about doing it against Kentucky.[24]

Adolph Rupp, Kentucky's legendary patriarch, has been remembered as the villain in the story, a powerful symbol of white supremacy, basketball's version of Alabama governor George Wallace, "the bigot blocking the gymnasium door." But in 1966, few fans and writers viewed the game as a morality tale, a confrontation between black and white, integration and segregation, good and evil. Undoubtedly, coaches, writers, and fans were well aware of each team's skin color, but few were conscious of the game's social implications. Still, Texas Western's victory was a watershed in the history of the sport, a portent of desegregation, what Kentucky star Pat Riley later called the "emancipation proclamation" of southern college basketball.[25]

· By 1966 African Americans had enrolled at every major school in the former Confederate states, yet there were no black athletes on any Southeastern Conference (SEC) basketball team. It was one thing to accept token black undergraduates behind closed classroom doors, but it was another thing entirely to showcase African Americans wearing the same uniform as whites, a jarring violation of the "southern way of life." Increasingly, civil rights activists and journalists pressured southern university officials to desegregate their teams. The Civil Rights Act of 1964 declared that universities could no longer discriminate academically, socially, or athletically; refusing to comply with the law meant risking federal financial support, an untenable consequence for university administrators. The intense struggle over desegregation divided the SEC: if forced to accept black athletes, some coaches, athletic directors, and university presidents threatened to split the conference into a North and South. At Kentucky President John W. Oswald supported integration and pushed Rupp to recruit black players. The Baron bitterly complained to his assistant coach Harry Lancaster, "Harry, that son of a bitch is ordering me to get some niggers in here. What am I going to do?"[26]

After Kentucky defeated Duke in the semifinals and Rupp realized that his team would play Texas Western, he guaranteed that "no five blacks" would beat him. Early in the game, David "Big Daddy" Lattin, Texas Western's big, bruising center, dunked with rim-bending force over Pat Riley, scowling like boxer Sonny Liston after a knockout blow. Riley later recalled, "It was a violent game. I don't mean there were any fights—but they were desperate and they were committed and they were more motivated than we were." Throughout the game, whenever Lattin dunked over a white player, it symbolized the great fear of white supremacists: actualized black male superiority.[27]

Outside of Lattin's dunks and Bobby Joe Hill's steal-induced breakaway layups, much of the game was unspectacular and anticlimactic. Most observers could not believe that the third-ranked Miners, with only one loss all season, had defeated top-ranked Kentucky, 72–65. Although white journalists and coaches virtually ignored the racial makeup of each team in their postgame commentaries, racial stereotypes shaped their reactions. Most of Texas Western's black players came from northern cities—Detroit, New York, and Gary, Indiana—creating a false perception that they played an inferior playground style. According to the *Baltimore Sun,* the Miners exercised lackadaisical defense, but could "do more things with a basketball than a monkey on a 50-foot jungle wire." John Wooden stereotypically asserted, "To take a bunch of seemingly undisciplined kids and do what Haskins did is one of the most remarkable coaching jobs I've seen." But the Miners were not a group of showboating tricksters concerned with entertaining the crowd. Their success was based on disciplined defense, teamwork, methodical ball-control offense, and poise under pressure. Texas Western's victory challenged all the racial myths.[28]

Rupp offered a number of excuses for his team's downfall. Some of his players had been sick during the week, lacking the stamina to play back-to-back nights. He complained that the officials helped Texas Western by calling twenty-eight personal fouls on his players and only twelve on the Miners. "Hell, every time the referees called a foul on Texas Western," he claimed, "the boys on that bench yelled, 'Discrimination, discrimination.'" Ultimately, he said, Texas Western won for one simple reason: "They had some niggers on their team and we didn't." To Rupp, the game proved that black athletes inherited physical advantages that whites did not. He was convinced that black athletes had evolved from some Darwinian jungle. He once said in a radio interview that back in Africa, "the lions and tigers had caught all the slow ones." The success of a predominantly black team against the most respected lily-white program in the country helped affirm a new set of racial assumptions that black athletes were naturally stronger and faster and could jump higher than whites.[29]

O

No one expected Texas Western to repeat as national champions. With Lew Alcindor, an exceptionally talented pair of guards, and a deep, versatile bench, John Wooden, most sportswriters predicted, would continue building his dynasty, win three straight national championships, and never lose a game.

Sportswriters suggested that this team would become the greatest in college basketball history, a burden that weighed most heavily on Alcindor. Before the season began, Wooden lost two potential starters, both forwards, who were supposed to aid Lew on the boards. Senior Edgar Lacey, still recovering from a hairline knee fracture, had to have corrective surgery and would not return until after the season ended. *Sports Illustrated*'s "most underrated senior player in the country," Mike Lynn, was arrested for credit card fraud in a local department store, forcing Wooden to suspend the team's returning leading scorer and rebounder. Even without Lynn and Lacey, most observers still considered UCLA the "most feared college squad in a decade."[30]

Lew Alcindor's first varsity game hinted at the future of college basketball. On December 3, 1966, nearly thirteen thousand people jammed Pauley Pavilion, thousands more tuned in to a local television station, and dozens of writers from national newspapers and magazines filled press row, speculating about how many points Alcindor would score. He stood center stage, crouching for the opening tip, looking up toward the hot lights that illuminated his every move. Wooden's game plan was simple: pass the ball to Alcindor. USC coach Bob Boyd made a fatal mistake, instructing his team to defend Alcindor man-to-man, but there was not a man in the country who could guard him alone.[31]

He put on an unforgettable performance, attacking the rim on nearly every offensive possession. The "Little Stilt" exhibited extraordinary moves, grace, balance, a soft touch, and thundering dunks. The rapturous crowd rose to its feet when he bolted down the floor as Mike Warren lofted the ball near the top of the backboard. Then, in one motion, Alcindor leaped toward the basket, caught the ball with his right hand, and violently stuffed it. He scored at will, sending USC scurrying whenever he elevated above the rim. He finished with fifty-six points and twenty-one rebounds in a 105–90 win. After the game, Wooden said that his star was so good that "he even frightens me." The shrewd coach later admitted that he had deliberately allowed Alcindor to score more than fifty points because he "wanted to put the fear of God in some people." He thoroughly succeeded.[32]

After watching Alcindor play one game, the *Los Angeles Times* declared that he "stood on the threshold of becoming the most dominant player the college game has ever known." Duke coach Vic Bubas was equally convinced that Alcindor would shred his defense if he played him man-to-man, so he devised a different strategy, employing a 2-3 zone in consecutive games against the Bruins. Bubas hoped that double- and triple-teaming him would force Alcindor's teammates to shoot more. It was a futile strategy. When Alcindor caught the ball in the low post, Duke immediately swarmed him, but he quickly flipped the ball to his teammates cutting through the lane unmolested. When Duke sagged on Alcindor, Mike Warren and Lucius Allen coolly knocked down wide-open jump shots as if they were warming up before practice. Lynn Shackelford, the Bruins' best shooter, launched deep, high arcing jumpers from the corners. If open, Shackelford, "the Machine," was automatic. Duke limited Alcindor to just nineteen points, but Warren knocked in twenty-six and Allen added nineteen of his own. UCLA's shooters picked apart Duke's zone, resulting in an 88–54 win. On defense, Alcindor closed the lane, blocking seven shots and altering others that were never taken out of fear that he would reject them. "It is impossible for me to tell you what his presence means on the court," Bubas explained. "I don't even think the fans appreciate what he does. The biggest, or rather the best word I can use for him is intimidation. You just can't play all phases of your normal game with him in there."[33]

The next night, Bubas stuck with the zone, but Alcindor adjusted, converting eighteen of twenty-two shot attempts, finishing with thirty-eight points and twenty-two rebounds. The Machine efficiently made ten of thirteen shots from all over the floor, good for twenty-two points, while Allen continuously darted past his man, scoring twenty of his own. It was another blowout for UCLA, 107–87, a convincing demonstration of the Bruins' dominance. If the man-to-man defense did not work and the zone defense failed, how could any team stop "Lew-CLA"?[34]

A wave of panic swept over coaches who feared that Alcindor was simply "too tall" and "too good" for any team to beat UCLA. They whined that he made the game uncompetitive and unfair. The *Los Angeles Times* suggested that he was "capable of either destroying or making a farce out of the collegiate game." The *Saturday Evening Post* echoed these concerns, wondering, "Can basketball survive Lew Alcindor?" "Let's face it," one East Coast coach lamented, "there are two classes in college basketball this season: best and second best. UCLA is in a class all by itself. All the rest of us are fighting to be No. 2." A number of observers suggested new rules to make the game fairer. One coach advised raising the basket from ten feet to twelve feet, while another facetiously proposed sinking the baskets into the floor like golf holes. Later in the season, in USC's rematch against UCLA, the Trojans played "stall ball," monotonously holding the ball for minutes at a time, creating a lumbering, stale pace. Well before the shot clock was introduced, Bob Boyd's tedious strategy kept USC in the game, but it bored spectators and failed to change the outcome. UCLA won the dullest game of the year in overtime, 40–35. Writers and fans worried that every team would stall against UCLA because it gave them a better chance to keep the game close. A Colorado State fan held up a sign with a solution that would make the game fairer for other teams: "Rule Out Lew."[35]

Some coaches complained that the referees protected Alcindor, rarely calling fouls on the imposing center. Wooden completely disagreed, deploring the way opposing players pushed, pulled, hacked, scratched, elbowed, and kneed his star. "He's only a boy," he expressed with his usual fatherly concern. "No matter how tall he is, he'll get hurt out there if this continues." Opposing coaches figured that the wiry center might buckle under the pressure of a more physical game. The pounding collisions near the basket irritated him, but he never lost self-control. He maintained a fearless, stoic expression, channeling his frustrations into dominating performances.[36]

There was no question that he had become the "king of the college basketball world," "the No. 1 attraction on the No. 1 team in the land." He compelled record-breaking attendance, helping sell out every home and road game UCLA played. From Berkeley to Palo Alto, from Seattle to Pullman, and from Corvallis to Eugene, ticket sales boomed. J. D. Morgan credited Alcindor as the main reason that fans filled the Los Angeles Sports Arena during the L.A. Classic. "He's by far the hottest item in college athletics, and when you think of the whole sports scope you realize his appeal is greater than any other athlete right now," he explained. Washington State oversold their seating capacity, and the University of Washington sold out its arena for the first time since the 1950s, forcing university administrators to show the game on an eight-by-ten-foot screen in the student union. Alcindor fascinated the public, magnetizing people who had little interest in college basketball. He was, according to the *Los Angeles Times*, "the biggest attraction to hit the Northwest since the Space Needle."[37]

UCLA's journey to Chicago demonstrated that Alcindor was more than a regional attraction; he had become a national phenomenon. J. D. Morgan scheduled UCLA to play in Chicago Stadium on consecutive days in late January. The money-minded athletic director emphasized the importance of national exposure, showcasing the Bruins in front of packed professional stadia in big cities, games that generated national media coverage and increased the visibility of the basketball program. More than forty thousand tickets were sold in advance, a two-day record for any basketball arena. In the wake of the point-shaving scandals, the Chicago Stadium doubleheaders rarely attracted such large crowds. Consequently, the Chicago press gave little coverage to the sport. Joseph Petritz, the publicity director for college basketball at the stadium, complained that for years he struggled to promote the doubleheaders. But now, he explained, "everyone wants to write about Alcindor and almost everyone seems to be buying tickets for Lew's two appearances in the stadium. He has to be the biggest college basketball attraction of all-time." David Condon of the *Chicago Tribune* added, "You can thank Alcindor for reviving interest in college basketball." Fans and writers eagerly anticipated watching the biggest celebrity in the sport. But there was one tiny problem. No one could get to Chicago Stadium.[38]

A day before the basketball team left behind the warm, pleasant California weather, the greatest snowstorm in Chicago history pounded the city to its knees. Buckets of snow whitewashed the Second City, paralyzing traffic, immobilizing trains, and grounding airplanes. With freezing temperatures, howling winds that blew up to sixty miles per hour, and colossal snowdrifts as high as twenty feet, the city had become "a frozen wasteland." In two days, a record twenty-three inches of snow fell, trapping hundreds of schoolchildren, long-distance commuters, and tourists. Chicago newspapers described the danger throughout the state: widespread power failures, impassable expressways, and countless traffic collisions. Block after block, hundreds of abandoned cars lined the Chicago streets. The *Chicago Daily*

News reported that twenty-one people had died shoveling snow. Local police and the Chicago Transit Authority instructed people not to leave their homes. An eerie silence fell over downtown, occasionally interrupted by scraping shovels and roaring snowplow engines. Chicago looked like "a white ghost city" in the aftermath of an apocalyptic blizzard.[39]

There was not a snowball's chance in hell that UCLA's flight out of Los Angeles would make it to O'Hare Airport. On the way to Chicago, TWA pilots diverted the plane to St. Louis, where the team split into six different taxicabs, planning to board a small train headed for Chicago. Five of the cabs made it to the train depot, but one cabbie accidentally drove to the wrong station, stranding starters Lynn Shackelford and Ken Heitz. They would have to catch another train, even though the rest of the team had already left. After an exhausting eleven-hour train ride, most of the travel-weary team arrived in Chicago at around two thirty in the morning.[40]

After Chicago mayor Richard Daley declared a state of emergency, Art Morse, Loyola athletic director and host of the tournament, canceled Friday night's doubleheader and rescheduled the games for Sunday. No one really believed that the games would be played, especially since UCLA was the only visiting team that had arrived and nearly every high school basketball game in the city and suburbs had been canceled. With Daley's approval, on Saturday morning, a special snowplow cleared a three-and-a-half-mile path from UCLA's hotel to the stadium. Miraculously, more than seventeen thousand fans and fifty sportswriters braved the blizzard to watch UCLA play Loyola. Some came from as far as New York, Omaha, and Moline. Stunned by the turnout, *Chicago Tribune* writer Robert Markus commented, "In a city where homes burned down because firemen were not able to answer alarms, where looters went unchallenged in the streets because police could not get to the scene," and where "the mail didn't get thru," basketball fans ignored the dangerous conditions just to see Lew Alcindor.[41]

In both games, the UCLA star gave the fans more than they paid for. In an 82–67 win against Loyola, he scored thirty-five points and cleared twenty rebounds. On Sunday, another ten thousand fans came to see "the Lew Alcindor show." He destroyed Illinois, scoring forty-five points in a blowout, 120–82. When Wooden removed him from the game with more than six minutes left, the rhapsodic fans rose to their feet, chanting, "We want Lew! We want Lew!" Still, some writers complained that his play appeared "effortless" and that he seemed to "coast" or "loaf" on the court. These stereotypical descriptions deemed black athletes as supertalented but lazy and unmotivated. Some misread Alcindor's unexcitable, emotionless facial expression as aloofness, but beneath his dispassionate countenance was a young man in full control of his emotions, composed beyond any self-doubt. Wooden was dumbfounded at the press's expectations of Alcindor. He reminded the writers that Alcindor had just scored forty-five points and that he would have removed him from the game earlier, "but I wanted him to put on a good show for the fans here." "After all," he said with a grin, "I understand that Alcindor had something to do with the big crowds that turned out despite the bad weather conditions."[42]

O

A blizzard was not the only thing that threatened Lew Alcindor's chances of playing in the Windy City. Before the team left Los Angeles, he received racist death threats postmarked from Chicago. J. D. Morgan contacted the Chicago police, who assigned an undercover officer to shadow the basketball star during the weekend. The most visible black college athlete in the country had become a target of racial hatred. Everywhere he went—the train station, the stadium, the hotel lobby, the airport—strangers fixed their eyes on him. Alcindor had to wonder if those lingering stares came from a killer.[43]

None of the Chicago or Los Angeles writers quoted Alcindor about the death threats, but as the season wore on, they continued to press him for interviews. For many journalists, interviewing Alcindor proved a frustrating process. First they had to submit a letter of intent to the UCLA athletic department that outlined a proposed set of questions, the duration of the interview, and the location. Sometimes Alcindor showed up, and sometimes he did not. Sometimes he was punctual, and sometimes he was late. Sometimes he answered the questions, and sometimes he offered, "No comment."[44]

Most of the questions came from white strangers who were interested in him only as a basketball player, not as a black man. To them, he was nothing more than good copy, a story that sold newspapers and magazines. At times, Alcindor replied to journalists' inquiries with curt answers. Question: "How did you feel about the firing of [University of California president] Clark Kerr?" Answer: "I have no opinion." Question: "How do you feel about [Republican California governor] Ronald Reagan?" Answer: "I have no opinion on Ronald Reagan." Question: "But he's the governor . . ." Answer: "He's not *my* governor." Alcindor refused to play the role of the "good Negro," a Stepin Fetchit caricature, subservient to white demands. Instead, he defiantly played by his own rules, showed up when he wanted to, and answered the questions that he wanted to answer. He was his own man.[45]

Throughout the season, *Sports Illustrated, Sport,* the *Saturday Evening Post, Look, Life,* and *Newsweek* ran feature stories on the college basketball star, cultivating his celebrity. Writers chronicled his rise to fame from high school to college, his journey from New York to California, and his troubles with fame. They consistently described him as a sullen and detached loner who spent much of his free time reading and listening to jazz records in his Santa Monica apartment. He identified with the black icons of the avant-garde—Miles Davis, John Coltrane, and Thelonius Monk—cool, soulful artists who mastered the art of improvisation and pushed the boundaries of tradition. Alcindor read everything and anything he could get his hands on—novels, history, philosophy, poetry, newspapers, and newsmagazines. Chester Himes, Ralph Ellison, and Leroi Jones were among his favorite black writers. He began studying the Koran and stopped attending mass. But by far the most important book he read was the *Autobiography of Malcolm X.*[46]

More than anyone else, Malcolm X shaped the way Alcindor viewed himself as a black man. Many young blacks internalized Malcolm's message of black unity, black pride, and Black Power by reading his mass-marketed *Autobiography* and volumes of his collected speeches. He contested the idea that racial integration would bring full equality to African Americans and encouraged black people "to question the validity of their schoolbook- and media-inspired faith in an integrated American Dream." Historian William Van Deburg wrote that in the aftermath of Malcolm's 1965 assassination, "He came to be far more than a martyr for the militant, separatist faith. He became a Black Power paradigm—the archetype, reference point, and spiritual adviser in absentia for a generation of Afro-American activists."[47]

Alcindor absorbed every word that Malcolm wrote, inspiring his own racial pride and political empowerment. Malcolm's message deeply resonated with Alcindor, who delivered a lecture called "The Myth of America as a Melting Pot" in his sociology class. He exposed the facade of America's cultural homogeneity and emphasized the importance of celebrating racial differences in a positive way. Alcindor told *Ramparts* writer Jack Scott, "Malcolm was able to humanize the whole awakening that has happened to black people in this country. His [*Autobiography*] shows a black man becoming aware of himself and of what his environment does to him. That's why it's relevant. The brothers on the street, they've been asleep for a long time, and this can wake people up."[48]

On February 21, 1967, the second anniversary of Malcolm X's assassination, a group of about thirty-five black UCLA students held a vigil on the campus "Bruin Walk" in memory of the slain leader. Three of the students wearing black armbands stood out: Alcindor, Lucius Allen, and Mike Warren. The silent demonstration spoke volumes about Alcindor's developing racial consciousness and identification with Black Power sentiment. In an *Ebony* magazine article, he expressed concern with racial inequality and stressed the importance of self-determination and the internalization of the black freedom struggle. "We've got to stand by ourselves before we can make it. Nobody is going to help us," he said. In other interviews, he shared his frustration with racism and his dissatisfaction with Californians. He told *Life* and *Look* that he avoided the UCLA campus because he found California too conservative, too reactionary toward race relations, and full of "phonies."[49]

His displeasure with California made him consider transferring from UCLA to New York University, St. John's, or Michigan, which was near Detroit and seemed to have a more liberal, politically active campus and a strong presence of black athletes. Lucius Allen contemplated returning home, too, and playing at Kansas. Some writers believed that they were unhappy at UCLA because of "broken recruiting promises." The young men privately shared their discontent with Willie Naulls, who encouraged them to stay at UCLA and introduced them to his friend and business adviser, Sam Gilbert.[50]

"Papa Sam" was a stout, balding, middle-aged construction magnate, a booster with deep pockets and a web of business connections. The son of

Jewish Lithuanian immigrants, Gilbert grew up in Los Angeles. In the 1930s, he attended UCLA, where he studied political science and economics. During the Depression, when his family fell on hard times, Gilbert left school to help support them. He never graduated, but Gilbert always remained a Bruin at heart. After a brief and unsuccessful career as a part-time middleweight boxer, he worked as a technical worker in a Hollywood film-processing lab. Gilbert had bigger dreams of financial independence and decided to start his own construction company. In addition to building his own business, Gilbert made millions from a series of successful patents; he owned patents on a door lock, metal construction studs, and a water toothpick, among others. Most important, for UCLA basketball players, he was a man who knew the right people—the kind of people who owed him personal favors.[51]

After meeting with Alcindor and Allen, Gilbert convinced them to stay at UCLA. At the time, John Wooden and J. D. Morgan were probably unconcerned about Gilbert, who was an invisible part of the program. But in the coming years, his relationship with the players became impossible to ignore. He acted as the program's padrone, a counselor who kept the players happy with jobs, gifts, and whatever "help" they needed. Some writers and coaches grew suspicious of Gilbert and other UCLA boosters, especially since Alcindor drove a 1958 Mercedes-Benz, suggesting that he had been bribed with "payola." Gilbert made life easier for the players by helping them sell their complimentary game tickets. "Once the money thing got worked out," Alcindor later wrote, "I never gave a second thought to leaving UCLA." During the Alcindor years, the NCAA secretly investigated the basketball program, but found nothing improper. For now, Wooden had little to worry about. He could thank Sam Gilbert later.[52]

O

While the media focused its attention on Lew Alcindor, opposing coaches realized that the Bruins' success was based on more than one man. Alcindor's teammates complemented him perfectly, forming the ideal team: a dominant center, devastatingly quick guards, and strong forwards who could rebound and shoot. Captain Mike Warren provided steady ball handling and leadership. The team's second leading scorer, Lucius Allen, energized the offense with his swift first step, bold drives, and a quick shooting release. With Warren and Allen, it was impossible to press UCLA; either player could fly past the defense with a speed dribble, whipcord pass, or pull-up jump shot. Coming off set screens, Lynn Shackelford released long, looping jumpers that crippled the confidence of every man who guarded him. At the other forward, the less publicized Ken Heitz added solid defense and precise shooting. Even without Alcindor, UCLA would have been a great team. "Give those other four just an 'average 6-8 center,'" Loyola coach George Ireland claimed, "and they'd still have a good chance to win the whole thing—the NCAA championship."[53]

The Bruins coasted through the regular season, a perfect 26-0. John Wooden's success with such a young team—starting four sophomores and one junior—was unprecedented. The Association of Basketball Coaches and the U.S. Basketball Writers Association named Wooden Coach of the Year. Critics suggested that any coach could have had a flawless record with Alcindor, but talent alone did not guarantee a championship. Some of the greatest players in the history of college basketball never won a national title for their coaches, including Wilt Chamberlain, Oscar Robertson, Jerry West, and Bill Bradley. Predictably, the Associated Press named Alcindor a first-team All-American, one of five blacks honored—a first in the history of the sport. And every major news outlet named him Player of the Year. He finished the season averaging twenty-nine points and more than fifteen rebounds per game. Remarkably, he converted nearly 67 percent of his shots. He could have scored more points, as he did when he scored sixty-one against Washington State, but Alcindor was a smart and selfless player who realized that he improved his team's chances of winning by passing the ball to open teammates. It earned him respect among the other players and helped avoid any jealousies that may have hampered the team's performance.[54]

After easily discarding Wyoming and Pacific in their first two NCAA Tournament games, UCLA prepared to square off against Houston in the semifinals. Seventh in the AP poll, the Cougars were the first ranked team that the Bruins faced since they played Duke in December. Undoubtedly, Houston was the biggest, strongest, most physical team that UCLA played all season. Six of Houston's nine regular players stood at least six foot six.

All-American Elvin Hayes, a chiseled six-foot-eight, 240-pound leaper who put the *power* in power forward, seemingly pulled down every ball that bounced off the rim. Next to Alcindor, Hayes was arguably the best player in the country, an athlete who had completely transformed Houston's basketball fortunes. In 1964 head basketball coach Guy Lewis, determined to save his program from mediocrity, headed east to Louisiana, where he recruited Hayes and guard Don Chaney. For years Lewis struggled to attract the most talented players in Texas, but with the support of the administration, he began scouring the South for an untapped talent pool: black athletes.[55]

Guy Lewis was not a civil rights crusader following his moral conscience, dedicated to desegregating college basketball. He simply wanted to win. But convincing Elvin Hayes to entrust his future in the hands of a white man would not be easy. Hayes grew up desperately poor in Rayville, Louisiana, a small, rural Jim Crow town. It was a brutally violent place where white supremacists beat and killed blacks without consequence, confident that the local sheriff did not care what happened to the local "niggers." With little education past the second grade, Elvin's parents raised him and his five siblings with the meager wages they earned picking cotton for a white man, praying for the day when their children would not have to toil in the fields under the blazing Louisiana sun. He attended segregated schools and never played basketball with or against white players. The local white school had seven or eight outdoor baskets with chain nets, shiny tin backboards, and a smoothly paved playing surface. The black school had one basket nailed to a light pole, a creaky old wooden backboard, bent rim, and dirt for a court. It was not much, but it helped Elvin Hayes get out of Rayville.[56]

When Lewis and his assistant Harvey Pate walked into the Hayeses' home, Elvin looked at them with a distrustful eye. But something happened that changed his mind. The two men were polite and courteous, sincerely concerned about his education as well as his athletic ability. Most important, it was the first time he saw white men show respect toward his mother. Savannah Hayes was impressed. The widow had somehow sent her other five children to college, and now her youngest son would go to Houston.[57]

By 1967 Houston had quickly become one of the best basketball programs in the country. With three blacks starting, Lewis's team looked completely different than it had just three years earlier. Initially, the integrated roster angered many white alumni, and some of the white players refused to talk to Hayes or Chaney. Many whites may not have cared if southern sports were integrated, as long as *their* school did not give scholarships to blacks instead of whites. Gradually, Houston's bigoted fans tolerated black players because the Cougars won basketball games. But long-held racist attitudes did not disappear just because Houston had a few successful black athletes. On a plane ride home after a game, a local newspaper writer tried to get Hayes's attention, shouting, "Hey, boy!" Suddenly, the passengers became quiet. Hayes faced the reporter, looked him in the eye, and said, "Boy's on *Tarzan. Boy* plays on *Tarzan.* I'm no boy. I'm 22 years old. I worked hard to become a man. I don't call you boy." Embarrassed, the reporter apologized, "I didn't mean anything by it." "I hope not," Hayes replied.[58]

It was one of the few times that anyone heard Elvin Hayes speak up about racism. Hayes was not speaking out for civil rights as much as he was defending his own personal pride. Unlike Lew Alcindor, he was never outspoken or publicly complained about racism on campus or in Houston. If Alcindor symbolized a more assertive, militant black athlete, Hayes represented the "good Negro"—approachable, deferential on civil rights, and an emblem of racial progress in the South. One local writer explained that when Hayes first came to Houston, he was viewed as a smiling, "silent, doe-eyed country freshman out of the backwoods of Louisiana." Growing up in the rural Jim Crow South, Hayes confronted a different set of challenges than Alcindor. Segregation enveloped every facet of his existence, and he learned to never challenge the social order, whereas Alcindor came of age in an urban, racially diverse, politically charged environment that pushed the boundaries of civil disobedience. And whereas Alcindor shied away from desegregating college basketball in the South, Hayes quietly embraced his role as a racial pioneer. In his own way, each man advanced the role of the black athlete in America.[59]

Hayes was one of the few players in America who was not intimidated by Alcindor. Before Houston took the court against UCLA in the 1967 semifinals, reporters asked him how he planned to score on Alcindor. The Houston star boasted, "I'm gonna run right over him." Hayes's woofing had no effect on the Bruins. Early in the game, Houston took a 19–18 lead, but

Warren and Allen utilized their quick reflexes, blitzing their guards with pressure. The trapping UCLA defense forced Houston turnovers and led to a ten-point scoring run. When the Cougars finally made it past midcourt, thanks to Alcindor, they avoided close-range shots, pounding the rim from long distance with the basketball "as if they meant to straighten it out." Houston's defense swirled around Alcindor in a half-court zone. When Lew found himself surrounded in a three-man circle, he held the ball out of reach, thought for a second, and wisely zipped the ball to his cutting teammates. Although he scored "only" nineteen points, the rest of the Bruins consistently made their shots. While the Cougars concentrated on him, they failed to put a hand in Lynn Shackelford's face, and he made them pay for it with twenty-one points. Elvin Hayes scored twenty-five points, but it was not enough. UCLA won easily, 73–58.[60]

After the game, Hayes complained that his teammates had "choked" and that Alcindor, who had blocked five of his shots, played unimpressively. Alcindor was "not at all, you know, all they really put him up to be," he said. Dayton head coach Mickey Donoher did not believe a word of it. After his unranked team upset fourth-ranked North Carolina in the semifinals, he realized that his team stood little chance of stopping Alcindor in the championship game. From the opening tip, it was clear that UCLA was "too good to produce exciting basketball." Gordon White of the *New York Times* wrote that the Bruins were never really tested. "Alcindor, good as he is," White commented, "made victory so routine and easy that excitement vanished seconds after the start." The Flyers missed their first seven shots, and before Donoher had even looked up at the scoreboard, it read UCLA 20, Dayton 4. Ken Heitz bottled up Dayton's star, Don May, who went scoreless for the first fifteen minutes. Heitz's defense, Alcindor's imposing presence in the middle, the press, the fast break, Shackleford's sharp shooting—it was all too much to handle. UCLA 79, Dayton 64.[61]

Immediately, sportswriters looked to the future, suggesting that the NCAA might as well cancel the next two seasons because UCLA was a sure bet to win the national championship both years. Most commentators agreed that with the entire starting lineup returning and the addition of Mike Lynn and Edgar Lacey, the Bruins would be even better next season. It was clear that UCLA had surpassed Kentucky as the best basketball program in the country. John Wooden had won his third national title in four years and coached his second undefeated team during that span. Many observers were convinced that the Bruins would win the next two championships and never lose a game.[62]

○

Three days after UCLA won the championship, the National Basketball Committee banned the dunk. The NBC defended the rule change because there was "no defense against the dunk, which upsets the balance between offense and defense." What they really meant was that there was no defense against Lew Alcindor, who upset the balance between offense and defense. Alcindor felt targeted, claiming that the rule "smacks a little of discrimination. When you look at it . . . most of the people who dunk are black athletes."[63]

It was a good point. During the sixties, as black athletes became increasingly visible on college basketball teams, dunking became largely a black phenomenon. For black players, dunking was a symbolic display of virility, aggression, and power at a time when many black men felt politically powerless. College basketball reflected the power structure of America: it was an institution controlled mostly by white men—coaches, athletic directors, and boosters. In the 1950s, when black athletes integrated predominantly white basketball teams, white coaches and fans expected them to defer to whites on the court and avoid any "fancy" plays that attracted individual attention. But in the 1960s, as black players became integral members of successful teams, they could express themselves on the court in ways that were previously unacceptable. Dunking for black men, therefore, reflected their desire for freedom and individual recognition. Dunking embodied the politics of resistance.[64]

Even if the all-white members of the NBC did not explicitly say that the rule was aimed at black athletes, the dunk ban reflected the conservative and reactionary politics of the sports establishment. Cultural critic Nelson George astutely observed that dunking "establishes a player's physical mastery of an opponent." So when black athletes like Alcindor, Elvin Hayes, and David "Big Daddy" Lattin dunked on white players, it threatened whites' sense of security and place within the game. Conservative coaches and fans perceived dunking as showboating, an individual act in a game that had historically discouraged individualism. Kentucky coach Adolph Rupp, perhaps still burning with the image of Lattin dunking on his players, commented, "I'm glad to see [the rules committee] do something about it. It doesn't belong in basketball." Alcindor later wrote, "There was no good reason to give it up except that this and other niggers were running away with the sport."[65]

The dunk ban could not stop Alcindor from dominating the game. In fact, the ban only made him better. Historically, African Americans have adapted to conditions of racism and oppression. Consistent with this tradition, Alcindor adapted to the restrictive forces of the new rule. He developed a soft touch near the basket and cultivated an array of shots, including his indefensible "skyhook." It became his new weapon, a reflection of his intelligence and artistic creativity. Time and time again, Alcindor cupped the ball in his hand, extended his arm toward the sky, pivoted toward the basket, and then gracefully flipped the ball over the outstretched arms of any player who tried to guard him. There was no rule to stop the skyhook.

5

Everybody's All-American

There was no place to hide. Wherever Lew Alcindor went, reporters poked him with microphones and prodded him with questions, photographers stalked and blinded him with the flash of a camera, and strangers gawked and pointed as if it was impossible to miss a seven-foot black man standing among white Lilliputians. John Wooden recalled that some whites viewed him as an object or some kind of creature, "some*thing* rather than someone." One time, a white woman shouted, "Look at that big black freak!" Wooden tried to convince Alcindor that the woman was startled by his size and that his black skin had nothing to do with her crude comment. Alcindor disagreed. "Do you think, coach," he asked, "if Mel Counts walked in she would have said, 'Look at that big white freak?'"[1]

To avoid uncomfortable confrontations with strangers, Alcindor often disappeared from his teammates, skipped out on social activities, and avoided hotel lobbies. Frequently, he retreated to his hotel room until it was absolutely necessary for him to come out. While the team sat at the airport gate waiting for an airplane, Alcindor slouched awkwardly in his seat, avoiding eye contact with strangers. Occasionally, he looked up and watched the planes take off, wishing that he too could fly away.[2]

At times the most visible black college athlete in the country wondered what life might be like if he were invisible. There was a loneliness hidden in his face and an anger disguised behind his soft brown eyes. He was torn by a "double-consciousness," what African American scholar W. E. B. DuBois described as "this sense of looking at one's self through the eyes of others." In 1903 DuBois wrote, "One ever feels his two-ness—an American, a Negro; two souls, two thoughts, two unreconciled strivings; two warring ideals in one dark body, whose dogged strength alone keeps it from being torn asunder." Frustrated by black powerlessness, Alcindor searched for an identity beyond the court, a way to assert himself as a black man. His dual existence of being black and being an American was even more complicated by his desire for privacy and a sense of obligation to help less fortunate members of the African American community.[3]

Alcindor was more than a symbol of his times—he helped shape his era in two fundamental ways. As a Black Power activist, he stood at the forefront of more militant black college athletes on campus. Before him, America had never witnessed such a successful college athlete speak out against racism. At the same time, the game's biggest star helped launch a new era of college basketball on television. For years the major networks showed little interest in the sport, but more and more fans wanted to watch Alcindor and the unstoppable Bruins. Soon producers and advertisers responded to the growing demand.[4]

In the sixties, television brought the civil rights movement into America's living rooms, and sports became an important part of the networks' entertainment programming. Television provided a forum for athletes to promote themselves, endorse products, and connect with sports fans and casual viewers. With more basketball, football, baseball, and boxing on television, black athletes became increasingly visible in American popular culture and helped shape the country's racial consciousness. In July 1968, Alcindor appeared on NBC's *Today* show to discuss his involvement with Operation Sports Rescue, a New York City youth program that used basketball clinics to teach kids the importance of education. Although Alcindor intended to discuss his role as a youth mentor, the host of the show, Joe Garagiola, asked him a question that weighed on the minds of viewers. Garagiola wondered why the college basketball star had refused to play in the Olympic Games. For months, newspaper writers, television reporters, coaches, and athletes had criticized Alcindor's decision. They could not understand why he had supported an

Olympic boycott movement in protest against racism in America. Alcindor answered, "Yeah, I live here, but it's not really my country." Then Garagiola suggested, "Well then there's only one solution, maybe you should move." As the tension mounted, the television station cut to a commercial break. Like the *Chicago Defender*'s A. S. "Doc" Young, many viewers wondered of Alcindor, "Where is YOUR country?"[5]

O

Lew Alcindor was not the only black athlete questioning democracy in America. On the early morning of April 28, 1967, a steady mist fell beneath a cloudy, gray Houston sky. A crowd of reporters, photographers, and television cameramen descended on the Armed Forces Examining and Entrance Station. At around eight, the taxicab that everyone had waited for pulled up to 701 Jacinto Street. When the door opened, Muhammad Ali appeared, and photographers began snapping pictures. Ali immediately noticed SNCC activist H. Rap Brown standing near the crowd of onlookers. The two men acknowledged each other by raising their fists in a Black Power salute. Five other black men demonstrated their solidarity with Ali by burning their draft cards. College students protested outside the induction center, carrying placards that read, "Draft beer—not Ali," "We love Ali," and "Ali, stay home." Hours after the champ entered the building, nearly two-dozen black activists gathered in front of the building. They marched in a circle, singing songs and chanting, "Hep! Hep! Don't take that step."[6]

Inside, Ali met forty-five other men who had been called for induction. "You all look very dejected," the champ said. "I'm gonna tell you some jokes." It was classic Ali. He was about to make the most important decision of his life, one that could send him to prison, cost him his boxing title and millions of dollars, yet he could not resist channeling his nervous energy into making people laugh. He cracked about how if "he went into the Army and the Viet Cong didn't get him, some red-neck from Georgia would." When the proceedings finally began, an induction officer instructed the inductees to take one step forward after he called their names. A step forward meant accepting induction into the armed forces. One by one, the names were called. When the induction officer called "Cassius Marcellus

Clay," Ali refused to step forward. His name was called two more times. Again, he did not move.[7]

Ali refused induction, claiming conscientious-objector status on religious grounds. He defended his position as a Muslim, maintaining that the Nation of Islam eschewed wars of any kind. As the Vietnam War escalated in 1966, President Lyndon Johnson increased American draft calls. Needing more ground forces, the military lowered its mental aptitude requirements, which now changed Ali's draft classification from 1-Y (not qualified for draft) to 1-A (qualified for draft). Before he became eligible for the draft, Ali had never given any serious thought to the Vietnam War. But after learning that he was eligible to serve in the military, Ali was forced to take a position. When he refused to be inducted into the military, the New York State Athletic Commission suspended his boxing license and stripped him of his heavyweight title; soon, other commissions followed suit. In Ali's view, the Vietnam War was a war of oppression, an imperialistic conquest that benefited white people. He wondered, "Why should they ask me to put on a uniform and go ten thousand miles from home and drop bombs and bullets on brown people in Vietnam while so-called Negro people in Louisville are treated like dogs?"[8]

Whereas most whites disagreed with Ali's decision, African American reactions varied. Initially, Jackie Robinson felt that Ali was "hurting the morale of a lot of young Negro soldiers over in Vietnam," but later applauded him for refusing to "stay in his place." Joe Louis, who raised money for the government with boxing exhibitions during World War II, said he was "ashamed" of Ali for turning down a similar path offered to him. In June former Cleveland Browns football star Jim Brown invited eight black athletes, including the Boston Celtics' Bill Russell and Lew Alcindor, to meet with Ali in Cleveland. Sportswriters speculated that they would ask Ali to reconsider his draft position and enter the army, but no one actually asked him to fight in Vietnam. At a press conference, Brown explained that the athletes supported Ali and that they discussed the problems confronting black America. Although the meeting seemed inconsequential, it was the first time that black athletes unified across various sports to rally behind a single cause. The Nation of Islam's newspaper, *Muhammad Speaks,* observed that it demonstrated "a growing unity among outstanding figures of the black athletic world."[9]

It was an important moment for Lew Alcindor. As a teenager, he admired Bill Russell because he was intelligent, politically aware, and uncompromising in his principles. And now, as a young man, he stood beside Russell and some of the most important black athletes in the country. "I remember being very flattered and proud to be invited to the meeting," Alcindor later reflected, "because these were professional athletes and I was just in college. And I was one hundred percent behind Muhammad's protesting what I thought was an unjust war." For many African Americans, Ali was an inspiring symbol of black liberation. Although he may have been the only college athlete at the meeting, Alcindor's presence revealed his growing identification with politically conscious black professional athletes. In Cleveland Alcindor realized that as a prominent college athlete, he shared a responsibility with Brown, Russell, and Ali to challenge the status quo.[10]

Alcindor spent the rest of the summer in Harlem, working as a youth mentor for Jim Brown's Negro Industrial and Economic Union and the New York City Housing Authority. He conducted basketball clinics for inner-city youths, encouraging them to stay in school, support community action groups, and take pride in their racial and ethnic heritage. Sporting a "natural" Afro, his message conveyed the importance of black pride and black self-determination. In the rhetoric of Ali, he told a group of youngsters that "black is beautiful, don't ever forget that." African American sportswriter Howie Evans praised his grassroots activism, comparing the basketball hero to Father Divine, Daddy Grace, and Malcolm X. It was a rewarding experience, a reinforcement of Brown's emphasis on self-help and community leadership among black athletes. In an interview with *Sport's* Phil Pepe, Alcindor explained that he identified with the kids as much as they did with him: "I'm one of them. I was born and brought up on 100th Street and Seventh Avenue. These are the guys I grew up with. They're my people. I'm responsible for them."[11]

Before Alcindor returned to California, he attended a Nation of Islam rally in Harlem at Muslim Mosque No. 7, Malcolm X's former headquarters. He came to hear Muhammad Ali lecture. In exile Ali crisscrossed the country, speaking at the Nation's mosques and on college campuses. He had become the Nation's greatest propaganda tool, an unquestioning foot soldier, a mouthpiece regurgitating Elijah Muhammad's lessons of Black Nationalism. In front of one thousand blacks, the champ extolled Muhammad's teachings, advocated racial separatism, and criticized integrationist civil rights leaders. He claimed that the civil rights movement aimed to keep blacks in their place, that it was a disguise for white paternalists who would force African Americans to ask, "Boss may I eat with you?" "Boss can I work for you?" Alcindor listened closely, agreeing with Ali's message of racial pride and self-determination. But he rejected the Nation's religious tenets, rigid moral code, and racial separatism. Unlike Ali, Alcindor thought independently of any organization or ideology.[12]

In October Harry Edwards, a relatively unknown, twenty-five-year-old associate professor of sociology, invited Alcindor, Lucius Allen, Mike Warren, and other black athletes to attend the Los Angeles Black Youth Conference. At San Jose State College, Edwards and a small group of black athletes and student activists planned the Olympic Project for Human Rights (OPHR), a Thanksgiving Day workshop organized to discuss the possibility of boycotting the 1968 Mexico City Olympic Games. Edwards, a former basketball player and discus competitor, cut an imposing figure, standing six-foot-eight, 240 pounds. He consciously cultivated an image of a Black Power radical, wearing a neatly trimmed Afro, goatee, dark sunglasses, beaded necklace, black leather jacket, and a black beret. He maintained that the sports establishment exploited black athletes as symbols of democracy, while black people were "categorically delegated to the sphere of sub-humans, second-class citizenship (20th century slavery)," and "subjected to the most vile of abuses." Inspired by Malcolm X, Edwards believed that black athletes had to use "whatever means necessary" to gain freedom. His skillful, provocatively dramatic, fiery orations captured the attention of the American public: "Is it not time for black people to stand up as men and women and refuse to be utilized as performing animals for a little extra dog food?"[13]

For decades many Americans, black and white, believed that sports were a progressive social force that allowed African Americans to break down racial barriers. But Edwards argued that the achievements of a select few black athletes did little to erase racial injustice. "What value is it to a black man to win a medal if he returns to be relegated to the hell of Harlem?" he asked. "And what does society gain by some Negro winning a medal while other Negroes are burning down the country?" Edwards understood that black athletes had real power in American society, and collectively they could use that power to define themselves beyond the athletic field. "I think the time is gone when the black man is going to run around and jump when the white man says so, and then come back home and run and jump some more to keep from being lynched," he said. It was time for "the auction block to come down." "Black masculinity," Edwards declared, was "no longer for sale."[14]

At two o'clock, Edwards began the workshop by making a case for a boycott. After he lectured for nearly thirty minutes, a number of athletes shared their own views, arguing for and against the boycott. Standing in front of a packed Sunday-school room on the second floor of the Second Baptist Church, Lew Alcindor rose from his chair and delivered what Edwards called "perhaps the most moving and dynamic statements in behalf of the boycott." According to Edwards, Alcindor said, "Everybody knows me. I'm the big basketball star, the weekend hero, everybody's All-American. Well, last summer I was almost killed by a racist cop shooting at a black cat in Harlem. He was shooting on the street—where masses of black people were standing around or just taking a walk. But he didn't care. After all we were just a bunch of niggers." He continued in a firm, steady voice, "I found out last summer we don't catch hell because we aren't basketball stars or because we don't have money. We catch hell because we are black. Somewhere each of us has got to take a stand against this kind of thing. This is how I make my stand—using what I have. And I take my stand here."[15]

His powerful speech elicited a standing ovation. After discussing the boycott for more than two hours, Edwards asked the room of two hundred people, "Well what do you want to do?" Chants of "Boycott! Boycott!" rang from every corner of the room. Outside the church, a violent confrontation broke out between the Black Power organization "US" and a group from the American Communist Party, forcing Edwards to take a roll-call vote instead of a private one. Although it is unclear how individual athletes responded to Alcindor's speech, his stance signified an important shift in the revolt of the black athlete. Before the OPHR, only a select few professional athletes—Jackie Robinson, Ali, Brown, and Russell—spoke out about racial discrimination. But Alcindor made it clear that as the most publicized black college basketball player, he would use his celebrity to facilitate change within the Black Freedom Struggle, and he encouraged others to do the same.[16]

When Harry Edwards emerged from the church, he claimed that the fifty or sixty black athletes in attendance voted unanimously to boycott the 1968 Olympic Games. When sportswriters asked San Jose State sprinter Tommie Smith about Edwards's boycott announcement, the track star refused to verify the professor's claim: "Harry has taken it upon himself to make a statement. He was not authorized to do so." *Sports Illustrated*'s Johnathan Rodgers, an African American sportswriter who witnessed the proceedings, wrote that Alcindor voted in favor of the boycott. But when Alcindor left the church, he refused to comment on his position.[17]

The next day, sportswriters incessantly called the UCLA athletic department, demanding to know if the program's black players would boycott the Olympics. When Mike Warren explained that he had not even attended the meeting, writers turned their attention to Alcindor. His account of the Black Youth Conference differed from Edwards's version. Alcindor remarked, "I can't comment on what Mr. Edwards said. All I can say is that everybody agreed it would be a good idea to boycott. That does not speak for any one person. Actually there is no boycott as of now. There can be no boycott until it's time for anybody to boycott." He explained that he had not made a final decision and that if he did play, he would miss a quarter of school, lose eligibility for UCLA's first nine games, and not graduate on time, all of which was true.[18]

Sportswriters seemed unsatisfied with Alcindor's answers. They pressed him further. One reporter asked the twenty-year-old what he would to do to solve America's "racial problem." Agitated, Alcindor snapped: "Look man, why do you ask me these questions? I am a basketball player. I am not a sociologist. I am not a politician. And I am not a political scientist." He had purposefully used his celebrity to speak out against racism in America, but when writers challenged his position, he recoiled, uncomfortable with the responsibility that came with being politically outspoken. Resentful of the writers' persistent questions, Alcindor fumed, "I'm not someone who's supposed to change the world." Yet he had directly challenged the uninvolved black college athlete standing alongside Ali, Brown, and Russell in Cleveland. By joining them, Alcindor, unlike lesser-known college athletes, became the most visible symbol of the college revolt. He had become an activist, demonstrating with black students at UCLA in memory of his hero, Malcolm X, and working with underprivileged Harlem youth. When the NCAA banned the dunk shot, he called it discriminatory. And he even compared racism in California to that in Alabama. For most whites who believed that sports were free of racism, Alcindor's views were unacceptable. Consequently, the UCLA star carried a great burden to answer the questions of the media who demanded more of him than points scored and games won.[19]

Most whites viewed the boycott movement as unpatriotic and nonsensical. Melvin Durslag of the *Los Angeles Herald-Examiner* echoed the sentiments of most whites who believed that "sports is an area in which discrimination is least prevalent, it is almost amusing that black racists would choose this field as their showcase." Syndicated political commentator Bob Considine wrote that black athletes were "stupid" for believing that a boycott could create any meaningful social change. *New York Times* columnist Arthur Daley suggested that Harry Edwards manipulated Alcindor because he was a prominent athlete, claiming that the UCLA star was "victimized by those who would use [him] to promote a boycott that has no chance of serving its purpose." Edwards denied the accusation: "I think that charge is sheer idiocy. How can you manipulate anybody like Lew Alcindor?"[20]

Although most white sportswriters denounced the boycott, those involved with the OPHR did find a few liberal sympathizers. Robert Lipsyte, a twenty-nine-year-old Jewish writer for the *New York Times,* had become increasingly interested in race and civil rights. In the early sixties, Lipsyte covered black protests, interviewed Malcolm X and Cassius Clay, and helped African American comedian and civil rights activist Dick Gregory write his autobiography. He was one of the few white journalists who openly questioned why the sports establishment accepted black athletes, arguing that integrated athletics was the result of economic interests, not the sports establishment's exceptional moral values. He reminded readers that the black athletes supporting the boycott were all college students and that on many campuses, black students were expected to be politically active. He suggested that many of these black athletes considered competing in the Olympics "hypocritical," especially "to those who believe that this country has offered black Americans only 'tricks and tokenism'; civil rights legislation that doesn't work, an antipoverty war that doesn't help the poor, political oppression and police-state tactics on the street." Few sportswriters recognized, as Lipsyte did, that sports could not be divorced from racial politics.[21]

While many whites criticized the boycott movement, not all African Americans supported it. Former UCLA Olympic champion Rafer Johnson maintained that boycotting the Games made little sense, since he believed that the Olympics "always have been fair to the Negro." A score of potential Olympians viewed participation in Mexico City as a patriotic duty, an important contribution to racial progress, and a demonstration to the world that the United States did not discriminate against black athletes. Houston basketball star Elvin Hayes typified this attitude, adamantly disagreeing with Alcindor. "This is my country and I would do anything for it," Hayes said. "I have seen prejudice—I have lived in it all my life," Hayes said. "But, sports have enabled me to get a good education and have a better life than my parents had." Triple jumper Art Walker echoed Hayes: "This country is no Utopia, by any means—but it's my country." For sprinter Charlie Greene, it was quite simple: "It comes down to a matter if you're an American or if you're not. I'm an American and I'm going to run."[22]

In the aftermath of Alcindor's boycott pronouncement, bigots sent him hate mail, branding him unpatriotic, a national disgrace, and an "uppity nigger." Critics demanded that UCLA dismiss him from the basketball team, but neither J. D. Morgan nor John Wooden ordered him to play in the Olympics or prevented him from speaking out on political issues. When Wooden first heard about Alcindor's involvement in the boycott, he avoided the racial controversy. "I don't want to get involved with the way a boy feels about society—whether he is black, yellow, or white. The way he feels about things is his own business." Wooden struggled to understand why black athletes would consider boycotting the Olympics. Like many whites, he thought that Alcindor had been exploited. "I feel it's outside influences trying to use Negro athletes," he told *Newsweek*. Privately, the conservative coach disagreed with college athletes using sports as a political forum. He hoped that questions about the boycott would go away once the season started. Alcindor shared his coach's wish. In December he predicted, "I don't think anything will develop about the boycott. It will pretty much be forgotten by the time the games come around."[23]

O

John Wooden frequently reminded his players that in one night or one week-end, they could tear down everything the team had worked toward. He discouraged his players from unhealthy and, what he deemed, immoral vices—cigarettes, alcohol, and drugs. Despite his lectures about permissiveness and moral conduct, his players were not immune from experimentation. Lucius Allen lived for fun. Friendly and charming, Allen was "the most likeable guy in the world," teammate Ken Heitz recalled. "Mr. Cool" enjoyed socializing at late-night parties, meeting the ladies, drinking, and smoking marijuana. Lew Alcindor remembered that wherever the Bruins played, the hippies came out to see Allen; "he was *their* player." The pair once received a letter from an admirer in St. Louis that read, "This is for you, hope you enjoy it." Inside the envelope was a tightly rolled joint. Alcindor and Allen smoked it with pleasure.[24]

In the late sixties, drug use became increasingly popular on college campuses, a reflection of the growing pleasure ethic among American youth. For some young people, smoking marijuana was more than a high; it was political statement, a rejection of authority, and an intentional violation of the law. A wave of panic swept over Californians concerned with what many believed was rampant drug abuse among youths. *Time* reported that LSD use among UCLA and Berkeley students had "grown into an alarming problem." Many conservatives associated illegal drug use with lawless rioters, long-haired hippies, communist-influenced protesters, free sex, "filthy speech," and the collapse of America's moral values. A 1966 poll showed that Californians were most worried about "crime, drugs, and juvenile delinquency." Republican gubernatorial candidate Ronald Reagan successfully exploited these fears, campaigned on public morality, and promised that he would restore law and order in the streets and on campus.[25]

On Tuesday morning, May 23, 1967, the long arm of the law showed up at 2627 South Hobart Boulevard. Lucius Allen opened his front door, relieved to see the policemen. He woke up that morning thinking that his car had been stolen, but the police informed him that the vehicle had been impounded overnight because it had no license plates. When the police looked inside the car, they found four marijuana joints in a plastic bag and four grams of marijuana in a jacket pocket. Allen tried to explain that he did not know how the weed ended up in his car, but the police did not believe his story. They handcuffed him and took him to jail under suspicion of possession of marijuana. After posting the eleven-hundred-dollar bond, Allen was released. John Wooden told the *Los Angeles Times* that he would wait to see how the court handled the matter before deciding on disciplinary action. "If this happened during the season then I'd take immediate action," Wooden conveniently commented. Apparently, an athlete could be held to his standards of conduct only from October to March. Fortunately for Allen and Wooden, a judge dropped the charges, citing insufficient evidence.[26]

Allen was not the only player on the team smoking grass. Lew Alcindor later admitted that during his college years, he smoked marijuana, briefly experimented with LSD, and even tried heroin. Truthfully, the only difference between Allen and Alcindor was that Allen got caught. If the public learned that Alcindor or other players on the team used illegal drugs, UCLA's athletic department would have faced a firestorm of criticism. A "source" close to the basketball program told two *Los Angeles Times* writers that if Allen had been dismissed, Alcindor and Mike Warren would have quit, and then the Bruins would have had an all-white team, and perhaps some of the white players would have quit in sympathy, too. But when the judge dismissed the charges, it relieved Wooden from having to suspend Allen and investigate whether other players shared his interest in marijuana. Still, many college coaches and administrators became increasingly concerned about the growing influence of America's drug culture. For years the establishment naively believed that college athletes would not poison their bodies with dope. Somehow the supposed ethics of sport—discipline, character, respect for authority—made athletes immune from turning on, tuning in, and dropping out. Coaches feared that if one athlete ignored team rules and got high, then the whole team might do it, and then the coach would lose control of his team. Some critics began to wonder if John Wooden already had.[27]

○

Despite the off-court controversies, the sporting press and most college basketball coaches believed that another UCLA championship was inevitable.
This was the deepest, most talented team John Wooden had ever coached.
The second string probably had enough talent to make the NCAA Tournament. The entire starting lineup returned more mature and more experienced.
Edgar Lacey had recovered from knee surgery, and Mike Lynn's suspension
ended, giving Alcindor extra help on the boards. Watching the defending
champions practice, Wooden admitted, "There's just not as much to teach."[28]

UCLA fans eagerly anticipated watching what many believed would be the
greatest team in the history of college basketball. A month before the season
began, J. D. Morgan announced that every home game at Pauley Pavilion
had been sold out. Fortunately for ticketless fans, UCLA's home games were
shown on television. For more than fifteen years, KTTV televised sporting
events for UCLA and USC. In the fall of 1966, KTLA sports director Bob
Speck approached Morgan about an exclusive package for the Bruins' basketball, football, and spring sports, knowing that UCLA's contract with KTTV
would expire in 1967. Speck believed that interest in Lew Alcindor would
generate high ratings for the station, and an exclusive television deal would
bolster the athletic department's income and increase the basketball program's visibility. Previously, KTTV televised fifteen events for *both* schools.
KTLA offered to showcase forty-two UCLA events, including twenty-five
basketball games. But there was a minor problem with televising UCLA's
basketball games. Morgan had signed a contract with KMPC, Southern
California's leading sports radio station, which guaranteed that UCLA would
televise only five home games live. Morgan and Speck struck a deal to show
road games live and home games on tape delay at 11:00 p.m., an appealing
schedule for "12 insomniacs" in Southern California. Don Page of the *Los
Angeles Times* wondered, "Who's going to stay up until 2 A.M. to watch a
basketball game?" Surprisingly, a cult of late-night viewers consistently followed the Bruins, a testament to the popularity of UCLA basketball.[29]

Until the late 1960s, most college basketball fans could watch only regional
teams live on television. Unlike college football, the three major networks—

ABC, NBC, and CBS—remained unconvinced that there was a profitable national audience for regular-season games. At the same time, the networks virtually ignored the commercial possibilities of televising the championship game live. In 1962 ABC showed the national championship between Ohio State and Cincinnati on tape delay, *a day after* the game was actually played. Only viewers in Ohio watched it live. Despite the major networks' lack of interest in college basketball, two independent syndicates, Sports Network, Inc. (SNI), and Television Sports, Inc. (TVS), built a market for the sport on television. In 1963 SNI broadcast the first championship game live nationwide. Over the next five years, SNI and TVS continued to build interest in college basketball by distributing regional broadcasts. Every weekend SNI telecast games in the Big Ten, Atlantic Coast Conference (ACC), and Pacific Eight, which often featured UCLA, while TVS had purchased the rights to show games in the Southeastern Conference, West Coast Conference, Southwest Conference, Missouri Valley Conference, Big Eight, and independents like Notre Dame, DePaul, and Houston.[30]

TVS founder Eddie Einhorn built his television company on regional college basketball, but his biggest break came in 1968 when he put together a deal for the first national broadcast of a regular-season game in prime time and in color. The idea for the game originated in March 1966, when Houston played in the first round of the NCAA Tournament at Pauley Pavilion. Houston coach Guy Lewis suggested to his athletic director, Harry Fouke, that the Cougars and the Bruins play each other two years later in the Houston Astrodome. Initially, Fouke thought it was a terrible idea. At the time, Houston played their home games in an on-campus gym with twenty-five hundred seats or at the Delmar Fieldhouse, a high school gym that held fifty-five hundred fans. There was no way, Fouke thought, that they could fill even half of the colossal Astrodome, which could accommodate more than fifty thousand fans. Besides, in Texas, football was king, not basketball. But Lewis persisted and told him that he would pay Houston and UCLA ten thousand dollars each out of his own pocket. Lewis thought of it as an investment in his program and a chance to promote college basketball. Fouke finally agreed and said, "Let's go see the Judge."[31]

Anyone who visited the Judge could smell cigar smoke wafting from his two-story office in the Astrodome. Roy Hofheinz smoked San Souci Perfectos, usually a box per day. Hofheinz loved to sip Jack Daniels and diet Dr. Pepper while he rotated a cigar between his fingers, tapping it into a gilded ashtray as he proselytized about how the Astrodome would change the way fans experienced sports. Charming and flamboyant, Hofheinz had an ego large enough to fill the stadium. The paunchy, round-faced fifty-four year-old millionaire had slick black hair and stained teeth and wore heavy black-rimmed glasses that made him look like "an enormous owl." He wore handmade shirts with cuff links the size of half-dollars and saffron silk suits. Hofheinz even drove his own black Cadillac limousine because he could not find a driver willing to work his twenty-hour day. He decorated his office with Oriental rugs, Moroccan furniture, lush velvet chairs, and a pair of giant lion statues, fit for a kingpin.[32]

In 1960 Hofheinz and his business partner, oilman Bob Smith, formed the Houston Sports Association. The two entrepreneurs bought 497 acres of flat swampland and sold nearly half of it to Harris County for the site of the Astrodome. Two public bond issues paid for the thirty-one-million-dollar dome, while Hofheinz and Smith successfully gained control of the lease of the stadium and brought a Major League Baseball team to Houston. Eventually, the Judge bought Smith out, becoming the "absolute monarch of the Houston Sports Association and the Astrodome."[33]

The Astrodome was unlike any other arena ever built. It was a modern Colosseum, "a gleaming hemisphere of glass and chrome and polished concrete with a revolutionary domed roof and an air-conditioning system." Its broad white crown stretched 642 feet, twice as big as any other structure, and it was tall enough to fit an eighteen-story building in the center of the field. The 474-foot electric scoreboard, four stories high, cost two million dollars, more than it cost to build Houston's old Colt Stadium. Whenever an Astros player hit a home run, the scoreboard's fifty thousand colored lights flashed with cowboys firing bullets, a snorting bull, and launching rockets. Without any beams, pillars, or supporting columns impeding the fans' view of the field, Hofheinz believed there was not a bad seat in the house. And who could complain about the seats? Every fan sat comfortably in a foam-rubber theater chair, color-coded to match a patron's ticket. A spectrum of burnt orange, red, black, purple, bright yellow, pale yellow, and teal fabric seats colored the interior. "A person that gets lost in this stadium will have to be color-blind or an idiot," the Judge said. "For those, we will have ushers, beautiful ones." The Astrodome offered a beer garden, five separate restaurants, two private clubs, and fifty-three luxury skyboxes, perfect for entertaining business guests, politicians, and socialites. Each suite included a balcony, a small living room with a closed-circuit television, radio, Dow Jones ticker, refrigerator, bar, and bathroom. It was *the* model sports arena of the future. The Astrodome, evangelist Billy Graham said, was "one of the great wonders of the world."[34]

The "Eighth Wonder of the World," as the Judge called it, was built for baseball and football. It was also the home of boxing, stock-car racing, soccer, tennis, bullfights, rodeos, concerts, the circus, and the "Billy Graham Crusade." When Guy Lewis and Harry Fouke approached Hofheinz about playing a college basketball game under "the big top," the Judge was not sure that it would work. He wondered where they would put the basketball court, and he questioned whether the fans could see the action. Lewis explained that they would place the court in the middle of the field, and he reminded Hofheinz that if the fans could watch a sport with a little white ball, certainly they could follow a big orange one during a game with much taller athletes. Once Lewis and Fouke told him that Houston would play UCLA, Hofheinz finally agreed. But no one had talked to J. D. Morgan or John Wooden about scheduling the game. Morgan needed little convincing. The UCLA athletic director believed that playing in front of at least twenty-five thousand people, on national television, would help create wider interest in college basketball and generate a nice check for the school. At first Wooden did not want to play. He worried that it would professionalize the game and that the fans would be too far from the court. He said that it would make "a spectacle" out of college basketball. But that was the whole point.[35]

For weeks sportswriters filled their columns by promoting "the Game of the Century." It had all the ingredients of a Hollywood drama that "not even Warner Bros. or Cecil B. DeMille could have dreamed of it." It was "a battle of the unbeatens," an "epic struggle" between number-one UCLA and number-two Houston. After winning their first seventeen games of the season, the Bruins had won forty-seven consecutive games, the second-longest winning streak in the history of college basketball. Writers built their stories around the sport's two biggest stars, Lew Alcindor and Elvin Hayes, even though they would not guard each other. The Astrodome ticket office sold more than fifty-two thousand tickets, including standing room only. It was the largest paying audience in the history of the sport, twice as large as any other college game ever played. Astrodome ticket manager Dick McDowell claimed that he had so many ticket requests that "we could have sold 75,000 tickets, no doubt about it." Houston sports information director Ted Nance reported that he had distributed 175 press passes to newspaper reporters and national magazine writers. Never before had so many Americans paid attention to a college basketball game. *Houston Chronicle* columnist Wells Twombly hyperbolically wrote that during the game, "the world seemed to stop spinning."[36]

Despite the tremendous media buildup, the three major networks showed no interest in televising the game. Eddie Einhorn outbid SNI for the rights to televise it, paying twenty-seven thousand dollars. Einhorn had the support of J. D. Morgan, whom he had known since the midsixties when TVS began broadcasting UCLA basketball games at Chicago Stadium. Morgan and Einhorn shared a common interest: each wanted to build his brand. Morgan realized that promoting UCLA basketball meant playing on national television, and Einhorn believed that he could build TVS around the best team with the game's biggest star. On 150 stations in forty-nine states, from Portland, Maine, to Fairbanks, Alaska, TVS distributed the "biggest show in sports" to the largest television audience in the history of college basketball. More than twenty million viewers tuned in to watch what many believed was impossible: a UCLA loss.[37]

From a patron's brightly colored seat, it all looked so artificial. The eighteen-ton basketball court had been disassembled, shipped all the way from the Los Angeles Sports Arena, and reassembled like a jigsaw puzzle in the middle of the Astrodome floor. The turf had been lifted, leaving the court surrounded by a layer of dirt. Hot television lights were placed above both baskets, momentarily blinding players who looked up from beneath the rim. Workers dug one-foot ditches on both sidelines for the players and press to preserve the view for the paying customers. The closest fans sat one hundred feet from the court, separated by a barren area of dirt. On the first level, obtrusive television equipment blocked the view of some fans. In the highest reaches of the dome, unless spectators had binoculars, the players looked like ants. Before the game, one fan grumbled from the nosebleeds, "I can't see what's going on, but I don't care [as long as] Houston wins."[38]

From the opening tip, it was clear that each team's star would define the outcome of the game. UCLA was the clear favorite, averaging one hundred points per game and beating their opponents by an average of thirty points. Most writers believed that the Bruins were simply too quick and that their press would rattle the Cougars. To decelerate UCLA's fast break, Houston employed a 1-3-1 zone. The zone slowed the Bruins, but Houston could thank Cal for a little help. A week earlier, a California player had accidentally poked Lew Alcindor in the eye while swiping at the ball. For three days, Alcindor experienced extreme pain and blurred vision and was forced to rest in a darkened room at UCLA's Jules Stein Eye Institute. John Wooden explained that it looked "as though somebody had rubbed a piece of sandpaper across his eye." A day before the game, Wooden doubted that his star would be able to play. On the morning of the game, Alcindor was still experiencing blurred vision and impaired depth perception. After six days of inactivity, he moved lethargically, bereft of his usual quick reflexes. Frequently, Elvin Hayes sprinted down the court before Alcindor could set himself in the paint, making it easy for him to score inside. When Alcindor tried to score, Houston's zone collapsed on him, and three times Hayes blocked his shots. Despite clear signs that Alcindor was not himself, Wooden left him on the court for all forty minutes of the game.[39]

In the first half, UCLA had no answer for Elvin Hayes. Edgar Lacey started the game guarding him. The Houston All-American dissected UCLA's defense, penetrated the lane, and hit a series of soft jumpers. After ten and a half minutes, Wooden pulled Lacey out of the game, but by that point Hayes had found his rhythm and was well on his way to scoring twenty-nine of Houston's forty-six first-half points. No player ever wants to be taken out of the game, especially when the man he is supposed to defend has outperformed him.

Lacey had been humiliated, and when Wooden took him out, it bruised his pride. When he approached the sideline, Wooden told him, "Come here and sit next to me," but Lacey walked right past him and sat down at the end of the bench.[40]

The Bruins trailed the Cougars by three at the half, 46–43. UCLA kept the score close, but they looked sluggish, like somebody woke them in the middle of the night to play a basketball game. Houston's zone defense worked just as planned, slowing the tempo in their favor. With little ball movement on offense, UCLA settled for too many long jump shots. Alcindor never found his shooting touch, missing fourteen of eighteen attempts. Mike Warren wanted to push the ball, but the Bruins could not move fast enough, with Alcindor gasping for air. Warren contemplated asking the coaches to take Alcindor out so that they could speed up the tempo, but kept his mouth shut. At halftime Wooden made one important adjustment, starting Jim Nielsen in place of Edgar Lacey. In the Houston locker room, Guy Lewis told his players, "Just take it to 'em and pray—pray real hard." Eddie Einhorn had instructions for play-by-play announcer Dick Enberg, too. Einhorn handed Enberg scribbled pieces of paper with ten-second spots from advertisers who had bought airtime in the middle of the game. With millions of viewers watching, more and more advertisers finally decided to cash in on college basketball.[41]

In the second half, neither team gained a real advantage. The crowd kept waiting for the Bruins to go on one of their patented runs, but it never came. For most of the second half, UCLA played from a few points behind. Over the course of seventeen minutes, Houston had scored only nineteen points, while UCLA had added just twenty-two. With three minutes left in the game, Alcindor sank two free throws, tying the game at 65. In the next minute, Hayes and Don Chaney hit back-to-back shots, giving Houston a four-point lead. Lucius Allen responded, drove hard down the baseline, and scored. With forty-four seconds remaining, Allen went inside again, where he met a cluster of Houston defenders. Ken Spain fouled him. Allen, UCLA's leading scorer with twenty-five points, made both free throws to tie the game, 69–69. At that point, everyone in the Astrodome knew where the ball was going. Elvin Hayes received a pass on the left block with his back to the basket. He turned to shoot, but Jim Nielsen blocked his shot. Hayes recovered the ball, rose up to shoot, and was fouled by Nielsen. Now, the pressure was on. He toed the free-throw line and calmly sank both shots, giving Houston a 71–69 edge. Hayes had performed brilliantly, scoring thirty-nine points, grabbing fifteen rebounds, and blocking eight shots. And he had made two clutch free throws when it mattered most.[42]

With twenty-eight seconds left on the clock, Mike Warren advanced the ball past midcourt. When Warren tried to pass the ball, it was tipped into the hands of Spain, who then traveled. The ball went back to UCLA. Lucius Allen dribbled left at the top of the key, looking inside for Alcindor, who was sandwiched between defenders. Allen spotted Lynn Shackelford in the far-right corner and attempted a skip pass, but Warren darted for the ball, failing to recognize that it was not intended for him. As Warren cut in front of Shackelford, the ball bounced off his hands. Only twelve seconds remained, and Houston had the ball. Spain passed it in to Hayes, who then dribbled in a semicircle with his head down. Just as Alcindor and Allen swarmed him, he passed the ball up-court to George Reynolds, who dribbled until time expired. Dozens of Houston fans stampeded over the top of Dick Enberg, who called the game from his foxhole, "The Houston Cougars have snapped UCLA's 47-game winning streak!"[43]

The Game of the Century advanced the commercialization of college basketball, proving that there was a major market for the sport. Suddenly, the three networks expressed interest in showing the NCAA Tournament. At the end of the 1968 season, NBC purchased the rights to broadcast the championship, paying more than a million dollars for a two-year contract, more than twice the amount that SNI had previously doled out. With its successful broadcast of the game from the Astrodome, TVS continued its national game of the week, sponsored by major advertisers, including Shell Oil, R. J. Reynolds, John Hancock Insurance, American Motors, and Uniroyal. These advertisers paid for more than competitive college basketball games; they paid for a brand of entertainment, and UCLA helped provide it.[44]

The UCLA-Houston game also represented racial progress on the court. Since Kentucky won the national championship in 1958, no other segregated team had won the title. Although the majority of programs in the Deep South remained lily-white, segregated college basketball was fast becoming a relic of the past. Without a doubt, the two best teams in the country had been built around exceptional African American athletes. UCLA and Houston each featured four black starters. Two years after Texas Western beat Kentucky in the national championship, Houston's victory over UCLA signaled a crushing blow against segregated college basketball. While Texas Western had recruited most of its black players outside the South, the majority of Houston's black players were southern born and raised. Recruiting southern black athletes allowed Guy Lewis to build Houston into a basketball power almost overnight and beat the once insurmountable UCLA Bruins, a fact that southern college basketball coaches could not ignore. Gradually, black athletes integrated college basketball in the Deep South. In 1967–68, North Carolina, Wake Forest, and Vanderbilt desegregated their varsity teams, and the following year North Carolina State followed suit. Still, by the end of the 1969 season, twelve schools in the SEC and the ACC had failed to successfully recruit black athletes. Many southern coaches resisted integration, fearful of upsetting Jim Crow custom and angering influential boosters. In the late sixties, while many southern coaches ignored protests from liberal students and civil rights groups, coaches above the Mason-Dixon line confronted a different source of pressure: Black Power.[45]

O

For the first time in a long time, UCLA boarded the team bus with no reason to celebrate. The players replayed the game in their minds, wondering what had gone wrong. Lucius Allen questioned John Wooden's strategy, asking him, "Coach, why didn't you put our best forward back into the game?" While Wooden asked Allen to discuss the matter with him privately, Edgar Lacey complained to Lew Alcindor about his limited playing time. Before the Houston game, Lacey had become an important contributor, the team's third leading scorer and second-best rebounder. But he was frustrated with his role. Although he had started every game of the season, the senior forward shared much of his playing time with Mike Lynn. Both Lacey and Lynn believed that they should have played more than Lynn Shackelford, but Wooden disagreed. Without question Lacey and Lynn were more talented than Shackelford, but both players thrived in the post.

With Alcindor clogging the lane, it did not make sense for Wooden to start them both. Shackelford, on the other hand, was a better fit for the team's offense because he could shoot from long distance, which helped prevent defenses from double-teaming Lew. Plus, Wooden believed that Shackelford worked hard and had a better attitude than his other forwards. But none of that mattered to Lacey. In his mind, he had been unfairly benched, and now, he told Alcindor, he was going to quit.[46]

On Monday a sportswriter asked Wooden why Lacey did not play in the second half against Houston. Wooden explained, "Edgar got his feelings hurt early. He wasn't effective guarding against his man [Elvin Hayes]. He didn't especially feel like coming back in anyway, so I didn't feel it was right to use him." Wooden said that he had considered putting Lacey back in, but when he looked down the bench, he saw him sulking. Lacey disagreed with Wooden's version, claiming that he was bouncing up and down on the bench, ready to go back into the game. On Tuesday morning, he visited Wooden's office, asking if the quote in the newspaper was accurate. Wooden answered, "You gave me the impression you didn't want to play. That's exactly what I told the papers and I'll tell you that." Lacey seethed, "That's all I wanted to know. I quit!"[47]

On Wednesday a sportswriter from the *Los Angeles Times* called Wooden at home. Wooden told the writer that Lacey had missed two practices and would not accompany the team to New York City, but he would allow him to return. Four days later, Lacey made it clear that he had no intention of returning. "I've never enjoyed playing for that man," he told the *Times* writer. "I'm glad I'm getting out now while I still have some of my pride, my sanity, and my self-esteem left." Lacey revealed that he had been frustrated for years, annoyed that the coach had tried to change the way he shot the ball and "misused" his talents. To Lacey, Wooden clearly favored Lynn Shackelford. "He is sacrificing my ability and Mike's ability to promote Shack," he complained.[48]

Alcindor understood Lacey's frustration. From his perspective, Wooden played Shackelford more than Lacey and Lynn because he fit into the coach's value system. Lacey was a loner who distanced himself from most of his teammates and coaches, whereas Shackelford accepted the coach's criticism, worked hard, and was a real "team player." In 1969 Alcindor told *Sports Il-*

lustrated's Jack Olsen, "Wooden had this thing about players being 'morally' ready for play," which prevented him from getting "along with 'problem' players." Alcindor claimed that if a player did not attend church "every Sunday and study for three hours a night and arrive 15 minutes early to practice and nod [in] agreement with every inspiring word the coach said, they were not morally fit to play—and they found themselves on the second team."[49]

According to Alcindor, Lynn Shackelford was Wooden's ideal player. Shack was the "All-American boy," studious, selfless, and conservative. Shackelford told the *Daily Bruin,* "For our team to do well, we can't be fighting the coach. By playing ball, you learn to work with your superior and your fellow students." Shackelford's perspective conformed to athletes' traditional attitudes toward authority. Lacey's actions reflected a more militant, questioning attitude among black athletes that threatened the very foundation of the college establishment. *Los Angeles Times* columnist John Hall lamented that Lacey's behavior symbolized "the celebrated and still growing rebellion of our youth—a noble term employed ruthlessly to cover up everything from simple bad manners and selfishness to ingratitude and disloyalty."[50]

Edgar Lacey was not the only black athlete who had publicly criticized his coach. At California Rene Herrerias ordered Bob Presley to cut his "natural" Afro. When Presley cut practice instead of his hair, Herrerias suspended him for the rest of the season. Most white coaches failed to realize that a natural was more than a hairstyle; it symbolized black pride, group unity, and self-love. For some, it was a political statement, a rejection of white standards of beauty, chemical straighteners, perms, and hot irons. It was a silent gesture that loudly spoke, "Black is beautiful." Although Presley had not trimmed his hair, Herrerias reinstated him two days later. Herrerias claimed that the decision was his alone, but the team's eleven white players believed that the administration forced him and Cal athletic director Pete Newell to bring Presley back to avoid further "racial problems." The white players defended their coach, claiming that there was no racial discrimination on the team and announced a mass resignation until the administration restored all coaching authority to Herrerias. In response, twenty-five black athletes, including Presley and four other basketball players, issued an ultimatum of their own. They demanded the dismissal of Herrerias, two assistant football coaches, and the athletic department business manager for "incompetence" and an "inability or unwillingness to relate to black athletes." If the university failed to comply with their grievances, they too would boycott all athletic events.[51]

The revolt at Cal was symptomatic of a larger movement of black athletes protesting real and perceived racial discrimination in athletic departments all across the country. Harry Edwards claimed that during the 1967–68 academic year, black athletes confronted white coaches and administrators on nearly three dozen campuses. Black athletes complained that they were exploited on the field; endured discrimination by coaches, teammates, and athletic directors; and received inadequate academic counseling. In response, they exercised collective power by negotiating the hiring of more black coaches, academic counselors, and trainers. At Cal, after mediation, the black and white players returned to the court without any major incidents, but at season's end Pete Newell and Rene Herrerias resigned. Cal filled Herrerias's position with his top assistant, Jim Padgett, and hired Earl Robinson as the school's first black assistant coach. At other schools, coaches and athletic directors hoped to avoid racial conflicts by recruiting fewer black athletes. One track coach admitted, "Unless we can find a way to separate the decent ones from the trouble-makers and militants, we're going to stop recruiting all Negroes."[52]

In the aftermath of the Berkeley revolt, a sportswriter asked John Wooden if Edgar Lacey's defiant actions were race related. "I have no knowledge of it," Wooden answered. When another writer asked J. D. Morgan about Wooden's relationship with black players, the UCLA athletic director responded, "There's no need for me or anybody else to defend Wooden. His record speaks for itself . . . not only his won-loss record as a coach but his record with men." Morgan suggested that former UCLA black athletes Walt Hazzard, Walt Torrence, or Fred Slaughter would stand up for Wooden. African American sportswriter L. I. Brockenbury defended Wooden for being fair to all of his players, noting that Lacey was the first black player to publicly criticize the UCLA coach.[53]

Wooden was well aware that UCLA's image as a racial paradise had played a decisive role in his program. "We've been very fortunate to have outstanding talent," Wooden acknowledged. "And you, as well as I, know that a large share of this talent has been the Negro athlete." In 1969 Wooden said,

"Black athletes know they will be treated well at UCLA and this is the true secret to our success in recruiting." Mike Warren, Lucius Allen, and Lew Alcindor recognized that their importance on the court empowered them off the court. They ignored Wooden's rules about hair length, eschewed suits and ties when they wanted, and broke curfew. "It was a much tighter ship the year before," a white player said, "until the blacks started going out and coming in at all hours. That's when things started changing. The whites were a little backward in that respect. We had been observing the training rules." When the white players realized that their black teammates had challenged the system without consequence, they too ignored team rules. Wooden had bent his authority more than ever before, mostly to keep Alcindor happy. It was easier that way.[54]

After leaving UCLA, some of Wooden's black players complained that the coach had made little effort to relate to them. "His relationships with blacks have no meaning," Mike Warren lamented in 1970. "The coaching staff was seriously interested only in us playing, studying, and keeping out of trouble. Our individual progress in terms of maturing as black men was of no concern. It's all superficial, the same kind of dialogue every day." Two seasons after Fred Slaughter helped Wooden win his first national title, he inquired about becoming an assistant coach, which would have made him the first black assistant on the staff, but the job went to Jay Carty, a former Oregon State center who volunteered his time. Slaughter shared Warren's frustration, suggesting that Wooden simply did not "understand the black man in terms of social values, needs, and moods." But Slaughter still believed that UCLA was a relatively good place for black athletes. "Coach Wooden," he observed, "is a product of his experience and background and he relates to the black as well as his background lets him. That's better than most."[55]

Perhaps the black players underestimated Wooden. He may not have completely comprehended the meaning of Black Power, but his relationships with black players helped him reevaluate his own attitudes about race. "I think I've had good discussions with various black members of my teams," he said. "I've tried to understand and adapt." He often told the story about a sportswriter who had asked Wilt Chamberlain if Los Angeles Lakers coach Van Breda Koff could "handle him." Chamberlain answered, "You 'handle' farm animals. You work with people." Wooden realized that he often said that he "handled" his players, but after listening to Chamberlain, he ceased using the dehumanizing term. And for years, Wooden referred to his players as "his boys." He considered it an endearing reference, but his integrated teams of the late 1960s made Wooden consciously aware that blacks considered "boy" an emasculating and paternalistic label. Wooden recognized this and tried not to use the term. It was his way of telling the players that he respected them as men.[56]

John Wooden had coached many black players before, but he had never met an athlete who confronted racism the way that Lew Alcindor did. Although they did not have a close relationship, Wooden had heard bigots spew racial epithets from the stands and knew that Alcindor received venomous hate letters and death threats. Still, Alcindor believed that Wooden could never really understand the depth of his wounds because Wooden was white. "Well, Lewis," Wooden asked, "I can at least try to understand, can't I?" Alcindor replied, "Yes Coach, but you can't fully because you're not black." The comment made a strong impression on Wooden, who reflected that Alcindor's experience was "something everyone should think about." For all of the life lessons Wooden shared with young men, no player taught him more about humanity than Lew Alcindor.[57]

○

In late February, Lew Alcindor, Mike Warren, and Lucius Allen announced that they would not play in the 1968 Olympic Games. J. D. Morgan maintained that their decision was "purely academic" and had nothing to do with the proposed boycott. In March Alcindor admitted to *Life,* "We don't want to get caught in the middle of anything." The angry backlash, the bitter criticisms, and the constant media attention discouraged the players from discussing their feelings about the boycott, but they conceded that their refusal to play was an implicit approval of the movement. Morgan told the press not to call requesting interviews because the players were done talking about it. They were focused on one thing: winning a national championship.[58]

After Houston defeated UCLA in the Astrodome, Alcindor sat near his cubicle, sullen, muttering to himself, "Never again, never again." *Sports*

Illustrated's cover photo featured Elvin Hayes rising above Alcindor's out-stretched arm for a jump shot next to a headline, "BIG EEEE OVER BIG LEW." Alcindor hung the photo in his locker as a reminder that he had unfinished business. It seemed inevitable that they would meet again. After the Houston loss, the Bruins won fourteen consecutive games. They looked hungrier, sharper, and more focused. If anything, that single loss gave them a renewed sense of purpose. Whatever improvements UCLA had made, Hayes seemed unimpressed. Before the NCAA semifinals, he boasted that if there was a rematch, UCLA "couldn't play us as close now as they did" in January. "If we played 'em again," he claimed, "we'd beat 'em worse, and it couldn't matter if it was on their own floor."[59]

On March 22, 1968, a record throng of 15,742 fans packed the Los Angeles Sports Arena to watch UCLA and Houston in the NCAA semifinals. Early in the game, the two teams matched each other basket for basket. With every passing minute, the disquieted home crowd grew impatient for a UCLA scoring run. At 10:46, UCLA led 20–19. Then the Bruins turned up the pressure. UCLA's 2-2-1 zone press frustrated Houston's guards, creating eleven first-half turnovers. The Cougars clearly missed starting point guard George Reynolds, who was ruled ineligible after Houston suddenly learned that he did not have enough transfer credits from a California junior college. His teammates suspected that UCLA had tipped off the NCAA before the tournament, an unproven accusation. Without Reynolds's cool ball handling, UCLA's swarming defense ignited a 17–5 scoring spurt. Guy Lewis called time-out, but it was too late. UCLA had already broken Houston's spirit. After a referee blew his whistle for the action break, Don Chaney slammed the ball in frustration, while Lewis tossed his red-and-white polka-dot towel onto the hardwood floor.[60]

By halftime UCLA had built a 53–31 lead. In the second half, UCLA picked Houston apart, scoring easily on fast-break layups and sharp outside shooting. When the Cougars managed to set up their half-court offense, Elvin Hayes could not penetrate inside. Jerry Norman devised a defensive strategy that prevented Hayes from dominating like he did in the Astrodome. Norman realized that Houston's success depended almost entirely on Hayes's scoring. The UCLA assistant coach believed that without an exceptional performance from Hayes, Houston could not win. He suggested to Wooden that the Bruins employ a "diamond and one" half-court defense, with Mike Warren at the top of the key, Alcindor underneath, and Lucius Allen and Mike Lynn on the wings. That left Lynn Shackelford free to blanket Hayes and prevent him from receiving the ball. If he did get it, the zone tilted toward Hayes, trapping him and forcing him to take a difficult shot or pass the ball back out to a teammate.[61]

The plan worked beautifully. Houston shot 28 percent, and Hayes scored only ten points. Lewis called the Bruins' dominating performance "the greatest exhibition of basketball I've ever seen." Alcindor redeemed himself with nineteen points and eighteen rebounds, but Lucius Allen was the star of the game, cutting through Houston's defense with his deceptive stop-and-go moves. He scored nineteen points on acrobatic layups and jumpers, dished twelve assists, and grabbed nine rebounds. Every UCLA starter excelled; Mike Lynn added nineteen points, Lynn Shackelford chipped in seventeen, and Mike Warren contributed fourteen. The Bruins destroyed the Cougars, 101–69. After the game, a writer asked Warren about beating Houston and playing North Carolina in the championship. "We haven't really said anything publicly," Warren admitted, "but we're a vindictive team. We've been looking forward to this game a long time. And we're not looking past North Carolina. We'll run them back down South too."[62]

"It wasn't a game," Jim Murray wrote, "It was a DEATH WATCH." Against North Carolina, Alcindor controlled the tempo, pace, and outcome of the national championship. North Carolina head coach Dean Smith mistakenly assigned Rusty Clark to guard Alcindor one-on-one. But it did not matter what player Smith put on him. For most of the night, Mike Warren, Lucius Allen, and Ken Heitz lobbed the ball inside, where Alcindor spun, reeled, and whirled with finesse, laying the ball in the basket. He relied less on strength and more on skill, agility, and grace. With every poetic hook shot Alcindor made, North Carolina moved closer to defeat. Watching him score, UCLA fans shouted with exhilaration, while the Carolina faithful somberly looked on with despair. Alcindor scored thirty-four points, made fifteen of twenty-one shots, snatched sixteen rebounds, and blocked five shots. UCLA's 78–55 victory was not nearly as impressive as the night before, but, then again, it did not have to be.[63]

After the game, observers began considering the significance of UCLA's championship run. For Dean Smith, there was no doubt that North Carolina had lost to "the greatest basketball team of all time in college circles." His colleague John Wooden had become only the second coach, next to Adolph Rupp, to win four national championships, and UCLA was the only basketball program that had won consecutive titles twice. Now, the question was, could UCLA win three straight championships? "It's difficult to do, very difficult," Wooden said. He reflected on the history of the game, noting that no school had ever won three consecutive titles. For most coaches, it was an unimaginable achievement. Wooden wondered, "Isn't it difficult?"[64]

○

In the summer of 1968, critics continued to wonder why Lew Alcindor refused to play in the Olympics. After saying that America was not really his country on the *Today* show, he tried to explain what he meant. He saw two Americas—one white, one black, separate and unequal. One group had full rights, and the other was treated as second-class citizens. "I've been fortunate because of my basketball ability," he said. "But I'm only one of many black persons in this struggle. I can't run around hollering I'm grateful for what I've received." His detractors argued that he had an obligation to represent his country, but he adamantly disagreed. He maintained, "Yes, I owe an obligation to my country, but my country also owes an obligation to me as a black man, an obligation that has not been fulfilled for 400 years. For too long I have been a second-class citizen. Not me personally; I have been very fortunate. I'm talking collectively, about me as a black man."[65]

Few sportswriters commented on how other prominent college basketball players, black and white, turned down Olympic invitations. Wes Unseld, Larry Miller, Don May, and Elvin Hayes offered various excuses, though their absences did not prevent the United States from winning the gold. Hayes had signed a contract with the NBA's San Diego Rockets. Yet he was never attacked like Alcindor, even though he had placed his economic interests ahead of any patriotic duty. Although there was never any unified Olympic boycott by black athletes, critics attacked Alcindor, ignoring his reasons for refusing to play. The *Los Angeles Times* received piles of hate mail, excoriating the UCLA star. One reader wrote, "When Lew Alcindor states on television that 'America is not really my country,' I have to agree that he is a black nigger." Another bigot, infuriated by Alcindor, vented, "I used to call them Negroes, but I'm getting to the place where they are just plain . . . niggers." Reading these venomous letters, Charles Maher, a white columnist for the *Times*, began to finally understand what Alcindor really meant. He observed of the last author, "This man unhappily expressed the attitude of more white people than we would care to admit. One wonders how these people can expect the black man to take great pride in calling himself an American when they still take perverse satisfaction in calling him a nigger."[66]

6

Woman Chasers and Hopheads

n the summer of 1968, on a sweltering hot day, Lew Alcindor swaggered
down the sidewalks of Harlem, soaking his long, brightly colored African
robe with sweat. He did not care about the cruel summer heat. When he
wore that loud red, orange, and yellow striped robe, he felt cool and hip. It
was his way of saying, "This is *me*. I am black and I am proud to be black." At
125th Street, just off Eighth Avenue, he stopped and entered a mosque. Since
he came to UCLA, Alcindor had searched for the meaning and substance
of his own faith, renounced Catholicism, and studied African history and
culture. Reading about Malcolm X inspired his own spiritual transformation.
Malcolm had served as a minister in the Nation of Islam, a religious sect that
practiced an unorthodox brand of Islam, preached racial separatism, and
claimed that white men were devils. But by 1964, Malcolm had repudiated
the Nation of Islam and its leader, Elijah Muhammad, and visited Africa,
where he embraced orthodox Islam. In his pilgrimage to Mecca, he learned
that white- and dark-skinned Muslims worshipped together. Malcolm's story
convinced Alcindor that he needed to abandon his own deep animosity
toward white people and accept the idea that the "genuine Muslim bears
witness that there is one God, that His name is Allah, and that all men—
black and white—are brothers."[1]

At the Sunni mosque, Alcindor discovered that he knew very little about
practicing Islam and began seriously studying the faith. Shortly after his

appearance on the *Today* show, his father passed on a message from Hammas Abdul-Khaalis, a former drummer that Ferdinand Sr. knew from their days playing jazz in New York City nightclubs. During Alcindor's television interview, Abdul-Khaalis noticed that the young basketball star wore a star-and-crescent pendant. When they first met in Abdul-Khaalis's Harlem apartment, Alcindor's future mentor firmly reprimanded him, "The first thing I want to tell you is, don't ever say that this isn't your country." Abdul-Khaalis reminded him that his ancestors lived and died in America and that he had a responsibility to make it a better country for his black brothers and sisters.[2]

From that point forward, they discussed what it meant to be "a believer." Over the next two weeks, Abdul-Khaalis taught him how to pray properly, how to make his ablutions, and the importance of the five *kalimas*. At the end of the summer, Abdul-Khaalis renamed his pupil Kareem Abdul-Jabbar. He explained that *Kareem* meant "noble and generous," and *Abdul* stood for "servant." "But," Abdul-Khaalis added, "we're missing your spirit." He thought for a moment and said, "Jabbar. That means powerful. That is where your spirit is."[3]

Alcindor's conversion to Islam symbolized his evolving identity as a black man. Like many African American Muslims, Alcindor's name change reflected a quest to reclaim his African heritage and a rejection of white Christian values. He learned that a French planter named Alcindor had enslaved his Nigerian ancestors, the Yoruba, and brought them to Trinidad. Knowing that Christians subjugated black West Africans, Alcindor discarded his Catholic name and rejected a heritage bonded to slavery, signifying his resistance to racial oppression and affirming black independence. It also revealed his deep dissatisfaction with compromising Christian leaders within the civil rights movement. In 1963, when he was just sixteen years old, the Ku Klux Klan bombed Birmingham's Sixteenth Street Baptist Church, killing four little girls. Alcindor burned with anger, outraged that black preachers and Washington liberals failed to bring down the white vigilantes who murdered innocent children. His faith shattered, he later wrote in his autobiography that "God certainly wasn't stepping in; they'd just bombed His house!"[4]

In early December 1968, during a midwestern road trip from Ohio State to Notre Dame, Alcindor and his teammates started talking about religion.

A team of Protestants, a Jew, a Catholic, and a coach who drew inspiration from the New Testament surrounded Alcindor as he shared his religious conversion. Shocked by the news, at first his teammates did not know what to say, but their curiosity propelled them to ask questions about a religion that most knew little about. They asked him which name he preferred, Lew or Kareem, and he told them that he would respond to both. He was torn between two worlds—one reflected how the public perceived him, and the other signified how he would define himself. Unlike Muhammad Ali, he did not make any major announcement about his new name. That would have invited the public into his private life, and he was not interested in explaining himself to sportswriters. For now, most people still knew him as Lew Alcindor.[5]

○

The 1968–69 season presented John Wooden with a new set of challenges. Thanks to the unexpected departure of Lucius Allen, the Bruins returned only two starters—Lew Alcindor and Lynn Shackelford. On May 23, 1968, exactly one year after Allen was arrested, the police jailed him again for two counts of marijuana possession. Allen had academic troubles, as well, and had dropped out of school before his arrest. Wooden had planned for the second-team All-American to replace graduating senior Mike Warren at point guard, but now he had to replace two exceptional guards instead of one.[6]

Wooden's moral code convinced him that "saving troubled players" was "the single most important thing" that he could do. But sometimes the devout Protestant could not reach his players. He knew that some players imbibed, caroused with coeds, and, *goodness gracious sakes alive*, smoked marijuana. From his perspective, such wild recreation not only corrupted their bodies, but also harmed their performance. In 1971, during a time-out of a close game against Washington, Wooden lamented, "It's not your fault but you've given in to a permissive society. You've lost the conference race and a chance at another national championship." Later that season, in the second half of the Western Regionals against Long Beach State, he scolded his players, "You're nothing but a bunch of All-American woman chasers and hopheads!" The coach who supposedly downplayed the importance of winning worried that youthful rebellion would tarnish his program and destroy the dynasty.[7]

Lucius Allen was not the only person who left the UCLA basketball program. A few days after Allen's arrest, the athletic department announced that assistant coach Jerry Norman had resigned and would be replaced by former Bruins guard Denny Crum. Athletic directors all around the country targeted Norman as their next head coach, but the Wooden disciple never seriously entertained the offers. Norman was dissatisfied with his meager salary and the way basketball consumed his life. So he retired from coaching to become a stockbroker, leaving behind a legacy that few assistant coaches could match. For more than a decade, Wooden showed little interest in recruiting, but in the early sixties, Norman convinced him that they needed to expand their recruiting efforts if they wanted a more successful program. The young assistant did most of the recruiting work—traveling, scouting, and pursuing prospects in Southern California and out-of-state standouts that Wooden otherwise would have ignored. And it was Norman who suggested employing the zone press, a crucial strategic change that helped transform UCLA from a competitive program into a championship one. In the view of *Los Angeles Times* beat writer Dwight Chapin, there was no doubt that Norman was "as much an architect of UCLA's early success as Wooden himself."[8]

Looking back on his time at UCLA, it is clear that Norman believes that Wooden did not fully appreciate him. Nearly forty years after he left UCLA, Norman bitterly commented, "Some head coaches, they recognize people that have helped them—and some don't." While Wooden's admirers have elevated him to sainthood, Norman has refused to deify his former mentor. He maintains that UCLA's success was built not on the Pyramid of Success, but by an infusion of exceptionally talented players—players that he recruited. "I don't mean to sound derogatory," Norman said, "but if you look at Wooden's record, he was at UCLA fifteen years and he never won anything." For years Wooden employed the same coaching philosophy, and then "all of a sudden" UCLA won the national title in 1964. "Why?" Norman asked sarcastically. "Overnight he became a genius?"[9]

If there was tension between Norman and Wooden in the late 1960s, it remained unexposed by the press. But by 1968, it was clear that Wooden no longer enjoyed coaching as much as he once did. Coaching Lew Alcindor increased the pressure to win, or more accurately not to lose. The media, fans, and alumni placed more demands on him. At the same time, Wooden worried about disunity among the players; sportswriters heard whispers that the Bruins socialized along racial lines, a common issue on many college basketball teams. Plus, the Westwood campus was no longer the same peaceful place that it had been when he began coaching there twenty years earlier. The students had changed, and so had the players. Campus unrest fueled more rebellious athletes who resisted discipline and defied his authority. And now, in the same week that Lucius Allen was arrested for drug possession, his top assistant coach had resigned. Wooden admitted that he had given considerable thought to stepping down sometime in the next three years. Perhaps, he wondered, his time as a college coach had passed.[10]

With virtually no experienced player at guard, Wooden feared that slower, unproven guards would limit the team's ability to execute the zone press and run the fast break, essential components of his system. In the early part of the season, he rotated senior Bill Sweek, a steady substitute the previous year; John Vallely, a sharpshooting junior-college transfer; and Ken Heitz, a fine defensive performer who started at forward on the 1967 championship team. While Wooden doubted the offensive strength of his guards, he was equally uncertain about who would start at forward. Shackelford had started the previous two seasons, mostly because of his shooting ability. Curtis Rowe and Sidney Wicks, two sophomores far more talented and athletic than Shackelford, had now joined the varsity. With Shackelford playing mostly on the perimeter, Wooden needed a forward who could complement Alcindor on the interior. Rowe, sinewy and swift, thrived in the paint, bouncing off the floor, rapidly jumping and tapping the ball to himself for rebounds and tip-ins. Wicks, on the other hand, liked to drive toward the basket, but this did not work well with Alcindor cemented in the post. He was faster and more spectacular than Rowe, a sensational scorer who, according to Wooden, seemed to care too much about scoring and little else. For this reason, the coach started Shackelford and Rowe until Wicks learned how to integrate his game into the team offense. Some writers predicted that without Mike Warren and Lucius Allen, this untested cast would fall short of a national championship. "Don't believe it," the *Sporting News* maintained. "UCLA is still the best—by far."[11]

After UCLA defeated its first three opponents—all ranked in the top fifteen—it was clear that the team's deficiencies were exaggerated. If they lacked the kind of quickness that opponents expected from UCLA, the team made up for it with depth, strength, and size. Although he was not the speediest floor general, John Vallely emerged as an outstanding point guard. He excelled at passing the ball inside, cutting to the basket, and hitting short jumpers. Rowe and Wicks consistently hovered above the basket, retrieved missed shots at both ends of the floor, and finished fast breaks with acrobatic layups. When the offense scuffled, Wooden relied on Alcindor to carry the team. By his senior year, he was stronger, quicker, and more confident shooting the ball. But, after watching him play at Madison Square Garden, *New York Times* columnist Robert Lipsyte commented that although Alcindor dominated opponents, he was rarely "spectacular or overwhelming." Phil Pepe of the *New York Daily News* noticed the same thing and suggested that Alcindor only "put out his best in spurts."[12]

For Alcindor, college basketball was no longer fun. Game after game, he played against weak competition in a conference that lacked any real challengers. After each game, reporters surrounded his locker and asked him the same tired questions about his height, whether he liked California, and his future playing professional basketball. His two best friends on the team—Edgar Lacey and Lucius Allen—were gone, and they had left under stressful circumstances. In the past two seasons, Alcindor had become increasingly withdrawn, distancing himself from his teammates and the public. He had few close relationships with white players and spent little time socializing with the team's other black players—Sidney Wicks and Curtis Rowe—because they were younger and had separate interests. In the world of basketball, he was most comfortable on the court because it insulated him from the conflicts of everyday life. The games provided a ritual of order, clearly defined boundaries, and a satisfying conclusion.[13]

Few people could relate to Alcindor or understand the incredible pressure he faced from the public and the press. With Lucius Allen gone, he gradually became more social with his senior white teammates, Bill Sweek and Ken

Heitz. Off the court, Sweek learned a lot from Alcindor, who shared his views about race, his love for jazz records, and his interest in samurai movies. Looking back, Heitz thought that after Alcindor had spent the summer of 1968 in New York, he returned to California with less anger toward whites. Like Malcolm X, Alcindor's religious conversion inspired him to reject all forms of racial bigotry. "I think he recognized that his white teammates weren't part of the problem," Heitz said. "They were part of the solution."[14]

When the Bruins traveled to New York City for a holiday tournament in late-December 1968, the team expected a warm welcome from Alcindor's hometown fans. Instead, New Yorkers greeted him "like he was the Hong Kong flu," booing him and cheering any time he experienced a hint of adversity. During the team's first game against Providence, a noticeably fat man sitting near the court shouted racial epithets at Alcindor. After the game, Wooden sent Sweek and Heitz, a lean, bespectacled senior, to meet with the press. Heitz was considered the "intellectual of the team," a serious student who would later graduate from Harvard Law. Like many white college students of the late 1960s, Heitz developed a social consciousness on campus, protesting against the Vietnam War and debating racial politics. He grew up in Santa Maria, a small town in Southern California with few blacks. Playing on an integrated basketball team exposed him to the harsh realities of racism. After Alcindor boycotted the 1968 Olympics, a bigot from North Carolina sent Heitz a letter asking how he could play with "that nigger." By the time he met with sportswriters after the Providence game, he was still fuming over the "racist crap" he had heard from the court, and he had no problems telling the press about it.[15]

The next morning, Wooden arrived at breakfast visibly upset. When the team arrived in New York, he had given the players a pep talk on the team bus. No one could remember what he had said. One player read a book; a few others slept. He reminded them that he expected the team to observe a 10:30 p.m. curfew (7:30 p.m. California time). When a writer asked the players if they would adhere to their coach's instructions, one Bruin replied, "We'll all ignore the man as usual." What if Wooden caught players breaking curfew? "It all depends on how you're playing," Lynn Shackelford answered. "If you've been playing good, he'll let you go pretty much as you please." Only this time, Wooden was not pleased to find out that four players came in at midnight the night before. After scolding the players for violating curfew, he tore into Sweek and Heitz for talking about issues other than basketball. "You're supposed to be a couple of basketball players," he said, "not a couple of liberal civil rights workers! Who do you think you are talking about this stuff?"[16]

Heitz had clearly crossed Wooden's political lines. Wooden made it perfectly clear that he did not want anyone talking to the media about issues other than basketball. Sports and politics, he thought, should not mix. It invited nothing but problems. After Wooden lectured the team, Heitz got the message. When another sportswriter approached him in New York, Heitz begged, "Please don't quote me. I just want to play."[17]

In a "behind-the-scenes" story in *Sport,* one player who wisely refused to be quoted said, "No one can knock Wooden. He's a genius as a coach. But we all wonder how he got the grandfather image. To the outside world he's always smiling, and very modest, like a nice old man. But we see him as he really is when he plays the role of the coach. He can be tough, uncompromising, totally humorless." For the players, there were two sides to John Wooden: a mythical public image—the Wizard of Westwood—and an inflexible authoritarian who imposed his social values on the team. The players respected him, but they also found him to be a hard man, obdurate and "too dogmatic." The last thing they wanted was a father figure telling them how to behave beyond the bounds of the basketball court. They resented that their coach, in the words of one writer, "was trying to make them prototypes of his own Horatio Alger, rural America, Christian upbringing." Another player complained that there was a striking generation gap between Wooden and the team: "What bothers most of us is when coach throws in his 'going through life' philosophy, and tells us this is how we should run our lives. We feel it's a little outdated."[18]

The more college athletes changed, the more convinced Wooden became that his rigid coaching methods were necessary. To his consternation, college basketball players increasingly identified with a youth culture that challenged authority. Sometimes it led to confrontations between him and his players. In early January of 1969, UCLA traveled to Corvallis to play against Oregon

State. The Beavers' 2-3 zone defense made it difficult for the Bruins to find open shots. At halftime, with UCLA leading by just three points, Ken Heitz asked Wooden if he and John Vallely could switch spots on offense so that he could act as a playmaker at the top of the key. Wooden did not answer him, so Heitz went ahead and made the change. In the second half, Heitz exploited the holes in Oregon State's zone, hitting Vallely, Shackelford, and Sweek on the wings for long-range jump shots. The next day, the local papers credited Heitz with making the key tactical adjustment in UCLA's 83–64 victory.[19]

In the following game against Houston, the Bruins struggled again in the first half. Alcindor was recovering from the flu and sat on the bench for most of the game. When he was on the court, UCLA could not push the ball and fell into a slower, more deliberate pace that favored Houston. During a break, Heitz told Wooden that he should substitute sophomore Steve Patterson for Alcindor so that UCLA could use its high-post offense. Incensed, Wooden grabbed Heitz by the jersey, pulling him close to his face, and yelled, "I don't care that you got your name in the paper for coaching this team! I'm the coach of this team! Sit down!" Heitz knew he was in deep trouble now. At halftime Wooden continued tongue-lashing Heitz. He reminded him over and over again that he was the coach of the team, nobody else. Finally, Heitz had enough and started ripping off his uniform, ready to quit. "This is bullshit!" he exclaimed. After nearly everyone filed out of the locker room, Denny Crum tried to assuage Heitz's anger. "Doggone it, just put everything back on," Crum said. "You know how [Wooden] is. Just go back out there and sit on the bench and clap really hard for the team and you'll be starting again in a week." Heitz followed Crum out onto the court and did as he said. Seven minutes into the second half, Wooden put Heitz back into the game. With Patterson playing in the high post, UCLA rolled over Houston, 100–64.[20]

Wooden's critics argued that he was not a great strategist. To his credit, he openly agreed. But when sportswriters attributed a UCLA victory to a player's strategy and not the head coach, it struck a nerve with Wooden. He had heard numerous times that any coach could win with Alcindor, a slight that he could not understand. Even if some outsiders did not respect his coaching methods, he made sure that his players did. "My teams have to play *my* way," Wooden maintained. "They *must* play by my way." Wooden imposed a clear chain of command, a structural hierarchy based on top-down leadership, and there was no arguing with him. Heitz said years later, "He was the coach, you were the player. There was no question who was in charge."[21]

O

Looking back, Ken Heitz thought that UCLA "always seemed like Wonderland." In 1969 a blond coed agreed. "It's always been quiet here at UCLA," she said. "Nothing ever happens the way it happens at all the other colleges in California." Throughout the sixties, UCLA evaded the dramatic large-scale disruptions that swept through Berkeley. Compared to Berkeley, the majority of students in Westwood were, in the words of Governor Ronald Reagan, "a decent, law-abiding group interested in getting educations, not in rioting and disrupting the campus." Many Californians viewed UCLA as "the classic Hollywood image of an All-American college," a sunny, spacious, serene environment, replete with sumptuous green grounds, redbrick buildings, beach-blond surf boys, glamorous coeds, and winning sports teams.[22]

For years the Bruins' integrated athletic teams projected an image of racial harmony at UCLA. But beneath this facade, the university experienced rumblings of racial discontent. Excluding UCLA's varsity sports teams, most student institutions remained overwhelmingly white. On a campus with approximately 29,000 students, in 1968, UCLA enrolled only 514 black students. Many of them felt invisible and underrepresented in the university power structure, so they joined the Black Student Union (BSU) to promote racial consciousness, black unity, and greater autonomy over their own education.[23]

On January 17, 1969, UCLA's BSU organized a meeting in the basement of Campbell Hall to discuss who would serve as the director of the university's newly established Afro-American Studies Center. Before the meeting, tensions simmered between the Black Panthers and a group known as "US," two black factions waging war over political power on campus and in Southern California. In the previous weeks, black men eyed each other suspiciously, roaming the campus with M-16 rifles hidden under long, black trench coats. Moments after the meeting ended, students filed out of the building, talking and laughing. Suddenly, those laughs turned to piercing screams when gunmen from US sprayed two Black Panthers with bullets.[24]

In the aftermath of the shooting, a wave of terror gripped the UCLA campus. Fearing deadly retribution, black students refused to talk with reporters about the murders. Chancellor Charles Young was so concerned about the safety of the BSU's leadership that the university hid the students for several days. Before the shootings, two basketball players, Sidney Wicks and Curtis Rowe, had joined the BSU. For Wicks and Rowe, membership in the BSU was a point of racial pride and an expression of who they were as men beyond the court. Wooden worried that their involvement in the student organization might interfere with their education and playing basketball. After the shootings, Wooden's concerns deepened, and he warned them to avoid further activity for the sake of their safety.[25]

Competing for a third consecutive national championship was difficult enough without the distractions of campus unrest. But the Bruins made it look easy. From December to March, the Bruins pounded opponents by twenty points per game, and it looked like another championship was inevitable. But late in the season, just before the NCAA Tournament, the team lost its focus. The guards played sloppily, turning the ball over more frequently, and Alcindor looked uninterested. In the last conference game, USC employed a calculated stall and beat UCLA 46–44, snapping the Bruins' forty-one-game winning streak. Still, the road to glory looked promising. The NCAA Tournament field offered no great threats to the Bruins' dominance. If UCLA won the Western Regionals, they would play the winner of the Midwest Regionals, which did not have a single team rated in the top ten. After UCLA whipped Santa Clara by thirty-eight points in the Western Regional finals, Steve Bisheff of the *Los Angeles Herald-Examiner* declared, "UCLA is simply the class of the country. Period."[26]

No one expected Drake to challenge UCLA during the NCAA semifinals. Like UCLA's 1964 championship team, Drake did not have a single starter taller than six-foot-five. The Bulldogs could not match the Bruins' strong front line, so they relied on backcourt quickness, a run-and-shoot offense, and an aggressive, swarming full-court defense. Drake coach Maury John believed that his team needed to press the UCLA guards to force a faster tempo, an inconceivable strategy against previous Wooden teams. The Bull-dogs' harassing defense created twenty turnovers and drew Alcindor away from the basket, as he tried to help John Vallely and the other guards who were trapped from the moment they crossed midcourt. Sensing an upset, the fans at Louisville's Freedom Hall gradually began cheering for the underdog, clapping and chanting with every Drake score and UCLA miss. As usual, Alcindor played effectively, scoring twenty-five points and snagging twenty-one rebounds, but it was Vallely who prevented Drake from running away with the game. He silenced the crowd with his baseline scoring drives, twisting and leaning for close layups and jumpers over a web of arms. Vallely's twenty-nine points helped the Bruins build a 78–66 lead with 3:48 left on the clock. Some Drake fans started looking for the exits.[27]

For Vallely, a point guard who averaged eleven points per game, this was by far his best game of the season. Unfortunately for him, it ended early when he fouled out with 1:23 remaining. With a nine-point lead, Wooden summoned senior sub Bill Sweek to check into the game. When he casually walked toward the scorer's table, Wooden barked at him for moving too slowly. Irritated by Wooden's biting criticism, Sweek began arguing with his coach. Seething over the player's disrespect, Wooden told him that if he did not want to play, then he should sit back down. At that point, the obstinate player turned around, walked right past the bench, and headed for the locker room. With few options left, Wooden inserted seldom-used sophomore guard Terry Schofield. In the next minute, Drake charged back and cut UCLA's lead to three points. The pressure was on. With 18 seconds left, a Drake player fouled Schofield. After the UCLA reserve missed the front end of a one-and-one free throw, Drake secured the rebound. Ten crucial seconds remained when the Bulldogs' best player, Willie McCarter, launched a jump shot nearly twenty feet away from the basket. As the ball caromed off the rim, six-foot-four forward Dolph Pullium leaped toward the basket and tipped the ball through the net, closing UCLA's lead to just one point with 7 seconds left on the clock. On the next possession, Sidney Wicks passed the ball in to Alcindor, who flipped it up-court to Lynn Shackelford. Drake fouled Shack as the buzzer sounded. He hit two meaningless free throws, and UCLA survived, 85–82.[28]

After the game Wooden stormed through the locker room doors. Steam escaped the shower entrance as he approached Sweek "with his fist cocked." Incensed, Wooden hardly cared that water sprayed his suit as he berated the disobedient player. The shouting continued when Sweek stepped out of the shower, dripping wet as he dressed. Like many subs on the team, he believed that Wooden treated players differently according to their playing status, punishing only those who did not start when team rules were broken. What angered Sweek most was Wooden's sanctimonious indignation. He told Wooden that it was not necessary for all of the players to join the Fellowship of Christian Athletes or make the honor roll or dress a certain way. Sweek reminded him that two players—Edgar Lacey and Don Saffer—had quit the team because of the way Wooden treated them. "Maybe you've got to realize that the trouble isn't always with them," he fumed. "Maybe some of it's with you!"[29]

The next morning, Wooden organized a team meeting before practice. He and Sweek apologized to one another, shook hands, and agreed that they both needed to improve their communication. After that, "all was happy in Bruinville," Sweek recalled. It appeared that they had become a closer group, but the shouting match revealed real discontent behind the dynasty's gilded doors. Sportswriters did not report the tension between the team and coach, but clearly the pressure to win a third consecutive title had taken its toll. The players were ready for the season to end, to get away from it all and each other. Lynn Shackelford later admitted that playing basketball "was so easy it didn't mean much and it had long since stopped being any fun. We'd had so many players with so many problems we'd long stopped feeling love for each other as teammates, we weren't all that proud as a team." Before the playoffs, Wooden had made sure that the players did not discuss private conflicts with the press, requiring a strict ban on player interviews until after the tournament ended. For Wooden, the protective order was necessary to prevent outside distractions from disrupting the team's chances of winning the national championship. The truth was that he failed to recognize that the program's problems were internal and would not go away, even if they won it all.[30]

If the UCLA players were distressed before the championship against Purdue, outsiders could hardly tell. Purdue's only hope of beating the defending champs hinged on three-time All-American Rick Mount, who possessed one of the purest, smoothest jump shots ever seen. Wooden had seen enough of the country's second leading scorer in two previous meetings to know that they had to keep the ball out of Mount's hands. After "the Rocket" hit his first two shots, Ken Heitz perpetually shadowed him, forcing the Purdue star to miss his next fourteen shots. While Mount struggled to locate the basket, Alcindor punished Purdue in the paint, scoring thirty-seven points and grabbing twenty rebounds. Midway through the second half, the Bruins owned a comfortable twenty-point lead. UCLA was simply too strong, too athletic, and too good. The next morning, the *Los Angeles Herald Examiner* headline said it all: "LewCLA: THREE IN A ROW: Purdue Blasted, 92–72; Big A Gets 37."[31]

When the horn sounded, photographers swarmed Alcindor, whose face broke a rare, wide smile, a genuine expression of joy and relief. Beaming with pride, he walked across the hardwood floor, a net draped around his neck and his arm at his father's side. After changing into slacks, a maroon turtleneck, and a blue sports jacket, Alcindor made his way to the pressroom, relaxed and reflective. He talked about the expectations of never losing a game, the constant interview requests, and the strain of public scrutiny. The intense pressure caused him excruciating migraine headaches, an intolerable pain that felt like his head was being squeezed between the jaws of a metal vise. "Everything was up in my throat all week," he admitted. "I could see ahead to the end, but there was apprehension and fear. Fear of losing. I don't know why, but it was there." Alcindor overcame those fears, won his third straight tournament Most Outstanding Player Award, and finished an incomparable career with an 88-2 record and three national championships.[32]

His legacy cannot be measured exclusively in hardware. Alcindor, more than any other college player of the sixties, left a cultural imprint on the game. From New York City to Los Angeles, Alcindor attracted unprecedented public interest in college basketball. In the process, he inspired the growing commercial relationship between network television and the sport. At the same time, his career encompassed important changes in college basketball shaped by the civil rights movement—the infusion of a black aesthetic, desegregation, and the revolt of the black athlete. At a time when most black college athletes avoided overt political protest, Alcindor injected black politics into college basketball. And although he succeeded on an integrated basketball team, Alcindor eschewed integration as a measure of racial equality.

When the team returned to Westwood, sportswriters asked John Wooden about the challenges of coaching during the last four seasons. He maintained that no college athlete had ever faced a more glaring media microscope or endured more criticism than Alcindor. He recognized that coaches all across the country popped champagne bottles, celebrating the end of the Alcindor era. Now, he wondered, "Did the rules committee put the dunk back in yet?"[33]

During the 1963–64 season Walt Hazzard and Gail Goodrich led UCLA to the school's first national championship and a perfect 30-0 record. Together, the most dynamic scoring backcourt in the country led the "Bruin Blitz": a suffocating full-court zone press that created turnovers and fast-break scores. (Los Angeles Public Library Photo Collection)

Before J. D. Morgan became UCLA athletic director in 1963, he coached the men's tennis team to six national championships. Over the course of the 1960s and 1970s, he became one of the most powerful athletic directors in the country. As an influential member of the NCAA Basketball Committee, Morgan helped transform college basketball into a big business and negotiated lucrative television contracts for UCLA and the NCAA.

In 1965 Coach John Wooden welcomed four talented freshmen to UCLA (*from left to right*): Lew Alcindor, Lynn Shackelford, Ken Heitz, and Lucius Allen.

In 1966–67, Lew Alcindor dominated opponents—and his teammates—in the annual varsity-freshmen game. At the end of the season, the National Basketball Committee banned the dunk. Critics called it the "Alcindor Rule," implying that the rule was designed to prevent the best player in the country from making a farce of the sport.

Alcindor's incredible combination of size, agility, and skill made him the most dominant college basketball player in history. In his three varsity seasons, he led UCLA to three consecutive championships and an overall 88-2 record. In Alcindor's two losses, against Houston in 1968 and USC in 1969, the Bruins lost by only two points in both games. Alcindor is the only player in history to be named the Most Outstanding Player of the Final Four three times.

Mike Warren's quickness and deft ball handling made him a dangerous offensive player. Here, he knifes through the defense to deliver a pass to Alcindor. In 1968 Warren was named a First-Team Consensus All-American.

In the 1969–70 and the 1970–71 seasons, Curtis Rowe emerged as one of UCLA's most consistent frontcourt players and best rebounders.

Whether he was tipping the ball into the basket or driving down the lane, Sidney Wicks could always find a way to score. After Lew Alcindor graduated in 1969, Wicks emerged as the team's best player and was named a First-Team Consensus All-American in 1970 and 1971.

Andy Hill played as a backup guard for UCLA from 1969 to 1972. Hill clashed with Coach Wooden over playing time and politics. In October 1969, Hill approached Wooden about skipping practice so that he and his teammates could march in the national Vietnam Moratorium. "Andy," Wooden said, "you don't *ever* have to come to practice. But there is no way that I am calling off practice for this moratorium." Later that season, in May 1970, Hill played a leading role in drafting an antiwar letter that the entire team sent to President Richard Nixon.

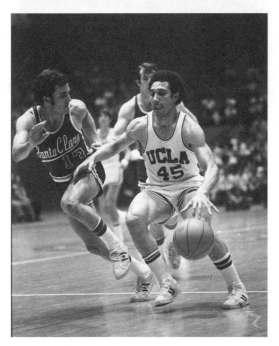

Henry Bibby was one of the most outstanding long-distance shooters to play for UCLA during the dynasty. In 1972 Bibby was named a Consensus All-American.

During a 1971 home game against crosstown rival USC, Coach Wooden shouted instructions to his players on the court. On offense UCLA ran very few set plays. Wooden wanted his team to push the ball up the court, fan out, and hit the open man. The players often heard him yelling from the sidelines, "Be quick but don't hurry!"

Keith Wilkes was one of the most talented players of the UCLA dynasty. An excellent midrange jump shooter, Wilkes was an ideal forward for Wooden's high-post offense. In 1973 Wilkes was named a Consensus All-American.

Bill Walton was a remarkable defender and rebounder. He seemed to cover the whole court, leaping for blocks, chasing loose balls, and snagging errant shots out of the air.

On May 9, 1972, UCLA All-American Bill Walton and about two thousand demonstrators paraded through Westwood Village in protest of the Vietnam War. When police met Walton and other peace activists at the intersection of Wilshire Boulevard and Veteran Avenue, the demonstrators sat down in the middle of the street, blocking traffic. On May 11, Walton was arrested with student protesters for barricading Murphy Hall, the administration building.

On January 19, 1974, despite Walton's best efforts to lead the Bruins to victory, the University of Notre Dame broke UCLA's record eighty-eight-game winning streak.

At UCLA every two-hour practice was planned to the exact minute and recorded on white three-by-five index cards. Wooden used his meticulous note-card system to organize drills that ran for five to ten minutes, never any longer. His basic coaching philosophy emphasized conditioning and drilling players on the fundamentals.

In the 1970s, Sam Gilbert was the most well-known booster in college basketball. The *Los Angeles Times* and *Time* published feature stories about the man the players called "Papa Sam" and "the Godfather." Throughout the dynasty years, Gilbert acted as "a one-man clearinghouse." He provided loans, bought airline tickets, and arranged for players to receive goods and services at a discount or gratis. The NCAA did not expose these violations at UCLA until after John Wooden retired.

7

The Desperate Coach

On the evening of May 4, 1970, eleven hundred UCLA alumni, fans, and parents gathered at the Beverly Hilton ballroom to celebrate another Bruins championship at the annual basketball team banquet. The night began like many other banquets, with boosters shaking hands with coaches, parents boasting about their sons, and players reminiscing about the season. Every year the seniors gave a farewell address. This season John Vallely and Bill Seibert were the featured speakers. Vallely, a two-year starter, gave a traditional senior farewell, praising the team for the discipline, dedication, and unity they displayed throughout the season. Few people in the audience knew anything about Seibert except that he rarely played. His teammates did not know him very well, either. Andy Hill recalled that he was a "loner" and "enigmatic." Seibert spent the previous four nights working on his speech, carefully crafting a testimonial about his experiences playing for John Wooden.[1]

Seibert nervously gripped the lectern as he looked out at the audience. His parents and his girlfriend smiled as they looked at him from their front-row seats. He began by thanking everyone in attendance, his family, teammates, and coaches. Then he launched into a long speech, blasting Wooden for upholding a double standard of team rules. The starters, he said, were exempt from punishment, but the reserves were not. Seibert claimed that Wooden's concern for each player was based entirely on who started and who did not. He said that he did not enjoy his experience at UCLA and that Wooden failed to communicate with the players. And then he basically called Wooden a hypocrite. For years Wooden defined success as "peace of mind," knowing that "you did your best to become the best that you are capable of becoming." But, Seibert suggested, that was not true. "The aim of the team was to win and that was the definition of success."[2]

Shocked by Seibert's words, the audience grew quiet. The celebration had suddenly become an uncomfortable experience for everyone in the room. Parents and boosters could not believe that one of Wooden's own players would criticize the most successful coach in the country. As Seibert continued, angry spectators heckled him. They did not pay ten dollars a plate to listen to this. While Seibert's mother quietly wept, his father encouraged him to sit down, but he pressed on anyhow. When he finished speaking, his teammates rose from their seats, clapping in unison, validating that there was some truth to what he had said. One man, "shaking with anger," walked up to Seibert and threatened to punch him in the mouth.[3]

Seibert claimed that the purpose of the speech was not to complain about playing time, but rather to comment on the values of the program. UCLA, he said, embodied a distortion of American ideals. The success ethic created a culture where "the more important people" did not have to follow the same rules as everybody else. While most people believed that the content and the occasion of the speech were completely inappropriate, he maintained that the banquet was the *only* time and place to express his frustrations. His attitude reflected a youth culture that demanded to be heard. When he publicly criticized the basketball program, Seibert rejected the traditional restraints imposed by the sports establishment. Athletes were not supposed to speak out or question the nature and conduct of sports organizations. But by the late sixties, more and more critics from within the sports world challenged the old sporting ideals. When Seibert questioned Wooden's methods, he questioned everything the coach stood for. And now someone would have to pay for it.

○

By 1968 antiwar demonstrations, teach-ins, and pickets against Dow and CIA recruiters occurred with increasing regularity at UCLA. In Westwood it was not unusual to watch young men burn draft cards. Yet there was no organization that led an antiwar movement on campus. In Southern California, a center of political conservatism, many citizens disapproved of student protesters who violated campus rules. One California poll found that "large majorities" of Californians felt that college students who disrupted campuses should be expelled. Most surveyed supported the suspension of antiwar demonstrators and draft dodgers. With conservative and radical voices competing on campus, neither side inspired mass mobilization at UCLA.[4]

In the spring of 1969, a confrontation at Berkeley provoked UCLA's student protest movement. It began when Cal students attempted to seize a vacant piece of off-campus university property. After administrators announced that they intended to build a playing field and a parking lot on the "People's Park," student activists tore down "No Trespassing" signs, staged a large rally that attracted thousands, and moved to take over the heavily guarded park. Chaos erupted when the police and National Guard engaged the demonstrators and fired buckshot pellets into the flesh of the unarmed crowd, injuring close to one hundred and killing one. Ronald Reagan declared marshal law and ordered a helicopter to strafe the protesters with tear gas. For seventeen days, the police, highway patrol, sheriff's deputies, and the National Guard occupied Berkeley. Once the battle lines were crossed, Reagan believed, it was his duty to prevent communists, militants, and hippies from taking over California's campuses one by one, like falling dominoes, as in Southeast Asia. "This is guerilla warfare," he maintained, and "the only thing that can win in campus guerilla warfare is . . . you eliminate them by firing the faculty members and expelling the students." Casualties were a part of war, he argued a year later: "If it takes a blood bath, let's get it over with. No more appeasement."[5]

The next day, Friday, May 16, Reagan and the California Regents convened at the UCLA Faculty Center for their rotating monthly meeting. Nearly fifteen hundred students surrounded the building, demanding their own meeting with the regents so that they could discuss the violence in Berkeley, the presence of ROTC on campus, and the regents' involvement with war corporations like Dow and aircraft manufacturers. When the regents refused to come out, protesters hurled rocks through the glass windows, while the Los Angeles Police Department and California Highway Patrol blocked the entrance doors, bracing for an attack. A police bullhorn blared, "If you have on glasses take them off. If you have pierced ears, take your earrings out." When a student jammed a metal stake into the building, another demonstrator grabbed the makeshift weapon and said, "We want to be heard, we're not here to fuck up the building." Chancellor Charles Young and a group of faculty members urged the agitated throng to disperse and meet with him on Monday. Ultimately, the police pushed the crowd back, and the regents escaped, avoiding any serious violence. Five days later, more than twelve hundred protesters peacefully occupied the administration building for twenty-four hours, leading Young to cancel classes. On May 26, student activists at UCLA and the other eight UC schools staged a two-day strike in protest against police-state tactics. Excessive force at Berkeley and the presence of police at UCLA radicalized students who did not necessarily view themselves as activists. As long as police clutched batons and the National Guard marched on campus, the *Daily Bruin* argued, students feared that they could not resolve their concerns without physical retaliation, and this was unacceptable.[6]

The spring protests marked a political awakening at UCLA. The demonstrations shook the very foundation of the university, energizing moderate students who sympathized with those who put their bodies on the line in the name of democracy. The protests at UCLA and Berkeley convinced many students that the university establishment repressed dissent and student political power. The *Los Angeles Times* reported this was the first time a significant number of UCLA students participated in any form of "action movement." These politically conscious youths were not the stereotypical "wild-eyed, bushy-haired radicals intent on anarchy." They were ordinary students who simply wanted to be heard.[7]

By 1969 most Americans had become disillusioned with Vietnam, saddened by the mounting death toll and angered that U.S. troops continued to fight what many considered an immoral war. On October 15, more than two million Americans—ordinary citizens, clergymen, businessmen, housewives, schoolteachers, congressional Democrats and Republicans—participated in the Vietnam Moratorium, a national protest that spread beyond the universities. It was, according to *Life,* "a display without historical parallel, the largest expression of public dissent ever seen in this country." At UCLA more than thirty-five hundred students marched from Royce Hall down Westwood Boulevard to the Federal Building, joining fifteen thousand supporters of the moratorium. A campus referendum revealed that 67 percent of students supported immediate troop withdrawal, a significant figure considering that two years earlier, only 55 percent approved such action. The moratorium indicated that the antiwar movement had become mainstream, a unifying force among Americans with divergent political views, and that it was no longer unpatriotic to demonstrate against the war for the sake of peace.[8]

Unfortunately for Andy Hill, he knew one person at UCLA who still supported the government's position in Vietnam. Coincidentally, the moratorium fell on the first day of basketball practice, and Hill, inspired by the zeitgeist, thought that the team should demonstrate alongside students and faculty. The sophomore guard from Los Angeles approached his closest friends on the team, John Ecker and Terry Schofield, hoping that they would share his enthusiasm for marching. When Hill explained that he wanted to ask John Wooden if he would cancel practice, Schofield instantly refused, though Ecker reluctantly agreed to go with him. When the idealistic athletes met Wooden in his office, Hill did most of the talking, arguing against the war and in favor of the moratorium. He was unsure whether Wooden would agree to his plan, but he was certain that he would identify with his antiwar sentiments. "Andy," the coach said, "you don't *ever* have to come to practice. But there is no way that I am calling off practice for this moratorium."[9]

Aggravated by the request, Wooden assailed the young men's political convictions. Hill was shocked at his coach's reaction. After all, who wasn't against the war? Although most Americans admitted that the war was a mistake, 69 percent believed that the antiwar movement was "harmful to American life." Wooden, a World War II veteran, fit into this group of patriots who viewed the antiwar movement as antithetical to "the American way of life," which included supporting the country during a time of war. For Wooden, social order and national unity trumped civil disobedience. He refused to allow the players' politics to interfere with the team's goals. Grudgingly, Hill and Ecker dressed for practice, though their minds drifted outside Pauley Pavilion. Wooden never again brought up the incident, but he never forgot about it, either.[10]

In an age of dissent and campus demonstrations, Wooden belonged to that group of Americans that Richard Nixon called "the great silent majority." They were "the non-shouters, the non-demonstrators," who resented loud protests, urban riots, rising crime rates, the growing use of illegal drugs, a permissive youth culture, and the failed leadership of intellectual elites. The silent majority included whites who were neither poor nor rich, blue-collar workers and the lower ranks of white-collar workers, urban ethnics, and rural families. According to *Time,* these frustrated middle Americans represented "a contradictory mixture of liberal and conservative impulses," "a state of mind, a morality, a construct of values and prejudices and a complex of fears." They cherished "a system of values that they see assaulted and mocked everywhere—everywhere except in Richard Nixon's Washington."[11]

In Nixon's America, Wooden personified the virtues of the silent majority. He represented the "backbone of America," decent, God-fearing, law-abiding citizens. Journalist Herbert Warren Wind wrote, "He is an anachronism, John Wooden—an island of James Whitcomb Riley in a sea of Ken Kesey, the Grateful Dead, Terry Southern, and Jerry Rubin." Like Nixon, Wooden projected an image of consensus in a period of dissent, a champion of middle-American values under attack. "In a world on fire and with his own university in ferment," one sportswriter commented, "John Robert Wooden stands as a kind of monument to the Establishment."[12]

Many Americans applauded him as "the upholder of virtue against vice," a counterforce to dissident youth. When a group of Bruins showed up on the first day of practice without visiting the barbershop, Wooden reminded them about his rules on hair. In the past, he allowed black players to grow naturals, but he strictly prohibited shaggy locks, flaring sideburns, bristly mustaches, and woolly goatees. The players resented the way that Wooden dictated their personal appearance, but he firmly believed that long hair made players perspire more, which could hinder their performance or possibly lead to colds or the flu if they went out into the cold. More important, long hair was an affront to Wooden's authoritarian sensibilities. Long hair, John Ecker said years later, "really irritated him deep down." If Wooden amended his rules on hair, the players might contest his decision-making power, an objectionable notion to the man in charge.[13]

Wooden's inflexible position against long hair was not based solely on his grooming standards. In a way, he was taking a stand against the counterculture, a group that he often called the "antiestablishment." In the late 1960s and early 1970s, coaches and college athletes frequently clashed over hair, a politically divisive issue that reflected the cultural tensions of the period. Coaches demanded clean-shaven, clean-cut appearances that could pass ROTC inspection, while many athletes preferred longer, unkempt hair, muttonchops, and goatees. In some instances, young men disobeyed their coaches, refused to cut their hair, and quit the team. For many youths, hair symbolized a rejection of crew-cut Cold War conformity. Long hair was an act of defiance, a declaration of freedom. Conservative adults associated long hair with insidious rebellion, dirty "freaks," campus dissidents, and commies. UCLA football coach Tommy Prothro lamented that half of the athletes on campus had smoked pot. "The boys who are giving in," he claimed, "you can spot. The long hair, not bathing, not caring," these were telltale signs of militant radicals.[14]

College coaches like Prothro and Wooden believed that they were in the business of making boys into men and that long hair undermined that effort. Real men cut their hair short. Women wore long hair. Short hair represented manliness, respect for order, and discipline. Long hair signified effeminacy, weakness, and empathy for subversives. For decades many Americans clung to the idea that "jocks" were clean cut, square-jawed, brutishly obedient reactionaries uninvolved in demonstrations, unless of course they were restoring law and order on campus by beating up protesting hippies. According to this narrow line of thinking, a real man pummeled protesters; he did not join them in a demonstration line. But by the late 1960s, it was clear that college athletes were no longer a monolithic group. Never before had so many college athletes—black and white—publicly confronted coaches, questioned their autonomy, ignored their rules, and dropped out of competitive athletics. College coaches firmly believed that sports were "the last stronghold of discipline on the campus," preserved by a patriarchal system where athletes never seriously defied their authority. Suddenly, it seemed that college athletes enthusiastically challenged the old order, refusing to abide by an autocracy that resisted the rebellious politics of America's youth. Most coaches agreed that it was time to fight back.[15]

In 1969 hysteria over protesting college athletes reached a fever pitch. Although the overwhelming majority of college athletes did not join campus demonstrations, boycott athletics, or rebel against their coaches, the establishment feared that Black Power militants, New Left radicals, and the counterculture would break up college athletics. In his three-part series "The Desperate Coach," *Sports Illustrated* writer John Underwood interviewed panicking coaches and angry athletic directors who talked about "the problem." One small-college basketball coach bemoaned, "I read somewhere—I clipped it out—that the aim of the New Left is to replace the athlete with the hippie as the idol of kids. I don't know if it can be done, but it seems society is intent on destroying Horatio Alger Jr." This coach pointed out that most confrontations between coaches and players involved militant black athletes, but now it appeared that white athletes were increasingly defiant too, though black players made more headlines than whites. Alarmed at the increasing number of confrontations, Oklahoma State basketball coach Henry Iba anxiously declared, "We are facing the greatest crisis in sports history. In the next eight months we could see sports virtually destroyed. Nobody seems to realize how critical the situation is."[16]

In January coaches and athletic directors roamed the tense halls of the Los Angeles Hilton Hotel, where they debated how to wrestle authority from disobedient athletes. The key issue of the National Collegiate Athletic Association annual convention was a proposed rule that would allow any "member institution" to "terminate the financial aid of a student-athlete if he is adjudged to have been guilty of manifest disobedience through violations or established athletic department policies and rules applicable to all student-athletes." In other words, coaches and athletic directors would reserve the right to punish athletes guilty of dissent of any kind by withdrawing their scholarships. This legislation was about more than a haircut; it was about power. After a 167–79 vote, the rule passed, bolstering the ability of coaches to quell athletic protest. NCAA executive director Walter Byers insisted that the NCAA was apolitical, but this rule reflected the reactionary politics of the Right, further evidenced by a sensational editorial Byers published in the *NCAA News* that suggested that the Black Student Union, SNCC, SDS, and the Black Panther Party were responsible for the tumultuous dissension in college athletics. In an ominous tone familiar to J. Edgar Hoover, Byers cited "government sources" that linked these organizations to "Communist-oriented, revolutionary groups in other nations." Supposedly, this "hard-core revolutionary force" recruited and exploited college athletes for the sole purpose of advancing some unclear political agenda. Byers had officially warned the athletic directors and coaches of America. Now it was up to them to stop "hard core insurrectionists" from taking over college athletic departments.[17]

Critics of the new legislation charged the NCAA with racism, arguing that the rule blatantly targeted protesting athletes, most of whom were black. In his *New York Times* column, Robert Lipsyte argued, "The rule was ostensibly passed to give coaches a bigger whip over the rambunctious black scholarship athletes whose disobediences have ranged from the growing of Bushman haircuts to the boycotting of matches with colleges that practice discrimination." What concerned Lipsyte and other detractors most was that coaches could interpret the legislation as grounds to dismiss under-performing athletes, regardless of race. Essentially, the rule fundamentally changed the relationship between student athletes and the university. Joe College was no longer a student athlete. He was simply an athlete, hired to win and keep his mouth shut.[18]

With the departure of Lew Alcindor, in 1969–70, UCLA returned to the high-post offense, a freer, more balanced scoring attack of screens, cuts, and quick passes. Wooden also planned to employ the press more often. This team would run, shoot, and run some more. Including Alcindor, the Bruins lost three of their top six players from the previous year and returned only one starting senior, guard John Vallely. Nobody could replace Alcindor, probably the greatest player in the history of college basketball, but Steve Patterson, a muscular, six-foot-nine junior proved more than capable as a scorer and rebounder. He was ideally suited to play in the high post, where he could face the basket, drill ten- to fifteen-foot jumpers, and fire the ball to his darting teammates. Few UCLA fans knew much about him except that he had been Alcindor's backup. He explained his previous role to one writer: "You know how [Boston Celtics head coach Red] Auerbach had his victory cigar? Well, I'm Wooden's cigar. When the game is clinched, he pulls Lew and puts in Patterson."[19]

An intelligent, introspective, and complex young man, Patterson often challenged Wooden, debating him in practice and wearing his sideburns longer than the coach allowed. He was raised in a strict Baptist home, an environment that he viewed as repressive and socially limiting. Attending UCLA liberated Patterson. He joined the Fellowship of Christian Athletes and organized a Bible-study group. At the same time, he questioned middle-American values, the win-at-all-costs attitude in sports, and the role of the college athlete on campus. "I've seen students who have long hair, smoke dope, dig rock music, and flash the peace sign who are still from the success mold," he said. "But I believe there is a percentage of people who are getting away from the idea that the performance and success ethic is the most important thing—who cringe at the thought of living in middle-class suburbia. I'm one of those."[20]

Patterson believed that athletes could be more constructive on campus, leading students in discussions about religion, politics, and social concerns. In the fall of 1970, Patterson and Sidney Wicks approached Wooden about skipping practice to participate in an antiwar rally. Practice was important, but these players could not ignore the war, not while their friends risked their lives in the jungles of Southeast Asia. Wooden told them the same thing he told Andy Hill and John Ecker: if they missed practice to join a peace rally, then they could not return to the team. The war, the peace movement, the campus protests—all of it inspired them to want to do something. "There were half a million soldiers in Vietnam and tens of thousands of young men getting drafted," John Ecker said. "It was something that really dominated our thoughts during those years. That was certainly motivation enough to write protest letters, to get out there and march in the streets, and to demonstrate against the war in Vietnam."[21]

There was no doubt that Patterson and Wicks would start on the front line with forward Curtis Rowe, but Wooden was uncertain about who would play opposite Vallely in the backcourt. Surprisingly, sophomore Henry Bibby emerged as one of UCLA's best players, a fine shooter with even greater range than Vallely. Bibby grew up in tobacco country, Franklinton, North Carolina, a small segregated town of six thousand people. In the summers, he labored beneath the blistering sun alongside his parents and brothers. When the work was done, he practiced shooting in the flickering light emanating from the one bulb outside his house. All that practice made him one of the most sought-after players in the country; Duke, North Carolina, North Carolina State, and other southern schools believed that Bibby's scoring talent and gentle, likable disposition would make him an ideal player for programs confronting integration. After attending a poorly funded all-black high school, he decided to leave the rural South, set west for California, and follow the path of many other out-of-state African Americans athletes who enrolled at UCLA.[22]

UCLA's other black starters, Curtis Rowe and Sidney Wicks, were the most talented forwards Wooden had coached. They were inseparable off the court, having regularly competed against each other in high school and on the playgrounds of Los Angeles. Strong, athletic, and aggressive with the ball, the forwards drove each other to be the best player on the court. Rowe was probably UCLA's most consistent performer, a fierce rebounder who planted himself beneath the boards, squeezed between defenders, and anticipated where the ball would bounce off the rim. His offensive game was steady and predictable, unremarkable but effective. Wicks, on the other hand, was UCLA's most dynamic player, lithe, quick, and explosive. For a six-foot-eight, 220-pound forward, he was exceptionally fast and a remarkable ball handler. Sometimes he dribbled the ball up the court and ran the offense from the top of the key, an unprecedented talent for a player his size. He was also the team's best leaper, a devastating shot blocker, and an ideal "outfielder" in the zone press. When the opposing team charged at him on a fast break, Wicks could flick the ball loose, scoop it up off the floor, zigzag around defenders, flip the ball to an open teammate, or finish the break all by himself. It was his combination of skills—a combination of strength, speed, and body control—that made him the best forward in the country.[23]

Wicks was the star of the Bruins. Though not of the same class as Alcindor, he was the team's best player, and he made sure that everybody knew it. He was loud, brash, and boastful, confident in his ability to take over a game. He jived his teammates, partied past curfew, and verbally sparred with Wooden, offering endless opinions about how the team should operate. Usually, Wicks was charming and engaging, but sometimes his braggadocio unnerved his teammates. John Vallely recalled, "Sidney could be very difficult at times. He was AC/DC. One day he'd throw his arm around you, the next he'd walk right past you. Only Sidney knew what turned him on and off. Most of the time he was fun to be around. But when he was in one of his dark moods, you kept your distance." Despite his loud, animated personality off the court, he swaggered onto the court wearing a serious, cold Bill Russell scowl, flexing his muscles, and clapping his hands together. With his boundless energy, Wicks exhorted his teammates to play hard, push the ball, and attack the basket.[24]

The break was back at UCLA. It was fast, fun, exciting basketball, an entertaining style that energized Pauley Pavilion. But before the season began, most coaches did not know what to expect from a UCLA team without Alcindor. Miami coach Ron Godfrey read a scouting report that claimed that the Bruins could not shoot from the outside. Godfrey followed the scout's advice and used a zone defense. After UCLA destroyed the Miami zone, setting a school scoring record in a 127–69 drubbing, Godfrey met with reporters and said, "I'm not gonna pay for that scouting report." The Bruins steamrolled their opponents, winning six of their first eight games by twenty-five points or more, including a thirty-one-point victory over number-thirteen Notre Dame. The Bruins were good, but they benefited from a weak nonconference schedule. They also played nine of their first thirteen games at home, a favorable arrangement designed by J. D. Morgan. Of their four road contests, none of the teams cracked the polls' top twenty. In fact, Notre Dame was the only ranked team that UCLA played before the NCAA Tournament.[25]

UCLA could lose one of two ways: if the opposing team slowed the tempo to a crawl or if the Bruins beat themselves. When they played together, UCLA's starters were far better than any other five in the country. Every starter averaged ten or more points, a balanced attack that made it difficult for opposing defenses to focus on stopping any one player. The Bruins were quick, agile, and versatile, a relentless force that thrived on defensive pressure, ball movement, and accurate shooting. Everything seemed to be going fine until February 21, when the Bruins played sloppy, careless basketball against Oregon. The team did nothing Wooden told them to do. They did not attack the zone, drive the baseline, or hustle on defense, and it cost them their twenty-one-game winning-streak.[26]

Although sportswriters did not predict the defeat, Wooden saw it coming. There was discernible tension among the starters and a lack of trust that seemed to divide along racial lines. At one point in the season, Wicks and Rowe asked Wooden to segregate hotel room assignments on road trips. They did not dislike their white teammates, but they felt more comfortable around other blacks. More problematic, Wicks thought that Vallely shot too much. Vallely believed that if he passed him the ball, he would never see it again, so he gave it to Patterson more often. Vallely recalled, "Sidney was upset because I was leading the team in scoring. He said, 'We can't have a white guy leading the team in scoring with so many great black players.'" There was no question that Wicks wanted to be the star. From his point of view, he was more naturally talented than Vallely. After the Oregon loss, Wicks sent Bibby and Hill to talk to Vallely. Rather than argue with Wicks, Vallely decided that he would shoot less and distribute the ball more democratically, creating a more harmonious team dynamic.[27]

By the playoffs, all seemed right with UCLA basketball. The team completed the regular season 24-2, and Wooden won his fourth Coach of the Year honor. Still, winning the national championship would not be easy. Although *Sports Illustrated*'s Joe Jares picked UCLA as the clear favorite, he also believed that there were seven or eight legitimate contenders entering the NCAA Tournament. But that's all they were, mere contenders. Against Long Beach State, Utah State, and fifth-ranked New Mexico State, UCLA's physical, high-scoring frontcourt and efficient backcourt shooting fueled three consecutive victories by an average of twenty points.[28]

UCLA's playoff victories were not as smooth as they appeared in newspaper headlines. During a second-half time-out in the semifinals against New Mexico State, Wooden, obviously upset, berated Wicks for doing something wrong, and the player did not shy away from a caustic rebuttal. The team huddled around them, shielding the television cameras from the argument.

After the time-out, cameramen zoomed in on Wicks, sulking, wiping his face with a towel on the bench as Wooden towered over him, admonishing him with the final word. After the game, not a single writer spoke with Wicks, thanks to Wooden's imposed code of silence. Later, a reporter ran into Wooden in the lobby of Washington, D.C.'s Shoreham Hotel. The writer asked him why he refused to allow his team contact with the press. Wooden, irritated by the question, took off his thick black-rimmed glasses, rubbed his eyes for a moment, and looked quizzically at the interrogator who pried into his program. "Are they big boys now, John, or what?" the reporter asked. "Newsmen," Wooden answered with a furrowed brow, "are too smart for college kids. They are in the business of selling papers. They will trick players into saying things, then twist it for purposes of controversy. I do not want controversy."[29]

Wooden distrusted the media. He preferred simplicity, order, and complete control over his program. Meddlesome reporters threatened all of those things. When the sportswriter pressed him further, Wooden maintained that he did not want anything interfering with his players' focus on basketball. He disapproved of players "talking about politics and racial issues and social change." "Such things," he claimed, "have a negative effect on the team as a whole." Some players seemed "distracted" by racial issues, the Vietnam War, and social causes, and it made his job increasingly difficult. He had heard stories about colleagues who lost players to the counterculture or, worse yet, lost their jobs over arguments about hair or charges of racism. Wooden refused to allow destructive outside issues to tear down everything he had built in Westwood. He refused to become another desperate coach.[30]

On the morning of the national championship game, Wooden again walked through the hotel lobby, worrying about how his team would perform later that afternoon against Jacksonville University (JU). When Andy Hill spotted him, he asked if he and his teammates could wear Yale T-shirts after they won the game. Puzzled at first, Wooden quickly realized that Hill wanted to make a political statement. Steve Patterson echoed Hill's request, arguing that the NCAA had unfairly ruled a Yale basketball player ineligible after he played in the Maccabiah Games. Although the NCAA allowed its athletes to play in the Olympics and the Pan American Games, after the point-shaving scandal of 1961, the NCAA banned summer basketball competition to prevent players from participating in resort leagues where gamblers preyed. But the Maccabiah Games were far from a corrupt summer league. Every four years, Jews from all across the globe represented their country in international athletic competition staged in Israel. When Yale refused to suspend the Jewish basketball player and actually played him during its games, the NCAA prohibited all Yale athletes from competing in its championship events. At the NCAA indoor-track championships, three Harvard athletes wore blue Yale T-shirts on the victory dais in solidarity with their Ivy League brethren. For these young men at Harvard and UCLA, the NCAA's repressive policy limited the freedom of athletes, and athletic events, therefore, were an ideal forum for political protest. Although Wooden disagreed in principle with the NCAA's ruling, like many conservatives he strongly disapproved of demonstrations, favoring more diplomatic appeals instead. So, the answer was no, UCLA could not wear Yale shirts.[31]

Most sportswriters would not have been surprised to hear Wooden's answer. Leading up to the national championship, journalists portrayed the UCLA coach as a symbol of conservative America and his counterpart, Jacksonville's Joe Williams, as a liberal free spirit. It was more than the way the two coaches dressed, Wooden in his drab brown suit, Williams in blue pants, pink shirt, and a snowy white sports jacket. It was even more than the way the two teams warmed up, UCLA in two crisp straight lines, Jacksonville bouncing, spinning, and dazzling the crowd in their green-and-yellow bell-bottoms, whipping passes behind the back and through the legs, as the speakers blared "Sweet Georgia Brown," the Harlem Globetrotters' whistling theme song. Their entirely different coaching philosophies represented the tensions within the profession: Wooden the traditionalist, resistant to change, and Williams the modernist, secure in his authority. Wooden was "a product of the old school," a rigid disciplinarian who instructed his players not to talk to strangers or leave their hotel rooms unless accompanied by a teammate. Williams had no dress code or training rules at all, except that his players give 100 percent on the court. Writers could almost hear Wooden gasp when the thirty-six-year-old coach questioned the very foundation of coaching: "What is discipline?"[32]

To most coaches, Williams's permissive approach invited players to challenge authority. Dwight Chapin of the *Los Angeles Times* observed that each team's image reflected the personality of its coach. "UCLA represents everything that is entrenched, solid, the disciplined, the ordered, and the sure," he wrote, and "Jacksonville represents the new and the now, the free flight, the experimental, the who-gives-a damn." When UCLA took the court against Jacksonville, Chapin commented, "It will be sort of like Richard Nixon running against Dr. Timothy Leary."[33]

Basketball fans could easily recognize that Artis Gilmore played for Williams. Gilmore embodied black "soul power," stylized in his Afro, muttonchops, and a bristly goatee that Wooden would never have allowed. He drew comparisons to a young Wilt Chamberlain, standing seven-foot-two with muscular thighs, sinewy torso, rangy arms, and powerful shoulders. Not only was he built like Chamberlain, but he played like him too, dropping hook shots over defenders like he was flipping a wad of paper into a wastebasket. Frequently, the nation's leading rebounder (twenty-two per game) sprang off the floor, snatched the ball with his left hand, slapped it with his right, and swung his sharp elbows, an intimidating tactic that kept opponents at a safe distance. And for a big man, Gilmore could really jump. One time he leaped so high that he blocked another player's shot with his elbow.[34]

It seemed that Jacksonville's entire front line was built like Gilmore. The Dolphins were, according to the school's media guide, "the tallest team in the nation—giant by giant." With Gilmore, seven-foot forward Pembrook Burrows, and six-foot-ten forward Rod McIntyre towering in the paint, and six-foot-five shooting guard Rex Morgan making deep jump shots, Jacksonville became the first team in history to average more than one hundred points per game. Fourteen years earlier, Jacksonville was a meager junior-college team, but now thanks to this richly talented group, JU entered the national championship game with only one loss and a chance to topple a dynasty.[35]

Right before the game started, Wooden informed Sidney Wicks that he would guard Gilmore, a difficult assignment considering he gave up six inches in height to the Jacksonville center. In the early minutes of the game, Wicks positioned himself on Gilmore's hip, extending an arm across his chest, trying to deny the ball. This strategy failed, as Gilmore scored unin-hibited, forging an early 24–15 JU lead with more than nine minutes left in the first half. At that point, Wooden knew he had to wrest control of the game away from Gilmore. During a time-out, Wicks exhorted Wooden to let him play behind Gilmore. "You can't guard him from behind," Wooden countered. "Yes, I can!" Wicks fired back. "I'll show you." Wooden conceded, and after the time-out, Wicks let Gilmore take two uncontested jumpers, but the third time Gilmore shot the ball, Wicks launched like a rocket, timed his jump with the ball's arc, and swatted it. Throughout the game, Wicks stuffed Gilmore's shot four more times. His series of blocks deflated Gilmore's confidence and, more important, forced him to miss twenty of his twenty-nine field-goal attempts. With his boundless energy, Wicks outrebounded Gilmore 18–16 and ignited a burst of fast-break scores that gave the Bruins a 41–36 halftime lead.[36]

Both teams opened the second half ice cold. In five minutes, UCLA missed nine of ten shots, and the two teams combined for only seven points. While Gilmore's first five shots bounced off the rim, the Bruins gradually built a lead to eight, eleven, and as high as sixteen points. In the final nine minutes, UCLA calmly operated under a more deliberate, patterned offense, success-fully outscoring JU 26–12. UCLA controlled the boards, neutralized JU's size, and won the game 80–69. Afterward, tournament MVP Sidney Wicks explained that Lew Alcindor was the difference in the game. "The dunk rule really helped me," Wicks said ironically. "If Gilmore could have dunked, he would have killed me."[37]

O

The day after the championship, John Wooden spent the evening relaxing at his daughter's house. As the family prepared to go out for dinner, the phone rang. When he picked up the phone, an operator asked him if he would wait while she connected him to a long-distance call. He was in a hurry to get out the door, but when she told him it was the president, the UCLA coach said that he would gladly wait. Wooden fought back tears when Richard Nixon's voice finally came over the line. Nixon had called to congratulate him for winning his fourth straight national championship, a remarkable achievement. Wooden told sportswriters that it was a "tremendous thrill" to hear from Nixon and "a wonderful gesture" that he would never forget.[38]

When Wooden hung up the phone, he had no idea that Nixon—the man he had voted for—would make a political decision that directly affected the UCLA basketball team. Like many Americans who traditionally voted Democrat, in 1968 Wooden voted Republican. Perhaps he voted for Nixon because they shared traditional values, or possibly because he promised to restore law and order, or maybe because Nixon said that he would end the war. If it was the latter, Nixon deceived him and millions of Americans. On April 30, 1970, the president announced that U.S. forces had invaded Cambodia to prevent the North Vietnamese from infiltrating South Vietnam. Ten days earlier, Nixon claimed that he would withdraw 150,000 American troops over the next year, an assurance that the war was winding down. Suddenly, he had expanded the war, breathing new life into an exhausted antiwar movement.[39]

Nixon's invasion enraged college students. If the war expanded into Cambodia, draft calls would increase and more students would be sent to fight in Southeast Asia. "We thought we might have to go and we might be killed," Andy Hill said. The Cambodian invasion provoked widespread protests across America's campuses, though UCLA's burgeoning antiwar movement did not organize any mass demonstration. Student strikes hit more than sixty campuses. Most of the protests were peaceful, but that all changed after Kent State. On May 4, Ohio National Guardsmen retaliated against taunting protesters, took aim at a crowd of two hundred Kent State students, and fired sixty-seven shots in thirteen seconds, wounding nine and killing four. After the bloodshed at Kent State, university administrators across the country prepared for a student uprising, but there was no way to prepare for what would come next.[40]

Later that night, at the Beverly Hilton ballroom, the UCLA basketball team, coaches, boosters, and parents escaped the tragic news at the annual basketball team banquet. After Bill Seibert finished his jeremiad against the basketball program, Wooden stepped to the podium and gave a brief, conciliatory response. In public Wooden said that he respected Seibert's right to express himself, but privately, Wooden chafed over his speech and the team's standing ovation. He suspected that there were players that agreed with everything that Seibert had said, and if they did, he wanted them off the team, though he would not revoke their scholarships.[41]

Determined to "eliminate all possible sources of trouble," Wooden planned to meet with Andy Hill, John Ecker, and Terry Schofield, players who "indicated that they were anti-establishment." The morning after Seibert's speech, on May 5, Wooden pulled Terry Schofield from his 8:00 a.m. class, a clear indication of his anger since he never wanted his players to miss class. When Schofield arrived, Wooden and his assistants Denny Crum and Gary Cunningham confronted him. For three and a half hours, the coaches argued with Schofield. At one point, Wooden called him a left-wing activist, a negative influence on the black players, and foulmouthed. Wooden claimed that it was obvious that Schofield and Ecker were "political activists," since they wore long hair and grew beards in the off-season. Schofield recalled that Wooden basically said that he "was not what a white ball player should be." Eventually, Schofield broke down crying, and the coaches declared a truce, agreeing to let him stay on the team.[42]

Shortly after the meeting ended, at noon, about four thousand students assembled at Meyerhoff Park, UCLA's free-speech area, joining more than five hundred campus strikes that occurred in the week after Kent State. "On strike, shut it down!" echoed throughout Meyerhoff. An hour after the rally began, about seventy-five students marched to the Men's Gym, home of UCLA's ROTC program and a potent symbol of the war, the draft, and the university-military-industrial complex. Enraged protesters hurled concrete chunks, rocks, and pieces of wood—anything that they could use to smash windows and batter the doors down. A small band of demonstrators attacked a plainclothes policeman, beating him on the back of the head, kicking him in the ribs, and stealing his loaded pistol. At 2:00 p.m., after Vice Chancellor David Saxon learned that violence between protesters and University Police had spread beyond the Men's Gym, he declared the first state of emergency in campus history, notifying the LAPD that their presence was needed in Westwood.[43]

Between 2:35 p.m. and 3:05 p.m., Saxon, a UC Police Department officer, and an LAPD officer made three separate announcements over the loudspeaker, instructing students to disperse from the area near the Men's Gym. Two LAPD buses arrived, bringing the number of officers on campus close to two hundred. Within a half hour, the police had cleared the area near the Men's Gym, with few arrests and evenhanded force. Afterward, squads of white-helmeted officers advanced through the upper campus, an area where many people were leaving class or work. They were completely uninvolved in a demonstration that started nearly four hours earlier, and they had not heard the evacuation command. Soon the campus erupted into an orgy of violence, as policemen furiously chased, clubbed, kicked, strangled, and dragged innocent bystanders before *and* after they were handcuffed. Eyewitness accounts reported numerous episodes of wanton police brutality. One policeman barked at a student, "Get moving, you motherfucker." After the young man asked the officer to repeat himself, the enraged officer cracked him in the knees with a baton and whacked him again and again across the back and hands. When the student tried to rise, the officer struck him again. Satisfied, the policeman walked away without arresting the student.[44]

After violence erupted at UCLA, Governor Reagan closed every college and university in the state for the rest of the week. For the first time since the Watts riots, the entire LAPD force worked in twelve-hour shifts. The next day, more than one hundred riot-ready police shadowed Westwood, squad cars and motorcycles circled the campus, and helicopters surveyed the area. But UCLA's state of emergency did not prevent Wooden from meeting with Hill and Ecker. Convinced that the reserve players agreed with Seibert's sentiments, Wooden suggested that they leave the team, but Hill and Ecker maintained that they wanted to stay. Afterward, Hill, Ecker, and Schofield met with their teammates at Sidney Wicks's apartment and talked about how Wooden targeted them as subversives. They resented Wooden for imposing his conservative values on the team during the off-season. He told them to cut their hair and avoid campus demonstrations and that they should not get involved in political organizations. Infuriated at their coach's reaction, the whole team—minus graduating seniors Seibert and Vallely—decided that they would meet again, this time with Sam Gilbert.[45]

Since 1967, when he convinced Lew Alcindor and Lucius Allen to stay at UCLA, Gilbert had grown increasingly close to the players. After Alcindor was graduated, Gilbert helped him negotiate his professional basketball contract, supposedly gratis, and he later did the same for Wicks, Rowe, and Patterson. He exuded fatherly warmth and a sincere concern for the players' welfare, inspiring the nickname "Papa Sam." The players expressed a genuine affection for Gilbert, who routinely threw parties for them at his Malibu home on Sundays. During "Sunday school," the players ate as much as they wanted, swam in his pool, and talked with Gilbert about race, religion, politics, and their personal problems, topics that Wooden avoided. But Gilbert doled out more than hamburgers and free advice. He helped players acquire cars, stereos, airline tickets, clothing, and whatever else they wanted. Knowing that the players frequently visited Gilbert's home, Wooden suspected that they benefited from his overzealous generosity. When he noticed that Wicks and Rowe wore flashy, expensive clothing, he inquired, "Did Sam Gilbert get these for you?" The players denied that the booster purchased them, but when Wooden asked if Gilbert arranged a discount, the players answered, "Don't you shop around for better prices when you get things?" When Wooden did not hear the answer that he wanted, he stopped asking questions, ignoring clear NCAA violations in his program.[46]

During the meeting with Gilbert, the players agreed that they would deliberately disobey Wooden's rules about political demonstrations by writing a letter to President Nixon, in care of H. R. Haldeman, a UCLA alumnus and the White House chief of staff. Gilbert, an opponent of the Republican administration, encouraged the players to write the letter. From a distance, Nixon, like much of the public, admired Wooden's players for what they supposedly represented: the triumph of traditional values, discipline, respect for authority, and success. But the players made it perfectly clear that they were not Nixon's team.[47]

The letter, signed by the whole team, began, "We, the undersigned, are thirteen U.C.L.A. students who wish to express our grave concern and disapproval over the President's policy of expansion of the immoral, genocidal and imperialistic war the United States is now waging in Southeast Asia." The team denounced violence, whether by protesters or police, but they fully supported "meaningful and peaceful demonstrations." "We further wish to clarify that we are not 'bums' as we college students have been so wrongly accused" by Richard Nixon. "Rather we are concerned with the well being of America and its democracy which should function as a reflection of the American people. But when massive demonstrations concerning the policies of this country are suppressed or dismissed as unwarranted or unlawful dissent, then there is something seriously wrong." Frustrated by Nixon's "unwillingness to carry out the will of the people," the team closed the letter with four demands: the immediate withdrawal of all American troops, the rapid de-escalation of the war, a public investigation of the Kent State shootings, and "the end of harassment of youth . . . by those in authority," an issue with which some players strongly identified.[48]

UCLA's antiwar letter was not an isolated protest among college athletes. In the aftermath of the Cambodian incursion, college athletes all across the country demonstrated against the war with their fellow students. Princeton's track team withdrew from the New Jersey intercollegiate track and field championships. The lacrosse, golf, and freshmen baseball teams at Williams College canceled their respective contests, as did the Dartmouth lacrosse team. At Columbia eighty-five football players sent a petition to Richard Nixon. A group of eighty San Diego State athletes marched across campus, demonstrating for peace. At Berkeley Cal athletes from ten sports held a press conference where they issued a joint statement similar to UCLA's basketball team, which read in part, "We, the overwhelming majority of California athletes, find that we can no longer live in the so-called 'apolitical atmosphere' which has permeated the athletic community. We find it necessary now to voice our opposition to President Nixon's oppressive policies at home and abroad. We condemn United States activity in Southeast Asia and call for a unilateral withdrawal of all United States forces in Southeast Asia."[49]

These student athletes were not militant radicals, commies, hippies, or bums. Rather, this was a radical moment, because entire teams of athletes unified against the war. At UCLA the basketball players viewed themselves as concerned students, part of the mainstream, frustrated with the way that Nixon dismissed dissent as unwarranted and unlawful. Nixon's escalation of the war provoked a new student activist, the "active moderate," which included athletes who rejected the idea that they belonged on the sideline of political activism. By 1970 college students did not have to join radical organizations to participate in the antiwar movement. These athletes showed that they could express dissent in different but effective ways— organizing political action, passing out leaflets, holding press conferences, and writing letters.[50]

UCLA's team letter was as much an act of rebellion against Wooden as it was an act of protest against the war. For these players, the letter symbolized a declaration of political independence from a coach who imposed limits on freedom of speech. Being politically active was an important part of their identity as students, and they refused to be denied the right to exercise that freedom. "[Writing the letter] made me feel like I was still a student not just an athlete," Andy Hill said later. "Being a student-athlete at UCLA," he said, meant not going "through school just as an athlete but to truly experience the entire spectrum of college life."[51]

When Wooden learned that the players had met with Gilbert, he called the team into his office for a meeting. He heard a rumor that the players were going to present him with a list of demands, but he would resign before acceding to any ultimatum. He prepared an alphabetical list of player names on a piece of notebook paper and started asking each player what made them unhappy, intending to show that most individuals were not dissatisfied. But Wooden could not control the conversation. After Kenny Booker answered his questions, Steve Patterson interrupted Wooden's orderly process and said that they did not want to talk as individuals, that they had team problems and wanted to address him as a group. Patterson and Wicks led the conversation, explaining that they did not want Wooden to dictate their personal lives, appearance, or political activity. But Wooden feared that player rebellion endangered the dynasty. He said, "By the mere fact that you're here demonstrating against me has done away with our chances of winning another national championship."[52]

The players maintained that they did not intend to undermine his authority. They simply wanted to discuss their grievances in a democratic way. "You shouldn't feel threatened by this," Wicks said. "We're here as a team and you taught us that." Wicks convinced Wooden that although they disagreed about some things, the players respected him, and his lessons about team unity inspired them to support one another, even if it meant incurring the coach's wrath. Wicks helped defuse the tension and moved the coach and team closer to understanding each other, though Wooden still believed that college athletes "should not use their position as stars to try to influence the public politically." But writing an antiwar letter to the president was basically a harmless demonstration. It could have been much worse if his star player got arrested for barricading the administration building.[53]

8

The Red Menace

On October 14, 1971, a day before Bill Walton's first varsity practice, a *Sports Illustrated* photographer asked him to take a picture with Coach Wooden. Walton hated taking pictures and detested individual attention, especially because basketball was a team game. At six-foot-eleven, the rawboned teenager posed awkwardly in his clean white uniform, pale skin exposed, his hands crossed in front of his body. His angular shoulders, wiry arms, and tender right knee wrapped in a heavy bandage suggested that his body might not hold up for the entire season. With a boyish freckled face, lantern jaw, and shaggy red hair, he looked like "Huckleberry Finn on stilts." Wooden, wearing his customary brown pants and gray sport coat, propped his left leg up on a chair, smiling for the camera. Walton shyly closed his lips, refusing so much as a weak grin.[1]

For a photographer, capturing any genuine expression from Walton required taking pictures of him on the basketball court. Right before tip-off, as the team huddled around Wooden, Walton swayed back and forth, rocking on the balls of his feet, snapping his fingers to the rhythm of the music. He played with boundless exuberance, jumping, shouting, and directing his teammates like a traffic cop. He celebrated great plays by clapping his hands and pumping his fist, as if to say, "Yes! That's how we do it!" Frequently, after rebounding the ball and triggering a fast-break outlet pass, Walton sat back and watched the action unfold with a wide smile on his face, laughing, soaking up every joyful minute of a game that he truly loved.[2]

When it was over, Walton hid his youthful enthusiasm from reporters. Uncomfortable around strangers, the shy star offered monosyllabic answers to their questions, stammering with a speech impediment. When Walton did speak, he guarded his privacy and deflected questions about himself, preferring to talk about his teammates. Initially, sportswriters found the quiet, soft-spoken "Merriwell folk hero" refreshingly modest and selfless, an ideal white athlete. During his sophomore year, as reporters pressed him for interviews, he opened up, revealing strong beliefs about political and social issues. Disillusioned with the dominant Cold War culture, Walton was deeply committed to changing America, eliminating poverty, eradicating racism, and ending the Vietnam War. He became a visible symbol of dissent, outspoken in his denunciation of authority and the war, making him the most controversial white basketball player of his generation.[3]

Nothing angered him more than watching Vietnam veterans return home in wheelchairs and body bags. He was frustrated by the government's empty promises that the war was winding down and that American soldiers would come home soon, but not soon enough. It seemed that every night, television newscasts showed images of napalm bombings ravaging entire villages, and still the war continued. Walton could not understand how the government allowed American teenagers to die every day in far-away jungles for a senseless, immoral war. "I want to see the end of wars," he said. "There are some people on this campus who agree and intend to act. I intend to act with them."[4]

○

By the early 1970s, sportswriters proclaimed UCLA basketball a dynasty, a term that Wooden disliked. He preferred to think of his program's success as a cycle—one that could come to an end. For Wooden, winning championships was not simply an end goal; it was part of a continuum, an experience that offered important teaching lessons. Every October on the first day of practice, the cycle started anew, a day when Wooden outlined his expectations for the upcoming season. He reminded his team that this was a new year; what happened the previous season no longer mattered.[5]

Wooden was a perfectionist, driven by an insatiable quest for self-improvement. The teacher in him viewed the basketball season as a process, a journey of lessons about effort, personal growth, success, and (however infrequent) failure. Every year, on October 15, the season began with Wooden instructing the players about how to put on their socks, how to lace their shoes, how to tuck their jerseys into their shorts, and how to dry their wet hair after showers. During practice he taught the basics, drilling players on inside turns, change of pace and direction, quick starts and stops, defensive sliding, passing, and rebounding. Over and over, the players ran the same drills, gradually accelerating with speed and efficiency. Wearing white shorts, a thick navy-blue and gold-trim warm-up jacket, and white socks pulled up high on his shins, Wooden demonstrated proper execution. Between drills he referred to his three-by-five index cards, exhorting the players to hurry to the next station on the court. While the players scrimmaged, he eagerly paced the sideline with a whistle hanging around his neck, his clear blue eyes alertly following the ball. The players could hear the bespectacled gray-haired coach shouting above squeaking sneakers, "The worst thing you can do is hurry!" "Be quick! But, for gracious sakes," he shouted, "don't hurry!"[6]

Wooden had one simple rule during practice: no player could ever stop moving unless he blew the whistle. He pushed the players past exhaustion, forcing them to run, jump, and slide for several minutes without resting. Backup center Swen Nater remembered that five minutes into the first day of practice, he could hardly breathe. Gasping for air, he felt like someone had stepped on his sternum. With his head spinning and a piercing pain in his side, Nater paused to catch his breath while the throbbing subsided. "Swen!" Wooden shouted in his flat Hoosier voice. "You are not to stop running! Catch up with the team!" Wooden required intensity, absolute focus, and maximum effort for every minute of practice. When a player made a mistake, he corrected him. He never stopped teaching. "Swen! There's no reason in the world somebody should take that ball away from you! C'mon now!" Wooden urged, "You're strong as a bull out there." Sometimes, no matter how hard the players tried, nothing was ever good enough for the demanding coach. Frequently, he became impatient, disgusted with the players' effort. When the team did not practice to his satisfaction, he ordered the team off the court, turned off the lights, and locked the gym doors.[7]

Wooden's coaching philosophy was rather uncomplicated: "Get the players in the best of condition. Teach them to execute the fundamentals quickly. Drill them to play as a team." Of course, recruiting talented players was the most important aspect of his philosophy. All season long, Wooden devoted his practices to the same drills, running the fast break, and executing the press. On offense UCLA used very few set plays. Basically, he wanted his team to quickly push the ball up the court, fan out, and hit the open man. Bill Walton later said that Wooden's system essentially came down to getting the ball to the best players and giving them the freedom to make plays. Wooden's basic philosophy mirrored the approach of Green Bay Packers legendary football coach Vince Lombardi. Both coaches strongly believed in simplicity, repetition, and execution, caring little if the other team had scouted them as long as their team was well prepared. "You do what you do best—and you do it again and again," Lombardi once said. Like Lombardi, Wooden agreed that perfection came from simplicity. "My feeling is that if we execute soundly— exactly the way we're supposed to—they'll have a rough time stopping us," he maintained. "We're an easy team to scout, but we're not easy to stop."[8]

For the past five seasons, no one had stopped the Bruins from winning the national championship. In 1971, with Sidney Wicks, Curtis Rowe, and Steve Patterson leading the way, UCLA defeated Villanova for the national championship, the Bruins' seventh title in eight seasons. But it was not a season without problems. The tensions between Wooden and the team from the previous year continued. Observers noticed that although UCLA won with regularity, some players appeared more interested in impressing pro scouts and padding their scoring statistics than passing the ball to open teammates. Curtis Rowe admitted, "Everyone has been too concerned about their future." Such selfishness divided the team. Another player complained to the school newspaper, "Off the court, everyone goes their own way."[9]

No player tested Wooden more than Sidney Wicks. Larry Farmer, Wicks's backup, recalled that Wooden sometimes brought freshman Bill Walton over to practice with the varsity. One time, during a two-on-one fast-break drill, Walton stood alone at the end of the court, prepared to defend the basket. On three consecutive fast breaks, Walton blocked the shot attempt. Aggravated that a freshman was dominating "Sidney's court," Wicks told his teammates that he would put an end to Walton's fun. "Oooh, something's gonna happen now," Farmer thought to himself.[10]

Henry Bibby and Sidney Wicks raced down court at full speed. Bibby dribbled with the ball and passed it to Wicks on the wing. As Wicks received the pass, Walton slid over to defend the shot. In a flash, Wicks leaped off the floor, propelling all of his momentum upward toward the rim, and forcefully slammed the ball over Walton's outstretched arms. "Sidney let a dunk rip that was probably one of the best dunks I've ever seen," Farmer recalled. The players stood, mouths agape, disbelieving what they just saw. A hush came over the gym until Wooden broke the silence. "Sidney! Sidney! You know there is no dunking in practice!" he shouted over the cackling players.[11]

Wicks knew—and so did Wooden—that he was the most important player on the team. Whenever the Bruins struggled on offense, Wooden relied on him to take control of the game. He even allowed Wicks to play one-on-one while his teammates watched. Exploiting one player's talents was inconsistent with Wooden's team-oriented coaching philosophy, but necessary for this team to win. Off the court, Wicks challenged Wooden's coaching principles as well. *Los Angeles Times* writer Dwight Chapin recalled that during an airplane ride home from Washington, Wooden noticed Wicks standing in the aisle, wearing sagging Levis that revealed the crack of his butt. Wooden turned to Chapin and said, "Isn't that *disgraceful?*" But Wooden said nothing to the star player about his appearance. Some things were not worth arguing about.[12]

After the 1971 season ended, Wooden looked forward to coaching an almost entirely new team. With three sophomores in the starting lineup—Walton, forward Keith Wilkes, and point guard Greg Lee—Wooden was surprised that such a young team dominated opponents right away. Despite their youth, the team played unselfish, textbook basketball. Unlike the previous championship team, these players relied less on physical strength and more on quickness and finesse. Wooden devised a basic 1-3-1 offense with Lee at the top of the key, shooters Henry Bibby and junior forward Larry Farmer on the wings, Wilkes at the foul line, and Walton down low.

Wooden positioned each player according to their offensive strength: Lee had strong hands and passed with precision; Bibby shot most accurately on the wing; Wilkes offered quickness and a soft shooting touch from the high post; Farmer worked effectively in the interior; and Walton, who possessed remarkable quickness for a center, could shoot, dribble, and pass better than any other man his size. On defense Wooden utilized a full-court 2-2-1 zone press, with Walton playing as the deep man and calling the signals.[13]

Walton was the key to everything. He seemed to cover the whole court, leaping for blocks, chasing loose balls, and snagging errant shots out of the air. He was an intelligent player, consciously aware of his teammates' exact position on the court. If Walton knew where his teammates stood, he could anticipate where they would be after he rebounded the ball, and then he could immediately throw a quick outlet pass, starting the break. It all happened so fast: in a single blurry motion, Walton swooped high above the rim, clutched the ball with his large hands, turned—sometimes in midair—and rifled the ball to a teammate, who accelerated the break with a pass or finished it with an easy layup. There was no defense for Walton's instantaneous fast-break trigger. From the moment he grabbed the ball, his teammates sprinted down the floor, while the defense backpedaled, never quite quick enough to catch up with the streaking Bruins.[14]

There was no question that this was the most explosive scoring team that Wooden had ever coached. The Bruins played with ceaseless energy, relentless on the break, fluid and smooth, persistently charging the basket. In their first seven games—all at Pauley Pavilion—UCLA averaged 112 points and defeated their opponents by a 47-point margin. But not everyone was impressed with the number-one team's early-season dominance. *Sports Illustrated*'s William Reed dryly noted that the Bruins' opponents "probably couldn't hold their own against the pom-pom girls." *Los Angeles Herald-Examiner* beat writer Doug Krikorian credited J. D. Morgan with building the Bruins' confidence with a soft schedule of "lollipops." These were fair criticisms, but Morgan cared little as long as UCLA won and cashed in with sold-out attendance at Pauley Pavilion.[15]

Three days before Christmas, UCLA hosted Notre Dame at Pauley Pavilion, their first rematch since the Irish upset the top-ranked Bruins the previous season, 89–82. There was absolutely no chance that Notre Dame would pull off another surprise victory against UCLA. After four consecutive seasons of winning more than twenty games, Notre Dame head coach Johnny Dee left South Bend and returned to practicing law. The new head coach, Richard "Digger" Phelps, a fiery thirty-one-year-old Irish Catholic from Dutchess County, New York, inherited a woefully inexperienced roster decimated by graduation. After one season as the head coach of Fordham, Phelps accepted the job at Notre Dame with a team of sophomores and walk-ons. The first year of his dream job turned out to be a nightmare. In the first game of the season, Indiana drubbed Notre Dame 94–29, causing many Irish fans to wonder if the wire service had misprinted the score. And now Notre Dame had to play UCLA at Pauley Pavilion where the Bruins had lost only two games since the arena opened in December 1965. From the opening tip, it was clear that Notre Dame was completely overmatched. During one stretch of the first half, UCLA outscored Notre Dame 36–3. Wooden unleashed an unmerciful press that completely crushed Notre Dame, creating numerous three-on-one fast-break layups. At halftime UCLA led 53–16. With about eight minutes remaining, and UCLA leading by 41 points, Wooden continued to press the Fighting Irish with his starting players. Phelps fumed that Wooden was running up the score with the game out of hand. Late in the game, he knelt near the scorer's table with a scowl on his face, locked eyes with UCLA assistant coach Gary Cunningham, and mouthed, "Fuck you! And the guy next to you too!"[16]

After UCLA pounded Notre Dame 114–56, the second-worst defeat in their school's history, Phelps hid his contempt. "I think John Wooden is the best man in college basketball history," he said. After both coaches spoke to the press, Wooden approached Phelps and tried to apologize for leaving his best players on the court long after the game was decided. "Now Digger," he explained, "this past week we were in our final exams and we didn't get to practice that much. We have our conference season starting next week, so I needed to work on my press." Infuriated, Phelps saw beyond Wooden's celebrated image. Wooden was intensely competitive, proud, and still bitter over losing to Notre Dame, a team that he considered inferior. Phelps did not believe a word Wooden said. "John," Phelps replied, "you do anything you have to do to beat me, because someday I am going to kick your ass."[17]

Maybe someday Phelps would beat Wooden, but few coaches believed that they had any real shot at doing it this season. No team in the country could match UCLA's talent and depth. The substitutes had more ability than most teams' first string, which meant that whenever Wooden inserted a player from the bench, he expected that they would execute as well as his starters. After watching the Bruins rout their early opponents, *Sports Illustrated*'s William Reed was convinced that UCLA was "so deep that their second team could probably win a Big Eight or SEC championship." By the end of February, UCLA had won twenty-three straight games, most by margins of around 30 points. Sportswriters asked Wooden how this team compared to his past UCLA squads. "I'd have to say at this stage that this team is certainly as good as any I've had," he said. "But everything is relative now. You can't really make any valid comparisons until the season is over. If we go on to win the title, I would have to rank this team as stronger than any I've ever coached."[18]

The Bruins' success transformed Walton into a national celebrity, though he was not interested in being a campus hero or everyone's best friend. He simply wanted space. After too many burdensome campus conversations with random students and hounding reporters, Walton decided to ride his bike whenever he left home, furiously pedaling through Westwood. That bike offered more than transportation; it gave him a sense of freedom—freedom to live by his own rules, freedom to talk only when he wanted, and freedom to escape the pressure of fame.[19]

More than anything, Walton loathed talking about his individual basketball accomplishments. It annoyed him when reporters ignored his teammates during postgame interviews. "It hurts me when people talk as if I'm the only player on the team," he said without a hint of false modesty. "I wish sportswriters wouldn't ask me anything personal at all. I would like to see them get the whole team together to talk. I don't like to be singled out as an individual because we don't play as individuals, we play as a team." Walton's genuine selflessness endeared him to the public, who admired him not only for his incredible basketball skills but also for his humble rejection of celebrity.[20]

"The most talked about player" in the country could not avoid the press forever. In March *Sports Illustrated*'s William Reed wrote a cover article titled "UCLA's Red Hot Red-Head." The story began in a modest middle-class house in La Mesa, California, a hilly suburb of San Diego. Ted and Gloria Walton raised their four children in a warm yet strict Catholic home centered on family unity. The Waltons did everything together: church picnics, music, games, mountain hikes, and camping trips. Large family dinners always started at 6:15, and from the moment they sat down, the children never stopped eating or talking. Ted and Gloria were college-educated, old-fashioned liberals who encouraged their children to express themselves, ask questions, and get involved. Everyone had a voice at the dinner table, where they discussed politics, school, and social issues. During the day, Ted helped the disadvantaged as a social worker and taught adult education at night. He bristled when people criticized the poor or when television stations showed grainy World War II footage, which he thought glorified war and violence.[21]

Bill's parents refused to purchase a television until the mid-1960s, so Walton often laid in bed next to a transistor radio, listening to KMPC's Fred Hessler call the play-by-play for UCLA games. Like so many kids growing up in Southern California, he dreamed of playing basketball for the Bruins. The first game he ever watched on television—at a friend's house—was the 1965 national championship between UCLA and Michigan. Seeing the Bruins—a team of skinny, scrappy players who relied on quickness, ball movement, and teamwork—convinced him that he wanted to play for UCLA. During his sophomore year of high school, Denny Crum sent Walton a letter of interest. After Crum watched Walton play during a recruiting trip, he told Wooden, "I've just seen the greatest high school prospect ever." Astonished at such an outrageous claim, Wooden reminded Crum that he had seen Lew Alcindor play as a teenager in New York City. "Yeah," Crum said, "but this kid is better." Wooden raised his eyebrows, motioned toward his office, and said, "Come inside—and close the door."[22]

It was not long after Crum's scouting trip that the secret got out: Helix High had the best basketball prospect in California. Scouts were most impressed by Walton's quickness, anticipation, and superb passing ability. In junior high, before his two big growth spurts, Walton played guard and frequently dribbled the ball up the court, which helped him develop acute court vision and keen passing skills. Between his sophomore and junior years of high school, he grew almost overnight from six-foot-one to six-foot-seven. During his junior year, he grew another two inches, and by his senior year he shot up to six-foot-eleven, though he weighed only 195 pounds. Whereas most exceptionally tall teenagers would have lost some coordination, Walton matured into a complete player, intelligent and decisive with the ball in his hands. The more he improved, the more attention he received from writers, scouts, and fans. Walton sacrificed easy shots and passed the ball, hoping that his teammates would receive more publicity for scoring points. During his senior year, he averaged twenty-nine points and twenty-four rebounds and led Helix High to a 33-0 record and a second straight California Interscholastic Federation district championship.[23]

Recruiting letters poured in from all over the country. Walton stopped counting them after he received 110 scholarship offers. He really wanted to go to UCLA, but that did not stop recruiters from doing all they could to change his mind, offering him cars, cash, and cushy jobs. Those crooked deals turned off Walton's parents, who had experience turning away shady characters a few years earlier, when football scouts approached Bill's brother Bruce, who ultimately chose UCLA. Crum knew that Wooden did not enjoy recruiting visits, but he pressured him into making an exception so that the Waltons could meet the UCLA coach. Wooden broke bread with the family and impressed them by promising only that Bill would receive an excellent education and a chance to earn a starting spot on the basketball team. Ultimately, Walton chose UCLA because he wanted to play for Wooden on the best college basketball team in the country. He also liked the idea of joining Greg Lee and Keith Wilkes, two of the best high school prospects in the state who had also committed to UCLA.[24]

In William Reed's cover story, Walton appeared as a traditional sports hero: hardworking, exceptionally talented, a winner—and white. *Los Angeles Times* reporter Jeff Prugh wrote that the "Great Silent Majority" celebrated him as a "Great White Hope"—a white savior who could rescue a sport overrun by blacks. In American sports, the search for a Great White Hope began in 1908, after Jack Johnson became the first African American to win the heavyweight boxing title. By the mid-1970s, as black athletes increasingly dominated boxing, baseball, football, and basketball, some whites feared that they had been permanently displaced. White college basketball fans and alumni complained that blacks received too many scholarships. And while it appeared that blacks had taken over college basketball, Walton's presence reassured the white silent majority that the "right kind" of athlete still represented *their* school. For many conservatives, not only were there too many black athletes on college basketball and football teams, but they were also the ones who complained about racism, joined protests, and boycotted athletics. *They* were the radicals. *They* were the outspoken troublemakers. White athletes, on the other hand, were the good boys, "a conservative force on campuses," rarely involved in demonstrations or controversial political statements.[25]

But Walton was not a traditional sports hero. He was a child of the sixties, a liberal's son with strong opinions about race, poverty, and war. He consciously followed the civil rights struggle and grew frustrated by racial inequality. At UCLA he studied African American history and talked about racism with his black teammates. When he was a teenager, his librarian mother brought home a copy of Bill Russell's *Go Up for Glory*. In Russell's autobiography, the Boston Celtics star shared his experiences with racial injustice. He bitterly complained about racism, questioned the effectiveness of nonviolence, and claimed that sport did not promote racial equality so much as it reflected patterns of inequality. After reading the book, Russell became Walton's hero.[26]

Like Russell, Walton seethed over racism. "I don't blame the blacks for hating the whites," he told William Reed. "They've gotten such a raw deal for so long." In March the *Los Angeles Herald-Examiner*'s Doug Krikorian and Bud Furillo interviewed Walton at a fancy Beverly Hills restaurant. Walton slouched in his chair with a dour expression on his face, picking at his food as the writers prodded him for answers. When they asked him about being a great basketball player, he retorted that one of the main reasons he had received so much attention was because he was white. After all, he said, he had not accomplished anything yet. Shocked at such a claim, the writers pressed him further. "If I was black, I wouldn't get as much publicity," he said. "I would be just another big black center who plays basketball and does things well." Walton understood that in the view of many whites, he represented an idealized savior, a Great White Hope, in a sport increasingly dominated by blacks. Yet he rejected any characterization as a Great White Hope: "It's been so long since there's been a big white player who make[s] people say, 'this guy is good.'" "You have to realize," he said, surprising the writers with his interpretation on race and sports, "that people who support basketball are white, upper middle class. So the white fans dig on me because I'm white." Furillo admitted that what Walton said made sense. "I'd be a damned liar if I didn't think it was important to me that you're white," he replied. "This is the day of emerging prides. But this is no reason for white people to lose theirs."[27]

Walton's racial views demonstrate how the civil rights movement politicized college athletes, black and white alike. In the 1960s and early 1970s, basketball played an important role breaking down racial barriers and teaching fans, sportswriters, coaches, and athletes about race in America. Walton's relationships with his black teammates and his admiration for black players such as Bill Russell inspired him to speak out against racism. While most whites looked at integrated sports teams as evidence that conditions had improved for blacks, Walton pointed out how African Americans continued to confront the abuses of racial discrimination. Moreover, his defiant rejection of being college basketball's "Great White Hope" demonstrates that the "Athletic Revolution" was defined not only by the revolt of the black athlete, but also by rebellious, politically conscious white athletes who refused to conform to the conservative values of the sports establishment.

○

If Wooden was concerned about Walton's controversial racial comments, he did not share his distress with sportswriters. His main worry was Walton's knees. When he was fourteen years old, Walton twisted his knee and tore cartilage. He underwent knee surgery and endured endless hours of therapy. After recovering, he grew six inches, and by the time he was eighteen, he developed tendonitis in both knees. It did not help that he constantly ran, jumped, and twisted on the hardwood floor, further pounding his knees and inflaming the aches of his joints. At times he limped off the court, grimacing. A half hour before every practice and game, Walton applied heating pads to his knees. Afterward, he soothed his stinging knees with ice. To make matters worse, in January, Walton tore tendons in his big toes, which required cortisone shots. The throbbing pain in his knees and toes became so unbearable that he started skipping Monday practices. Yet he still managed to play at an elite level, convincing some coaches that his pain did not exist. One coach called him "a hell of an actor." An opposing player suggested that Walton was "a con artist . . . seeking sympathy." Such gross accusations hurt him. "My problem *is* real," he said, "and it is not easy to overcome."[28]

By the end of the Bruins' perfect regular season, it was clear that only Walton's knees could stop them from winning a sixth consecutive national title. UCLA devastated opponents with their suffocating full-court press, relentless fast breaks, and frequent scoring bursts. The Bruins were never in any real danger of losing a game. UCLA, Doug Krikorian wrote, "made a mockery of the 1971–72 season by beating foes by abnormal margins." They averaged ninety-six points per game and allowed only sixty-three, a remarkable margin considering that the starters rarely played an entire game. Walton and Bibby made All-American, and Walton won the Naismith Player of the Year Award. Quite simply, no team could match their talent, depth, and quickness. Long Beach State coach Jerry Tarkanian, who had lost to Wooden twice in the past two years of the NCAA Tournament, declared, "This is the best UCLA team ever."[29]

After UCLA defeated Long Beach State for a third consecutive time in the Western Regional finals, 73–57, Tarkanian's players were less complimentary of the Bruins. It was a physical contest underneath the basket, with the players pushing, grabbing, and elbowing one another. Henry Bibby claimed that during a fast break, a Long Beach player pushed him from behind. Incensed at the way his players were mugged, Wooden fiercely shook his rolled-up program and yelled at the referee, "This is disgraceful!" With ten minutes left in the second half, Walton had to leave the game after getting hit in the ribs. At that point, Wooden leaped from his chair, marched to the scorer's table, and chided Long Beach assistant coach Dwight Jones for his team's "disgraceful and unethical" rough play. Then, according to Jones, Wooden complained to one of the officials that Long Beach State had intentionally fouled Walton. At that point, the referee calmly explained to him that he would watch for flagrant fouls. Afterward, one of the 49ers groaned that the "officials protect UCLA. They were fouling us a lot and we didn't get the calls." Another player called Walton "a crybaby."[30]

After soundly defeating the 49ers, the Bruins did not have to travel far for the Final Four. For their next game against Louisville, UCLA fans packed the Los Angeles Sports Arena with blue and gold shirts, pennants, and banners, excited to see if former Bruins assistant Denny Crum could defeat his mentor. Crum had played for Wooden, served as his top assistant for four years, and helped build the dynasty by recruiting some of UCLA's best players. And although he knew UCLA's system inside out, his Louisville squad would have to play a perfect game to win. They did not. Louisville simply could not stop Walton inside. The All-American center scored thirty-three points and grabbed twenty-one rebounds, easily leading the Bruins past the Cardinals, 96–77. Afterward, Louisville center Al Vilacheck echoed Long Beach State's complaints, lamenting, "Walton is strong, but you can't touch him. The officials put him in a cage. He cries a lot. I just don't think a man of his ability should cry so much."[31]

Occasionally, Walton lost his temper and became distracted in a fit of frustration. He had extremely high expectations for himself and his teammates, and when the team fell short of those expectations or he felt slighted by the officials, he erupted. Goaltending calls, turnovers, and uncalled fouls gnawed at him. When opposing players hit, slapped, or collided with him, as Louisville often did, he complained to referees with a distressed, almost wincing facial expression. In March, when UCLA defeated USC in one of the roughest contests of the year, Walton told sportswriters that the Trojans' Ron Riley hit him "with the cheapest shot ever seen." After that episode, he developed a fragile reputation, and opposing teams attacked him with a more physical, bruising style, hoping that he would crack under the pressure.[32]

Before UCLA met Florida State in the national championship, some coaches expressed disappointment that the NCAA allowed the Seminoles to play in the tournament. For the previous three seasons, Florida State was on probation, mainly for providing recruits with "lavish entertainment," which prevented them from participating in the playoffs. Before the 1972 tournament, some coaches suspected that three Seminoles had illegally signed contracts with professional agents. Again, the NCAA investigated the program and forced three players to sign affidavits swearing that they did not have agents. Before the championship game against UCLA, Bill Wall, president of the National Association of Basketball Coaches and head coach at tiny MacMurray College, publicly complained that Florida State did not belong in the tournament.[33]

Florida State head coach Hugh Durham adamantly defended his program. Durham believed that he drew scrutiny because he had fully integrated the basketball team—nine of ten players were black—at a predominantly white southern school. He resented accusations that he "bought" players and wondered why similar accusations were not charged at other major programs. "It was speculated that Lew Alcindor got more than he was supposed to receive," he said. "It's all right with schools like UCLA, North Carolina, or South Carolina. But if it's Long Beach State or Florida State, somebody's eye gets cocked and he says, 'Why did he *really* go to Florida State?'" To Durham and many other coaches, it appeared that UCLA played by a different set of rules. Some coaches perceived that referees favored Wooden and that the NCAA ignored UCLA's illicit relationships with boosters. It was bad enough that UCLA had the best players. But it seemed even worse when the system privileged the Wizard of Westwood.[34]

The Bruins paid little attention to the off-court controversy surrounding Florida State. They maintained their focus on a single objective: winning the national championship. When UCLA swaggered onto the court, the Los Angeles crowd rose to its feet, thundering with applause. One fan held up a sign: "WELCOME TO THE SIXTH ANNUAL BRUIN INVITATIONAL." Early in the game, Florida State, a sixteen-point underdog, delivered a surprising blow, hitting seven of its first ten shots. When things went well, Wooden sat with his rolled-up program in hand, lightly tapping it against his knee. But when he was worried, he nervously twisted and unrolled the program. Wooden rarely called the first time-out because he believed that it gave the opposing team a psychological advantage; it suggested a sense of panic. When he finally gave in and called time-out, a sportswriter sitting along the press row turned to his colleague and mockingly suggested that perhaps Wooden had made a mistake during his superstitious pregame ritual. "Maybe John did it wrong this time," the other writer sarcastically wondered. "Maybe he crossed the right leg over the left." During the break, Wooden knelt down in front of the team bench and said something to his nodding players. "OK?" he asked. "OK!" they all replied, affirming his instructions.[35]

The UCLA time-out did not help. The Bruins fell behind 21–14, the biggest deficit they had faced all season long. The crowd was shocked. The most UCLA had ever trailed was at Oregon, 4–0. But the Bruins never panicked. They started hitting some shots, slowly building their confidence. First, Bibby hit a jumper. Then Walton made a free throw. Bibby sank another jump shot, followed by a Walton bank shot. Suddenly, the score was tied at 21, and the Seminoles looked stressed and confused. Florida State tried double-teaming Walton, but he quickly zipped the ball to Keith Wilkes for open midrange jumpers. UCLA surged past Florida State and gained a commanding 50–39 halftime lead.[36]

In the second half, Florida State fought back, cutting UCLA's lead to seven points on three occasions. Walton was visibly annoyed when the Seminoles trapped and hacked him underneath the basket. He complained to officials and jawed with opponents. Nonetheless, the Bruins remained poised, and their defensive pressure forced the Seminoles into costly turnovers. In the last four minutes, Florida State turned over the ball three times. With 1:05 left on the clock and UCLA leading 79–72, Wilkes scored a layup, clinching the Bruins' sixth straight national championship, their eighth in nine years. The *Los Angeles Times* called UCLA's 81–76 victory—the closest of the year—the "perfect ending to a perfect season." UCLA's star players all performed well: Walton scored twenty-four points and snagged twenty rebounds, Wilkes finished with twenty-three points, and Bibby contributed eighteen points.[37]

Afterward, Walton met with reporters in the Sports Arena pressroom. He was tired and bruised, and his knees ached. He wanted to be left alone. When sportswriters asked him to raise the microphone so that they could better hear his answers, he snapped, "I can hear myself. My voice is bouncing off the back wall." After another writer again asked him to adjust the microphone, he suggested that he move to an open seat in the front row. When he finally talked about the game, he expressed extreme dissatisfaction with his performance. "I'm not that elated because we didn't play that well," he said. "Florida State is an excellent team but we didn't dominate the game like we know we can." Walton moped behind the microphone, shaking his head in disbelief. "I felt like we lost it," he muttered. Shortly thereafter, he headed to the Bruins' dressing room, ignoring autograph requests along the way. As he worked his way through a crowd of reporters and UCLA fans, Walton peevishly complained, "Whose locker room is this anyway?"[38]

For Walton, winning the national championship was not enough. He was competing not only against the opponent on the court but also against an unmatched standard of success built by past UCLA teams—an ideal of perfection. Walton's disappointment, then, stemmed from the pressure of knowing that he and his teammates would always be compared to past UCLA teams—teams that never lost the championship game. For the UCLA players, beating Florida State in the national championship by only five points—the lowest margin of victory in UCLA title-game history—was unimpressive. Such a close victory felt like losing, which was completely unacceptable to those who wore the UCLA uniform. Sitting near his locker, surrounded by strangers, Walton unwrapped his bandaged knee and removed his sweaty socks. He admitted that he feared playing for "the UCLA team [that] didn't win the national championship." It was a revealing moment: here was the best player in the country who had just won the national championship, but all he could think about was how he had *almost* lost.[39]

○

In March 1972, a junior high school teacher in Cincinnati, Ohio, wanted to learn what his forty students knew about current events. It was a complex and confusing time for many young people. In an election year, five men were caught breaking into the Democratic National Headquarters office at the Watergate Hotel. President Richard Nixon visited China and the Soviet Union, hoping to reduce the threat of nuclear war. At the Olympic Village in Munich, Palestinian terrorists attacked Israeli athletes in a bloody hostage takeover. By midyear in Vietnam, American troop levels declined to sixty-nine thousand. Harry Truman, Walter Winchell, and J. Edgar Hoover all died. So did Jackie Robinson and Roberto Clemente. *Life* magazine folded, and *Ms.,* the first magazine run by and for women, appeared on the news-stand. Don McLean sang about the day the music died, Marlon Brando played the Godfather, and Major League Baseball players went on strike for the first time in history.

The teacher questioned the students about a number of events. He also asked them what the letters *U-C-L-A* stood for. Of the forty students, thirty-seven correctly wrote: "University of California, Los Angeles." One student offered a more memorable answer. U-C-L-A, the student wrote, stood for "BASKETBALL." This junior high school student was not the only one who immediately thought about basketball when he read the letters *U-C-L-A.* Clearly, the dynasty played a significant role in shaping the university's identity. When Wooden first came to UCLA, the university was considered a provincial college, an extension of the University of California, Berkeley. But by the early 1970s, UCLA had built a preeminent reputation in athletics and academics, ranking among the top ten universities in the country in teaching, research, and service. Looking back at UCLA's phenomenal rise, Chancellor Charles Young maintained, "I think it is safe to say that UCLA would not have gained the stature, nationally or internationally, that it has as quickly as it did had it not been for athletics."[40]

UCLA administrators realized that the basketball program's national success and visibility could attract economic support from multiple sources. In the 1970s, under the governorship of Republican Ronald Reagan and the fiscally conservative Democrat Jerry Brown, the University of California operated under a tight budget, slowing UCLA's growth. With shrinking state funding, UCLA increasingly relied on private donors. At a time when UCLA "experienced comparatively little excitement or unusual distinction . . . except for its men's basketball team," Wooden served a critical role in generating financial support. In 1972 he served as the national chairman of UCLA's Annual Fund, appealing to alumni and friends of the university for generous donations. Wooden was an ideal speaker for the university. There was no one better to represent UCLA. His folksy speeches put people at ease. "He was somebody you knew when he spoke was telling the truth," Charles Young said. Wooden reminded basketball fans that their donations would benefit UCLA's educational, research, and cultural programs. Without their help, the faculty, the students, and the school's reputation would suffer, but with their support, UCLA would prosper, just like the basketball team. The dynasty, then, served a larger purpose beyond promoting school spirit. The Bruins basketball program became a promotional vehicle for building the university.[41]

O

By 1972 the antiwar movement at UCLA had faded into the background. Since the Kent State protests swept the country two years earlier, many college students became disillusioned with the peace movement. Activists were exhausted from participating in mass demonstrations that failed to convince the Nixon administration to withdraw immediately from Vietnam. Others hoped that the war would end soon, especially because draft calls and American causalities had declined. At the same time, the antiwar movement became less radical as more liberal and moderate Americans supported total withdrawal. Many Americans distrusted what the government told them about the war. In June 1971, the *New York Times* and the *Washington Post* published what became known as the *Pentagon Papers,* the Defense Department's secret history of how the American government deliberately deceived the public about its role in Vietnam, dating back to the Truman administration. After the government documents were published, polls showed that more than 70 percent of Americans thought that the war was "a mistake," which meant that radical activists did not have to persuade middle America that the war was wrong.[42]

In January 1972, the editors of UCLA's *Daily Bruin* complained that there was a "lack of commitment to the cause of peace among a supposedly enlightened student body of 28,000." In late April, the editors lamented the "silence" among Westwood students and reminded readers that "we cannot afford to drop out of the fight against the [war] because of boredom or fatigue." Still, there were some UCLA activists who refused to remain quiet until every American soldier returned home. Bill Walton was one of them. He sympathized with those who refused service and avoided the draft. The young men who were drafted, he said, were "told to go and kill" and "risk their lives for no real reason." To him, war simply did not make sense. "I hate when people say you should be proud to die for your country," he fumed. "What does death prove? Wouldn't it be better to live for your country?"[43]

Like many Americans, Walton doubted Richard Nixon's hollow peace promises. "I don't think Nixon can bring about peace," he said. "He's too wrapped up in fascist ways, imperialism, and all this bullshit." On May 8, the president announced that he had authorized the mining of North Vietnam's ports and ordered an intensified bombing campaign. Nixon claimed that mining Haiphong Harbor would prove a "decisive military action to end the war." Peace activists were outraged that the president had ignored their cries for withdrawal and that he had blatantly escalated the conflict in Southeast Asia. Turbulent campus demonstrations erupted all over the country, though they were smaller and far less violent than those that occurred immediately after the Cambodian invasion two years earlier. On May 9, shortly before noon, as many as two thousand antiwar demonstrators marched through UCLA's campus, where they denounced the presence of ROTC and persistently shouted, "On strike, shut it down!"[44]

About five hundred protesters, including Walton and teammates Greg Lee, Keith Wilkes, and Larry Farmer, paraded from campus through Westwood Village; some students carried signs that read, "STOP THIS ILLEGAL WAR!" Shortly after 2:25 p.m., the chanting demonstrators made their way to Wilshire Boulevard and Le Conte Avenue, where fifty LAPD officers confronted them. The demonstrators ignored police orders to remain on the sidewalk and continued down Wilshire until they reached Veteran Avenue. When the police instructed them to disperse, some protesters, including Walton, refused and sat down, blocking traffic. The LAPD threatened to arrest them if they did not leave the area. A group of demonstrators wanted to march back to campus, while others, like Walton, were committed to disrupting the intersection. About a half hour later, after the LAPD issued a second dispersal order, the group gradually headed back to campus, though Walton and about ten others sat down again at the intersection of Wilshire and Gayley Avenue. After five minutes passed, Walton straggled back toward campus, where students listened to military veterans denounce the war.[45]

Throughout the next day, peaceful protests continued. Some of the demonstrators entered classrooms and exhorted other students to join them.

The *Daily Bruin* reported that Walton and Greg Lee interrupted a class and urged students to "shut this school down." The professor suggested that those who wished to leave class could do so, and those who wished to discuss the war could stay. "You can't get anything accomplished by just debating the war," Walton groaned. "You should be out there demonstrating!" Later that evening, Walton and about two hundred students staged an overnight occupation at Murphy Hall, where they barricaded the outside doors with furniture, tables, and trash cans. He was convinced that shutting down the administration building would "raise the consciousness of the people."[46]

The next morning, riot-ready university police ordered the throng of protesters to evacuate Murphy Hall. After the students peacefully complied with the command, nearly one thousand protesters marched from a rally at Janss Steps and joined the Murphy Hall demonstration. At that point, a six-foot-eleven, shaggy redhead in blue jeans and a white short-sleeve shirt led a small group of students who piled chairs, garbage cans, scooters, and wooden barricades in front of Murphy Hall's main entrance. Then Walton helped a few others drag a janitor's cart in front of the doorway. Shortly after 2:00 p.m., the LAPD arrived, wielding batons. Chancellor Charles Young did not want to call the city police, but he feared that an overturned maintenance vehicle, leaking with gasoline, had become a fire hazard. After the LAPD instructed the protesters to disperse, about two hundred students sat down in the street, including Walton, who repeatedly shouted, "The whole world is watching!" He offered no resistance when the LAPD helped him to his feet and into the paddy wagon. Before Walton entered the police bus, he turned toward Chancellor Young, extended his middle finger, and yelled, "Fuck you, Chuck!"[47]

The police booked Walton at the Valley Services Division in Van Nuys and charged him with disturbing the peace, failure to disperse, unlawful assembly, and rioting. According to *Los Angeles Times* writers Jeff Prugh and Dwight Chapin, Walton's brother Bruce paid the five-hundred-dollar bail with money from Sam Gilbert. *Sports Illustrated* also reported that Bruce bailed him out, though the magazine made no mention of Gilbert. In recent interviews, Walton has offered a different version of what happened after he was arrested. He claims that Wooden came down to the jail, paid the bail, and drove him home. Supposedly, during the car ride, Wooden lectured him for getting arrested and disrupting the campus. He suggested that Walton protest the war by writing letters, an ironic proposal given his disapproval of the 1970 championship team's letter denouncing Nixon's Vietnam policies. Perhaps Walton's account is exactly what happened. Or perhaps Prugh and Chapin's reporting further confirms that Gilbert helped solve the legal and financial problems of UCLA basketball players.[48]

In the wake of Walton's arrest, conservative critics accused him of associating with communists and "a hardcore group of militants." Los Angeles mayor Sam Yorty called the antiwar demonstrators "young American dupes of the Communist Party." The *Orange County Register,* a leading voice for the Right in Southern California, suggested that if Walton had taken "a history lesson from the mayor," then communists could not have manipulated him. The *Register* also maintained that if the antiwar demonstration had taken place during the basketball season, Wooden would have prevented Walton from participating. Meanwhile, anticommunist zealots sent Walton vitriolic hate letters, calling him an unpatriotic, subversive commie pinko. Even J. D. Morgan believed that communist agitators manipulated athletes such as Walton to promote their political agenda. Walton's critics noted that he called himself a "socialist," "a revolutionary," and "an internationalist," clear evidence that he was a Red Menace. A Republican voter from Long Beach complained to Governor Ronald Reagan that Walton wanted "to destroy UCLA" and that he should be removed from the basketball team. Many of his detractors demanded that Chancellor Young punish him immediately and dismiss him from school.[49]

Walton's antiwar demonstration and the conservative backlash it engendered reflected the fracturing of America during the Vietnam era. His protest reveals that the Athletic Revolution was defined not only by politically active athletes on the Left, but also by politically conservative fans, coaches, and commentators on the Right—critics who resisted political and social change within sports. For many conservatives, Walton's political activism threatened two important American institutions—the college campus and college athletics. His opponents believed that college athletes were supposed to act, in the traditional sense, apolitically, failing to recognize that their own conservative attitudes about the ways athletes should behave had important political implications.

While Walton waited to learn about his punishment at UCLA, rumors about his future circulated throughout the campus. Radio station KMPC reported that his teammates drafted a letter requesting that he sit out the following season. When a reporter from the *Los Angeles Free Press*—an alternative newspaper with a leftist bent—asked him about the situation, Walton said, "Some were for me, some were against me. Nobody from the team really came out and said they thought I was a motherfucker. I know that some of them disagreed with my actions but I'm not leading my life so that people will say what a good guy I am." After *Sports Illustrated* asked Wooden how he would deal with Walton, he replied, "That's not in my bailiwick. It's out of season and a student's conduct is out of my hands." UCLA dean of students Byron Atkinson placed Walton on probation for two years, but did not suspend him from school or the basketball team. The best basketball player in the country was too important to UCLA's national championship hopes and the commercial benefits that came with winning for him not to play. The Van Nuys Municipal Court leniently fined him fifty dollars and put him on probation for twelve months.[50]

Clearly, Walton was an incredibly complex individual. The All-American basketball player respected authority, accepted discipline, and obeyed team rules. The outspoken activist, on the other hand, defied authority, rejected the old order, and rebelled against the sports establishment's political norms. He was not a hard-core militant, a communist sympathizer, or a radical intent on anarchy. He was a committed peace advocate, who, like many American youths, viewed confrontation with authority as a normal and necessary part of life. Above all, Walton was an idealist who sought individual freedom and eschewed conformity.

"I tend not to bend under pressure," he said. "I don't let other people control my life. I like to lead my own life."[51]

9

The Rebel and the Saint

ill Walton loved to argue with John Wooden. They debated everything: the war, politics, religion, clothes, curfew, and team rules. It seemed that every day, Walton irritated Wooden in practice, persistently asking the same questions. "Why do we have to do it this way? Why? Why? Why?" Before the first practice of Walton's senior year, the All-American center tested Wooden again. On team picture day, he arrived unshorn. Walton's thick red hair covered his ears, and his scraggly chinstrap beard made him look like he played for the American Basketball Association's (ABA) San Diego Conquistadors, not the UCLA Bruins. Wooden took one glance at him and said, "Bill, your hair's too long." Walton had read the team letter Wooden wrote during the summer, which reminded the players about his rules on hair: "Wear no mustache, beard or goatee; have sideburns no longer than the top of the lobes of your ears; have the hair of reasonable length with the coaches being the judge as to what is reasonable length."[1]

For Walton, Wooden's rules about hair were completely unreasonable. He believed that no one, not even his coach, had the right to tell him to cut his hair. Asking him to get a haircut not only infringed on his personal freedom but also violated his political sensibilities. His convictions about hair reflected the attitudes of the counterculture.[2] His long hair symbolized a rejection of conformity, a desire for independence, and a direct challenge to the establishment. He defied the stereotypes that All-American athletes wore short hair and only dirty hippies wore long hair. "Everybody expects me to be a certain way," he said. "They have their own idea of what a college basketball player should be like—short hair and all that—but I'm not that way. I'm myself. I love long hair. I wish coach Wooden would let us wear it as long as we like to have it."[3]

Walton, firm in his convictions, was determined to take a stand against Wooden's arbitrary rules. After all, he was the NCAA Player of the Year and had led UCLA to two undefeated national championships. How could Wooden tell him what to do? "Coach," he began, "I've thought about it for a long time and I think I should be allowed to grow my hair as long as I want."

"I'm sorry, Bill," Wooden replied, "but you know how I feel about the subject."

"But, Coach, I don't think it's fair that we can't decide for ourselves what the proper hair length is."

"You feel strongly about this, do you?"

"Yes, very strongly."

"Well, Bill I feel strongly about this particular rule too. So we're going to miss you, but it was nice having you here."[4]

At that moment, Walton had to make a decision: accept Wooden's authority or defy him. Almost immediately, he sprinted through the gym doors, hopped on his bicycle, and sat down in a barber's chair. Walton later said that there was nothing more important to him than playing basketball for UCLA. He would never let anything get in the way of playing for a national championship. Not even a haircut.[5]

This story is about more than a haircut; it's a story about the Athletic Revolution, a culture clash between politically conscious athletes and the conservative sports establishment, a conflict between athletes' desire for autonomy and coaches' sense of authority. In his refusal to let Walton play with long hair, Wooden rejected the infusion of liberal values onto the court and scored a victory for conservatives who believed that coaches had to draw the line against rebellious athletes like Walton.[6]

For the good of the team, Wooden refused to tolerate dissent or anything that suggested radicalism, even long hair. Winning was too important. Sportswriter Arnold Hano observed, "There is something almost unreal about Wooden, in his dedication to the team. If anything gets in the way, it is wrong, be it woman-chasing, or pot, or hair that may fly in a man's eyes, and for a split second, impair his vision. Or a goatee that in no way can affect a man's play, but may annoy the people who support the team—alumni, fans, press, people of influence." Wooden often reminded the players that the letters on the front of their jersey—U-C-L-A—represented something more than the team itself, which meant that his players would not wear long hair during the season.[7]

The defiant attitudes of some players made Wooden's coaching job far more challenging. He complained that his players were not as malleable as they once were when he first started coaching. What America's youth needed, more than anything, was discipline, he said. Discipline not only was the foundation for a winning basketball team, but would also help solve the problems of society. Despite the resistance of some players, Wooden successfully convinced them to accept his message and sacrifice their individual concerns for the good of the team. Sportswriters often noted that what made him a great coach was his ability to overcome off-court distractions and "narrow the generation gap."[8]

Throughout the 1960s and 1970s, conservatives decried the politicization of college sports, claiming that athletes who participated in political demonstrations or adopted the attitudes of the counterculture would destroy American sports. But Wooden's teams defied this myth. Although some UCLA players were politically active, the Bruins continued to win. Wooden understood that he had to change with the times; he bent some of his rules and compromised without completely giving in. Although he often disagreed with his players about politics, dress, and hair, he tried to understand their perspective.[9]

Walton respected Wooden not for his beliefs, but for the strength of Wooden's convictions. Both men lived their lives according to different, sometimes opposing, values, yet Walton admired his coach for treating him as something more than a basketball player. Whereas most people saw Walton exclusively as an athlete, Wooden was interested in him as a human being, fully concerned about his welfare off the court. And most important, both men respected the social hierarchy of college basketball. If the athlete wanted to play, if he wanted to win, he had to follow the coach. Through basketball, Walton and

Wooden found common ground and a mutual admiration for one another. "I don't have blind reverence for authority," Walton said. "People I respect earn my respect. Coach Wooden has earned it."[10]

○

In the fall of 1972, after spending the summer backpacking in the California Sierra Nevada, Bill Walton returned to campus, where he lived in a tiny room in an old fraternity house. Few people knew his address, and no one could reach him by telephone because he did not own one, of course. He often lay on his large custom-made bed, reading Tolstoy, Vonnegut, and Michener. Sometimes he stayed up late, listening to his favorite rock records—the Rolling Stones, Country Joe and the Fish, and Bob Dylan. Dylan's poetic lyrics resonated with Walton. In Dylan's folk-rock music, he could identify with his contempt for authority, celebration of "noble outlaws," and distrust of the establishment.[11]

That distrust shaped Walton's attitude toward the mainstream media. Before the season began, he met with Bill Libby for an extended interview that was later published in the magazine section of the *Los Angeles Times* and formed the basis of Libby's book *The Walton Gang*. Walton had avoided interviews since March, ignoring requests to discuss his antiwar demonstration and subsequent arrest. Sharing his opinions with Libby worried him; he was afraid that it would create more negative publicity. Walton hated the idea of journalists shaping a false image of who he really was, but he never allowed them to get close enough to really know him. "I don't want to be made into some cardboard cutout, and I don't want people to be disappointed when they find out that I'm something other than what they want me to be," he said. "Some people have the idea that a UCLA athlete is an all-American boy," he commented. "But what is an all-American boy? Someone who wears his hair cut short. . . . Someone who thinks it's the most important thing in the world to win games or the most noble thing on earth to give your life for your country?"[12]

In many ways, he adopted the broader values and attitudes of the counterculture—a counterculture that had infiltrated the mainstream and become more political. Like many youths who identified with the counterculture, Walton defined himself by what he was not. At a time when many Americans were increasingly hostile toward those who looked or acted "different"—hippies, "freaks," beatniks, and peaceniks—Walton rejected labels that categorized him as threatening or as acceptable. He was not the typical all-American boy or All-American athlete. Nor was he "the world's tallest hippie" or a fanatical ideologue. In the world of American sports, Walton was an iconoclast: the antihero who defied traditional views of what a white athlete was supposed to represent. He was "a rebel with a cause," "a free thinker and a free speaker," an individual set on his own path. In essence, he echoed Muhammad Ali, who said, "I don't have to be what you want me to be. I'm free to be who I want."[13]

Walton's opinions were driven by his disillusionment with the establishment. Like many American youths, he was alienated by what Tom Brokaw later called the "greatest generation"—Wooden's generation—a generation that raised its children to avoid controversy, respect authority, and believe in America's democratic ideals. During the Vietnam War, young people lost trust in America's institutions, the government, and their parents. One activist wrote, "What's happening is that a whole generation is starting to say to its parents, 'You can no longer get us killed & be killed for your uptight archaic beliefs.'" By the early 1970s, as the war continued, many young people believed that there was something wrong with America. They blamed the endless war on the government, the military, and their parents. It seemed that everywhere they looked, American institutions were failing. The greatest generation had failed them.[14]

The contradictions between American ideals and American realities frustrated Walton. The history major pointed out that although blacks had won freedom after the Civil War, they were still fighting for racial equality more than one hundred years later. He believed that blacks had the right to do whatever was necessary to achieve freedom. Although many whites feared that the angry rhetoric of Black Power would provoke a violent uprising, Walton considered it as a potent source of black empowerment. "I wouldn't blame the blacks if they took up arms and went into outright revolt," he said. "I don't like violence, but violence scares people, and sometimes you have to scare people into doing right, into acting." The more Walton talked about racism, the more intense and agitated he became. His eyes widened and his brow furrowed as he looked at Libby. "If a black man gunned me down right now," he said, his voice rising, "I'd figure it was all right because of what whites have done to blacks."[15]

It was an extreme statement, one that shocked Libby and the readers of the *Los Angeles Times*. It revealed the depths of his outrage over injustice and his uncertainty about how to react to a country tearing itself apart. Like many young activists on the Left, Walton believed that speaking out against racism, poverty, and the war would lead to real change. But in his mind, the establishment refused to acknowledge what young people were saying. Such obstinacy created a sense of powerlessness and desperation among America's youth. It radicalized some, while others dropped out of politics all together. Walton's alienation with the establishment forced him to question everything—politics, poverty, the war, his coach, even his own sense of purpose.

Walton and Libby continued their interview at a popular restaurant on Wilshire Boulevard, where customers immediately noticed the six-foot-eleven basketball star. Strangers stretched their necks just to get a glimpse of him. He tried to ignore their stares, but the attention made him uneasy, especially when people approached the table and asked for his autograph. He barely acknowledged his admirers when they came over. Without lifting his head, he quickly scribbled his signature, nodded, and said very little. He hated signing autographs. "Autographs," he said, "are the most meaningless things I can imagine."[16]

He could not understand why people idolized and celebrated athletes as heroes. "People make too much of sports and athletes," he said. "It's all out of proportion to its place in the overall scheme of things." He often wondered why other students stood in line for hours outside Pauley Pavilion just to watch a game. Why did they cheer so loud? Why did they get so excited? Why was the UCLA basketball team so important to people? In the sixties, sports offered much-needed relief, a diversion at a time when the country was deeply conflicted, fighting over the war and civil rights. It was a morally ambiguous, complex, and often confusing time for America. But basketball provided simplicity: two opposing sides, struggling for the same prize, competing for victory. At the end of the game, there was a clear winner, and it always mattered who won.[17]

During the Vietnam Era, it seemed that winning became more important in American life than ever before. Americans were obsessed with winning—winning the war, winning the election, winning the big game. "We play our games, or watch them contested, with the same tenacious ferocity with which we fight a war in Vietnam and with as little reason or sense," journalist Leonard Shecter observed. "We are taught from the cradle that we have never lost a war and that winning is everything, tying is like kissing your sister and losing is nothing." In sports, Vince Lombardi repeatedly said, "winning isn't everything, it's the only thing."[18]

Americans' cultural preoccupation with winning inspired a countercultural backlash against competition. On the West Coast, many youths turned to Frisbee and "New Games," alternative sports that de-emphasized competition. In Southern California, during the seventies, "soul surfing" became more popular within the counterculture. Soul surfers rode the waves exclusively for personal enrichment, in opposition to competitive commercialized surfing. Even Walton, an elite college basketball player on an undefeated championship team, questioned the importance of winning in every facet of American life. "I don't know why players can't just play the game," he said. "Is it so important to win? Why do we have to win all the time? Why does this country have to win all the time? We could end this war so easily and we don't do it. Why not just end it?"[19]

Walton's devotion to winning in basketball ran contrary to his renunciation of America's competitive ethic. Every time he stepped onto the basketball court, he played to win. He *had* to win. His greatest fear, he admitted, was playing for the UCLA team that failed to win a national championship. There was no question that Walton loved competing. When he graduated from UCLA, he turned down a more lucrative offer to play in the ABA because he believed that the competition in the NBA was superior. Walton expressed his competitive zeal not only as an athlete, but also as an activist. Like many activists on the Left, Walton saw social and political causes in competitive terms. Real change, he believed, resulted only from action. During UCLA's antiwar protests the previous May, he told a class of students, "You can't get anything accomplished by just debating the war. You should be out there demonstrating!" The antiwar movement offered Walton a competitive physical outlet. Marching in the street and barricading the administration building expressed his willingness to put his body on the line.[20]

No athletic event better reflected America's preoccupation with winning more than the Olympics. The Cold War rivalry between the United States and the Soviet Union further intensified Americans' competitive ethic. Every Olympic event seemed to represent the global struggle between East and West, communism and democracy, socialism and capitalism. The Games, then, were not really games. For the United States and the Soviet Union, winning an event signified ideological supremacy. So when Bill Walton announced that he would not compete in the 1972 Summer Olympic Games in Munich, many superpatriots claimed that that he had let his country down. Without the best amateur player in the country, critics groaned, the United States risked losing an important event to the Soviet Union. Some commentators accused him of refusing to play out of protest against the Vietnam War, though he never faced the kind of backlash that Lew Alcindor did for not playing in 1968. Walton claimed that politics had nothing to do with his decision. His doctor, he said, recommended that he rest his aching knees instead of participating in the Olympics. When pressed further about his decision, he said, "I just don't want to play."[21]

Walton was not the only prominent college player who chose not to represent U.S. basketball. Outstanding collegians such as Bob McAdoo, David Thompson, George McGinnis, Len Elmore, and Julius Erving all turned down the chance to play in the Olympics. The U.S. Olympic Basketball Committee worried that with so many elite players declining invitations, mostly because they had signed professional contracts, the U.S. team would be shorthanded in Munich.[22]

Perhaps the biggest surprise of the Olympic basketball trials was the performance of UCLA backup center Swen Nater. Few people knew how good Nater was until he was given the chance to play regularly at the trials. His soft shooting touch and fierce rebounding impressed Olympic head coach Henry Iba. As the leading scorer in camp, Nater proved that he could start anywhere in the country—except UCLA—and would provide the Olympic team with much-needed strength near the basket. But Nater never made it to Munich. Iba's rigid coaching methods and arduous practicing conditions convinced six players to leave the trials during the first week. After making the team, Nater tried to adapt to Iba's strict regimen, but he ultimately quit the team because the practice and eating schedule led him to lose nearly twenty pounds in five days. With each practice, he became weaker and weaker, unable to jump, run, and scrap for rebounds with his usual intensity.[23]

After Nater quit the team during the Hawaii training camp, *Los Angeles Times* columnist John Hall criticized the UCLA players for failing "to give a little of themselves to the general public which has paid their way to the top of the mountain." Hall lamented that it had become a tradition for UCLA basketball players not to represent their country. Not since 1964, when Walt Hazzard made the U.S. team, had a UCLA player competed in the Olympic Games. Hall wondered why John Wooden had failed to encourage Walton, Nater, and Keith Wilkes to suit up for the red, white, and blue. "The indifference displayed by his athletes is unlike John and hardly a tribute to the great UCLA basketball coach," he wrote. Saul Shapiro of the *Daily Bruin* argued that critics like Hall were "placing their own patriotism above individual prerogative." He wondered, "Was Wooden supposed to fly to Hawaii and tell Swen that for the future of 'truth, justice, and the American Way,' he must clout the Russians a mighty blow?"[24]

When Walton announced that he was not interested in participating in the Olympics, Wooden shared his own opinion on the matter. He lamented how the "spirit of the Games" had "become more political." What bothered him most was that the Olympics were no longer a celebration of individual achievement and international brotherhood, but rather a Cold War competition. "When you ask the average person about the Olympics," Wooden groaned, "he'll ask: 'How are we going to do against the Russians?' Is that what the Olympics are? Are we participating against just one team, or are we participating against all countries?" he wondered. "I'm just as patriotic as anyone," he said, "but I've become a bit disillusioned with the political nature of the Olympics and other things."[25]

When the Soviet Union defeated the United States in a surprising and controversial gold-medal game—the first loss in U.S. Olympic basketball history—some dejected Americans pointed the finger at Walton and Wooden, suggesting that had Walton played, there was no way that the United States would have lost by one point to the Soviets. In a letter to the *Sporting News,* Major David G. Cotts placed the blame for the U.S. defeat squarely on UCLA. "The U.S. sent an inferior team, because John Wooden, the greatest basketball coach of all-time in my opinion, refused to expose Bill Walton's knees to the test and failed to influence Swen Nater from leaving the team." Walton cared little that some Americans considered losing a basketball game to the Soviet Union tantamount to suffering a serious defeat in the Cold War. And he dismissed any suggestion that the United States would have won with him in Munich. "Anyway," he casually asked, "is it so terrible we didn't win for once?"[26]

O

In the world of college basketball, winning was all that mattered. It defined UCLA and made Wooden an important cultural icon. Without his unprecedented basketball success, the public would have cared little about his coaching philosophy or his principles of leadership. But because he won more than any other coach and because his teams were emblems of perfection, Wooden helped inspire a desire for success among many Americans. Thousands of admirers wrote him letters—servicemen in Vietnam, college professors, students, business owners, movie producers, high school coaches, ministers, mothers, and children. They often asked him for advice or for a copy of his Pyramid of Success. After the *New York Times Magazine* published a story about him with the pyramid on the cover, readers sent letters to the editor praising the coach for his values. One college admissions director wrote, "John Wooden's 'Pyramid of success' so impressed me that I have mounted it and have it hanging in my office. It has become the credo of this admissions office." A young lady from Lenox, Massachusetts, decided to keep the cover image "as an inspiration," reminding her "of the principles one must strive for to reach success."[27]

Reading beyond the magazine cover revealed that Wooden's success was based on more than his principles. Although many Americans admired him for his ethics and his character-building-above-winning philosophy, the truth was that Wooden was first and foremost a basketball coach who was paid to win, which meant that he did everything possible to succeed. The coach who considered himself an educator acknowledged that the athletic department scheduled classes that were considered much easier and helped the athletes maintain athletic eligibility. He also admitted that he ran the team "like a machine," suppressing individuality. He wanted the players to focus on basketball and avoid outside distractions, such as campus demonstrations or interviews with the press. Arnold Hano, the article's author, implied that Wooden exploited out-of-state blacks' interest in California. Hano pointed out that UCLA's greatest black players came mostly from outside California, while the overwhelming majority of the Bruins' white players were from the Golden State. It appeared that UCLA recruited black players not because it was a liberal institution, but because it helped the university win basketball games. One critical reader wrote that Wooden's conservative values and "narrow" coaching methods reminded him of President Richard Nixon and Ohio State football coach Woody Hayes—leaders who believed that winning was truly the only thing that mattered in life. Whatever the readers thought of Wooden, one thing was certain: he was a winner.[28]

For many frustrated coaches, it seemed that Wooden never lost. Entering the 1972–73 season, UCLA had won 45 straight games. The last time the Bruins lost was against Notre Dame on January 23, 1971. Now, if the Bruins won the first 16 games of the season, they would break San Francisco's record 60-game winning streak set in 1956. UCLA had come close to breaking USF's record once before in 1968, when Houston snapped their 47-game winning streak. Most observers had no doubt that this UCLA team would break the record. As long as Bill Walton stayed in school, they predicted, UCLA would finish this season and the next undefeated, running their winning streak up to 105 games.[29]

Since winning had become the norm at UCLA, the players rarely mentioned the streak. Wooden was confident that the team had the right attitude and the proper makeup to be even better than the year before. Even without All-American guard Henry Bibby, UCLA returned four starters from its undefeated championship team. Larry Hollyfield, an explosive scoring guard, replaced Bibby in the backcourt, though he could not replace Bibby's deep shooting accuracy. *Sports Illustrated* noted that although

"Bibby's long-range bombing is gone, the Bruins are so deep and talented his departure will hardly be noticed." UCLA had so much more talent than any other program in the country, the magazine noted, that their "second team could be ranked No. 1."[30]

UCLA fans expected few obstacles on the way to another national title. But on December 12, 1972, the *Los Angeles Times* reported worrisome news: John Wooden had spent the night at St. John's Hospital in Santa Monica. At 1:15 a.m., he awakened with severe chest pains. After a half hour, he finally woke Nellie and told her he needed to go to the hospital. At first the press inaccurately reported that he had a gastrointestinal problem. Then came the news that he suffered from exhaustion. Finally, his doctor told the media that the sixty-two-year-old coach had not experienced a heart attack, but had a "mild heart condition." Undoubtedly, the tremendous pressure of winning—perhaps more accurately, the pressure of never losing—contributed to Wooden's elevated stress and heart trouble. "At UCLA," a *Los Angeles Times* writer observed, "pre-eminence in basketball isn't just expected, it is DEMANDED. Anything less is intolerable in the eyes of loyalists." Nellie admitted that the weight of public expectations was, at times, overwhelming for her husband. "These past few years haven't been the most enjoyable for us," she said. With her husband in the hospital, fans and writers wondered if he would have to retire from coaching.[31]

After Wooden spent seven days in the hospital, he rested comfortably at home. One afternoon, while Nellie was out at the store, he heard the doorbell ring. When he opened the door, he was surprised to see that one of his players had ridden a bicycle ten miles from campus just to see him. It warmed his heart when Bill Walton appeared at the door and asked him how he was feeling. For all of their disagreements about hair, politics, team rules, and strategy, Walton and Wooden shared a deep appreciation for one another. The veteran coach never forgot about the visit from his young pupil.[32]

Wooden resumed his coaching duties on December 21, after missing only one game—the first time he had ever missed a game in twenty-five years at UCLA. Before practice, each player greeted him with a handshake and a smile. During practice, he rarely rose from a chair near the court; instead, he sat, observing in silence while his assistants orchestrated the drills. Occasionally, he offered instruction or corrected a player's mistake. It was difficult for him to sit still. Sometimes he strolled across the court for a different perspective of the action, mindful of his doctors' orders. "I've always told my players to be quick, but don't hurry," he said with a grin, "but my doctors have told me that I can't follow my own advice. I can't be quick or hurry."[33]

The next night, against Pittsburgh, after the starting lineups were announced, more than twelve thousand UCLA fans stood and cheered wildly when they heard his name. At halftime Wooden received the loudest standing ovation of the night when he was presented with a Grecian urn for being named *Sports Illustrated*'s Sportsman of the Year, an honor he shared with the first Sportswoman of the Year, tennis star Billie Jean King. Each winner embodied a different set of values in the world of sports: Wooden represented the establishment, tradition, and paternal authority. King, on the other hand, was a forerunner of change, an advocate of women's liberation, and a feminist symbol in a male-dominated arena.[34]

When King and Wooden met with *Sports Illustrated*'s Curry Kirkpatrick, they discussed the importance of sport in society and in their own lives. The UCLA coach deplored the commercial excesses and corruptive forces of sports: overpaid professional athletes, labor-management disputes, athletes who endorsed tobacco and liquor, and illegal recruiting in big-time college athletics. On the last issue, he proposed that the NCAA disallow recruiting altogether, a surprising suggestion, considering much of his success was based on recruiting talented players outside of Southern California. He had always disliked recruiting, which he considered a form of salesmanship. He was not a salesman. Wooden decried the way that college basketball had moved away from its amateur roots and had become a big business. Ironically, his teams had helped drive these changes within the sport, including the high-stakes competition for talented recruits.[35]

He also believed that UCLA's success had made a positive impact on college basketball. "The winning streak is the best thing that can happen to the college game," he said. "It gives incentive to other teams to beat us." The streak also created a clear narrative for reporters: UCLA was college basketball's Goliath, the invincible giant; every other team played the role of David, the fearless and honorable challenger. As the season progressed, win after win, the media repeatedly asked Wooden if UCLA could continue its winning streak and break USF's record of sixty consecutive wins. On early Wednesday morning, January 24, the Bruins boarded TWA Flight 24 for Chicago, where they would finally answer those nagging questions.[36]

Thanks to J. D. Morgan, the team traveled first class, just like the pros. The jet cabin was filled with blue and yellow pennants, TV cameras, reporters, and attractive stewardesses dressed in UCLA T-shirts. After the Bruins stopped in Chicago and defeated Loyola for their sixtieth consecutive victory, they boarded a Greyhound bus and headed east toward South Bend, Indiana. As the bus rolled through the Hoosier flatlands, the players told jokes and jammed to the sounds of Mick Jagger and the Rolling Stones on a portable cassette player. At one point, Walton looked at Wooden and sarcastically asked, "You like this kind of music, don't you coach?" "I wouldn't turn him on. But he doesn't bug me," he answered. Later, in the back of the bus, a reporter asked Greg Lee if he was worried about losing to Notre Dame. "I never think about losing," Lee replied. Even now, one victory away from breaking USF's record, the UCLA players seemed relaxed and loose, unaffected by outside pressure. Wooden had prepared them for this moment. "If we win at Notre Dame Saturday, we'll win without excessive exuberance," he promised. "If we lose, we'll lose without excessive dejection."[37]

For more than two months, the nationally televised game had been sold out. Notre Dame prepared for a monumental upset, holding a pep rally an hour and a half before tip-off, while the "poor fathers" worked "overtime conducting masses." It would take more than a Hail Mary and a pep rally to defeat UCLA. The Bruins took the court, focused and ready, determined not to let the rowdy Irish fans screaming obscenities distract them. Walton enjoyed playing in front of a hostile crowd more than at home because it made winning more challenging. From the opening tip, UCLA controlled the tempo, scoring in waves, pressing and running free for uncontested lay-ups. Keith Wilkes scored twenty points, connecting on midrange jumpers and baseline drives. Walton dominated every aspect of the game, finishing with sixteen points, fifteen rebounds, and eleven blocked shots. UCLA routed Notre Dame, 82–63. The game was not nearly as close as the score indicated. When it was over, a reporter asked Walton if he would remember the record-breaking game more than all the others. "No. The game I'll remember most," he answered, "is the game UCLA loses."[38]

When it was over, none of the players leaped into each other's arms at the sound of the buzzer, and no one climbed ladders to cut down the nets. Photographers grumbled about the players' routine reaction. On behalf of the team, Wooden accepted the game ball. In front of a live television audience, he said with a smile, "This isn't the greatest thing that's happened on this day. It's my granddaughter's birthday." He continued, "But the most important thing is that this was cease-fire day in Vietnam. That's much more important than this." It was vintage Wooden—the coach who "loves God, country, family, and winning" seemed to always say the right thing at the right time. The humble, lovable, great American sports hero honored America in its early hours of peace.[39]

Not everyone was impressed with Wooden's performance against Notre Dame. *Philadelphia Inquirer* columnist Frank Dolson suggested that Wooden's modest, scholarly, gentlemanly image was inconsistent with the UCLA coach's behavior on the sideline. As evidence, Dolson recounted an incident midway through the second half. Throughout the game, UCLA and Notre Dame pushed, shoved, and bodychecked each other under the basket. At one point, Larry Hollyfield's elbow bloodied the nose of Notre Dame's Pete Crotty. Wooden believed that the Irish were playing too rough. Incensed that the referees had done nothing to clean up the game, he marched over to Notre Dame's sideline, leaned over Digger Phelps, and "waved a finger under his nose like a teacher scolding an errant schoolboy." He criticized Phelps for allowing Notre Dame center John Shumate to crash into Walton. "If Shumate doesn't knock it off," he warned, "I'll send Swen Nater in and you know what I'll have him do." Wooden later justified his unsportsmanlike behavior: "Shumate lost a little control there." The truth was, it was Wooden who had lost control.[40]

Dolson could not believe that of all coaches, John Wooden, the moral paragon of college basketball, had reacted so vindictively. Dolson wondered why he had allowed Hollyfield to continue to play, even though his flagrant foul had knocked Crotty out of the game. Why, after Phelps had been charged with a technical foul for stepping onto the court, did Wooden point it out to the officials, indicating that Phelps had indeed crossed the line? And why did Wooden threaten to send in Nater? "Because," Dolson answered, "apparently, he is a man who wants—and expects—every edge he can get. Winning does that to people. Even to nice, sweet, lovable, scholarly people like John Wooden."[41]

Dolson was one of the few sportswriters who actually criticized Wooden in print, and many readers did not like it. Wooden's loyal fans wrote letters to the *Philadelphia Inquirer* defending the UCLA coach, arguing that Dolson had unfairly attacked him. Dolson replied that "just because a man practically always wins doesn't mean he is [incapable] of being wrong. The fact is John Wooden WAS wrong that Saturday afternoon at Notre Dame." Wooden agreed. After thinking it over for a few days, he penned a letter of apology to Phelps and Shumate.[42]

O

The war was over. In 1972, after America's "Christmas bombing" failed to break the will of the North Vietnamese, the United States signed a peace treaty with the Communists in late-January 1973. American soldiers and prisoners were finally coming home from Vietnam. The draft had ended, and the antiwar protests on campus had disappeared. Walton stopped talking about the war, and Wooden no longer worried about players' joining demonstrations. Like the Vietnam War, for the past decade, UCLA basketball had become a constant feature of American life. Critics had grown tired of UCLA's never-ending dominance. If UCLA kept winning, they claimed, college basketball would become irrelevant. *Los Angeles Times* columnist John Hall claimed that outside Westwood, interest in college basketball had dwindled. As long as UCLA never lost, and as long as there was no chance of UCLA ever losing, basketball fans outside Southern California had little reason to follow the sport. Some commentators complained that college basketball lacked drama. It had become too predictable. "Winning," a UCLA student complained, "has become a bore."[43]

After winning eight championships—six in a row—and breaking the consecutive-victories record, UCLA had nothing left to accomplish except build on its own records. Curry Kirkpatrick wrote that UCLA had "reached that inevitable yet harrowing point at which accomplishment becomes commonplace. In fact, a bore. It seems almost as if winning is no longer invigorating or weighty; challenging or recreative; fresh, fun, or gay. No cause for celebration. Sad to say, no longer even news. UCLA winning again is a weather outlook, a traffic report, dog-bites man stuff."[44]

Even the Bruins seemed uninterested with winning all the time. Greg Lee admitted that he did not enjoy the games very much. Without any real competition, he said, it was nearly impossible to get excited about winning. Basketball was no longer simply a game that the team played for fun and recreation; it had become, in the words of one player, "a job," a full-time profession that demanded results. The pressures of winning and sustaining the streak required that the values of success prevailed over the values of sportsmanship. Their entire lives were shaped by public expectations that they would always win. After the Notre Dame game, Wooden noticed that the players looked "blasé," unimpressed with their own achievements.[45]

Kirkpatrick suggested that although fans had grown tired of UCLA victories, they were still interested in what the players did off the court. After the Notre Dame game, the *Sports Illustrated* writer filed a feature story that took readers behind the scenes. Kirkpatrick wrote that the team was just like any other group of young college men searching for fun. On the road, they broke Wooden's curfew and sneaked beer and women into their hotel rooms. One player recalled that during a layover at the Chicago airport, the team imbibed freely, unconcerned about any punishment Wooden might hand down. According to one player, when they boarded the plane home, they were "thoroughly plastered out of [their] minds." They engaged in a peanut- and water-throwing fight until Wooden finally ended their fun after a flying peanut hit him in the head.[46]

In Westwood the players were treated like heroes. Whenever they visited Hollis Johnson's Soda Fountain in the Village, they received complimentary meals. Frequently, the team ate, drank, and swam at Sam Gilbert's sprawling home in Pacific Palisades. They lived the good life. But not all was well with the UCLA team. Kirkpatrick suggested that a rivalry for playing time between Greg Lee, who was white, and Tommy Curtis, who was black, created racial dissension on the team. He reported that Walton preferred Lee, his best friend on the team, especially because Lee passed him the ball more effectively near the basket. Supposedly, Walton informed Wooden that he wanted Lee to play instead of Curtis. Walton's black teammates had long considered him a "soul brother," not a Great White Hope. But after the *Sports Illustrated* story came out, some black players questioned the authenticity of his liberal attitudes. Walton was hurt by their reaction, further convinced that little good came from talking with reporters.[47]

Despite the internal tensions within the team, nothing could prevent them from making the NCAA Tournament, renamed the "UCLA Invitational" by one magazine. By the early 1970s, the tournament had become a national phenomenon, a cultural event shaped in large part by the UCLA dynasty. "As a sports attraction," *Los Angeles Times* writer Jeff Prugh commented, "the NCAA [Tournament] has moved from backstage to center stage almost in concert with the phenomenal rise of UCLA's prominence year after year."[48]

The Bruins' unprecedented success added tremendous commercial value to college basketball and helped reconfigure the format and visibility of the NCAA Tournament. Before the UCLA dynasty, local television stations determined whether to broadcast the national championship game. But after the 1968 UCLA-Houston game in the Astrodome, college basketball proved that it could compete in prime time with other forms of entertainment on national television. The NCAA recognized the growing popularity of the tournament and made important changes to attract more profitable television exposure. In May 1972, the NCAA Basketball Tournament Committee announced that it was expanding the number of teams in the tournament for the 1974–75 season, from twenty-five to thirty-two. This meant that NBC would make more money televising more games and that the NCAA would collect larger revenues. For the 1973 tournament, the Tournament Committee moved the semifinals from Thursday night to Saturday night and the final game from Saturday night to Monday night. The new schedule allowed NBC to show both semifinal games instead of one. The network hoped that the final game would be a prime-time hit with fans and casual viewers in the same way as *Monday Night Football*. Lawrence Laurent of the *Washington Post* wrote, "NBC would be quite happy, of course, if the prime-time telecast includes UCLA in quest of its seventh national championship and its attention winning center Bill Walton."[49]

By the early seventies, the NCAA Tournament had become a big business, and UCLA represented a brand of excellence that enhanced the sport's image and the tournament's viability. UCLA's championship games attracted record-breaking crowds, millions of television viewers, and sold-out tickets a full year in advance of the tournament. In 1973 the NCAA's decision to move the national championship into prime time paid off: thirty-eight million fans—the largest television audience to ever watch a college basketball championship, tuned in to NBC to watch UCLA play Memphis State, shattering the previous season's national championship record of thirty million viewers. UCLA made the national championship an attractive investment for NBC, since most Bruins fans lived in the nation's second-largest market. In Los Angeles, the 1973 national championship earned a 36.0 rating, which meant that 36 percent of households with television sets were tuned in to the game. KTLA director of sports programming Bob Speck explained that UCLA generated higher ratings than any other program, making college basketball a highly profitable televised sport. "UCLA has done for college basketball what Notre Dame and USC helped to do for college football," Speck observed. "Wooden and his guys—Alcindor, Goodrich, Walton, Hazzard, Wicks, and Rowe—are owed a debt of gratitude from all universities and basketball programs."[50]

Millions of basketball fans tuned in to see if somebody, anybody, could stop UCLA. On Saturday evening, Indiana tried and failed during the semifinals. Now it was Memphis State's turn. The twelfth-ranked Memphis State Tigers were an exciting, athletic team that ran the fast break and pounded the ball inside with Ronnie "Big Cat" Robinson and Larry "Dr. K" Kenon. They were also one of the hottest teams in the country; entering the national championship, Memphis State had won twenty-two of its last twenty-four games. Larry Finch, an explosive All-American scoring guard, energized the Tigers with his dynamic drives and quick pull-up jump shot.[51]

On the eve of the championship, while basketball fans boasted predictions over dinner and drinks, UCLA ran through its final practice at the St. Louis Arena. Usually, Wooden structured his playoff practices with disciplined precision, commanding the players to move and execute drills in a serious tone. The only sound he wanted to hear was the ball bouncing on the hardwood floor. But this practice was different. Wooden sensed that his team was tense. In the semifinals against Indiana, UCLA built a 54–34 lead. Then, in a matter of four minutes, UCLA allowed Indiana to score seventeen unanswered points, reducing the Bruins' lead to three points. Although UCLA successfully regrouped, Wooden had never before seen his team lose its composure like that, so he broke away from his regimented practice routine. At the end of practice, he surprised the players and told them to finish practice by dunking the basketball. Slamming the ball through the net seemed to help the players release whatever pressure they had bottled up over the course of the season. For a moment, basketball was fun again. Suddenly, the team became more energized, more relaxed, and more focused.[52]

As usual, Wooden was concerned about off-court distractions, especially with the press. Throughout the tournament, sportswriters bemoaned his refusal to open up the locker room. Wooden replied that he did not want anyone in the dressing room that did not belong there. "Besides," he added, "I don't think the players want all these people in there when they are running around naked." When a writer from a national magazine inquired about interviewing the UCLA coach for a cover story, J. D. Morgan suggested that all the answers to his questions could be found in Wooden's recently released autobiography, *They Call Me Coach*.[53]

At the end of UCLA's final practice, a reporter approached Walton with a few questions. He had dodged writers all year long, but in St. Louis they seemed to follow him wherever he went. Every time a writer cornered him, Walton escaped with curt replies. "I don't know. I can't talk," he said. "You'll have to see the Wizard." When the Wizard saw the writer talking with Walton, he immediately intervened. Wooden accused the writer of biased reporting and claimed that he had cheered for Indiana during the semifinals. Then he barked at the startled writer, "Get away from my players!"[54]

Later that evening, after practice, Walton returned to his hotel room. The night before, on the eve of the finals, he tossed and turned. His bed was too small, and he could hear roaring trucks on the expressway outside his window. When J. D. Morgan heard about Walton's sleepless night, he offered to switch rooms. Walton gladly accepted and switched rooms from Stouffer's Riverfront Inn, where his teammates were staying, to the Chase Park Plaza. He slept peacefully until about three, when he heard someone trying to enter the room. He nervously got out of bed and peered at the door. Then the phone rang. When he picked it up, no one answered. He had no idea what was going on. As he started dialing the number to Morgan's room, he heard a loud bang at the door. "Police! Open the door now!" The police asked him to come down to the lobby. Earlier, the Chase staff had seen Morgan leave with his bags and assumed that he had checked out of the hotel. Thinking that Morgan's room was vacant, someone at the Chase gave a key to another guest. When the guest could not get into Walton's room, the hotel staff contacted the police. Finally, at four in the morning, Morgan came back to the Chase and helped straighten out the whole mess. Exhausted, Walton finally went back to bed.[55]

On Monday morning, sportswriters speculated that Walton had switched rooms because he was negotiating a pro contract and would make an announcement from the Chase Park Plaza. Reporters predicted that he would forego his senior year and sign a contract with the NBA's Philadelphia 76ers or the ABA's San Diego Conquistadors. When the *Los Angeles Times'* Dwight Chapin and Jeff Prugh asked Sam Gilbert—whom they described as "Walton's financial adviser"—if he would sign a pro contract after the championship, he brusquely answered, "No." The writers pressed him further: "Will you deny it?" "Yes," Gilbert said. Unconvinced with Gilbert's answers, the press consulted with Wooden, Morgan, and Walton's teammates, all of whom said that he would be back for his senior year.[56]

Sportswriters failed to ask one critical question: how could Sam Gilbert represent Bill Walton, an amateur athlete, without the NCAA investigating their clear professional relationship? Under NCAA rules, any player who entered into an agreement with a professional organization or agreed to be represented by an agent in the marketing of his athletic talent automatically became ineligible. Sportswriters clearly knew, as did the NCAA, that Gilbert had negotiated contracts for past UCLA players and that many of them spent an extensive amount of time in his home. In the past few years, the NCAA had taken a hard-line stance against agents and the ABA for pursuing college players and signing them to professional contracts while they were still under scholarship. In 1972 the NCAA sued the ABA for concealing contracts with college players who had remaining eligibility. At the same time, the NCAA investigated college basketball programs with athletes who signed pro contracts before their eligibility expired or who were rumored to have received extra benefits that exceeded their scholarships.[57]

Testifying before a House Education subcommittee, Marlow W. Cook, a Republican senator from Kentucky, claimed that the NCAA's criteria for investigating violations excluded programs that made money for the NCAA. Cook reminded his colleagues, "The NCAA is big business. It deals in economics; its power comes from money; and its power is wielded in economic terms." Furthermore, he wanted to know why every investigation he read about involved only black athletes. "Was UCLA investigated when Bill Walton was recruited?" he wondered. He asked the same question about Louisiana State University's Pete Maravich and other white stars, implying that the NCAA protected programs with outstanding white players. Although there is no evidence that Walton received any gifts from UCLA recruiters and there is no evidence that the NCAA deliberately investigated programs with black stars, Cook asked a fair question about UCLA, a question that would linger until after John Wooden retired.[58]

Even if reporters and fans did not believe that Walton would return to UCLA for his senior year, he still had one more important game to play this season. More than 19,300 fans filled the St. Louis Arena, screaming and shouting, eagerly anticipating the biggest game of the year. Most of the crowd cheered for Memphis State, though hardly anyone in the Gateway City gave the Tigers a chance of beating the Bruins. Walton took the court wearing a stoic expression, tightlipped and focused, uninterested in bantering with his teammates. His controlled expression never changed. Early on, against Memphis State's man-to-man defense, Walton dominated inside. He scored from all angles, making shots from the low post and the high post, off the glass and touching nothing but the net. Feinting, faking, and fluidly moving through the defense, he dropped shots into the basket. On numerous possessions, Greg Lee looked for Walton underneath the hoop. When they locked eyes, Walton pointed his index finger up in the air and nodded, signaling Lee to lob him the ball. The two displayed remarkable rhythm and timing: over and over again, Lee lofted the ball above the rim for Walton to tip it in over the outstretched arms of Larry Kenon. With 7:49 left in the first half, and UCLA leading 29–22, Memphis State coach Gene Bartow had seen enough of Walton and changed to a 1-2-2 zone defense.[59]

Unfortunately for Bartow, there was no defense that could stop Walton. Not even Kenon, arguably the best big man in the South, could stop him. In the first half, Walton performed nearly flawlessly. He made eleven of twelve shots, mostly on high, arcing lobs from Lee and Larry Hollyfield. After missing one short jump shot, he immediately tipped it back in. He controlled the paint for the entire game, intimidating the Tigers with his sweeping rebounds and devastating blocks. He grabbed thirteen rebounds, blocked seven shots, and was called for three defensive and four offensive goaltending violations. A chorus of boos rained from the stands when he voiced his displeasure with the referees. With 4:14 left in the half, he was whistled again, this time for his third foul. After that, Memphis State went on an 8–2 run, tying the score at halftime, 39–39.[60]

In the second half, UCLA repeatedly beat Memphis State's zone defense, mostly on lobs to Walton. With 11:42 left in the game, UCLA led by just two points, 49–47, fueling Memphis State fans' hopes for victory. Walton shattered the Tigers' dreams of an upset with an eight-point scoring streak, bolstering UCLA's lead, 57–47. He scored on angled bank shots, twisting layups, and off-balance tip-ins. With 7:36 left on the clock and UCLA up by eight points, Walton made three baskets in less than a minute. Incredibly, Walton made twenty-one of twenty-two shots and two free throws, totaling forty-four points, breaking Gail Goodrich's championship-game scoring record by two points. During a time-out late in the second half, Greg Lee asked Coach Wooden if someone else should shoot besides Walton. Perplexed, Wooden replied, "Why?"[61]

With less than three minutes left and UCLA leading by fifteen points, Walton turned his ankle and collapsed onto the hardwood floor. When Memphis State's Larry Finch helped him limp to the sideline, the crowd rose to its feet, applauding the greatest individual performance in college basketball history. "They were appreciative of what they just witnessed," Doug Krikorian wrote, "just like fans who saw a Koufax no hitter, or a Louis knockout, or a Ruth calling his shot, were appreciative, too." The fans' one-minute standing ovation did not emote celebratory feelings from Walton. With his legs extended and his ankle wrapped, he sat sullenly on the bench, unmoved by the fans' cheers. But he never really played for them. He played for his teammates, his coach, and his love for the game. When it was over, and the scoreboard read UCLA 87, Memphis State 66, his teammates laughed and shouted, but he never smiled. A fan approached him with a program and asked for an autograph. Walton shooed him away. "Great game, Bill," the fan said. "It was just a game, forget it," he said coolly. "How is your ankle?" the fan wondered. Clearly annoyed, he answered, "I'll survive!"[62]

Afterward, dozens of reporters and photographers congregated outside the UCLA dressing room, expecting to talk with him. The press waited impatiently, complaining to each other about his surly attitude. After fifteen minutes, Wooden finally opened the doors. Those who wanted to talk with Walton had wasted their time. Someone asked him, "What happened to your ankle?" "I don't know," he said. "It just hurts, man." Another reporter asked, "Have you ever had a bigger thrill, Bill?" He murmured, "I don't want to talk about it, man." "Excuse me," he said, as he forced his way though the throng of reporters, heading for the locker room exit. "I'm really in a hurry to see my friends. I have nothing to say." Appalled at his behavior, the writers stared at one another, mouths agape, their notepads blank. Walton left the locker room, walked down the long hallway, and disappeared in the distance.[63]

O

"This was the tournament where Wooden finally reached super-celebrity status," Curry Kirkpatrick wrote in *Sports Illustrated*. Throughout the weekend, he was spotted in the hotel lobby, signing autographs, "greeting old ladies and small children," counseling young assistant coaches, talking about past championships, and answering reporters' questions. In St. Louis, fans, coaches, and writers stood in awe in his presence, accepting his word "as gospel." "He was Fred Astaire at a dance seminar; John Ford at a cinema exhibition; Maharishi Mahesh Yogi on the mount, accepting hosannas, dispensing advice, suffering fools gently."[64]

Wooden's admirers maintained that fame and glory had not changed him. Even the Wizard himself helped perpetuate the myth, dismissing any suggestion that he was different from the young man who once coached at a small teachers college in Indiana. He was still the same humble, good Christian, small-town midwesterner he had always been. *Los Angeles Times* columnist Jim Murray wrote, "John R. Wooden came to California 25 years ago, a shy, God-fearing, simple-as-a-corn-husk man—EVERYWHERE but on a basketball court. John R. Wooden remains today, a shy, God-fearing, simple-as-a-corn-husk man—EVERYWHERE but on a basketball court."[65]

The truth was that winning had changed him and his own sense of identity. The more he won, the surer he became of himself, his coaching methods, and his principles. Success not only shaped his place in the world of sports, but also elevated his standing in American popular culture. By the early 1970s, Wooden was more than a great basketball coach; he was a celebrity, conscious of his own saintly image.

Earlier in the season, two *Los Angeles Times* writers in their early thirties, Dwight Chapin and Jeff Prugh, published *The Wizard of Westwood: Coach John Wooden and His UCLA Bruins.* Chapin and Prugh aimed to write an objective portrait of the coaching icon, and they succeeded. They wanted to show him as a human being, flawed and at times hypocritical, not as a worshiped sports hero. They conducted interviews with players, rival coaches, officials, friends, family, and Wooden himself. *The Wizard of Westwood* documented subjects that Wooden preferred left uncovered: boosters paying the 1964 championship team for rebounds, Lew Alcindor's unhappiness at UCLA, Edgar Lacey quitting the team, Lucius Allen's troubles with the law, Bill Seibert's senior speech criticizing Wooden, Bill Walton's antiwar protest and subsequent arrest, and Sam Gilbert's close relationship with the program. The authors also revealed that beneath Wooden's "saintly demeanor" was an intensely competitive man who was consumed with winning. One former player told the writers, "He has this gigantic ego. He is sold on John Wooden. He has this thing about becoming the greatest coach of all time."[66]

Before they published *The Wizard of Westwood,* Chapin and Prugh offered to write their book with Wooden as an autobiography, but he preferred to wait until he retired to write a memoir. After Wooden learned that *The*

Wizard of Westwood and two other journalistic accounts of his program would be published, he became nervous about the contents and rushed to write his own version of the story. According to Wooden, he browsed through *The Wizard of Westwood* and found "some untruths and some half-truths. There was no truth to some of the things written." He was convinced that the *Los Angeles Times* writers "were digging for something controversial." Writing his own book would allow him to craft a pristine image of his program, free of any controversy or real conflict. Wooden's reaction revealed the depths of his insecurity, his concern that outsiders may expose him as something other than Saint John. A columnist from *Newsday* commented, "It sometimes seems that Wooden is fearful that the press might discover something about the Wizard of Westwood which would tarnish his golden image."[67]

After the national championship against Memphis State, Wooden appeared on national television in a postgame interview. At the end of the interview, he surprised the announcer by pulling out a copy of *They Call Me Coach*. Wooden clearly understood that most of the public viewed him—and his cultural image—as a moral force. His publisher promoted the book emphasizing his moral authority. One advertisement quoted him, "No coach should be trusted with . . . working with young men . . . unless he is spiritually strong. If he does possess the inner strength, it is only because he has faith in God and truly loves his fellow man." After reading *They Call Me Coach,* Jim Murray sarcastically opined, "Everything he says should be identified by testament, chapter, and verse, it seems."[68]

Wooden recognized that the national championship presented a commercial opportunity to attract admiring consumers to his product. He was selling a story to middle America—a story about a great American sports hero who rose above humble origins and achieved incredible success. His premeditated sales pitch on national television revealed that success had changed him. The more he won, the more concerned he became with what people thought about him. Dwight Chapin recalled that during a Bruins booster-club dinner in the mid-1970s, Wooden scanned the packed banquet hall, turned to Chapin, and said, "It wasn't always like this," a subtle reminder of how he had completely transformed the importance of basketball at UCLA. Yet Wooden seemed unsatisfied with what he had accomplished, adding that if the Bruins stopped winning basketball games, the crowds would stop showing up at Pauley Pavilion and the alumni dinners. Without winning, he would fail to please the people, the fans, the alumni, and the writers; without winning, they would stop applauding whenever he entered a room.[69]

In American popular culture, Wooden was supposed to represent the ideal sportsman, but when he violated public expectations of his behavior, critics questioned his moral authority. William Gildea of the *Washington Post* suggested that publicizing a book during an interview was a bit self-indulgent. "The Wooden sales effort—and gall—reached a rare level last Monday night," Gildea commented. "The jingle of cash registers was almost audible in bookstores throughout the land." Frank Dolson described Wooden's behavior as "petty," "petulant," and "insecure." Dolson wondered, "Did Wooden really have to take another verbal shot at the co-authors of a generally favorable book that depicts him, however, as a human being instead of god?"[70]

Wooden's cultural image created conflicting reactions from the press. Many writers admired him for his success and moral values, but there were others who had grown tired of UCLA's dominance and the coach who came across, at times, as pretentious. The more successful he became, the more the national press scrutinized his behavior. Dolson noted that there was a growing "dislike for UCLA—and in some cases for Wooden." Writers, opposing coaches, and fans complained that UCLA was winning too much and that it was ruining college basketball. "What John Wooden has to done to college basketball is to wreck it," the *Seattle Times'* Georg N. Myers lamented. L. H. Gregory of the *Portland Oregonian* groaned, "Gets rather monotonous, doesn't it? UCLA, week after week, month after month, season after season, winning every basketball game it plays."[71]

By the end of the 1973 season, UCLA had won seven consecutive national championships, nine of the last ten. After back-to-back undefeated seasons, the Bruins owned a seventy-five-game winning streak. Remarkably, Wooden's teams had won thirty-six consecutive NCAA Tournament games, which meant that UCLA never lost when it mattered most. And it seemed that there was no end in sight. What could possibly stop UCLA from winning? "Hopefully, something," Frank Dolson wrote. "The dynasty has lasted long enough."[72]

10

Cracks in the Pyramid

n 1974 the *Sporting News*'s Art Spander commented, "In these turbulent times, when other myths are being destroyed, when politicians have less veracity than circus pitchmen, when the economy is bouncing around like a free ball at midcourt, one thing remains constant, UCLA is still winning basketball games." By the mid-1970s, there was a growing sense that American institutions were failing, leaders could not be trusted, and the country's ideals had vanished. America had lost a war, its president disgraced in a cover-up scandal and its people frustrated by a stagnating economy. With swelling unemployment, increasing poverty, inflation, and endless gasoline lines, many Americans feared that the country had entered a period of decline. Against a backdrop of disillusion and cultural malaise, according to one historian, "Americans retreated to established ideals and old virtues—and they judged their leaders accordingly." Instead of seeking alternative values and emblems, people identified with traditional symbols. UCLA basketball remained an American institution that had not failed. Many admired John Wooden as a peerless leader, a man of integrity who produced constant prosperity. His dynasty, unlike much of America, appeared to have no limits. It was an enduring force of greatness, "one of the unaltered verities of life." While people questioned everything around them, "even mom and apple pie," Spander wrote, "America still has something left to believe in: UCLA basketball."[1]

○

"We have a fine team and any fine team has a chance of winning all its games," Wooden said on the eve of the 1973–74 season opener. "But I don't think you can come out and say you're going to do it. That's expecting too much." After winning nine national championships, Wooden was accustomed to high expectations. It seemed that before every season, he delivered the same speech, minimizing lofty expectations for his team. After winning seventy-five straight games and seven consecutive national championships, there was little doubt that the Bruins would keep on winning just like they always did. On paper UCLA was better than ever. Of all the teams Wooden coached during the dynasty, this squad was by far the most talented. Larry Hollyfield, Larry Farmer, and Swen Nater had graduated, but it did not matter. The Bruins returned two All-Americans, Bill Walton and Keith Wilkes, along with senior guards Greg Lee and Tommy Curtis, and versatile junior forward Dave Meyers, a rising star whose long arms and tenacious defense made him a key player in the Bruins' press. UCLA's depth extended all the way down to the end of the bench, where guards Andre McCarter and Pete Trgovich sat near promising center Ralph Drollinger. And for the first time in history, Wooden could play his most spectacular freshmen, Marques Johnson and Richard Washington. In all, eight players from the 1973–74 UCLA basketball team would go on to play in the NBA. Five players were first-round draft choices, and four of them were selected within the first three picks of the NBA draft.[2]

Although Wooden benefited from the most talented roster in his coaching career, the Bruins' nonconference schedule threatened UCLA's winning streak. UCLA would play three teams ranked in the preseason top ten: number-two North Carolina State, number-four Maryland, and number-eight Notre Dame. The first challenge came from the Maryland Terrapins, a team that coach Lefty Driesell boastfully called the "UCLA of the East." Maryland's formidable defense frustrated UCLA into one of the worst shooting performances ever witnessed by Bruins fans. Walton missed fifteen of twenty-three shots. Keith Wilkes missed thirteen of seventeen, and Tommy Curtis missed twelve of seventeen. Despite UCLA's anemic shooting, the Bruins barely prevailed, 65–64.[3]

Although the Bruins won, Wooden was concerned about his team's performance. Replacing two starters had not been as easy as he had imagined. UCLA shot poorly, relied too much on Walton, and looked uninterested on defense. Tommy Curtis dribbled the ball too much and sometimes drove out of control, convincing Wooden that he needed to move Greg Lee from the wing and play him more at point guard, where he effectively ran UCLA's set offense in the past. Curtis had not played himself out of his starting role, but the fact that Wooden had not settled on a consistent floor leader was a troubling sign, especially since UCLA was set to play the second-ranked North Carolina State Wolfpack.[4]

Wooden downplayed the significance of the upcoming contest against N.C. State, calling it a "rehearsal" for the conference schedule and a "meaningless" game for UCLA. But for the North Carolina State players, college basketball fans, and sportswriters, this game was far from meaningless. The Wolfpack had something to prove. The previous season, N.C. State finished undefeated but could not challenge UCLA for the national championship because the NCAA had placed the basketball program on probation for recruiting violations, barring the team from competing in any postseason tournament.[5]

The UCLA–N.C. State game was the most anticipated regular-season college basketball game since UCLA played Houston in the Astrodome in 1968. N.C. State fans flooded St. Louis, purchasing far more tickets than UCLA rooters, perhaps as much as four to one. Wolfpack boosters flew in from Raleigh, Greensboro, Winston-Salem, Charlotte, and Atlanta. Some drove cars with red-and-white bumper stickers that read, "Shoot Down the Walton Gang." The intriguing matchup between the top-ranked teams in the country—billed as "the Dream Game" by sportswriters—made this "the most profitable college game in college basketball history." UCLA and N.C. State each earned more than $125,000 from gate receipts and television, $40,000 more than UCLA made from their appearance in the 1973 Final Four.[6]

If there was any reason to believe that N.C. State could beat UCLA, it was David Thompson. Professional scouts considered Thompson one of the ten best players in the country, including NBA and ABA players. They compared him to some of the best athletes who had ever played the game: Oscar Robertson, Elgin Baylor, and Julius Erving. Like Erving's, Thompson's game was above the rim. The six-foot-four, 200-pound forward was incredibly quick and athletic. He could drive, accelerate, and vault to the rim unlike any other player in the country. Standing perfectly still, Thompson could explode straight up like a rocket, forty-two inches off the ground. Some claimed that he could grab a quarter off the top of the backboard and leave two dimes and a nickel.[7]

What made N.C. State so difficult to stop was its balanced attack. Tommy Burleson, a seven-foot-four white center who had played on the 1972 Olympic team, anchored the middle; Thompson operated from the wing; and Monte Towe, a diminutive playmaker from Converse, Indiana, controlled the tempo at point guard. In many ways, N.C. State's playing style mirrored UCLA's. The Wolfpack pressed on defense, crashed the boards, ran the fast break, and relied on a fluid, spontaneous offense rather than set patterns.[8]

When the Wolfpack took the court against UCLA, they looked "scared to death." The Bruins, on the other hand, appeared confident and cool, unfazed by the bright lights and the boisterous crowd. From the sideline, Wooden studied the Wolfpack, clutching a tiny silver cross in his left hand. Just nine minutes into the game, Wooden squeezed his cross a little tighter when a referee whistled Bill Walton for his fourth foul—one short of disqualification. Although UCLA led 15–10, suddenly the partisan crowd cheered a little louder. Without Walton, the crowd sensed that this might finally be it for the Bruins. The score remained close for the rest of the half, though neither team shot very well. Even with Walton on the bench, N.C. State failed to take over the game. Keith Wilkes hounded David Thompson on defense, blanketing his every move. In the first half, Thompson missed ten of thirteen shots. It was as if both teams were playing without their best player. But thanks to Monte Towe's speedy low dribble and effective passing, N.C. State broke through UCLA's press and gained a one-point lead at halftime.[9]

When the second half started, Walton continued to sit on the bench. For twenty-one minutes, he sat helplessly, nervously bouncing his leg up and down. All he could do was cheer on his teammates and stare at the scoreboard clock. He pleaded with Wooden to let him play. Finally, with 9:54 left, and UCLA leading 54–52, Walton sprang from his seat. In the next 4:19, UCLA outscored N.C. State 19–4. Walton energized his teammates, blocking shots, grabbing rebounds, and firing quick outlet passes. At one point, he stuffed Tom Burleson's shot twice in thirty seconds. When the play was over, Walton smirked. He did not have to say anything. Everyone in the arena knew that the game was over. Wooden put the cross back in his pocket.[10]

O

As Walton walked off the court, smiling with his index finger pointed high in the air, Tommy Curtis jogged past him and yelled, "What an ass-whippin'!" UCLA's 84–66 victory convinced many commentators that N.C. State was not nearly as good as ACC rival Maryland, let alone the defending national champions. Most writers believed that there was only one team left on the schedule that could possibly beat UCLA: Notre Dame.[11]

On January 16, 1974, UCLA flew to the Midwest to play two games in three days. First they would play Iowa in Chicago, and then they would travel to South Bend to take on an undefeated Notre Dame team. During the flight, Wooden sat comfortably in first class next to *Los Angeles Times* writer Jeff Prugh. They discussed UCLA's eighty-seven-game winning streak and the pressures of success. Wooden could not imagine another team ever repeating what the Bruins had accomplished. It had been three years since UCLA lost a game—against Notre Dame in South Bend. Could Wooden envision the Bruins losing again? "Anything can happen," he suggested, though he seemed unconcerned about the streak coming to an end. "It's probably hard for people to believe," he said, "but the streak is meaningless to us now, when it comes to motivating us to win."[12]

Wooden spent the flight focused less on the winning streak and more on Bill Walton's health. Ten days earlier, against Washington State, Bill Walton jumped high off the ground for a rebound when Rich Steele undercut him. Walton crashed to the floor. He lay on the court, writhing in pain. Years later he described the play as a "despicable act of intentional violence and dirty play." At the time, sportswriters reported that he had severely bruised his back, but Walton had broken two bones in his spine, an injury that would cause him lifelong pain. After missing the next two games against Cal and Stanford, Wooden seriously doubted that Walton could play against Notre Dame. When they arrived in Chicago, Walton practiced wearing a corset with steel rods. Every time he jumped, shot, or moved, he felt a sharp twinge in his back. When he did not suit up against Iowa, many fans wondered if Walton would ever return.[13]

UCLA's unimpressive performance against Iowa revealed a distracted and unmotivated team. Although they won by more than twenty points, the Bruins played carelessly on offense, blowing easy shots from close range. Wooden expressed concern about the team's focus and desire to play at the highest level possible for every game. After winning eighty-eight straight games, it was hard to get excited about any upcoming contest, even against rival Notre Dame, the second-ranked team in the country. "There's no rah-rah stuff about the game," Andre McCarter said. "We look at it like a business, like a job. That's how it is at UCLA. It's like the pros, except you don't have any income."[14]

For Phelps, this game was a long time coming. He never forgot how in his first season at Notre Dame, UCLA had humiliated his team by nearly sixty points. He was convinced that Wooden had intentionally run up the score against him. Now Phelps had the talent to beat Wooden, to exact revenge, and he wanted to do it in the worst way. For hours on end, he dissected UCLA's game films. After studying the Bruins, he was convinced that they were not as good as past UCLA squads. Phelps even bought a book about Wooden to better understand how he thought about the game and his coaching tendencies. No one was better prepared to coach against UCLA than Phelps. "I know them so well I could coach them myself," he claimed. Throughout the week, Phelps ran demanding practices. At times he could be harsh and critical, exploding in frustration when the team lost focus. But at the end of Wednesday's practice, he showed a lighter side, a confidence in his players. He told them that he expected victory on Saturday. Then he had the team practice cutting down the nets.[15]

In the Notre Dame locker room, the Fighting Irish were loose and relaxed, dancing to music blaring from twin speakers. An hour before tip-off, Phelps told the players to turn off the music and get ready. When the team left for warm-ups, Phelps stayed behind, quietly pacing the locker room with his eyes fixed on the floor. Twenty minutes before game time, the players returned, chatting and clapping their hands. When they gathered around Phelps for his final instructions, he warned the team, "Don't let them rattle you. Don't let 'em talk to you." He reminded them that Wooden was extremely competitive and would try to distract anyone within shouting distance of UCLA's bench. Finally, he said, "All right, I want you to act like men, play like men, and win like men!"[16]

After the lineups were announced, Bill Walton walked to center court, wearing a brace on his back and bandages around both knees. In less than a minute, he was hurt again. Adrian Dantley, a strong freshman forward, elbowed him in the face while the two fought for a rebound. Wooden called time-out so that the UCLA trainer could attend to Walton's bleeding lip. Notre Dame's aggressiveness did not seem to bother the Bruins. From the opening tip, UCLA looked unbeatable. The Bruins made 70 percent of their shots in the first half, leading by as many as seventeen points. Early in the second half, the Fighting Irish came roaring back, trimming UCLA's lead to two points. Notre Dame's aggressiveness inspired a nine-point scoring run from UCLA. With a little more than three minutes left on the clock, and Notre Dame trailing by eleven, Digger Phelps called time-out.[17]

Phelps made a lineup change and adjusted the setup of Notre Dame's full-court man-to-man press. In the next three minutes, UCLA fumbled the ball, threw it away, and missed easy shots. Notre Dame made six baskets, while UCLA missed six. Every time Notre Dame scored, the crowd roared louder and louder. Students rocked the bleachers, jumping up and down. With all the excitement and booming noise, adrenaline surged through the players' veins. At no point during UCLA's collapse did Wooden call time-out. He figured that everything would turn out all right, just like it did the previous eighty-eight games. When a coach called time-out, he thought, it showed weakness. Perhaps he should have stopped the game, but he did not.[18]

With less than a minute left, and UCLA leading 70–69, Keith Wilkes drove from the right wing, past his defender, and converted a layup. But the basket did not count. A referee called him for charging and waved off the basket. With thirty seconds left in the game, Notre Dame's Gary Brokaw looked inside for John Shumate, but he was covered. Then Brokaw spotted Dwight Clay in the right corner and passed him the ball. Clay caught it, set his feet, and let the ball fly. Swish! For the first time in the whole game

Notre Dame led, 71–70. The crowd erupted with jubilation. Finally, Wooden called time-out.[19]

On UCLA's next possession, John Shumate intercepted a pass intended for Walton, but could not hold onto the ball. Tommy Curtis picked it up and missed a long, desperate shot. Both teams flew to the ball, and it ended up bouncing out of bounds off of a Notre Dame player's leg. UCLA now had the ball with six seconds left. Walton received the pass and took a quick turnaround shot a few feet from the basket. The ball glanced off the rim. Pete Trgovich grabbed it for a layup. He missed. Dave Meyers wildly tapped the ball off the glass. Shumate secured the rebound and tossed the ball high up in the air as the final two seconds expired.[20]

The streak was over. Notre Dame fans stormed the court, shouting, hugging, and high-fiving one another. A few rowdy people yelled obscenities at Wooden. A group of Notre Dame students lifted the players onto their shoulders and carried them around the court like royalty. It was time to cut down the nets.[21]

Afterward, reporters asked the UCLA coach what went wrong. He complained that a few late calls did not go their way, including the Wilkes charge. He acknowledged that his team became complacent in the final minutes and failed to "play their own game," but he refused to say that they had lost their poise. Notre Dame's best players, Gary Brokaw and John Shumate, played very well, scoring twenty-five and twenty-four points, respectively. Wooden suggested that Walton's ailing back prevented him from playing his best, though he managed to score twenty-four points and missed only two shots. In the second half, the Bruins struggled mightily on offense, making only ten of twenty-nine shots. It did not help that Keith Wilkes converted only two of nine shots in the second half and failed to score in the final eight minutes. Most important, Notre Dame never quit. They never stopped believing that they could win. Their will to win was greater than UCLA's desire not to lose.[22]

A week after UCLA fell to Notre Dame, the top two teams played again in a rematch at Pauley Pavilion. After breaking the Bruins' winning streak, the Fighting Irish had become UCLA's indisputable national rival. Sportswriters framed the game as something far more significant than an intersectional contest; it was "war, revenge, salvation, and all those things." It seemed like there were sportswriters from every major newspaper covering the game, compelling UCLA to add an extra press row. UCLA's winning streak and the rivalry with Notre Dame generated incredibly high national ratings for TVS, belying any notion that the public had lost interest in the sport because of the Bruins' dominance. The *Los Angeles Times* reported that the first UCLA–Notre Dame game recorded a 13.5 rating and the second game 16.3, two of the highest-rated regular-season games in history.[23]

The UCLA–Notre Dame series helped make college basketball a more popular sport on national television. TVS founder Eddie Einhorn later explained that intraregional games attracted a limited audience, but intersectional games interested viewers from all across America. People wanted to watch the Bruins because they were the most dominant program in the country, and although the Fighting Irish were not a basketball power, Notre Dame was a nationally identifiable school with a large fan base. The outstanding ratings for 1974 series convinced NBC to sign a long-term agreement with TVS. Previously, most regular-season games were shown by local stations or broadcast regionally by TVS. In 1975, after televising the NCAA playoffs for six years, NBC announced that it would add regular-season games to its schedule. Together, NBC and TVS began broadcasting Saturday-afternoon doubleheaders; NBC televised the national games, and TVS showed the regional ones. The network's regular-season programming showcased the top teams, giving viewers a chance to see the very best games, regardless of where they lived. Consequently, viewers became more knowledgeable about the national landscape of college basketball and more familiar with the sport's biggest stars. UCLA's network television games helped usher in the modern era of college basketball, where fans experienced the sport not only on a regional basis, but also on a national level. By the mid-1970s, college basketball had become an integral part of America's national entertainment culture.[24]

The Bruins' basketball program provided great financial rewards for the university. The more UCLA won, the more they appeared on television and the more money the school earned. The basketball team's national television appearances, radio contracts, and ticket sales generated incredible profits. In the early 1970s, with spiraling inflation and rising travel costs, most athletic directors struggled to keep their basketball programs out of the red. While athletic directors worried about breaking even, J. D. Morgan did not have that problem. In most athletic departments, football was the top revenue-producing sport, but at UCLA basketball made more money than football. In 1974 the basketball program made a profit of more than $330,000, which was $90,000 more than the football program. The money UCLA received from tickets and television rights helped support the entire athletic department. Without question, UCLA's unique commercial success was dependent on one factor: winning.[25]

After losing to Notre Dame, few people thought that UCLA would fall again to the Irish at home. Wooden denied that this was a game of retribution, but it was clear by UCLA's practices that he was determined to win more than ever. Every afternoon, for two intense hours, Wooden exhorted his men, shouted out instructions, and demanded their very best. The players could not remember the last time he was so actively involved in practice. The team responded, appearing more animated and aggressive during drills. After Notre Dame held the top-ranked crown for one week, UCLA restored its ranking in a 94–75 blowout.[26]

That deep desire to win—the hard screens, sharp cuts, crisp passes, and swooping rebounds—seemed to disappear two weeks later in a narrow five-point win at home against an average Oregon State team. UCLA looked tentative, unorganized, and uninspired. After the game, reporters wondered why UCLA did not crush Oregon State. What was wrong with the Bruins? "Like I've been saying," Wooden said, frustrated with his players and questions about their inconsistent performance, "we're not a hungry team." He explained that the team worked hard in practice, but they lacked a "killer's instinct." They may have won, but Wooden's spirited halftime harangue did little to energize his team. The players had heard his lectures countless times before, and they were tired of them. In another game, it was clear that they had stopped listening to the Wizard. When Wooden instructed his team to apply a full-court press, the players simply ignored him.[27]

Before things got better, they got much worse. In mid-February, the Bruins lost consecutive road games against Oregon State and Oregon. After a Saturday-night loss to Oregon, the team returned to a Portland motel. Standing in the lobby, a fan, assuming UCLA had won, asked Bill Walton about the Bruins' margin of victory. Barely audible, Walton muttered that they had lost. The man could not believe it. "You lost! Why, you guys are the best!" Dejected, Walton shook his head and looked at Greg Lee like he was in mourning. Then he said, "Not anymore we're not." The players were shocked that they had lost to such inferior teams. It was the first time UCLA had lost consecutive games since 1966. Suddenly, the players panicked and starting questioning Wooden's wisdom. Aggravated, one player vented to Curry Kirkpatrick, "We've got to change things now so they're right. We've lost two games in a row. Something sure as hell is not working right."[28]

After the "lost weekend" in Oregon, rumors circulated throughout the press that team dissension led to a series of "secret meetings." The players grumbled about playing time, Wooden's lineup changes, and his offensive strategy. Some thought that he placed too much emphasis on the scoring of Walton and Wilkes. Throughout the season, Wooden rotated his starting guards and eventually shifted his offense from a two-guard set to a 1–3–1, with freshman forward Marques Johnson replacing former starting guards Greg Lee and Pete Trgovich. With Johnson starting, UCLA basically started three forwards, which meant that Lee and Trgovich played much less. "The right people are not playing," Lee complained after the Oregon trip. Lee, who had been a starter in 1972 and mostly a substitute in 1973, was not happy with his bench role. "I think we were playing better when I was in the lineup, but I don't make those decisions." A few substitutes considered transferring so that they could showcase their talents elsewhere. Wooden believed that some players were simply being selfish, too consumed with impressing professional scouts. One thing was clear: Wooden had lost the consensus in his locker room.[29]

In the wake of their two-game losing streak, sportswriters and fans compiled a list of what was wrong with the Bruins. Their schedule was too demanding, and the players were emotionally and physically drained. Walton had lost his enthusiasm. Tommy Curtis needed to pass more and dribble less. Keith Wilkes forced too many bad shots. Marques Johnson was too slow, Pete Trgovich too skinny, and Greg Lee too ornery. UCLA did not have superb ball handlers who could single-handedly break a press. Equally problematic, none of the guards were great outside shooters, which meant that defenses could collapse around Walton. And Wooden's 1-3-1 offense had become predictable, lacking movement and continuity. The offensive pattern always started the same way: Curtis or Lee brought the ball up and passed it to Wilkes or Meyers on the wing. Then the wing looked inside to Walton; if he was not open, the ball went back to the point guard, and the Bruins offense started all over again. When they could not feed Walton, the rest of the team stood and watched, waiting for someone else to do something.[30]

On defense, Wooden's three-forward lineup offered more size, but less quickness. Consequently, UCLA's trademark full-court press seemed to disappear, and so too did the steals that triggered the famed fast break. For years UCLA's press intimidated opponents who did know how to react to it. But by 1974, coaches had learned how to break it, and many countered with deliberate half-court offenses to slow the tempo in their favor. Critics suggested that Wooden was not a strong strategy coach and had failed to make the necessary adjustments. Some of those critics included his own players, who thought that he was indecisive in the face of adversity. One player told the *Washington Post*, "On the bench, he just sits there rolling up his program, growling at the officials and listening to Walton."[31]

The Bruins suffered from a crisis of confidence—confidence in themselves and their leader. The discontent within the UCLA basketball team reflected the great divide of the 1970s—"the divide of disillusionment." Since World War II, Americans had become conditioned to expect progress, to reach new frontiers. But over the course of the sixties and into the seventies, people became increasingly impatient with unresolved problems and leaders who failed to meet those challenges. America's leaders had failed to find the answers to the country's greatest crises: urban race riots, campus protests, and the Vietnam War. In the aftermath of the war and Watergate, the country's leaders—politicians, military generals, university presidents, and police commissioners—faced growing scrutiny and skepticism. "There is a very obvious dearth of people who seem able to supply convincing answers, or even point to directions toward solutions," Harvard University president Derek Bok observed. Against this backdrop of pessimism, after losing three games, it appeared that UCLA had finally reached a frontier, shattering the team's sense of invincibility and their faith in Wooden. The players turned to him for answers, but even the greatest coach in the country could not solve the complex problems of a fractious team.[32]

For more than a decade, national magazines, newspapers, and television networks saturated their sports coverage with stories about the greatness of Wooden. But by the mid-1970s, when the media became more skeptical about leaders and institutions, scrutinizing journalists exposed the myths of American sports. One of those myths revolved around Wooden's Pyramid of Success, credited by many as the foundation of UCLA's basketball achievements. The *Washington Post*'s Leonard Shapiro argued that Wooden's Pyramid of Success was a "cliché-cluttered credo" that had little to do with the team's accomplishments. "No one," Shapiro wrote, "really has to tell Bill Walton how to achieve success. Just throw him a basketball and everything else will fall into place." Of course, coaching the team was really not that simple. Wooden's stature as a leader was based on the idea that his moral virtues allowed him to transform divergent personalities into a cohesive unit. But the team dissension, the players' bitter complaints about his coaching, and their impatience with losing undermined Wooden's leadership, exposing cracks in the pyramid.[33]

○

For all the complaints about the team's listlessness and Wooden's coaching, the real key to the Bruins' success was Bill Walton. He still had not completely recovered from his back injury, making it very difficult for him to compete at the high level that he expected. At the same time, he felt incredible pressure to carry the team when they needed him most. Wooden believed that of all his players, only Walton could provide the kind of leadership necessary for the Bruins to regain their confidence. In the losses to Oregon State and Oregon, Walton looked nothing like college basketball's best player, scoring only five points in the second half against the Beavers and taking only five total shots against the Ducks.[34]

After UCLA's losses, Walton faced growing scrutiny from the media. Some writers questioned his drive, claiming that he had become complacent and distracted by the lucrative professional contract offers that awaited him after graduation. He had lost his desire for perfection, they said, and was more concerned with personal exploration. Detractors suggested that transcendental meditation dulled his competitive instincts and a vegetarian diet sapped his body. Others argued that UCLA "lost an ungodly three games" because the entire team "seemed more interested in eating, swimming, cycling, philosophizing, and politicking than playing basketball." Such complaints, according to historian Christopher Lasch, reflected the fears of some Americans who believed that "a way of life was dying—the culture of competitive individualism." For many critics, the politics of personal liberation had a negative influence on athletes who cared less about the sacred American ideals of sacrifice, teamwork, and industriousness. They worried that the emerging "Me Generation" and the "cult of the self" shaped a new breed of athletes who glorified more relaxed values and celebrated personal fulfillment. What was most troubling about UCLA, a team of "free thinking, liberated youngsters," was the way they blamed Wooden for losing instead of accepting personal responsibility, a disturbing sign to many fans.[35]

During the season, Wooden made changes with his offensive system, starting lineup, and team rules. After the "lost weekend" in Oregon—and complaints from Walton and Lee—he went back to the two-guard high-post offense and started Lee instead of Marques Johnson. He relaxed his rules on dress, allowing the team to wear sandals and jeans on road trips. The players ignored his rules for promptness, and he no longer required the whole team to eat together, accommodating the vegetarians who preferred to eat at the cafeteria. Looking back, he thought that this contributed to disunity on and off the court. Too often, Wooden gave in, allowing the team to chip away at his authority.[36]

In the back of his mind, Wooden worried that Walton—his most important team leader—had become a follower off the court. Walton talked like a radical and dressed like a radical. He became a vegetarian, practiced transcendental meditation, and lived with a woman. For Wooden, dealing with his moody star was sometimes very difficult. He considered Walton complex and enigmatic, almost fragile. "Sometimes with Bill I feel like I'm handling a piece of glass," he said.[37]

The pressures of winning gave Walton extreme anxiety. The stress was so immense that he asked Wooden for permission to smoke marijuana after games. Walton needed it, he said, to help him relax. Wooden absolutely refused. There was no way he could allow it. Walton persisted; he was so restless that he could not sleep, and he worried that it would affect his performance in upcoming games. Finally, Wooden gave in. Just don't tell your teammates, he said.[38]

Wooden had sent Walton a clear message: the rules did not apply to stars. And he gave Walton more than permission to smoke after games; he gave him a greater sense of entitlement. This story reflects the changing dynamic between college coaches and athletes during the Athletic Revolution. Twenty years earlier, no UCLA player would have dared to ask Wooden for permission to smoke marijuana. Wooden would have been appalled at the mere suggestion and likely kicked the player off the team. But in 1974, things were different. Marijuana use had become more common among America's youth, and, more important, the best college basketball players received certain privileges. Walton's status as an All-American and the most important player at UCLA empowered him to challenge Wooden's principles and prevailing cultural norms.[39]

During his senior season, *Time* ran a long feature article on Walton. The newsmagazine covered familiar ground: his outspoken socialist views, meditation practices, vegetarian diet, long hair, and antiwar protests—newsworthy material for a famous college athlete. The most remarkable aspect of *Time's* reporting was not about Walton, though, but rather a half-page story devoted to "a patron called Papa Sam." By 1974 Sam Gilbert's visibility had grown enormously. So had his ego. What other booster was featured in *Time?* Gilbert was no longer "the man in the shadows," operating behind the Wizard's curtain. He was the most publicized booster in the country. His name could be found in major newspapers right next to his most important clients—Kareem Abdul-Jabbar and Bill Walton, though the press never explicitly questioned his presence in the program in print. He had become a vital part of the basketball program, building personal and professional relationships with many UCLA athletes. By the time Keith Wilkes arrived in Westwood in 1971, Gilbert was already "an institution." Papa Sam was like family, a friendly uncle and a loyal friend, someone the players could entrust with their troubles. He counseled them about school, jobs, pregnant girlfriends, difficulties with their parents, and dealing with Wooden.[40]

Gilbert claimed that he was just "another fan," an avid observer of the program and a friend to the players. But J. D. Morgan knew better. Publicly, Morgan dismissed any controversy around Gilbert, calling him "a humanitarian . . . someone who is in a unique position to help the kids after they finish school." Privately, Morgan was concerned about Gilbert helping "the kids" before they graduated. He realized that if the players received special favors from boosters, then the boosters would feel more empowered to wield greater influence, a dangerous position for any athletic director or coach. Morgan worried that if the NCAA caught Gilbert doing anything that violated the rules or damaged the reputation of UCLA, then the university could lose not only the opportunity to compete for national championships, but also the major revenues that came with it.[41]

Without question, Morgan knew that Gilbert had breached NCAA rules, and as a result, so had UCLA. Gilbert and Wooden's assistant coaches helped players sell their tickets for a handsome profit, a common practice at schools all across the country. Greg Lee recalled that he and his teammates did not worry about violating NCAA rules because UCLA players had received special benefits for years. Gilbert's well-publicized professional contract negotiations for UCLA players before their eligibility expired made him a "representative of the school's athletic interests" and placed the university in direct violation of NCAA rules—yet the NCAA did nothing to punish UCLA.[42]

On numerous occasions, Morgan asked Gilbert to cease his involvement with the basketball program. It seemed that Morgan had complete control over the athletic department, but he could not control Gilbert. So Morgan chose a policy of accommodation with the influential booster, as did John Wooden. "I know [Gilbert] and J. D. had kind of an arm's length truce," Chancellor Charles Young acknowledged. "I don't think J. D. wanted to stir the pot too much."[43]

Wooden knew all about Sam Gilbert, too. Occasionally, Gilbert called him on the phone; what they discussed is unknown. He worried that Gilbert's munificent assistance would harm the program. He warned the players about getting too close to Gilbert, but they ignored him and continued to seek Papa Sam's counsel. Wooden resented the way Gilbert interfered with his team. Frequently, the players went to Gilbert to discuss their problems without talking to Wooden. This irritated the UCLA coach. But, said Greg Lee, "[Wooden] was glad about [Gilbert's] presence." For Wooden, "whatever was happening was going to be out of sight, out of mind." An anonymous UCLA player told the *Los Angeles Times* in 1971, "I'm sure there have been times when Sam and the athletic department haven't seen eye to eye. But I also know that they've gone after Sam's help when they've needed it."[44]

O

In late February, after UCLA crushed Washington, 99–65, reporters asked John Wooden about his coaching future at UCLA. He said that he welcomed the challenge of coaching the next group of players the following season— "if, I'm here next year." One sportswriter asked him if that meant that this was his last season coaching the Bruins. Wooden refused to comment, but it was clear that coaching the dynasty and all the inherent pressures that came with it were wearing on him. The stress lines on his weathered face and the distant look in his eyes suggested that he had seriously contemplated moving on. The following day, Wooden clarified his retirement plans: "I'm at UCLA until I tell you I'm not."[45]

With two conference losses, UCLA needed to defeat USC to secure the Pac-8 title and make the NCAA Tournament. Entering the game, the Bruins and the Trojans shared identical conference records (11-2). A loss would end UCLA's season. Before the season began, no one could have imagined that the Bruins would not make the playoffs. But after three losses and three victories by five points or less, UCLA's spot in the tournament seemed far from guaranteed. Facing elimination, UCLA responded, focused and aggressive. In the first half, the Bruins held the Trojans to just four baskets and outscored them 47–13. By the time it was over, UCLA had humiliated USC, 82–52, proving any suggestion of the dynasty's demise premature.[46]

Heading into the NCAA Tournament, UCLA was favored to win the national championship, though the polls ranked North Carolina State first and UCLA second. Wooden was not too concerned with the top-ranked Wolfpack. He had revenge on his mind. "I *really* want Notre Dame," he said, clenching his fist. Before UCLA could play Notre Dame or North Carolina State, the Bruins faced off against Dayton—an unremarkable team that had lost seven games during the regular season. Throughout his entire tenure at UCLA, none of Wooden's teams had ever played an overtime game in the NCAA Tournament. But against Dayton, after building a seventeen-point lead in the first half, UCLA needed *three* thrilling overtime periods to win, 111–100.[47]

After easily dispatching San Francisco, 83–60, in the West Regional Finals, the Bruins advanced to the Final Four. Since Notre Dame had lost to Michigan in the Mideast Semifinals, Wooden would not get the chance to coach against Digger Phelps again. Instead, college basketball fans would see the matchup that so many had predicted for the national championship before the season started. North Carolina State was much improved, having lost only one game—to UCLA—all season. Before the national semifinals, Wooden said, "I just want North Carolina State to remember that we played them on a neutral court with Walton out half the game and beat them by 18 points." At that point in the season, UCLA was an intimidating force and the clear favorite to win the national title. But that was no longer the case. N.C. State forward Tim Stoddard replied, "We know they aren't 18 points better than us, but what's more important is that *they* know it."[48]

Wooden rarely concerned himself with the opposition and did little advance scouting, even for UCLA's biggest games. He told his players not to worry about the other team. Execute our system, he said, and everything will be fine. And he never, ever talked about stopping a single opposing player—except for David Thompson. He knew that the Bruins would need whatever edge they could get playing the Final Four in the Wolfpack's home state. Therefore, Wooden sent assistant coach Frank Arnold to scout N.C. State in the Eastern Regional Finals in Raleigh. While Arnold watched State play Pittsburgh, his eyes followed Thompson all over the court. Midway through the first half, Thompson raced down court, burst from the free-throw line, and leaped three or four feet in the air to block a shot. As he came down, his foot hit a teammate's shoulder, causing him to cartwheel in midair. When his head hit the hardwood court, it sounded like a "bowling ball had fallen off the top of the backboard." An eerie hush fell over the Coliseum, as Thompson lay motionless on the court, his head cut open. For ten minutes fans looked on with grave concern as two doctors and a nurse attended to him.[49]

When he left the court on a stretcher, Wolfpack fans feared the worst. N.C. State assistant athletic director Frank Weedon saw blood trickle from Thompson's head and immediately thought that he was dead. An ambulance took him to the hospital, where he received fifteen stitches. Back at the Coliseum, the team struggled to concentrate, knowing that Thompson was hospitalized. Remarkably, he returned to the Coliseum late in the second half, wearing his red warm-up suit and a heavy white bandage around his head, looking "like a wounded solider." With Thompson watching from the bench, N.C. State soundly defeated Pittsburgh, 100–72. The following weekend, on the eve of the Final Four, six thousand fans showed up at the Greensboro Coliseum to see if he could even practice. Thompson forcefully dunked the ball, over and over again. He slammed it with one hand, two hands, and behind his head. There was no question that he was ready to play.[50]

For the Wolfpack, this was essentially a home game, with N.C. State's campus in Raleigh only seventy-nine miles from Greensboro. Sportswriters estimated that more than 90 percent of the fans attending the Final Four would cheer for the Wolfpack. As first-time hosts of the Final Four, North Carolinians swelled with southern pride, boasting about their great state as "basketball country." Governor James E. Holshouser Jr.—a University of North Carolina law grad—proclaimed Saturday as "Wolfpack Basketball Day." This was the first time that the college basketball championship was played in the South. Previously, the championship had been played in Louisville, Kentucky; College Park, Maryland; and Houston, Texas—none of which was truly the South, according to many North Carolinians. Under this line of thinking, the last time a truly southern team won the national championship was in 1957, when the North Carolina Tar Heels beat the Kansas Jayhawks. This meant that the game between the Wolfpack and the Bruins was about more than just a chance to play for the national championship. This game was a "veritable war to Southern folk, with their salvation, pride, and destiny on the line." Los Angeles had the Dodgers, Angels, Rams,

Kings, Lakers, Hollywood, and Disneyland. But in North Carolina, noted one L.A. writer, "They have only tobacco and basketball and North Carolina State is carrying their banner tomorrow."[51]

From the moment the game began, Bill Walton and Tom Burleson battled underneath the basket, scrapping for rebounds and contesting each other's shots. Burleson, Tim Stoddard, and Phil Spence all took turns guarding Walton, who scored on a series of bank shots, twisting layups, and tip-ins. He led both teams with twenty-nine points and eighteen rebounds, but Burleson challenged him the entire game, scoring twenty points of his own. The two teams traded baskets for most of the game, keeping the score close. With 4:58 left in regulation, David Thompson broke toward the basket, soared high above the rim, caught a pass, and gently dropped the ball into the net. After Thompson's "alley-oop," the Wolfpack led, 63–61. A thunderous salvo erupted in the Coliseum. It sounded "like the whole state of North Carolina" was cheering for the Wolfpack.[52]

Dave Meyers came back and made a close shot inside, tying the score. After each team made another basket, the game was tied once again, 65–65. With about a minute left, Walton misfired on a short hook shot. Burleson rebounded the ball, and the Wolfpack simulated a delay offense until only 23 seconds remained on the clock. Norm Sloan called time-out so his team could prepare to take the final shot. Ideally, Burleson, Thompson, or Monte Towe would take it, but with just 4 seconds left, burly forward Tim Stoddard was the only one open, and he missed a corner shot that would have won the game.[53]

In the overtime period, neither team gained control. On offense, N.C. State spread out, deliberately moving the ball around the perimeter, slowing the tempo. With the game tied and 15 seconds left, the Wolfpack had the ball and another chance to win, but Burleson failed to score on a short jumper. In the second overtime, UCLA raced out to a seven-point lead. With 3:27 remaining, Tommy Curtis fired a sharp pass underneath the basket to Keith Wilkes, who scored while he was fouled and then made the bonus free throw. Curtis jogged back, grinning and jumping, holding his index fingers in the air, reminding everyone in the arena that UCLA was *still* number one until someone knocked them off. After that play, the Bruins relaxed, and the Wolfpack played more aggressively. N.C. State pressed tighter, harassing Curtis and Lee, forcing them into critical errors. After two free throws from Towe and a basket from Thompson, N.C. State cut the lead to four points. At 2:48, Curtis ran into Towe and was called for charging. A few seconds later, Meyers let the ball fly right through his hands. He could feel the game slipping away.[54]

On the next Wolfpack possession, Burleson scored on an offensive rebound, cutting UCLA's lead to just two points. Moments later, he made one of two free throws, and N.C. State inched closer to catching UCLA. With 1:16 left, Meyers missed the front end of a critical one-and-one free throw. At the other end of the floor, Thompson flew past Wilkes, leaped toward the basket, and banked a clutch jumper off the backboard. N.C. State led 76–75. On UCLA's next possession, Lee missed a long shot from the corner, and Wilkes was whistled for shoving Thompson underneath the basket. Thompson sank both free throws. A few moments later, Lee attempted a pass to Walton, but Burleson intercepted it. Tommy Curtis fouled Monte Towe, who then made two more free throws, pushing State's lead to 80–75. Walton scored UCLA's final basket, but it did not matter. The game was over, and so was the dynasty.[55]

The Bruins hurried off the court, except for Lee, who strolled back to the locker room, shaking his head in disbelief. Shocked, UCLA's song girls looked at each with tears in their eyes, unsure of what to say or what to do. Wooden stood glumly just outside the press conference room, patiently waiting for Norm Sloan to finish his remarks. When Wooden entered the room, reporters and photographers greeted him with applause. He gracefully congratulated N.C. State, noting how well they had played. He explained that the Bruins made too many costly turnovers and took too many hurried shots with the lead. Holding a lead, he reminded the writers, had been a problem for his team all season.[56]

Twenty minutes after the game, J. D. Morgan finally opened up UCLA's dressing room to the press. Slumped on a bench with his back against the wall, Dave Meyers stared into space, still wearing his sweat-soaked uniform. Keith Wilkes did not have the words to describe his emotions. All he could say was that he was really tired. The players struggled to comprehend it all.

How did they lose? They had an eleven-point lead—twice—in regulation and blew a seven-point lead in the second overtime. "We did our best," Lee said, his spirit broken. Walton was determined not to talk to the press at all. He had brought a chair into the shower and lingered there for nearly forty minutes. When he came out, two dozen writers surrounded him while he dried himself with a towel. As Walton dressed, he ignored most of the writers' questions, shrugging his shoulders and nodding his head. A few reporters walked away, but most stayed, hoping that if they waited long enough, Walton would offer a quality sound bite. Finally, a writer spoke up, "What is your contempt for the media?" Irritated, Walton replied that he did not have any contempt for the media. He paused for a moment. "You're asking questions. I am not answering any of them. But when I pick up tomorrow's paper, I'll be quoted as giving answers to your questions."[57]

The next morning's newspaper headlines announced the end of an era in large bold print: "**The Dynasty Is in Ruins**"; "**The King Is Dead, Bruins Don't Cry**"; "**Sun Sets on Bruin Empire**." Curry Kirkpatrick predicted that North Carolina State's victory over UCLA would be more memorable than their win against Marquette for the national championship. In Saturday's double-overtime game against the Bruins, he claimed, "The Wolfpack truly won the title." When N.C. State defeated UCLA, the Wolfpack ended one of the greatest winning streaks in the history of American sports. Doug Krikorian of the *Los Angeles Herald-Examiner* suggested that UCLA's loss reflected the growing sense of defeatism in America. UCLA basketball was another fallen "American institution." A few years earlier, no one could imagine UCLA not winning the national championship, but as America's temper changed, it became "inevitable" that the dynasty would end, too. "It was only in keeping with the mood of our times that the Bruins would be beaten, would be made only a memory," Krikorian wrote. "After all, nothing in the United States is sacred any more."[58]

11

The Godfather

"We were just getting ready to celebrate," Marques Johnson explained. Only minutes earlier, with less than ten seconds left in overtime, Johnson had passed the ball to Richard Washington, UCLA's towering center. Standing about ten feet from the basket, Washington posted up against Louisville's Bill Bunton, maneuvered past him with one dribble, and released a soft, arcing shot. If Washington made it, UCLA would play in the national championship. If he missed, John Wooden would coach in the consolation finale for the second consecutive season. Fortunately for Wooden, the ball swished through the net, and Washington became an instant hero. With four seconds left on the clock, Louisville had just enough time for Allen Murphy to heave a desperate half-court shot that caromed off the rim.[1]

When the final buzzer sounded, the scoreboard read UCLA 75, Louisville 74. Wooden struggled through a crowd of exuberant fans who had rushed the court to congratulate him. After shaking hands with his former pupil and Louisville head coach Denny Crum, he headed for the pressroom. As Wooden walked through the corridor of the San Diego Sports Arena, he reflected on the game, the season, and his career. He was extremely proud of the way his team had competed in an incredibly close semifinal. When the season started, few prognosticators envisioned that this UCLA team—a team without any true "star"—would make a run at the national championship.

But Wooden found a way to weld the talents of an inexperienced group into an unselfish and cohesive unit, which he credited to reestablishing a stricter code of discipline that had eroded during the Walton years. This season, the entire team ate together, followed his rules about hair, and no longer wore Levis and flip-flops on road trips.[2]

For this team, following Wooden's rules was easier than following in the footsteps of the Walton Gang. UCLA fans frequently complained at court-side when the Bruins did not blow out opponents. The team lacked depth and a veteran point guard and returned only one starter. Despite these short-comings, UCLA had the ingredients of a championship team: athleticism, quickness, and a strong frontcourt. Captain Dave Meyers, an All-American forward, took the court with a permanent scowl on his face, looking like he was "mad at the world." He was intensely driven, aggressive, and scrappy, diving for loose balls as if they were ticking time bombs that might explode if he did not recover them. Richard Washington, a prized recruit, developed into a consistent inside force. Sophomore forward Marques Johnson, after battling hepatitis and fatigue through the first part of the season, emerged as an explosive scorer. Gradually, guards Pete Trgovich and Andre McCarter proved an effective backcourt tandem, actively disrupting the tempo of op-posing teams as they led UCLA's constricting full-court zone press.[3]

As the season progressed, the Bruins steadily improved, losing only three regular-season games. This group, described by Wooden as "fine, young Christian men," never bickered or pointed fingers at each other when things did not go well. Not once during the entire season did Wooden have to stop practice to prevent players from fighting. This team gave him few problems on or off the court. None of the players was involved in campus demonstra-tions or seriously challenged his authority. Those days were over.[4]

By 1975 most of the battles of the Athletic Revolution had passed, though the sport still felt its consequences. Protests by players on and off the court had changed the relationship between coaches and athletes. Over the course of the sixties, defiant college athletes had chiseled away the authority of coaches. In 1973 the NCAA responded by passing a piece of legislation that replaced the four-year scholarship with a one-year scholarship renewed at a coach's discretion. This measure represented a lasting victory for conservatives; it discouraged dissent and strengthened the authority of coaches. Under this rule, college athletes became more accountable to their coaches than their professors for the continuation of financial aid, forcing athletes to devote more time to their sport. Increasingly, then, big-time college basketball had become more like professional basketball, with a greater emphasis on winning and less emphasis on education.[5]

During the 1974–75 season, Wooden spent more time teaching his players than arguing with them. He often mentioned how much he enjoyed coaching this team, which is why, on the eve of the semifinals against Louisville, a group of Los Angeles sportswriters was surprised to hear him say that this might be his last Final Four. If he did retire, Wooden said, he would tell his players first, and he had not done that yet. "It's been a troubled time," he admitted. "I haven't slept well for the last couple of weeks." He did not really want to retire, he maintained, but there were "outside forces" influencing his decision. "I could never talk about them. Please don't ask me to," he pleaded.[6]

For weeks, rumors of Wooden's retirement circulated throughout the Los Angeles press, though he publicly denied that he was leaving UCLA. Signs of his departure had preceded the tournament: in early March, Washington State coach George Raveling wrote in his Sunday *Seattle Post-Intelligencer* column that Wooden was stepping down at the end of the season. Before UCLA's final game at Pauley Pavilion, Wooden told his team that it would be the last home game "for a few people in this room." His doctor advised him not to coach the 1976 U.S. Olympic basketball team. The *Los Angeles Times'* John Hall reminded readers that the sixty-four-year-old coach had a heart attack only two years earlier and suffered from insomnia and a burning stomach. Consequently, he had to watch his diet, take medication, and walk five miles every day at dawn to protect his health. Nell Wooden explained that it was not just the coaching responsibilities that wore on her husband. It was "all the things together that were getting him uptight. He had to get out from the pressure. I think that was the biggest thing. When you get to a certain age, it's hard to take those things any more."[7]

Standing in the spotlight drained him. The constant scrutiny, demanding expectations from alumni and fans, and the invasive media made coaching less enjoyable. He had set out to be a coach and a teacher, but success had transformed him into a celebrity, an unwelcomed role. Coaching a dynasty made it impossible for him to live the simple life that he strongly desired. By 1975 the "overwhelming attention, inspection, and curiosity" had become "more than an irritation. It was deeply disturbing." Wooden later wrote that he "felt more and more that crowds were closing in and enveloping" him; he "seemed to be constantly surrounded," and he could not take it anymore.[8]

After defeating Louisville, Wooden knew that it was time to walk away from it all. He did not want to meet with the media or deal with the crowds. His career in coaching was over, and now he had to tell his team. So, instead of entering the Sports Arena pressroom, he veered off to the UCLA locker room, where his players were celebrating their incredible overtime victory. The team gathered around him. In vintage Wooden fashion, he spoke briefly and to the point. "I'm bowing out," he said, his voice quivering. He looked around the room at the players' young, wide-eyed faces. "I don't want to. I have to." And with those three succinct sentences, he left.[9]

Silence fell over the locker room. The players were stunned and unsure what to say or do. Some sat in solitude, alone with their thoughts. Others talked in pairs, barely above a whisper. They were sad to see Wooden go, but not completely surprised about his decision, given the recent rumors in the media. At the press conference, Wooden's public revelation moved Denny Crum to tears. His hands shook as he thought about his mentor leaving coaching. "Basketball will miss him," Crum said softly. Moments later, J. D. Morgan reflected on Wooden's importance to UCLA and the sport: "He has been college basketball. He has been the game. He has compiled records nobody is going to equal." Inevitably, the press had one question to ask after Wooden's announcement. Who would replace him? Morgan refused to discuss potential candidates, though Crum seemed to be an obvious successor. He simply said, "We'll get the best man we can to replace him," though Morgan knew that no one could replace John Wooden.[10]

Wooden still had one more championship game to coach. On Monday evening, he took the court the same way he always did: wearing a dark-gray suit, carrying a game program tightly rolled up in his left hand, waving to the crowd with a little smile. Everyone in the San Diego Sports Arena was aware that this was his last game. During the introductions, the crowd cheered so loudly for him that it seemed like everyone in the building was rooting for UCLA, though one man clearly wanted Wooden to lose. "It will be sad if he loses," retired coach Adolph Rupp commented, "but he's got enough of those damn trophies. Johnny's in against me tonight."[11]

Wooden desperately wanted to beat Kentucky. Whenever the Bruins scored or made a good play, he raised and pumped his fist, exhorting his players to move quicker and run harder. During the game's most tense moments, he paced the sideline with a slightly pained expression on his face, directing his team, rolled-up program in hand, reminding the officials to watch the way Kentucky's bruising athletes checked his players. At least a half-dozen times, he leaped off the bench, barking at the officials in protest. With 6:23 left to play, and UCLA leading 76–75, Dave Meyers attempted a jump shot. As he came down, Meyers collided with Kentucky forward Kevin Grevey. An official called Meyers for charging. Stunned at the call, he slapped the hardwood with his palms and was assessed a technical foul for doing so. Wooden was so outraged that Meyers had to restrain him from walking out on the court. For the next few minutes, Wooden berated the referee, shouting, "You crook!"[12]

Kentucky could capitalize on a possible five-point play—a maximum of three free throws followed by possession of the ball. Grevey, an 80 percent free-throw shooter who finished the game with thirty-four points, missed the technical and the first of a one-and-one free throw. On the next possession, Kentucky turned over the ball on an offensive foul. UCLA recovered from the potentially damaging foul calls, reenergized. Instead of a five-point possession, Kentucky came away with nothing. In the next two minutes, UCLA built a five-point lead and never looked back. "There was no way we were going to lose coach's last game," Andre McCarter asserted.[13]

In John Wooden's final game, UCLA defeated Kentucky, 92–85. He collected his tenth national title and now had enough rings for every finger. With hundreds of people surrounding him on the court, he embraced his players, proud of what they had achieved. During the championship ceremony, Wooden stood beside his team on a platform, a shredded victory net around his neck, while the fans thanked him one last time with a standing ovation. He graciously waved back, smiling widely. It was the perfect ending to a storybook journey. He stepped away from coaching on top, leaving behind an unrivaled legacy and a lasting imprint on the sport. After the ceremony, a writer asked Wooden how the program would fare without him. Grinning, he insisted, "UCLA is not going to fall on hard times."[14]

○

Two days after the national championship, UCLA announced that Illinois head coach Gene Bartow had been released from his contract and would replace John Wooden. Sportswriters had speculated among a long list of potential successors, some of whom were extremely unlikely to take the UCLA job, including USC's Bob Boyd, Indiana's Bob Knight, North Carolina's Dean Smith, and N.C. State's Norm Sloan. Most UCLA fans had hoped that Denny Crum would return to Westwood, but J. D. Morgan did not consult with them or Wooden about the job search. Wooden would have preferred that Crum or his longtime assistant Gary Cunningham take over, but Cunningham stepped away from coaching when Wooden retired so that he could pursue a career in university administration, and Morgan had a cool relationship with Crum.[15]

Morgan respected Bartow's coaching intellect and the manner in which he worked with players. He was most impressed with the way Bartow had built Memphis State into a national contender, leading the Tigers to the 1973 national championship. In many ways, Bartow reminded Morgan of Wooden. "Clean Gene" did not drink, smoke, or swear. He was a midwesterner, a devout churchgoer, and a family man. He even looked like the ex-UCLA coach: slender, black spectacles, and short grayish hair, parted to the side just like Wooden. He exuded a quiet confidence, stressed discipline, and insisted on teamwork. His teams ran the fast break and pressed on defense. It all sounded very familiar.[16]

Critics were unimpressed with Bartow's track record, pointing out that Illinois must have been pleased to release him, since his team had just finished the season 8-18. Nothing he did, short of winning a national championship, would be good enough for many UCLA fans and alumni. He hoped that the "nostalgia for Coach Wooden" would pass in about a year, but that never happened. During his first six months at UCLA, Bartow shared an office with Wooden. He was constantly reminded of Wooden's presence, looking up at his plaques, trophies, pictures, and the man himself.[17]

Bartow's rocky first season was filled with ups and downs: four total losses, including an embarrassing twenty-point opening-game defeat to Indiana. Team dissension, bickering, and rebellion damaged his coaching reputation. Alumni voiced their displeasure, made obscene phone calls, and wrote nasty letters. They claimed that he had lost control of the team. The overwhelming stress of coaching at UCLA led Bartow to lose twenty pounds. Despite these problems, he led the Bruins to the Final Four, where they lost to eventual champion Indiana, this time by only fourteen points.[18]

According to the standards at UCLA, Bartow's second season was an epic failure. Although the Bruins finished the season with a 24-5 record, first in the conference, and ranked second nationally, Idaho State knocked them out of the NCAA Tournament in a stunning one-point upset in the West Region Semifinal. Critics blasted Bartow. John Wooden would have never lost to an undistinguished team like Idaho State, they said. The fans, the alumni, and the press expected too much, Bartow thought. They expected him to win every game, and when he did not, they attacked him, sometimes harshly and unfairly. The *Los Angeles Times* published numerous letters of disapproval, convincing Bartow that the media intended to ruin him. When a radio listener expressed displeasure with his coaching, Bartow stormed off the show. Wooden thought that he was "too sensitive" and that he had to learn how to ignore the criticism. But Bartow simply could not deal with it anymore. So, after two seasons at UCLA, two conference championships, and a 52-9 record, he left for the University of Alabama, Birmingham, where he would create an athletic program, coach the basketball team, and earn three times what he made in salary at UCLA. UAB was the complete opposite of UCLA: there was no tradition of excellence, no public expectations, and no media scrutiny. Bartow could not wait to leave Westwood. In Birmingham, he would have his own office.[19]

○

Gene Bartow's biggest problem at UCLA was dealing with meddlesome alumni and boosters—one in particular. When he first accepted the job, the man everyone called "the Godfather" sat him down over breakfast and explained his important role in the basketball program. Sam Gilbert fully embraced the Godfather image. Poor, powerless, exploited players came to him for help. He granted them favors and did whatever he believed was necessary to deal with their problems. He did not ask for retribution, though they would always remain indebted to him. In return, all he asked for were friendship and loyalty, perhaps an occasional small gift out of respect. Like Mario Puzo's fictional Godfather, Gilbert operated outside the system. He ignored the rules and let nothing stand in his way.[20]

Before the meeting, Bartow had never heard of Gilbert, but Sam made it perfectly clear who he was. Gilbert discussed everything he did for the players in detail, "almost down to the dollar amount per player." It made Bartow uncomfortable. He ignored Gilbert's advice and instructed the players to avoid him. The two developed an intense feud, a power struggle over the players' loyalty. Gilbert detested the way Bartow tried to undermine his influence and threatened to buy Bartow out of his contract, signifying Gilbert's growing influence over the program after Wooden retired. Bartow feared that Gilbert might actually hurt him. In 1991 he wrote a letter to an NCAA executive, claiming that Gilbert was "Mafia-related and was capable of hurting people." He had no doubt that if the NCAA had investigated UCLA when he was there, Gilbert would have thought that Bartow turned him in, and then his life "would have been in possible danger."[21]

In 1976, at the end of Bartow's first season at UCLA, juniors Richard Washington and Marques Johnson flew to Denver with Sam Gilbert to meet with the ABA's Denver Nuggets, a team coached by Larry Brown. Gilbert paid for the underclassmen's flights and helped both players negotiate with the team, but the Nuggets eventually withdrew their contract offer, fearing that improper signings with underclassmen might ruin the ABA's forthcoming merger with the NBA. Ultimately, Washington signed with the NBA's Kansas City Kings, and Johnson remained at UCLA for his senior year.[22]

The NCAA suspected that Gilbert had illegally represented UCLA underclassmen and assigned J. Brent Clark to probe the Bruins basketball program. In July 1975, Clark, a twenty-six-year-old attorney from rural Oklahoma, joined the NCAA's enforcement staff, the division that investigates member-school infractions. In early 1977, after canvassing the Westwood campus and interviewing key witnesses, including Gilbert, he determined that Gilbert,

Washington, and Johnson had violated NCAA rules and recommended a full-scale investigation of UCLA basketball. Clark's superior at the NCAA, Bill Hunt, however, ignored his report. He claims that Hunt pulled him aside and said, "We're just not going after [UCLA] right now."[23]

On February 27, 1978, during a congressional hearing on NCAA operations, Clark testified before the House Subcommittee on Oversight and Investigations. Clark was considered a controversial "star witness," since he had quit the NCAA enforcement staff and begun working as an investigator for the congressional subcommittee. Throughout the first day of hearings, he charged the NCAA of bribing informants during investigations, employing "manipulative and corrupt" tactics to obtain information from member schools, phone tapping, and collusion between the investigative staff and the Committee on Infractions. He claimed that executive director Walter Byers's opinion of a school dictated whether the NCAA investigated an athletic program, a charge that Byers vehemently denied. Clark also alleged that the NCAA denied member schools adequate due process and failed to provide information necessary for a defense.[24]

In his testimony, Clark claimed that Bill Hunt said that the NCAA had become suspicious of the activities of "a long time agent for basketball players at this particular major collegiate basketball power" and asked him to look into the matter. After Clark conducted interviews and documented "very serious evidence of wrongdoing," Hunt called off the investigation. Clark believed that Hunt's orders meant that "Mr. Byers [instructed Hunt] not to pursue the individual since it would involve one of the NCAA's leading moneymakers, a major basketball power." "In this instance," he concluded, "politics and balance sheets seemed to dictate that the NCAA take no action."[25]

Although Clark did not explicitly cite names, he was clearly talking about UCLA and Sam Gilbert. Nearly four years later, he told the *Los Angeles Times,* "Gilbert was well known to the NCAA for years and years. His name had appeared in print many times." Clark suspected that other NCAA investigators had talked with Gilbert before he did. He was convinced that if his superiors had allowed him to stay in Los Angeles for another month, he would have found more evidence of Gilbert's wrongdoing and that UCLA would have been placed on an indefinite suspension. But for the NCAA, "the negative repercussions" of placing UCLA on probation "outweighed the positive benefits." If the NCAA had punished UCLA, it would have ended UCLA's title streak and damaged the reputation of the most well-respected icon in college basketball. Equally important, suspending UCLA would have jeopardized the NCAA's commercial boom in Los Angeles, a major media market that attracted high television ratings when the Bruins played in the NCAA Tournament. The NCAA's failure to penalize UCLA was a clear case of selective enforcement. Clark maintained, "As long as Wooden was there, the NCAA would never have taken any action."[26]

○

Brent Clark was not the only person investigating Sam Gilbert. In 1978 Jack Scott published a book about Bill Walton's third season with the Portland Trail Blazers. In his first season, Walton told Gilbert that he wanted to be traded to the Los Angeles Lakers and that he was considering quitting basketball altogether. It was no secret that he was miserable in Portland, a damp, rainy city, and that he did not enjoy playing for a team that lost more games than it won. Gilbert leaked this private information to the press, violating Walton's confidence. Walton determined that he could no longer trust him and that it was time to break off their relationship. Gilbert retaliated and accused him of faking an ankle injury and refusing to play so that Portland would trade him to Los Angeles. Walton denied these charges, but his longtime critics refused to believe him. In their eyes, he was a deceitful, pampered athlete and a dirty political radical. Angry fans and cynical sportswriters attacked him for trying to "rip off" the Portland organization, never questioning the single source of these claims.[27]

By this time, Jack Scott had become his new business adviser and personal counselor. Scott was the one man whom Walton could trust. They shared political views, social ideals, and a commune in Portland. After the 1974 NCAA Tournament, they went backpacking together and soon became close friends. While he was a student at UCLA, Walton read Scott's *Athletic Revolution,* a "radical" critique of the relationship between sports and society. From a distance, Scott admired Walton because he was one of the few exceptional athletes who stood up for his political beliefs. During Walton's tenuous first professional season, hostile detractors vilified him for his political views, counterculture lifestyle, and alleged scheme to get paid while he sat out. *Newsday's* Sandy Padwe called the assault on Walton "the most vicious *ever* against a white athlete." Walton seriously considered quitting, but Scott convinced him not to give up the game that he loved. In the spring of that season, Scott endured intense media scrutiny as well when the FBI suspected—but did not accuse—him of harboring teenage newspaper heiress Patty Hearst during her underground hiding with a terrorist organization known as the Symbionese Liberation Army (SLA). Walton stood by him, denied any knowledge of Scott's involvement with Hearst or the SLA, and publicly denounced the FBI and the U.S. government.[28]

Scott's involvement in the complicated Hearst case and his politically charged writings on athletics made him one of the most controversial figures in American sports. Scott was a classic sixties radical: intense, zealous, and sincerely devoted to the causes that consumed him. What separated him from other radicals was that he focused on the injustices in American sports. After earning a Ph.D. in higher education from Berkeley, he wrote for *Ramparts;* cofounded the Institute for the Study of Sports and Society with his wife, Micki; and became the athletic director at Oberlin College. In his writings, Scott decried racism in college and professional sports, denounced the abuses of sports' medical practices—especially the use of painkillers—argued that athletes should have greater autonomy in athletics, and questioned America's obsession with winning.[29]

In *The Athletic Revolution* and other writings, Scott documented the influential role of wealthy alumni and boosters in "big-time" college sports. He railed against the abuses of college athletics: excess commercialism, backhanded recruiting deals, and the professionalization of athletes. He detested the hypocrisy of the NCAA's claim that college athletes were exclusively amateurs, countering that big-time college football and basketball were major American businesses where athletes were recruited and paid—in scholarships and sometimes other benefits—to win and generate profits. When Scott wrote *Bill Walton: On the Road with the Portland Trail Blazers,* he criticized the NCAA for selectively enforcing its rules against some programs and ignoring blatant violations at UCLA.[30]

Walton told Scott that UCLA basketball players received "help" from boosters like Gilbert. After talking with Walton, Scott claimed, "UCLA players were so well taken care of—far beyond the rules of the NCAA—that even players from poor backgrounds never left UCLA prematurely to turn pro during John Wooden's championship years." Walton admitted, "It's hard for me to have a proper perspective on financial matters, since I've always had whatever I wanted since I enrolled at UCLA." At the time, the NCAA had placed the University of Nevada, Las Vegas, on probation for providing its basketball players with illegal assistance. Walton believed that the NCAA had unfairly targeted UNLV head coach Jerry Tarkanian because he recruited black athletes whom many other coaches "branded as troublemakers." It seemed that the NCAA discriminatingly enforced its rules and ignored violations by premier programs such as UCLA. "I hate to say anything that may hurt UCLA," Walton said, "but I can't be quiet when I see what the NCAA is doing to Jerry Tarkanian. . . . The NCAA is working day and night trying to get Jerry, but no one from the NCAA ever questioned me during my four years at UCLA!"[31]

In his book, Scott quoted a telephone conversation with Gilbert, who was clearly irritated that he had dared to call him. "I think Walton's a walking asshole," Gilbert said in an agitated voice. "My research says you, too, are an asshole." According to Scott, Gilbert threatened him numerous times. The longer they stayed on the phone, the more incensed Gilbert became. "Mr. Scott," he warned, "I'll say it once more. Don't fuck with me! Don't fuck with me! Take my word for it." Gilbert could not intimidate Scott, who had been shadowed and surveilled by the FBI. Scott told Gilbert that he had in his possession a signed letter from a former UCLA basketball player. The letter stated that after the player turned pro, he was supposed to pay Gilbert back forty-five hundred dollars. "Are you going to use that letter?" Gilbert asked nervously. "UCLA would have to return four NCAA championships. What I did is a total violation of NCAA rules." Gilbert persisted, asking Scott over and over again if he would use the letter. Scott thanked him for verifying its authenticity and ended the conversation.[32]

This was the first time that anyone had published any evidence of Gilbert's improprieties. When sportswriter Ron Rapoport questioned Scott about the book's contents, Scott played a tape recording of his conversations with Gilbert and an unidentified athlete who was, in all likelihood, probably Walton. Walton told one writer that the book "accurately reflects the characters involved" in his career at UCLA. The NCAA called Scott, too, and inquired about his charges against Gilbert, but he refused to cooperate, maintaining that he did not intend to "bust UCLA, but to point out the hypocrisy of the double standards that exist." If Gilbert sued him for libel, then he would produce the letter and have five other UCLA players testify that they had received money under the table too, but Gilbert never did.[33]

Scott and Walton wrote the Gilbert section very carefully, hoping to expose him without harming UCLA. They clearly tried to protect Wooden, claiming that the distinguished coach was unaware of the "'support' his star players regularly received." When reporters asked Wooden about Scott's book, he steadfastly denied that there was any wrongdoing during his coaching tenure. He remained firmly convinced that his players never accepted illegal payments from Gilbert or anyone else. At least, that is what he said publicly. Even though Bill Walton—a player whom Wooden once described as "open and sincere"—had clearly stated that UCLA had broken NCAA rules, both Wooden and J. D. Morgan denied it. They reminded the press that the NCAA had investigated the basketball program in the past and found no violations, though Brent Clark would have disagreed with that conclusion. One thing was clear: as long as Wooden's and Morgan's reputations were in jeopardy, the NCAA's ruling mattered more than Walton's word.[34]

○

Gary Cunningham did not really want the job. He had never set out to be a head basketball coach, but after Gene Bartow left UCLA, J. D. Morgan needed a to find a replacement. Morgan appealed to Cunningham's emotions and told him that UCLA—his alma mater—needed him now more than ever. After working for the UCLA Alumni Association for two years, Cunningham missed the players, the competition, and the games. In two seasons as head coach, he won fifty-eight games and lost only eight, never by more than four points. The Bruins won two conference championships, though they failed to reach the Final Four. Equally important, Cunningham had won the full support of the alumni. So it stunned the UCLA community when, after just two seasons, Cunningham called it quits. Spending all of his free time on the road scouting and recruiting young athletes in one gym or another made him miserable when he really just wanted to be with his family. Coaching, he decided, was too demanding of his time and energy, and it really was not much fun.[35]

After Cunningham resigned, Morgan hired Larry Brown, who had recently departed from the Denver Nuggets. Morgan promised to do everything he could to help Brown succeed, and in return, he asked him to accomplish two things: "get Sam Gilbert out of the program and make sure you win." In the previous two years, Gilbert had expanded his role in the program, helping Gary Cunningham recruit. Cunningham made Gilbert feel even more important by soliciting his help, something John Wooden and Gene Bartow never did. It made Gilbert feel like the program actually needed him, boosting his already large ego. Brown, on the other hand, preferred that the players come to him with their problems and stay away from Gilbert. Although he never directly confronted Gilbert, Brown advised his players not to get involved with him, which only antagonized the Godfather. "I feared this guy would tear down the program if I fought him," Brown said, "so I tried to tolerate him." Over the next two seasons, the tension between the coach and booster became "very ugly and uncomfortable." Gilbert told a journalist that he could cut off Brown's testicles, and "he wouldn't know it until he pulled his pants down."[36]

After just two seasons, including a loss to Louisville in the 1980 national championship, Brown quit his job at UCLA. The fans unfairly criticized him, he thought, and certainly did not appreciate him. Brown claimed that the "people on the periphery" made his job far more difficult. They complained that he was not like Cunningham or Wooden. When the New Jersey Nets asked him if he was interested in returning to the pros and making more than five times his UCLA salary, Brown departed Westwood. Since Wooden retired in 1975, UCLA had hired three coaches, and none stayed for more than two seasons. For years, UCLA symbolized unity, consistency, and excellence, but the head basketball coach's revolving office door had diminished the program's prestige.[37]

For sixteen years, one man hired the coaches at UCLA. Had J. D. Morgan been around for Larry Brown's second season, perhaps he would have stayed longer. In October 1979, hypertension and heart problems forced him to retire early, and Brown lost his greatest supporter. On December 16, 1980, a year after open-heart surgery, Morgan passed away, leaving behind a legacy of unprecedented success and a model athletic department. Before he took over as athletic director in 1963, UCLA rarely won championships in any sport, save for Morgan's tennis teams. But during his tenure as athletic director, Morgan built UCLA into the "Athens of Athletics." Under his leadership, UCLA dominated the national sports competition, winning an astounding thirty NCAA championships—more than any other university in the country. The Bruins won ten titles in basketball, seven in volleyball, six in tennis, four in track and field, and three in water polo, and the football team played in two Rose Bowls.[38]

If John Wooden was the chief executive of the UCLA dynasty, Morgan was its architect. Morgan was a power broker, vibrant, forceful, and sometimes arrogant. He was an astute businessman and a visionary, responsible for the expansion of UCLA's athletic facilities, the construction of Pauley Pavilion, and quadrupling the athletic department's income from radio and television. In many ways, Morgan was a central figure in college basketball's commercial growth. From 1968 to 1974, he served as an influential member of the NCAA Basketball Committee, which managed the tournament's budget, selected game sites, and approved television contracts. He helped the NCAA Tournament sign a lucrative long-term contract with NBC and negotiated network television deals for UCLA. Wooden may have won the games, but it was Morgan who made UCLA the most visible basketball program in the country.[39]

After Morgan retired, his former assistant, Robert Fischer, took over the athletic department and hired Larry Farmer as UCLA's new basketball coach. For more than a decade, since he joined the Bruins as a freshman player in 1970, Farmer had been a constant figure in the program. As a varsity forward and two-year starter, Farmer played on the most successful Bruins teams of the dynasty, winning eighty-nine games and losing only one. Before Fischer named him head coach, he worked diligently as an assistant under Gene Bartow, Gary Cunningham, and Larry Brown. At thirty years old, Farmer was the youngest head basketball coach in UCLA history and its first African American at the position, though no one seemed to notice. He was extremely likable, gregarious, and popular with the press, fans, and alumni. Although he had never been a head coach, UCLA boosters were pleased with his selection because Farmer was not an outsider like Bartow or Brown. "To them," he said, "I *am* UCLA."[40]

No one was happier that Farmer got the job than Sam Gilbert. The two were incredibly close, like family, really. As an eighteen-year-old freshman living far away from his Denver home, Farmer could not make it back to his parents' house for Thanksgiving dinner, so he ate all alone at Hamburger Hamlet. After Gilbert heard about it, he promised that it would never happen again to Farmer or any other out-of-state player. Farmer never forgot his generosity. Gilbert offered him personal and professional advice and, in return, gained unwavering loyalty from one of his favorite players. After Farmer gave his first championship ring to his father, he offered his second to Gilbert, figuring he would win a third and keep it for himself. That ring was more than an emblem of their bond. It was a sign of respect to the Godfather, signifying the depths of his reach in the program. Here was Gilbert, an outsider, a booster, not an official member of the university, who owned a championship ring. When he wore that ring, it was his way of telling the world, "I am important. I am UCLA, too."[41]

By the time Farmer became UCLA's head coach in March 1981, Gilbert's influence among the players had waned considerably. Public suspicions and negative attention forced Gilbert to withdraw from the program. Out of all the players on Farmer's team, only one senior spent any time with Gilbert. The freshmen did not even know him, but that hardly mattered. In April the NCAA informed UCLA that they were investigating Gilbert and the basketball program. It was time to pay for past sins. The NCAA focused its attention on the period from 1977 to 1981. Under its enforcement code, the governing body could not investigate the Wooden years because of a four-year statute of limitations, unless there was information that indicated "a pattern of willful violations on the part of the institution or the individual involved." Apparently, Gilbert's news clippings, Bill Walton's comments in

Jack Scott's book, and Brent Clark's investigation did not show any previous pattern of violations. In December, just as Farmer started to make his imprint on the program, the NCAA announced that UCLA had been placed on probation for two years, prohibited from participating in any postseason tournament for the 1981–82 season, and ordered to return its second-place trophy from the 1980 NCAA Tournament.[42]

The NCAA charged UCLA with nine total violations, citing two unnamed "representatives" who were responsible for giving athletes rent reductions, cash payments, free use of cars, and paid lodging and meals for recruits and their families. One of these representatives cosigned a promissory note so that a player could finance the purchase of a car. According to the report, UCLA's violations involved two enrolled players and two prospective recruits. At various times, an assistant coach purchased meals for recruits and their parents and loaned a car to a recruit. As a result of the NCAA's investigation, UCLA was instructed to "disassociate" Gilbert "from participating in any recruiting activities," which meant that Farmer had to ban his friend from the program. Farmer immediately defended Gilbert: "For over a decade, I've seen him do so many good things for student-athletes. I believe to single him out is unfair."[43]

Although the NCAA did not name Gilbert as one of the "representatives" in its report, an investigative journalist from the *Los Angeles Times* confirmed that he was a guilty party. When the writer visited Gilbert's office, the famed booster denied any involvement. He even tried to convince the *Times* reporter that he was innocent by putting his wife, Rose, on speakerphone, but she accidentally revealed that her husband had "committed a few violations." Sam quickly interrupted her, saying, "I had some kids over for dinner." Gilbert suggested that having players over for Thanksgiving should not be a violation of NCAA rules, but if it was, he promised not to do it again.[44]

Gilbert was not the only one who had UCLA athletes over for Thanksgiving dinner. John Wooden admitted that he also had players at his house during the holidays. He understood that it was "technically" against the rules, but he could not allow his players to be alone on Thanksgiving or Christmas. If the NCAA punished him for it, he would have given his "last cent to fight it all the way," and, he said, "I would have won." He also admitted that he broke a few other rules when he was the coach, violations he deemed "minor." Wooden bailed players out of jail and even paid rent for a married player whose wife was ill in the hospital. He did not do these things to gain a competitive advantage or persuade a recruit to sign with UCLA. He acted because he thought that it was the right thing to do. He never solicited the help of a booster to recruit a player, nor would he have tolerated cash payments to his players. Besides, he said, the NCAA's investigation had found only "inconsequential" violations—violations that occurred after he left the program. "If there's nothing worse than what they came up with," Wooden commented, "then there's no great problem."[45]

But there was a problem. Two reporters from the *Los Angeles Times,* Mike Littwin and Alan Greenberg, were unsatisfied with the NCAA's investigation and decided to conduct one of their own, questioning forty-five players, coaches, and boosters who were involved with the UCLA basketball program dating back to Wooden's years as head coach. According to Littwin and Greenberg, Gilbert acted as "a one-man clearing house" during the dynasty, helping "players and their families receive goods and services usually at big discounts and sometimes no cost." He paid for players' airline tickets, bought and sold their season tickets well above face value so that they could use the money to purchase cars, and arranged for Lew Alcindor to live in an Encino guesthouse at little or no cost. The most shocking revelation was that Gilbert arranged and paid for abortions for players' girlfriends. According to Lucius Allen, this happened often. "If a ballplayer impregnated someone, there was always a hospital available," Allen said. "I never paid for it."[46]

The *Los Angeles Times* story demonstrated beyond a shadow of a doubt that at the height of Wooden's coaching career, a culture of corruption pervaded the basketball program. UCLA's most important players admitted that they had received improper benefits and gifts. Many of them had come to UCLA imagining that after playing for the Bruins, they would play in the pros. They figured that they would win multiple national championships in front of sell-out crowds and on national television and benefit not only from Wooden's teaching, but also from Gilbert's connections with professional teams. By the late 1960s, Gilbert was well known for negotiating contracts for numerous UCLA players and helping them fulfill their professional aspirations.

And before players turned pro, he made sure that they had everything they needed. In this way, Wooden and Gilbert were inextricably linked: together they made UCLA the most attractive basketball program in the country for prized recruits. "They may deny it now, and they may even mean it," Littwin and Greenberg asserted, "but the two—coach and booster—worked together. If not hand in hand, at least with the same purpose in mind: To serve the [program]. And maybe themselves."[47]

The corruption at UCLA was only a microcosm of what was happening throughout big-time college athletics. In the early 1980s, numerous newspapers and magazines published exposés on the excesses of commercialism in college sports, uncovering scandals, rampant financial abuses, and academic cheating. Investigators found numerous violations at schools all across the country, including illegal recruiting inducements, forged transcripts, slush funds, and improper benefits. In March 1982, the *New York Times* reported that, including UCLA, seventeen schools—the highest number for a single period—were on NCAA probation for rules violations, and that did not include the thirty-five other schools that the NCAA was currently investigating. NCAA officials, academics, university administrators, athletic directors, and sportswriters expressed alarm over the abuses, demanded harsher penalties, and proposed various reforms to clean up intercollegiate athletics.[48]

For at least three decades, commercialism and corruption were intertwined in the world of college basketball. In the aftermath of the 1951 point-shaving scandals, university administrators and athletic directors condemned Madison Square Garden and New York City as a hive of bribery and vice, though subsidizing college players had occurred in the Midwest and on the West Coast as well. In response, university presidents and athletic directors avoided the city arenas—at least for a little while—and moved to keep college basketball on campus. In the late 1960s and 1970s, many universities and colleges built large campus basketball arenas. Thus, a cycle of commercialism and corruption evolved: to pay for these arenas, the schools needed sellout crowds; to attract sellout crowds, they had to field winning teams; to field winning teams, some relied on boosters and provided recruits with extra benefits. At the same time, the popularity of college basketball grew, as did the potential revenues from television, which created a greater incentive for coaches and athletic directors to produce winning teams and cut corners.[49]

For all the outrage against the abuses in big-time college sports, calls for athletic reform and stiff penalties failed to change a culture of boosterism on college campuses. At UCLA, no one was truly held accountable for breaking NCAA rules: J. D. Morgan had died, John Wooden had retired, and Gene Bartow, Gary Cunningham, and Larry Brown had all moved on. The whole system depended on athletic department leaders and university administrators policing their own programs, but in the case of UCLA and so many others, everyone involved with the basketball program failed to act. Charles Young maintains that although Morgan asked Gilbert to stay away from the program, he could not push the Godfather too hard. "J. D. Morgan, at least, felt Sam was somebody you didn't want to cross," Young said. "And by that I mean, J. D. Morgan, who was fearless, felt his life might be in danger" if he challenged Gilbert.[50]

After the NCAA's investigation, UCLA barred Gilbert from the basketball program, but he refused to accept his banishment. In 1985 Gilbert paid a security deposit and rent for Carl Pitts, a UCLA basketball recruit. When athletic director Peter Dalis learned about it, he immediately turned him in and informed the NCAA that Gilbert had acted alone. Two years later, the NCAA took away two basketball scholarships for the 1988–89 season and again ordered UCLA to sever ties with Gilbert. But the damage was already done. He had left an indelible black mark on the UCLA dynasty.

On November 24, 1987, federal marshals surrounded Gilbert's house, intending to arrest him for laundering money in a thirty-six-million-dollar international drug-smuggling scheme that began in 1975. The news came as a major shock to former UCLA players who thought that they knew him. When the marshals arrived on Gilbert's doorstep, they were surprised to find that he was not home. He had died three days earlier at age seventy-four after battling cancer and heart disease. "It's a tragic thing," Larry Farmer said when he learned about the charges. "He always had great respect for the law. It's just a shame that he's not here to defend himself."[51]

○

Few commentators ever asked John Wooden to defend the way he dealt with Gilbert. In retirement he remained a popular figure in American culture, celebrated for his leadership and moral values. He conducted coaching clinics, provided commentary during college basketball telecasts, answered piles of fan mail, gave frequent interviews, spoke with students and business groups, and made annual appearances at the Final Four. For thirty-seven years, the Woodens attended the Final Four together, but by 1984, Nell had become terminally ill, and John feared that the only woman he had ever loved might not live much longer. That year, at the Final Four in Seattle, the elderly Wooden pushed his wife around in a wheelchair so she could visit with friends. It was the last thing Nell did that she really enjoyed. Sportswriter John Feinstein remembered that late one night, as Wooden wheeled his wife across a hotel lobby, someone started to clap. Then another person joined in, and soon the entire hotel lobby echoed with applause. It was like a scene from an old Hollywood movie. There were no wild cheers, "just warm applause and quite a few tears," Feinstein recalled. Before they reached the elevator, Wooden stopped and turned Nell around so that she could face the crowd. They both waved and nodded in gratitude. It was the last time they were seen together at the Final Four.[52]

After fifty-three years of marriage, Nell died on March 21, 1985. When she passed away, Wooden refused to return to the Final Four without her. It would be too painful, he said. He lived reclusively and turned away friends and former players who wanted to visit him. Inconsolable and clearly depressed, his friends and family were extremely worried about his will to go on. For a few years, he slept on top of the bed covers, so as not to disturb Nell's side. On the twenty-first of every month, he penned a love letter to Nell, crisply folded it, and neatly placed it on a stack tied with yellow ribbon atop her pillow. In time, the love of friends, family, and former players convinced him that his life was worth living. In 1995 Wooden finally returned to the Final Four in Seattle, where he watched UCLA win its first national title since he retired.[53]

Wooden was pleased to see the Bruins win the championship, but he disapproved of the excessive commercialism in college basketball. When he started coaching in the late 1940s, most schools played basketball in small gyms that seated about thirty-five-hundred people. By the 1970s, college teams played in nineteen-thousand-seat arenas designed to attract blue-chip prospects and national television cameras. Pete Newell, who began coaching college basketball at the same time as Wooden, said, "When I was young, college basketball was an extension of the college itself. Now it is a piece of some television network."[54]

Television drove college basketball's commercial boom. In the twenty years since Wooden retired, the NCAA Tournament had evolved into a cultural phenomenon known as "March Madness," a sixty-four-team, three-week-long, billion-dollar mass-media event. The tournament's growth in popularity and consistently high ratings made March Madness a profitable enterprise for the participating schools, the NCAA, and CBS. In 1979 the NCAA Tournament fielded forty teams. Over the next six years, it expanded twice, to forty-eight teams in 1980 and sixty-four teams in 1985. The expansion of the tournament enhanced college basketball's cultural significance. By the early 1980s, many sports fans considered the NCAA Tournament the greatest sporting event in America, rivaling professional baseball's World Series and professional football's Super Bowl in media attention.[55]

Since the 1970s, during every five-year period, television revenues from the tournament more than doubled. In 1979 the TV rights fees were $5.2 million; they doubled in 1980. In 1982, when CBS outbid NBC for the tournament, the price for the television rights soared to $48 million. By 1985 the television fees doubled again, to $96 million. In 1991 CBS paid $1 billion to televise the NCAA Tournament for seven years. Three years later, the network signed the biggest sports contract in television history, paying more than $1.7 billion for the rights to the Final Four through 2002.[56]

Television changed not only the way people watched college basketball, but also the way coaches ran their programs. When Wooden first arrived at UCLA, most of the players on the team were from California. But during the sixties, as television expanded its coverage of college basketball, and UCLA in particular, Wooden and his assistants lured outstanding out-of-state prospects, including Lew Alcindor, who proved that one extraordinary recruit could fundamentally change a program's fortunes. With Alcindor, UCLA dominated the sport and attracted greater network television exposure than any other program. Wooden was not the first coach to recruit out-of-state players, but his unprecedented success in this regard proved the benefits of the practice. At the same time, the top recruits dreamed of signing with the pros after college, and the best way to capture the attention of professional executives was to play extremely well, and often, on national television. Thus, it was during the dynasty that the role of coaches fundamentally changed. In the modern era of television, athletic directors were less concerned about hiring a coach for his character and teaching ability. Instead, athletic directors asked more important questions of a potential coach: Can he recruit? Can he sell the program? Can he build an entertaining team fit for television?[57]

After leaving the coaching profession, Wooden complained that television was "the worst thing that's happened to college basketball." Like many critics of the sport, Wooden argued that the cameras promoted showmanship, grandstanding, and individualism. He groaned that too many players were overly concerned with entertaining the crowd, making news highlights, and gaining personal attention. Even the coaches had become performers, he lamented, acting out on the sidelines for the cameras. Wooden advocated banning the dunk, an ironic suggestion given his disapproval of the "Alcindor Rule" in 1967. He also argued that the networks had too much control over scheduling and that no team should play on Sundays. Worst of all, television encouraged greedy athletic directors, coaches, and university presidents "to permit things they would otherwise not permit," all for the sake of winning, playing in the NCAA Tournament, and collecting a large paycheck, a hypocritical complaint given the culture of boosterism during the UCLA dynasty. "The impact of commercialism, of TV money is devious," he lectured in 1990. "Too many presidents today are nothing more than fundraisers [who] see athletics as a tool for tapping alumni treasure."[58]

To combat this corruption of educational values, he proposed that the NCAA allow every school to play in the tournament—just like the Indiana high school tournament he grew up watching and played in. As a counterbalance to the financial disparity between the teams that reached the Final Four and those that did not, he suggested a more equitable distribution of revenues among all the schools in the tournament. Wooden's complaints about commercialism and corruption in college basketball reflected a nostalgia for a more innocent time when coaches cared more about character than victory, before television transformed the sport into a big business, when winning a championship was a reason to celebrate school pride, not school profits.[59]

In his analysis, Wooden failed to acknowledge how the UCLA dynasty shaped the sport's culture of commercialism. In 1968, when J. D. Morgan asked him about playing "the Game of the Century" against Houston in the Astrodome, Wooden thought that it would turn college basketball into "a farce." Ultimately, he agreed to play the game because Morgan convinced him that the money from television and the gate would help finance UCLA's entire athletic department and promote college basketball, which it did. After the game, athletic directors realized that basketball's television dollars could help support nonrevenue sports in a way that football had done almost exclusively in the past. And most important, it demonstrated how television networks would pay top dollar to showcase the best teams with the biggest stars, which only further intensified the importance of recruiting and the illicit subsidization of athletes. If the dynasty accomplished anything beyond establishing a new standard of success, then, it proved that universities, corporations, and the NCAA could make major money from college basketball.[60]

Wooden had always known that college basketball was more than a game; it was a business, and UCLA played a central role in building that business. The dynasty's greatest achievement was the way that Wooden's teams made college basketball matter in a way that it had not previously. Before the dynasty, college basketball remained a regional sport, followed by local fans and media. In the process of winning ten national championships in twelve seasons, UCLA created a great American success story, compelling wider media attention and a national audience for college basketball.

Looking back at the dynasty, UCLA's achievements seem more impressive, considering that since Wooden retired in 1975, no other coach or school has come close to approaching UCLA's records. Duke's Mike Kryzewski has won four national championships, six fewer than Wooden. Building a dynasty now, in an era of competitive parity, seems almost impossible for coaches like Kryzewski. Perhaps the greatest challenge for contemporary coaches is convincing the best players to turn down a multimillion-dollar NBA contract and stay in college. None of Wooden's All-Americans ever left UCLA early for the pros; today, the NBA's top draft picks rarely play for four years in college. Critics claim that it was easier for Wooden to win the championship because his teams had to win only four games most years; now a championship team has to play six games. Those detractors have missed the point: the number of wins matters less than the times a team can lose: none. Under the incredible pressure of a single-elimination tournament, Wooden's teams won thirty-eight consecutive playoff games. Equally remarkable, in ten national championship appearances, Wooden never lost.

Wooden's success represents the greatest achievement in the history of coaching. In the pantheon of basketball coaches, only Red Auerbach and Phil Jackson compare to Wooden. Auerbach built a dynasty with the Boston Celtics, winning nine championships, including eight in a row from 1959 to 1966. Jackson, who has surpassed both Auerbach and Wooden with eleven championships, never won more than three consecutive titles, though he did it with two different teams, the Chicago Bulls and the Los Angeles Lakers. Yet unlike these two professional coaches, Wooden never benefited from coaching any varsity player for more than three years. Throughout the dynasty, Wooden lost players to graduation, leaving him to rebuild the foundation of the program over and over again. Walt Hazzard, Gail Goodrich, Lew Alcindor, Sidney Wicks, Curtis Rowe, Bill Walton, Keith Wilkes, and so many others came and went. And through it all there was one constant: John Wooden.

O

In our collective memory, John Wooden has been remembered as the patron saint of college basketball, revered as a virtuous achiever, sage, self-made man, and American icon. Many consider him the greatest coach in the history of American sports. Since his retirement more than three decades ago, Wooden's legend has grown in memory. In the popular culture, adulators have constructed a sanitized version of UCLA's past, a narrative that excludes or minimizes Sam Gilbert's presence in the program. The mythmaking surrounding Wooden's image originated during the 1960s and persisted long after he retired. In 1974 Bill Libby captured the mythical image of Wooden in *The Walton Gang*. According to Libby, the "brilliant" and "scholarly" coach had "beaten back and beaten down all his rivals without breaking any rules, without once swearing, without asking for any favors," and, most important, "without compromising his principles."[61]

Much of what Libby wrote about Wooden was true. Yet this image overwhelms the paradoxes of the man. Wooden compromised his principles when he allowed Gilbert to infect his program. He may not have sought Gilbert's help, but he failed to terminate the illicit relationship between the booster and his players. Over the years, many sportswriters and supporters have defended Wooden. Columnist Rick Reilly, who once wrote that Wooden was the best man he had ever known, claimed that he would "punch any man in the mouth who says Wooden knew" about Gilbert's crooked deals with UCLA players. According to Reilly, Wooden "couldn't have known it or he would have stopped it. He'd have sooner cut off his own hand than cheat."[62]

Reilly was right about one thing: Wooden would never have intentionally cheated. In his mind, he did all that he could to rid the program of Gilbert's corrupt influence by warning his players to avoid Papa Sam. Wooden maintained a clear conscience because he never really believed that he had actually cheated. Reilly and other apologists have refused to accept the contradictions of Wooden's character. They have failed to recognize that Wooden—a coach who commanded the full respect of his players, enforced rules for everything, distrusted outsiders, and never ceded his authority—knowingly permitted an outsider to undermine his authority, jeopardize the integrity of his program, and tarnish his reputation. In his failure to effectively confront Gilbert, Wooden surrendered his moral authority and invited legitimate questions about the veracity of his leadership.[63]

None of this changes the fact that Wooden was a wonderful person who touched countless people with his warmth, kindness, and generosity. Nor does it diminish the fact that he was an incredible coach and an even better teacher. But the whole man was a flawed man. Wooden was a man of virtue and foibles, extraordinary in some respects and ordinary in others. He exemplified exceptional drive, discipline, and intelligence. And although he never explicitly talked about winning, competition consumed him and sometimes impaired his ability to make decisions that conformed to his moral values. Yet what has and will persist about Wooden is a legacy of principles.

At his core, Wooden was a man who followed principles as goals for living; sometimes he lived up to those principles, and sometimes he did not.

People often asked him how he wanted to be remembered. He preferred that they would think of him as a teacher, family man, and devout Christian. Was he a saint or a pietist? A hero or a hypocrite? Perhaps Wooden had the answer. "You see," he said, "the truth is somewhere in between. It's wrong to turn people into idols. But it's wrong to lose hope, to believe that we can't find good examples to inspire us. We need role models. Maybe role models are getting harder to find these days. That doesn't mean that there aren't any worth finding."[64]

Notes

Abbreviations

Byers Papers	Walter Byers Papers, NCAA Archives, Indianapolis
CD	*Chicago Defender*
CDN	*Chicago Daily News*
CE	*California Eagle*
CEY	Charles E. Young Papers, UCLA Archives
Clark Testimony,	*NCAA Enforcement Program: Hearings before the*
NCAA Hearings	*Subcommittee on Oversight and Investigations of the House Committee on Interstate and Foreign Commerce,* 95th Cong., 2nd sess., 1978
CSM	*Christian Science Monitor*
CST	*Chicago Sun-Times*
CT	*Chicago Tribune*
DB	*Daily Bruin*
DC	*Daily Californian* (Berkeley student newspaper)
FDM	Franklin D. Murphy Papers, UCLA Archives
HC	*Houston Chronicle*
HI	*Houston Informer*
KCS	*Kansas City Star*
LAE	*Los Angeles Examiner*
LAFP	*Los Angeles Free Press*
LAHE	*Los Angeles Herald-Examiner*
LAS	*Los Angeles Sentinel*
LAT	*Los Angeles Times*
LCJ	*Louisville (Ky.) Courier Journal*
LH	*Lexington (Ky.) Herald*

MCA	Memphis Commercial Appeal
NYAN	New York Amsterdam News
NYDN	New York Daily News
NYT	New York Times
PI	Philadelphia Inquirer
PT	Philadelphia Tribune
RNO	Raleigh (N.C.) News and Observer
SBT	South Bend (Ind.) Tribune
SEP	Saturday Evening Post
SFC	San Francisco Chronicle
SI	Sports Illustrated
SJMN	San Jose (Calif.) Mercury News
SN	Sporting News
SPD	St. Louis Post-Dispatch
UCLA OHC	Oral History Collection, Department of Special Collections, UCLA
WP	Washington Post

Preface

1. "SN Conversation: John Wooden," *SN,* January 5, 2009, 41–46; Alexander Wolff, "Remembering the Wizard," *SI,* June 14, 2010, 32–37. I am grateful that Swen Nater generously allowed me to use his poem "Yonder."

2. Ramona Shelburne, "Abdul-Jabbar Remembers Wooden," *ESPNLosAngeles .com,* June 6, 2010.

3. Ibid.

4. *Torrance (Calif.) Daily Breeze,* June 27, 2010.

5. *Orange County Register,* June 27, 2010.

6. *NYT,* June 6, 2010; Andy Hill, phone interview with the author, March 20, 2011.

7. Surprisingly, there is no scholarly monograph on the history of college basketball, its greatest dynasty, or its preeminent coaching icon. My work aims to fill these gaps in the literature.

8. On the Athletic Revolution, see Jack Scott, *The Athletic Revolution* (New York: Free Press, 1971); and David Zang, *SportsWars: Athletes in the Age of Aquarius* (Fayetteville: University of Arkansas Press, 2001).

Chapter 1. Goodness! Gracious! Sakes Alive!

1. Dwight Chapin and Jeff Prugh, *The Wizard of Westwood: Coach John Wooden and His UCLA Bruins* (Boston: Houghton Mifflin, 1973), 79–80; Earl Warren, "California's Biggest Headache," *SEP,* August 14, 1948, 72. For a cultural history of Route 66,

see Arthur Krim, *Route 66: Iconography of the American Highway* (Santa Fe, N.M.: Center for American Places, 2005).

2. John Wooden with Jack Tobin, *They Call Me Coach* (Waco, Tex.: Word Books, 1972), 77.

3. Chapin and Prugh, *Wizard of Westwood*, 84–90; *UCLA Basketball Media Guide,* 1948–49, 4; John Wooden with Steve Jamison, *My Personal Best: Life Lessons from an All-American Journey* (New York: McGraw-Hill, 2004), 94–96; H. Anthony Medley, *UCLA Basketball: The Real Story* (Los Angeles: Galant Press, 1972), 2–3; *DB,* December 3, 1948; "Wooden and Staff Greet 1948 Basketball Aspirants," *UCLA Magazine,* November 1948, 14; Jerry Weiner, "John Wooden: The Hoosier Hotshot," *UCLA Magazine,* December 1948, 13.

4. Wooden with Tobin, *They Call Me Coach,* 22; Wooden with Jamison, *My Personal Best,* 6–7.

5. Wooden with Tobin, *They Call Me Coach,* 22–29; Wooden with Jamison, *My Personal Best,* 7.

6. Wooden with Jamison, *My Personal Best,* 3, 49.

7. Ibid., 17–19; John Wooden and Jay Carty, *Coach Wooden's Pyramid of Success: Building Blocks for a Better Life* (Ventura, Calif.: Regal Books, 2005), 130. John Wooden later added a seventh point to his father's creed: pray for guidance.

8. Wooden with Tobin, *They Call Me Coach,* 22–23.

9. Wooden with Jamison, *My Personal Best,* 1; John Wooden with Steve Jamison, *The Essential Wooden: A Lifetime of Lessons and Leadership* (New York: McGraw-Hill, 2007), 32. On manhood during the nineteenth and twentieth centuries, see E. Anthony Rotundo, *American Manhood: Transformations in Masculinity from the Revolution to the Modern Era* (New York: Basic Books, 1993); and Michael Kimmel, *Manhood in America: A Cultural History* (New York: Free Press, 1996). On Victorian values, see Daniel Walker Howe, ed., *Victorian America* (Philadelphia: University of Philadelphia Press, 1976); and Thomas J. Schlereth, *Victorian America: Transformations in Everyday Life, 1876–1915* (New York: HarperCollins, 1991).

10. Norman Jones, *Growing Up in Indiana: The Culture & Hoosier Hysteria Revisited* (Bloomington, Ind.: Author House, 2005), 6; Philip M. Hoose, *Hoosiers: The Fabulous Life of Indiana,* 2nd ed. (Indianapolis: Guild Press of Indiana, 1995), 88.

11. Bob Williams, *Hoosier Hysteria! Indiana High School Basketball* (South Bend, Ind.: Hardwood Press, 1997), 309–10.

12. Wooden with Tobin, *They Call Me Coach,* 29, 34; Hoose, *Hoosiers,* 98; Joanne Raetz Stuttgen, *Martinsville: A Pictorial History* (St. Louis: G. Bradley, 1995), 8–9, 24–25, 58, 88; Williams, *Hoosier Hysteria!,* 204; David G. Martin, "Gymnasium or Coliseum? Basketball, Education, and Community Impulse in Indiana in the Early Twentieth Century," in *Hoosier Schools: Past and Present,* edited by William J. Reese (Bloomington: Indiana University Press, 1998), 140–41.

13. *Indianapolis News,* March 21, 1927, March 19, 1928; *Indianapolis Star,* March 20, 1927; *The Debris* (Purdue University yearbook), 1931, 136; *Lafayette Journal and Courier,* December 15, 30, 1930, January 6, 1932; *Purdue Exponent,* December 4, 1929,

December 19, 1931, February 7, 1932; *Chicago Daily Tribune,* December 20, 1929, March 11, 1932.

14. Neville L. Johnson, *The John Wooden Pyramid of Success,* 2nd ed. (Los Angeles: Cool Titles, 2004), 26.

15. John Wooden and Steve Jamison, *Wooden on Leadership* (New York: McGraw-Hill, 2005), 41–43; "Ward Lewis Lambert Memorial" press release, ca. January 1958, Ward Lambert file, Purdue University Sports Information Office Records; Alan R. Karpick, *Boilermaker Basketball: Great Purdue Teams and Players* (Chicago: Bonus Books, 1989), 19; Ward L. Lambert, *Practical Basketball* (Chicago: Athletic Journal, 1932), 72, 125–27, 226–27, 238. On muscular Christianity and the origins of basketball, see Clifford Putney, *Muscular Christianity: Manhood and Sports in Protestant America, 1880–1920* (Cambridge, Mass.: Harvard University Press, 2001); Elmer L. Johnson, *The History of YMCA Physical Education* (Chicago: Association Press, 1979); William J. Baker, *Playing with God: Religion and Modern Sport* (Cambridge, Mass.: Harvard University Press, 2007); James Naismith, *Basketball: Its Origins and Development* (1941; reprint, Lincoln: University of Nebraska Press, 1996).

16. Wooden with Tobin, *They Call Me Coach,* 49–53; Wooden and Jamison, *Wooden on Leadership,* 23, 41–43, 157–58; Lambert, *Practical Basketball,* 3, 130–44, 185, 231–38.

17. Wooden with Tobin, *They Call Me Coach,* 56–58; Wooden with Jamison, *My Personal Best,* 51–58.

18. Wooden with Tobin, *They Call Me Coach,* 58, 69–74; N. Johnson, *Wooden Pyramid of Success,* 28.

19. *Terre Haute Tribune,* March 11, 1948; Wooden with Tobin, *They Call Me Coach,* 75–77.

20. *Indiana Statesman,* April 22, 1948; Wooden with Jamison, *My Personal Best,* 80–83; Wooden with Tobin, *They Call Me Coach,* 76–77; Chapin and Prugh, *Wizard of Westwood,* 71–72.

21. Gerald D. Nash, *The American West Transformed: The Impact of the Second World War* (Bloomington: Indiana University Press, 1985), 17–26, 56–74; Eric Avila, *Popular Culture in the Age of White Flight: Fear and Fantasy in Suburban Los Angeles* (Berkeley and Los Angeles: University of California Press, 2006), 29; Arthur C. Verge, "The Impact of the Second World War on Los Angeles," *Pacific Historical Review* 63 (August 1994): 289–314; *LAT,* December 18, 1945; Lisa McGirr, *Suburban Warriors: The Origins of the New American Right* (Princeton, N.J.: Princeton University Press, 2001), 25–26.

22. On the GI Bill and higher education, see Diane Ravitch, *The Troubled Crusade: American Education, 1945–1980* (New York: Basic Books, 1983), 12–15; Kurt Edward Kemper, "Reformers in the Marketplace of Ideas: Student Activism and American Democracy in Cold War Los Angeles" (Ph.D. diss., Louisiana State University, 2000), 11, 33; Andrew Hamilton and John B. Jackson, *UCLA on the Move during Fifty Golden Years, 1919–1969* (Los Angeles: Ward Ritchie Press, 1969), viii, 3, 107, 114–27; Andrew Hamilton, "California: The World's Largest University," *Coronet,*

May 1949, 36–40; "Boom at U.C.L.A.," *Newsweek,* February 9, 1953, 74; Martin Mayer, "University in the Sun," *Esquire,* November 1961, 113–14; *Southern Campus* (UCLA student yearbook), 1950, 1953.

23. *General Catalogue: Departments at Los Angeles, Fall and Spring Semester, 1960–1961* (University of California–Los Angeles, July 1, 1960), 2C.

24. Medley, *UCLA Basketball,* 3–4; Wooden with Jamison, *My Personal Best,* 107–8; *DB,* November 2, 30, 1948, February 7, 25, 1949; *LAT,* November 29, 1948, March 4, 1949, March 1, 1950, January 30, March 5, 1952. I have drawn much of Wooden's early coaching philosophy from his first published coaching article. See John R. Wooden, "U.C.L.A.'s Coaching Pattern," *Scholastic Coach,* December 1955, 12–14, 39–41.

25. Throughout the 1950s, coaches emphasized organization and efficiency. See Dale Hanks, "Organization Begins with the Coach," *Scholastic Coach,* October 1959, 66–68; Arthur J. Gallon, "For More Efficient Coaching a Weekly Chart," *Athletic Journal,* November 1956, 13, 37; Wooden, "U.C.L.A.'s Coaching Pattern," 13–14.

26. Wooden with Tobin, *They Call Me Coach,* 105–9; Wooden and Jamison, *Wooden on Leadership,* 153–62; 256; Wooden with Jamison, *My Personal Best,* 107–10; John R. Wooden, *Practical Modern Basketball* (New York: Ronald Press, 1966), 21–37; Marv Dunphy, "John Wooden: The Coaching Process" (Ph.D. diss., Brigham Young University, 1981), 103–19; Ronald Gallimore and Roland Tharp, "What a Coach Can Teach a Teacher, 1975–2004: Reflections and Reanalysis of John Wooden's Teaching Practices," *Sport Psychologist* 18 (2004): 119–37; Swen Nater and Ronald Gallimore, *You Haven't Taught until They Have Learned: John Wooden's Teaching Principles and Practices* (Morgantown, W.Va.: Fitness Information Technology, 2006), 5–8, 91–97.

27. Wooden, *Practical Modern Basketball,* 37, 44, 53–55.

28. Wooden with Tobin, *They Call Me Coach,* 106; Wooden with Jamison, *My Personal Best,* 106; John Wooden with Steve Jamison, *Wooden: A Lifetime of Observations and Reflections On and Off the Court* (Lincolnwood, Ill.: Contemporary Books, 1997), 60–61.

29. *DB,* November 30, December 3, 1948; *LAT,* January 11, 1949; Bruce Jenkins, *A Good Man: The Pete Newell Story* (Berkeley, Calif.: Frog, 1999), 120.

30. Wooden, *Practical Modern Basketball,* 10; I. R. McVay, "Small Men Win for UCLA's John Wooden," *Look,* March 12, 1963, 96.

31. At the time, the PCC was divided into a Northern Division and a Southern Division. Oregon State won the Northern Division and defeated UCLA in a three-game tournament for the conference title. *DB,* February 7, 25, 1949, February 7, 14, March 3, 1950; *LAT,* January 12, 1950.

32. *LAT,* March 6, 1950; "Baseball: The Gold Rush West," *Newsweek,* September 2, 1957, 84; Roland Lazenby, *The Show: The Inside Story of the Spectacular Los Angeles Lakers in the Words of Those Who Lived It* (New York: McGraw-Hill, 2006), 68–71. On the Dodgers' relocation to California, see Neil J. Sullivan, *The Dodgers Move West* (New York: Oxford University Press, 1989).

33. Wooden with Jamison, *My Personal Best,* 92–93, 98–100; Chapin and Prugh,

Wizard of Westwood, 82–83; Steve Bisheff, *John Wooden: An American Treasure* (Nashville, Tenn.: Cumberland House, 2004), 29–30; *LAT,* March 3, 1950.

34. Wooden with Tobin, *They Call Me Coach,* 81–82; Wooden with Jamison, *My Personal Best,* 99–100; *DB,* March 3, 1950; *LAT,* March 3, 1950.

35. "John Wooden: New Casaba Coach," *UCLA Magazine,* May 1948, 10; *LAT,* August 28, 1951; *The Hoop* (game program, Southern California vs. UCLA), March 1, 1952; *LAT,* March 4, 5, 1952; Bob Seizer, "Sizing It Up," *The Hoop* (game program, Washington vs. UCLA), December 13, 1952; *DB,* February 7, 25, 1949, January 1, 1952; *LAT,* January 11, 1953, February 26, 1954; *Southern Campus,* 1957, 248.

36. "Cage Champs Feted at Awards Banquet," *UCLA Alumni Magazine,* May 1956, 14; James H. Madison, *Indiana through Tradition and Change: A History of the Hoosier State and Its People, 1920–1945* (Indianapolis: Indiana Historical Society, 1982), 3–7; Herbert Warren Wind, "West of the Wabash," *New Yorker,* March 22, 1969, 101. On the conservative values of Southern California, see McGirr, *Suburban Warriors;* and Darren Dochuk, *From Bible Belt to Sunbelt: Plain-Folk Religion, Grassroots Politics, and the Rise of Evangelical Conservatism* (New York: W. W. Norton, 2011).

37. Wooden with Jamison, *Essential Wooden,* 31–32.

38. Wooden with Jamison, *My Personal Best,* 84–86.

39. Wooden with Jamison, *Essential Wooden,* 37.

40. Wooden, *Practical Modern Basketball,* 13–17; Wooden with Tobin, *They Call Me Coach,* 87–92; *Oxnard Press Courier,* May 9, 1956; N. Johnson, *Wooden Pyramid of Success,* 160–70.

41. Wooden with Jamison, *My Personal Best,* 109; Wooden with Tobin, *They Call Me Coach,* 94.

42. John Wooden and Steve Jamison, *The Wisdom of Wooden: My Century On and Off the Court* (New York: McGraw-Hill, 2011), pages not listed; Judy Arlen Hilkey, *Character Is Capital: Success Manuals and Manhood in Gilded Age America* (Chapel Hill: University of North Carolina Press, 1997); Richard Weiss, *The American Myth of Success* (1969; reprint, Urbana: University of Illinois Press, 1988).

43. *LAT,* February 17, April 21, 1956.

44. Aram Goudsouzian, "The House That Russell Built: Bill Russell, the University of San Francisco, and the Winning Streak That Changed College Basketball," *California History* 84 (Fall 2007): 1–12, 19; David Halberstam, *The Fifties* (New York: Ballantine Books, 1994), 694–98; Nelson George, *Elevating the Game: Black Men and Basketball* (Lincoln: University of Nebraska Press, 1992), 107–9; Bill Russell and Taylor Branch, *Second Wind: The Memoirs of an Opinionated Man* (New York: Ballantine Books, 1979), 77–82, 93–98; *LAT,* January 13, 1955.

45. *LAT,* December 5, 1954; Goudsouzian, "House That Russell Built," 7; *LAS,* January 13, 1955, November 15, December 13, 1956, February 21, 1957, August 28, 1958; Jenkins, *Good Man,* 80–81; *CE,* January 13, 1955. In 1929 Herman Hill became USC's first black basketball player. The next black basketball player for USC was Vern Ashby, who played from 1960 to 1962.

46. Brian Urquhart, *Ralph Bunche: An American Life* (New York: W. W. Nor-

ton, 1993), 37–40; Lane Demas, "Sport History, Race, and the College Gridiron: A Southern California Turning Point," *Southern California Quarterly* 89 (Summer 2007): 169–93; Lane Demas, "On the Threshold of Broad and Rich Football Pastures: Integrated College Football at UCLA, 1938–1941," in *Horsehides, Pigskin, Oval Tracts, and Apple Pie: Essays on Sports and American Culture,* edited by Jim Vlasich (Jefferson, N.C.: McFarland, 2006), 86–103; Gregory J. Kaliss, "Everyone's All-Americans: Race, Men's College Athletics, and the Ideal of Equality" (Ph.D. diss., University of North Carolina at Chapel Hill, 2008), 86–159; *LAT,* October 9, 1939.

47. Chapin and Prugh, *Wizard of Westwood,* 90–91; Hamilton and Jackson, *UCLA on the Move,* 165; *Southern Campus,* 1950, 22; Mary Daily, "Learning from a Legacy," *UCLA Magazine,* October 1, 2006, http://www.magazine.ucla.edu/features/admissions-crisis/index7.html; William Ackerman, *My Fifty Year Love-In at UCLA* (Los Angeles: Fashion Press, 1969), 152–53; Rafer Johnson with Philip Goldberg, *The Best That I Can Be: An Autobiography* (New York: Galilee, Doubleday, 1998), 57–59, 70–72; *LAT,* August 15, 1958; Sara Boynoff, "Los Angeles: A Race Relations Success Story," *Look,* March 19, 1957, 25–29; Al Stump, "Big Man on Campus," *Sport,* July 1959, 26–28, 93–94; "Student, Leader, and Athlete," *UCLA Alumni Magazine,* February 1959, 6–8. In 1941 Kenny Washington served on the student council. Willard Johnson was elected as the second black student body president in 1956. Rafer Johnson was elected two years after him.

48. Kemper, "Reformers in the Marketplace of Ideas," 50–53; *DB,* May 20, 1955; Willie Naulls, *Levitation's View: Lessons Learned from an Extraordinary Journey,* vol. 2, *The Wooden Years* (Laguna Niguel, Calif.: Willie Naulls Ministries, 2005), 40–43, 49; N. Johnson, *Wooden Pyramid of Success,* 391–92. Moore lived in the Zeta Beta Tau house, and Naulls stayed in the Sigma Alpha Mu house. For a discussion of black-Jewish relations during the civil rights era, see Cheryl Lynn Greenberg, *Troubling the Waters: Black-Jewish Relations in the Twentieth Century* (Princeton, N.J.: Princeton University Press, 2006).

49. During the 1953–54 season, Duquesne University's Donald "Dudey" Moore became the first coach of a major college team to start three blacks: Jim Tucker, Dick Ricketts, and Sihugo Green. *Pittsburgh Courier,* January 30, 1954, February 5, 1955; *NYT,* December 29, 1953; *Baltimore Afro-American,* December 27, 1955; *LAS,* January 13, February 24, March 3, 1955; *LAT,* February 28, 1955; Goudsouzian, "House That Russell Built," 9–11.

50. *LAT,* December 31, 1955, January 17, February 3, March 1, 11, 12, 17, 1956; *LAS,* December 22, 1955, January 12, March 8, 1956; *CE,* April 5, 1956; "Here Is Morris Taft's Famed 'Hanging' Jump Shot," *UCLA Alumni Magazine,* February 1956, 14.

51. *WP,* February 4, 1957; *LAT,* March 2, May 24, 1956; Tim Cohane, "Inside the West Coast Football Scandal," *Look,* August 7, 1956, 72–80; Al Stump, "Football's Biggest Stink," *True,* October 1956, 42–43, 95–99; John R. Thelin, *Games Colleges Play: Scandal and Reform in Intercollegiate Athletics* (Baltimore: Johns Hopkins University Press, 1994), 128–47.

52. *NYT,* May 20, 1956; "The Academic Senate Report on Athletics," *UCLA Alumni Magazine,* October 1956, 20–21; "Death of a Conference," *Newsweek,* December 23, 1957, 54; *LAT,* February 15, 1959; *DB,* December 11, 16, 1957, February 8, 1960. Eventually, Washington State, Oregon, and Oregon State joined the AAWU.

53. "The Man from U.C.L.A.," *Time,* October 21, 1966, 98; Margaret Leslie Davis, *The Culture Broker: Franklin D. Murphy and the Transformation of Los Angeles* (Berkeley and Los Angeles: University of California Press, 2007), 28, 46; Franklin D. Murphy interview in N. Johnson, *Wooden Pyramid of Success,* 394; "Murphy: The Man behind the Change," *UCLA Alumni Magazine,* Fall 1966, 8.

54. *DB,* November 16, 1962, February 11, 1963; Murphy interview with David Rose, "The Right Man at the Right Time: J. D. Morgan," transcript 1984, UCLA OHC, 75–76 (hereafter Murphy interview with Rose).

55. Murphy interview with Rose, 76; Charles Young, phone interview with the author, April 28, 2011.

56. Jerry Bowles, "Dawn of an Era," *UCLA Alumni Magazine,* February–March 1963, 32–3; *LAT,* December 17, 1961; J. D. Morgan, personal résumé, September 1, 1964, J. D. Morgan Biographical File, UCLA Archives; *DB,* February 11, 1963. Morgan retired from coaching tennis in 1966.

57. Much of my description of Morgan's personality is drawn from interviews in "The Right Man at the Right Time: J. D. Morgan," UCLA OHC. See also Chapin and Prugh, *Wizard of Westwood,* 112, 247–48; Wooden interview in Dunphy, "Wooden: The Coaching Process," 135.

58. Murphy interview with Rose, 57, 77–78; *DB,* July 2, 26, 1963; Bowles, "Dawn of an Era," 33.

59. *LAT,* August 11, 1963; brochure and letter from general chairman H. R. Haldeman to "Alumnus," n.d. (ca. 1963), Box 118, Folder 243, Pauley Pavilion (1963–70), FDM; Davis, *Culture Broker,* 30, 45–49, 61, 66; *LAHE,* December 19, 1963. Pauley's donation was the largest gift in UCLA's history.

Chapter 2. The Wizard of Westwood

1. Ray Cave, "Wizards in the Land of Oz," *SI,* March 19, 1962, 62; *LAT,* February 22, 1962; Nick Peters, "The Wooden Legacy: 10 Out of 12," in *Dynasty,* edited by Joe Hoppel, Mike Nahrstedt, and Steve Zesch (St. Louis: Sporting News, 1989), 84; *PT,* April 5, 1960.

2. George, *Elevating the Game,* 142 (see chap. 1, n. 44); *DB,* March 1, 1963; *PT,* April 26, 1960; Hazzard interview in N. Johnson, *Wooden Pyramid of Success,* 355–56 (see chap. 1, n. 14).

3. Cave, "Wizards in the Land of Oz,"62; *LAS,* March 19, 1964; *LAT,* December 9, 1984.

4. "Scouting Reports," *SI,* December 9, 1963, 47–54.

5. *LAT,* March 13, 1960; Wooden with Tobin, *They Call Me Coach,* 119–21 (see chap. 1, n. 2); Wooden with Jamison, *My Personal Best,* 110–12 (see chap. 1, n. 3).

6. *LAT,* March 2, December 14, 24, 1960.

7. *LAT,* December 24, 1960; Medley, *UCLA Basketball,* 11–12 (see chap. 1, n. 3); Chapin and Prugh, *Wizard of Westwood,* 97–98 (see chap. 1, n. 1); John Green, phone interview with the author, April 19, 2011.

8. On the 1951 point-shaving scandals, see Charley Rosen, *Scandals of '51: How the Gamblers Almost Killed College Basketball* (1978; reprint, New York: Seven Stories Press, 1999); Albert J. Figone, "Gambling and College Basketball: The Scandal of 1951," *Journal of Sport History* 16 (Spring 1989): 44–61.

9. *LAE,* May 30, 1961. The Associated Negro Press covered the Lawson story. See *HI,* June 17, 1961; Young, phone interview (see chap. 1, n. 55).

10. *HI,* June 17, 1961; Chapin and Prugh, *Wizard of Westwood,* 98–99.

11. "Basketball's Malignancy: Its Prognosis and Treatment," *Scholastic Coach,* May 1961, 5, 64–65; Jimmy Breslin, "Where the Basketball Scandals Will Lead," *Sport,* December 1961, 34–37, 91–95; Jeremiah Tax, "The Facts about the Fixes," *SI,* March 27, 1961, 18–19; *DB,* April 4, 1961; "College Sports Scandals," *School and Society,* October 7, 1961, 314; Henry Steele Commager, "Give the Games Back to the Students," *New York Times Magazine,* April 16, 1961, 27.

12. Jerry Brondfield, *The UCLA Story: Basketball at Its Best* (New York: Scholastic Book Services, 1973), 32–33.

13. Wooden with Tobin, *They Call Me Coach,* 16–17; *DB,* November 16, 1961, January 11, 1963; *PT,* February 8, 1964; Cave, "Wizards in the Land of Oz," 62; Chapin and Prugh, *Wizard of Westwood,* 120.

14. *LAT,* February 22, 1962; *Daily News of Los Angeles,* December 14, 1986; Thomas McLaughlin, *Give and Go: Basketball as a Cultural Practice* (New York: State University of New York Press, 2008), 16–17; George, *Elevating the Game,* xvi–xvii, 72–76.

15. *LAT,* December 3, 10, 1961; *DB,* December 4, 1961.

16. *HI,* December 2, 1961; *DB,* November 15, 22, December 8, 1961; *CE,* November 23, 1961; *LAT,* November 20, 1961; Kurt Edward Kemper, "The Smell of Roses and the Color of Players: College Football and the Expansion of the Civil Rights Movement in the West," *Journal of Sport History* 31 (Fall 2004): 317–39.

17. Kemper, "Reformers in the Marketplace of Ideas," 104–6 (see chap. 1, n. 22); Terry H. Anderson, *The Movement and the Sixties: Protest in America from Greensboro to Wounded Knee* (New York: Oxford University Press, 1995), 43–57; Robert Weisbrot, *Freedom Bound: A History of America's Civil Rights Movement* (New York: W. W. Norton, 1990), 55–63; Clayborne Carson, *In Struggle: SNCC and the Black Awakening of the 1960s* (Cambridge, Mass.: Harvard University Press, 1981), 9–18, 31–44. The best history of the Freedom Rides is Raymond Arsenault's *Freedom Riders: 1961 and the Struggle for Racial Justice* (New York: Oxford University Press, 2006).

18. *LAS,* August 3, 1961; *DB,* September 18, October 3, 4, 1961; Kemper, "Reformers in the Marketplace of Ideas," 104; Steve McNichols, interview with Donald J. Schippers, "The Houston Freedom Ride," 1961, transcript 1964, UCLA OHC, 49–168; McNichols quoted in Arsenault, *Freedom Riders,* 389.

19. *DB,* December 14, 1961.

20. Madison, *Indiana through Tradition and Change*, 4, 7–10 (see chap. 1, n. 36); Emma Lou Thornbrough, "Breaking Racial Barriers to Public Accommodations in Indiana, 1935 to 1963," *Indiana Magazine of History* 83 (December 1987): 301–3, 320; Randy Roberts, *"But They Can't Beat Us": Oscar Robertson and the Crispus Attucks Tigers* (Champaign, Ill.: Sports Publishing, 1999), 38–42; Charles H. Martin, "The Color Line in Midwestern College Sports, 1890–1960," *Indiana Magazine of History* 98 (June 2002): 98–105.

21. John R. M. Wilson, *The History of the National Association of Intercollegiate Athletics* (Monterey, Calif.: Coaches Choice, 2005), 25–26; *NYT*, March 6, 1948; Wooden with Jamison, *My Personal Best*, 79–80; *Kansas City Call*, March 12, 19, 1948; Clarence Walker, diary, November 27, 1947. Walker referred to Jim Crow as "J. C." His son, Kevin Walker, gave me a copy of the diary.

22. *DB*, December 15, 1961, January 5, 1962; *HI*, December 23, 1961.

23. Green, phone interview; *HI*, December 30, 1961. Cincinnati's Oscar Robertson and Bradley's Chet Walker have written about discrimination in Houston during their college years. See Oscar Robertson, *The Big O: My Life, My Times, My Game* (New York: Rodale, 2005), 88–92; and Chet Walker with Chris Messenger, *Long Time Coming: A Black Athlete's Coming of Age in America* (New York: Grove Press, 1995), 77–82.

24. *DB*, January 3, 1962; *HI*, December 30, 1961; *LAE*, December 30, 1961; Blackman interview in N. Johnson, *Wooden Pyramid of Success*, 332–33. Neither the *Houston Chronicle* nor the University of Houston's student newspaper, the *Houston Cougar*, discussed the racial tensions during the game.

25. *LAT*, December 24, 27, 1961; *CD*, December 28, 1961; *DB*, January 3, 1962. On black athletes at predominantly white schools, see Harry Edwards, *The Revolt of the Black Athlete* (New York: Free Press, 1969), 8–21; Scott, *The Athletic Revolution*, 80–81 (see preface, n. 8).

26. *DB*, January 4, 5, February 6, 15, 1962; *CE*, February 22, 1962; Ralph H. Turner to Franklin D. Murphy, December 27, 1961, Intercollegiate Athletics, 1961–1962 Folder, Box 27, FDM; Charles E. Young to Ralph H. Turner, January 16, 1962, FDM; Franklin D. Murphy to Wilbur Johns, January 24, 1962, FDM; Clark Kerr to Chancellor Glenn T. Seaborg and Chancellor Franklin D. Murphy, September 7, 1960, Folder 246-S Intercollegiate Athletic Advisory Council 1960, Box 123, FDM.

27. *LAS*, January 4, 1962; *HI*, December 30, 1961.

28. Cave, "Wizards in the Land of Oz," 60, 64; *LAT*, December 28, 29, 1961; Ray Cave, "A Parlay of Luke and the Rat," *SI*, January 8, 1962, 24–25; Hazzard interview in N. Johnson, *Wooden Pyramid of Success*, 364; Jaleesa Hazzard, phone interview with the author, April 19, 2011; *DB*, January 3, 1962.

29. *LAT*, January 3, February 2, 4, 25, 1962; *DB*, February 26, March 5, 7, 1962; Cave, "Wizards in the Land of Oz," 64; Green, phone interview.

30. *LAT*, March 17, 18, 1962; *DB*, March 19, 1962; Ray Cave, "A Grudge Match for the National Title," *SI*, March 26, 1962, 28; Ray Cave, "Cincinnati Is No.1, No.1, No.1!," *SI*, April 2, 1962, 30.

31. Cave, "Cincinnati Is No.1, No.1, No.1!," 30; Medley, *UCLA Basketball*, 14–15; Robert Stern, *They Were Number One: A History of the NCAA Basketball Tournament* (New York: Leisure Press, 1983), 184; *LCJ*, March 24, 1962; *LAT*, March 24, 1962.

32. Larry Bortstein, *UCLA's Fabulous Bruins: The Story of a Basketball Dynasty* (New York: St. Martin's, 1972), 49–50; Medley, *UCLA Basketball*, 15–16, 22; Prugh and Chapin, *Wizard of Westwood*, 127–28; *LAT*, January 9, 1964; John Underwood, "Five Midgets and a Wink at Nell," *SI*, February 24, 1964, 49; Bisheff, *John Wooden*, 122 (see chap. 1, n. 33); Goodrich interview in N. Johnson, *Wooden Pyramid of Success*, 348–49; Arnold Hano, "Gail Goodrich: Drive, He Says," *Sport*, April 1972, 38, 72; N. Johnson, *Wooden Pyramid of Success*, 63–64; Goodrich, phone interview with the author, April 26, 2011; Keith Erickson, phone interview with the author, March 26, 2011.

33. Medley, *UCLA Basketball*, 16, 35–36; Alexander Wolff, "Birth of a Dynasty," *SI*, March 19, 2007, 87.

34. Wolff, "Birth of a Dynasty," 88; Frank Deford, "The Team of '64," *SI*, March 26, 1979, 75, 80; *LAT*, March 11, 1964; Medley, *UCLA Basketball*, 31.

35. In his autobiography, Wooden calculated that from 1948 until 1960, 62 percent of his lettermen had attended junior colleges. From 1960 until his retirement, more than 56 percent of his players had come from junior colleges. See Wooden with Tobin, *They Call Me Coach*, 83.

36. Ibid., 17–18; Bortstein, *UCLA's Fabulous Bruins*, 97–98; Chapin and Prugh, *Wizard of Westwood*, 130; Underwood, "Five Midgets and a Wink at Nell," 49; Erickson, phone interview.

37. *DB*, December 13, 1962; Bortstein, *UCLA's Fabulous Bruins*, 43–44; Wooden with Tobin, *They Call Me Coach*, 16–17.

38. *LAT*, December 27, 1962; Wooden with Tobin, *They Call Me Coach*, 12–15; Medley, *UCLA Basketball*, 23–24.

39. *LAT*, March 15, 1963; *DB*, March 18, 1963.

40. *DB*, December 17, 1964; Chapin and Prugh, *Wizard of Westwood*, 243–44.

41. Chapin and Prugh, *Wizard of Westwood*, 105–11; Medley, *UCLA Basketball*, 25–29.

42. *LAT*, February 5, 1969; Wooden with Tobin, *They Call Me Coach*, 116–17.

43. Goodrich, phone interview; *DB*, November 26, 1963; *LAT*, November 23, 1963; Deford, "The Team of '64," 75; Anderson, *Movement and the Sixties*, 75; W. J. Rorabaugh, *Kennedy and the Promise of the Sixties* (Cambridge: Cambridge University Press, 2002), ix–21, 215, 229.

44. Erickson, phone interview; *LAHE*, December 7, 1963; *LAT*, December 28, 1963.

45. Chapin and Prugh, *Wizard of Westwood*, 116; *DB*, January 6, 1964; "Pressure—That's Our Game," *Time*, January 17, 1964, 74–75; *LAHE*, January 18, 1964.

46. *LAHE*, January 21, 1964; *LAT*, December 28, 29, 1963, January 21, March 11, 1964; Lazenby, *The Show*, 68–70, 76–82 (see chap. 1, n. 32).

47. *LAHE*, January 19, 1964; *LAT*, December 8, 25, 1963, January 16, 1964; *NYT*,

January 13, 22, February 8, 25, 1964; *CT,* March 3, 1964; *WP,* January 6, 13, February 19, March 7, 1964; "Pressure—That's Our Game," 74–75.

48. Gena Dagel Caponi, introduction to *Signifyin(g), Sanctifyin,' & Slam Dunking: A Reader in African American Expressive Culture,* edited by Gena Dagel Caponi (Amherst: University of Massachusetts Press, 1999), 3–12; Michael Novak, *The Joy of Sports: End Zones, Bases, Baskets, Balls, and the Consecration of the American Spirit* (New York: Basic Books, 1976), 98–114.

49. *NYT,* January 22, 1964; Sam Balter, "A Team with Heart and a Great Coach," *UCLA Alumni Magazine,* April 1962, 36; Cave, "Wizards in the Land of Oz," 61; McVay, "Small Men Win for UCLA's John Wooden," 93–97 (see chap. 1, n. 30); "Pressure—That's Our Game," 74–75; Underwood, "Five Midgets and a Wink at Nell," 49; *DB,* March 11, 1964.

50. Wooden with Jamison, *My Personal Best,* 109; Cave, "Wizards in the Land of Oz," 63; "Pressure—That's Our Game," 75; Underwood, "Five Midgets and a Wink at Nell," 46–49; Wind, "West of the Wabash," 94, 98–99 (see chap. 1, n. 36); *LAT,* May 3, 1964.

51. *NYT,* January 22, 1964, March 28, 1965; McVay, "Small Men Win for UCLA's John Wooden," 93–97; *DB,* May 15, 1963.

52. *LAHE,* March 17, 1964; Henry M. Littlefield, "The Wizard of Oz: Parable on Populism," *American Quarterly* 16 (Spring 1964): 47–58. On the images and language of populism, see Michael Kazin, *The Populist Persuasion: An American History* (New York: Basic Books, 1995).

53. Chapin and Prugh, *Wizard of Westwood,* 118, 288.

54. *WP,* June 21, 1973; Erickson, phone interview; Goodrich, phone interview.

55. *LAHE,* January 14, February 15, 1964; *LAT,* February 12, March 10, 1964; Medley, *UCLA Basketball,* 41. The other two championship teams that finished undefeated were San Francisco (1956) and North Carolina (1957).

56. *LAHE,* March 14, 15, 16, 18, 21, 22, 1964; *DB,* March 16, 1964; *LAT,* March 18, 1964; *NYT,* March 20, 1964; *KCS,* March 21, 1964.

57. Goodrich, phone interview.

58. Underwood, "Five Midgets and a Wink at Nell," 46; John Underwood, "The Two-Minute Explosion," *SI,* March 30, 1964, 16–19; Wooden with Tobin, *They Call Me Coach,* 97–98; Chapin and Prugh, *Wizard of Westwood,* 14, 20; *LAHE,* March 17, 1964; *LAT,* March 13, 1960, February 4, 1969; Cave, "Cincinnati Is No.1, No.1, No.1!" Various primary sources suggest that Wooden occasionally changed the order of his pregame routine.

59. *LAT,* March 18, 20, 1964; *KCS,* March 21, 1964; John Underwood, "Key Facts about 10 of the Best," *SI,* March 16, 1964, 22; Underwood, "The Two-Minute Explosion," 16–19.

60. Deford, "The Team of '64," 80; Medley, *UCLA Basketball,* 17–23.

61. Medley, *UCLA Basketball,* 42–43; *LAHE,* March 22, 1964; *KCS,* March 22, 1964; Underwood, "The Two-Minute Explosion," 19; *NYT,* March 22, 1964; "Play-

by-Play of Championship Game," in *The Unbeatable Bruins: A Souvenir of the 1963–4 UCLA Basketball Team National Collegiate Champions*, 1964, 3.

62. *KCS*, March 22, 1964.

63. Medley, *UCLA Basketball*, 44.

Chapter 3. The Promised Land

1. Goodrich, phone interview (see chap. 2, n. 32); "Gail Goodrich—UCLA," *Newsweek*, March 22, 1965, 56; Brondfield, *UCLA Story*, 45–46 (see chap. 2, n. 12); Chapin and Prugh, *Wizard of Westwood*, 127–28 (see chap. 1, n. 1).

2. Erickson, phone interview (see chap. 2, n. 32); Chapin and Prugh, *Wizard of Westwood*, 128; Underwood, "Five Midgets and a Wink at Nell," 49 (see chap. 2, n. 32).

3. "The Best and Littlest Bruin," *SI*, March 15, 1965, 27; *Southern Campus* (UCLA yearbook), 1965, 131; Dan Hafner, "Gail Goodrich—New Kingpin of Go-Go Bruins," *SN*, January 23, 1965, 31; *DB*, December 10, 1964; "Twig or Treat?," *Senior Scholastic*, February 25, 1965, 20.

4. George Gallup and Evan Hill, "Youth: The Cool Generation," *SEP*, December 23, 1961, 64–81; Kirse Granat May, *Golden State, Golden Youth: The California Image in Popular Culture, 1955–1966* (Chapel Hill: University of North Carolina Press, 2002), 136–37; Anderson, *Movement and the Sixties*, 127–30 (see chap. 2, n. 17); "Gail Goodrich—UCLA," 56; "The Man from U.C.L.A.," *Time*, October, 21, 1966, 98; Hirsch quoted in Deford, "The Team of '64," 76 (see chap. 2, n. 34).

5. Kevin Starr, *Golden Dreams: California in an Age of Abundance* (New York: Oxford University Press, 2009), 369; Chapin and Prugh, *Wizard of Westwood*, 230.

6. James J. Rawls and Walter Bean, *California: An Interpretive History*, 8th ed. (Boston: McGraw-Hill, 2002), 426–27; Davis, *Culture Broker*, 26–27 (see chap. 1, n. 53); Kevin Starr, *California: A History* (New York: Modern Library, 2007), 243–44; William Trombley, "The Exploding University of California," *SEP*, May 16, 1964, 22–28. On the baby boom generation, see Steven Gillon, *Boomer Nation: The Largest and Richest Generation Ever and How It Changed America* (New York: Simon & Schuster, 2004).

7. Kenneth J. Heineman, *Put Your Bodies upon the Wheels: Student Revolt in the 1960s* (Chicago: Ivan R. Dee, 2001), 11–12; Anderson, *Movement and the Sixties*, 89–90, 95; David Farber, *The Age of Great Dreams: America in the 1960s* (New York: Hill and Wang, 1994), 57.

8. George B. Leonard, "California," *Look*, September 25, 1962, 31; "California: Too Much, Too Soon," *Esquire*, May 1963, 65; "The Number One State: Booming, Beautiful California," *Newsweek*, September 10, 1962, 29–38; "The Call of California," *Life*, October 19, 1962, special issue; Eugene Burdick, "From Gold Rush to Sun Rush," *New York Times Magazine*, April 14, 1963, 36–37, 89–92; Richard Warren Lewis, "Those Swinging Beach Movies," *SEP*, July 31, 1965, 83–7; "The Mad Happy

Surfers," *Life,* September 1, 1961, 47–53; Farber, *Age of Great Dreams,* 53. In 1962 California claimed that it had exceeded New York's population, but other demographers figured that the Golden State became the country's most populous state in 1963, 1964, and 1965.

9. May, *Golden State, Golden Youth,* 24–26, 95–134; Patricia Coffin, "California Is Bustin' Out All Over," *Look,* September 29, 1959, 57–58; Stanley Gordon, "California Co-Eds: Beauties from Two Top Campuses," *Look,* September 29, 1959, 67–69.

10. May, *Golden State, Golden Youth,* 135–38; Burdick, "From Gold Rush to Sun Rush," 92.

11. Maurice Isserman and Michael Kazin, *America Divided: The Civil War of the 1960s* (New York: Oxford University Press, 2000), 166–69; W. J. Rorabaugh, *Berkeley at War: The 1960s* (New York: Oxford University Press, 1989), 19–47.

12. Rorabaugh, *Berkeley at War;* Anderson, *Movement and the Sixties,* 87, 97–105; Mark Hamilton Lytle, *America's Uncivil Wars: The Sixties Era from Elvis to the Fall of Richard Nixon* (New York: Oxford University Press, 2006), 168–73; Heineman, *Put Your Bodies upon the Wheels,* 106–10.

13. Richard Gilbert, "A Good Time at UCLA: An English View," *Harper's,* April 1965, 75–77; Kemper, "Reformers in the Marketplace of Ideas," 130–36 (see chap. 1, n. 22); Davis, *Culture Broker,* 86–87; *DB,* October 9, November 12, 13, December 1, 3, 15, 1964.

14. May, *Golden State, Golden Youth,* 147–15; Rorabaugh, *Berkeley at War,* 19; Alfred Wright, "To the Big Game and to the Barricades," *SI,* January 3, 1966, 50.

15. May, *Golden State, Golden Youth,* 151–55; Colin Miller, "The Press and the Student Revolt," in *Revolution at Berkeley,* edited by Michael V. Miller and Susan Gilmore (New York: Dell, 1965), 338; Robert Lipsyte, *SportsWorld: An American Dreamland* (New York: Quadrangle, 1975), 11.

16. *LAT,* March 30, 1965. For a scholarly monograph that explores Frank Merriwell and American culture, see Michael Oriard, *Dreaming of Heroes: American Sports Fiction, 1868–1980* (Chicago: Nelson-Hall, 1982), 25–68.

17. Goodrich, phone interview.

18. Ibid.

19. Ibid.; Harry Edwards, *The Sociology of Sport* (Homewood, Ill.: Dorsey Press, 1973), 71–78, 131–32, 141–43; Arnold Beisser, *The Madness in Sports: Psychological Observations on Sports* (New York: Meredith, 1967), 200–201; Cave, "Wizards in the Land of Oz," 63 (see chap. 2, n. 1); Underwood, "Five Midgets and a Wink at Nell," 49; *LAT,* May 31, 1964.

20. Goodrich, phone interview.

21. *DB,* December 4, 7, 1964; *LAHE,* December 5, 6, 8, 1964; *LAT,* December 5, 1964; Joe Goldstein, "Snazzy Cazzie, Buntin Give Michigan Cagers Big Edge," *SN,* December 12, 1964, 40.

22. Chapin and Prugh, *Wizard of Westwood,* 129–30; *LAHE,* December 12, 1964; *LAT,* December 12, 1964.

23. *LAHE,* December 27, 1964; *LAT,* February 5, 1965; Medley, *UCLA Basket-*

ball, 47–52 (see chap. 1, n. 3); Mervin Hyman, "A Press That Panics Them All," *SI,* December 6, 1965, 77–86.

24. Frank Deford, "Two Once and Future Champs," *SI,* January 11, 1965, 18–21; *LAHE,* January 14, 15, 1965; *LAT,* September 7, 1964, March 4, 1965.

25. *LAHE,* March 20, 21, 1965; *LAT,* November 25, 1964; *DB,* March 19, 1965; Medley, *UCLA Basketball,* 60.

26. "What? Sold Out, Already!," *NCAA News,* May 1964, 2; "Shall We Dance?," *Time,* December 25, 1964, 50; *LAHE,* December 2, 1964; Goldstein, "Snazzy Cazzie," 40; John Underwood, "His Hopes Hang by an Ankle," *SI,* March 23, 1964, 18–21; *CD,* December 19, 1964; *CT,* March 15, 1965.

27. *LAT,* March 20, 1965; Medley, *UCLA Basketball,* 60–64; Frank Deford, "The Power of the Press," *SI,* March 29, 1965, 21–22; *DB,* March 26, 1965.

28. *LAT,* March 22, 1965; *DB,* March 26, 1965; Bill Becker, "The Coach Who Arranges Chaos," *Sport,* March 1966, 56.

29. *LAT,* March 22, 1965; Medley, *UCLA Basketball,* 63; Deford, "Power of the Press," 22–23; *NYT,* March 21; *LAHE,* March 22, 1965; Goodrich, phone interview. The other four schools that had won consecutive national championships were Oklahoma State, Kentucky, San Francisco, and Cincinnati.

30. *LAHE,* March 22, 1965; *LAT,* January 10, 1964; Deford, "Power of the Press," 23.

31. Gilbert, "Good Time at UCLA," 75; Franklin D. Murphy interview in N. Johnson, *Wooden Pyramid of Success,* 394 (see chap. 1, n. 14). In 1962 *Life* called California the "Athlete's Promised Land." See "The Call of California," *Life,* October 19, 1962, 64.

32. *LAT,* November 20, 1966.

33. *LAHE,* February 23, March 16, 1965; *LAT,* January 4, March 17, 1965; *NYT,* January 2, 31, February 13, March 8, 28, 1965; *NYAN,* February 20, May 1, 1965; "The Character Builders," *SI,* December 10, 1962, 16–17; "Big A," *Newsweek,* December 24, 1962, 43; George Walsh, "The Wooing of a Seven-Foot Wonder," *SEP,* March 14, 1964, 70–71; Will Bradbury, "Big Lew's Message to Scouts: Shh! I'm Busy," *Life,* January 29, 1965, 53–54; William J. McKean, "High Alcindor—Basketball's Mt. Everest," *Look,* February 9, 1965, 86–90; "Don't Call Us . . .," *Newsweek,* February 15, 1965, 60–61; "Double Dribbles," *SN,* January 16, 1965, 32; Harold Rosenthal, "Rumors Outrunning Facts on Alcindor—Superman of Preps," *SN,* February 27, 1965, 42; "Basketball's Hottest Comer," *Sport,* March 1965, 44–47; "1965 All-American H.S. Basketball Squad," *Scholastic Coach,* May 1965, 62; Phil Pepe, *Stand Tall: The Lew Alcindor Story* (New York: Temp Books, 1970), 6.

34. Ibid.

35. *LAT,* November 20, 1966.

36. Ibid.; *DB,* April 5, 1965; Lew Alcindor with Jack Olsen, "My Story," *SI,* October 27, 1969, 98.

37. Medley, *UCLA Basketball,* 66–67; Dunphy, "Wooden: The Coaching Process," 46–55 (see chap. 1, n. 26); Chapin and Prugh, *Wizard of Westwood,* 246; John Wooden interview with David Rose, "The Right Man at the Right Time: J. D. Morgan,"

1982, transcript 1984, UCLA OHC, 345–49; Arnold Hano, "Winning: With Nice Guys and a Pyramid of Principles," *New York Times Magazine,* December 2, 1973, 134, 139–40; *LAT,* April 29, 1965, November 20, 1966.

38. *LAT,* May 5, 1965; *NYAN,* January 30, February 6, 1965; *NYT,* March 8, 28, 1965; *DB,* April 21, 1965; *PT,* January 25, 1964; Bradbury, "Big Lew's Message to Scouts," 53–54; Rosenthal, "Rumors Outrunning Facts on Alcindor," 42; Hano, "Winning," 140–42; Alcindor with Olsen, "My Story," 98; Kareem Abdul-Jabbar and Peter Knobler, *Giant Steps* (New York: Bantam Books, 1983), 103; Eddie Einhorn with Ron Rapoport, *How March Became Madness: How the NCAA Tournament Became the Greatest Sporting Event in America* (Chicago: Triumph Books, 2006), 23; Ralph J. Bunche to Lew Alcindor, March 26, 1965, Box 27, Athletic Department, 1965–70 Folder, FDM; *Daily News of Los Angeles,* March 21, 2004; Scott Howard Cooper, *The Bruin 100: The Greatest Games in the History of UCLA Basketball* (Lenexa, Kans.: Addax, 1999), 11.

39. *NYT,* March 28, April 15, 1965; *LAT,* April 14, 1965; *DB,* April 21, 1965; *NYAN,* May 1, 1965; Walsh, "Wooing of a Seven-Foot Wonder," 70; McKean, "High Alcindor," 86.

40. Abdul-Jabbar and Knobler, *Giant Steps,* 21–27, 48; Walsh, "Wooing of a Seven-Foot Wonder," 70; Alcindor with Olsen, "My Story," 87–88.

41. Frank Deford, "Lewie Is a Minority of One," *SI,* December 5, 1966, 40–41; Walsh, "Wooing of a Seven-Foot Wonder," 70–71; Abdul-Jabbar and Knobler, *Giant Steps,* 44–45; Joel Cohen, *Big A: The Story of Lew Alcindor* (New York: Scholastic Books, 1971), 26.

42. Abdul-Jabbar and Knobler, *Giant Steps,* 49–50; Walsh, "Wooing of a Seven-Footer," 71.

43. Abdul-Jabbar and Knobler, *Giant Steps,* 46.

44. Alcindor with Olsen, "My Story," 90; Pepe, *Stand Tall,* 39.

45. Alcindor with Olsen, "My Story," 90; Abdul-Jabbar and Knobler, *Giant Steps,* 67–68.

46. Kenneth B. Clark and Jeannette Hopkins, *A Relevant War against Poverty: A Study of Community Action Programs and Observable Social Change* (New York: Harper & Row, 1969), 5–8; Kareem Abdul-Jabbar with Raymond Obstfeld, *On the Shoulders of Giants: My Journey through the Harlem Renaissance* (New York: Simon & Schuster, 2007), 51–54; Abdul-Jabbar with Mignon McCarthy, *Kareem* (New York: Random House, 1990), 156. For a history of HARYOU, see Cyril Degrasse Tyson, *Power and Politics in Central Harlem, 1962–1964: The Harlem Youth Opportunities Unlimited Experience* (New York: Jay Street, 2004). For histories of the Black Power movement, see William L. Van Deburg, *New Day in Babylon: The Black Power Movement and American Culture* (Chicago: University of Chicago Press, 1992); Peniel Joseph, *Waiting 'til the Midnight Hour: A Narrative History of Black Power in America* (New York: Henry Holt, 2006).

47. Abdul-Jabbar with McCarthy, *Kareem,* 6. For a discussion of Harlem in the

1960s, see John Henrik Clarke, ed., *Harlem: A Community in Transition* (New York: Citadel Press, 1964).

48. Fred C. Shapiro and James W. Sullivan, *Race Riots: New York, 1964* (New York: Thomas Y. Crowell, 1964), 1–10, 43–47; "Harlem: Hatred in the Streets," *Newsweek,* August 3, 1964, 16; *Report of the National Advisory Commission on Civil Disorders* (Washington, D.C.: U.S. Government Printing Office, 1968), 19–20; Michael W. Flamm, *Law and Order: Street Crime, Civil Unrest, and the Crisis of Liberalism in the 1960s* (New York: Columbia University Press, 2005), 37.

49. "Harlem: Hatred in the Streets," 16–19; Abdul-Jabbar and Knobler, *Giant Steps,* 73.

50. Alcindor with Olsen, "My Story," 95; Abdul-Jabbar and Knobler, *Giant Steps,* 71–74; Abdul-Jabbar with Obstfeld, *On the Shoulders of Giants,* 56–57. The August 13, 1964, issue of *Jet* includes a picture of Alcindor standing near King at the press conference in Harlem.

51. Pepe, *Stand Tall,* 3–4, 59–60; Lipsyte, *SportsWorld,* 150–54; *LAT,* November 20, 1966; *NYT,* May 5, 1965.

52. *Newsday,* May 5, 1965; *New York Herald-Tribune,* May 5, 1965; *New York Post,* May 5, 1965; *NYDN,* May 5, 1965; *LAT,* May 5, 1965; Abdul-Jabbar and Knobler, *Giant Steps,* 108–9; Abdul-Jabbar with McCarthy, *Kareem,* 86–87.

53. "California, Here I Come," *Time,* May 14, 1965, 81; Lew Alcindor with Jack Olsen, "UCLA Was a Mistake," *SI,* November 3, 1969, 35; May, *Golden State, Golden Youth,* 160.

Chapter 4. Alone in a Crowd

1. Rex Lardner, "Can Basketball Survive Lew Alcindor?," *SEP,* January 14, 1967, 73; *LAT,* November 29, 1965; *CD,* December 2, 1965; *WP,* October 9, 1966; Medley, *UCLA Basketball,* 68–69 (see chap. 1, n. 3); Phil Elderkin, "Rimming the NBA," *SN,* November 12, 1966, 21; Rudy Langlais, "Exclusive: Kareem Abdul-Jabbar," *Black Sports,* January 1976, 16.

2. Phil Pepe, "For the First Time Lew Alcindor Sounds Off!," *Sport,* October 1967, 35; Phil Pepe, "What Next for UCLA's Man of the Year? An Interview with Lew Alcindor," in *Basketball Yearbook,* 1968, 6; *Newsday,* December 5, 1966.

3. Lipsyte, *SportsWorld,* 150–56 (see chap. 3, n. 15); *NYT,* October 15, 1966; *LAT,* February 3, 1967.

4. "Alcindor the Awesome," *Ebony,* March 1967, 96–97; John Lake, "The Making of a Legend: Towering Lew Alcindor," *Newsweek,* February 27, 1967, 62; Alcindor with Olsen, "UCLA Was a Mistake," 36 (see chap. 3, n. 53).

5. Matthew Dallek, *The Right Moment: Ronald Reagan's First Victory and the Decisive Turning Point in American Politics* (New York: Free Press, 2000), 128–43; Rick Perlstein, *Nixonland: The Rise of a President and the Fracturing of America* (New York: Scribner, 2008), 3–17; "Los Angeles: The Fire This Time," *Newsweek,* August

23, 1965, 15–17; "After the Blood Bath," *Newsweek,* August 30, 1965, 13–20; "Trigger of Hate," *Time,* August 20, 1965, 15–19; *LAT,* August 20, 1965.

6. Gerald Horne, *Fire This Time: The Watts Uprising and the 1960s* (Charlottesville: University Press of Virginia, 1995), 3; Perlstein, *Nixonland,* 16; Dallek, *Right Moment,* 129, 145–46.

7. Louie Robinson, "This Would Never Have Happened," *Ebony,* October 1965, 114, 122, 124; Horne, *Fire This Time,* 36–42; May, *Golden State, Golden Youth,* 160–64 (see chap. 3, n. 4); "After the Blood Bath," 16.

8. Chester Himes, *The Quality of Hurt: The Early Years* (New York: Paragon House, 1990), 73–74. On blacks in Los Angeles, see Josh Sides, *L.A. City Limits: African American Los Angeles from the Great Depression to the Present* (Berkeley and Los Angeles: University of California Press, 2003).

9. Jeanne Theoharis, "'Alabama on Avalon': Rethinking the Watts Uprising and the Character of Black Protest in Los Angeles," in *The Black Power Movement: Rethinking the Civil Rights and Black Power Era,* edited by Peniel Joseph (New York: Routledge, 2006), 34–36, 46–48; Dallek, *Right Moment,* 57–61; Horne, *Fire This Time,* 37. Later in 1964, the California Supreme Court nullified Proposition 14, declaring it unconstitutional.

10. Alcindor with Olsen, "UCLA Was a Mistake," 36–37; Lake, "Making of a Legend," 62.

11. Jack Olsen, "Pride and Prejudice," *SI,* July 8, 1968, 20–21; Curry Kirkpatrick, "UCLA: Simple, Awesomely Simple," *SI,* November 30, 1970, 43; Hano, "Winning," 143 (see chap. 3, n. 37).

12. Olsen, "Pride and Prejudice," 31; Pete Axthelm, "The Angry Black Athlete," *Newsweek,* July 15, 1968, 57; *DB,* February 9, 1967; John Riley, "Big Lew Measures His Lonely World," *Life,* February 17, 1967, 105–6; Arnold Hano, "The Heart of Lew Alcindor," *Sport,* April 1967, 74; "Lew Alcindor: Alone in a Crowd," *Look,* February 21, 1967, 95–98; Alcindor with Olsen, "UCLA Was a Mistake," 36–38.

13. Christian G. Appy, *Working-Class War: American Combat Soldiers and Vietnam* (Chapel Hill: University of North Carolina Press, 1993), 34–37; *DB,* September 23, 1965, January 7, May 17, 1966; *LAT,* January 30, 1966.

14. Anderson, *Movement and the Sixties,* 124–27 (see chap. 2, n. 17); Farber, *Age of Great Dreams,* 138–40, 153 (see chap. 3, n. 7); *LAHE,* December 21, 1965; *DB,* October 1, 5, 18, November 12, 15, December 15, 1965; "Students Talk about Students," *UCLA Alumni Magazine* ("Special Issue: Students in the Sixties"), Fall 1965, 4.

15. *DB,* October 5, 18, November 12, 1965, March 28, October 26, 1966; Perlstein, *Nixonland,* 80–82.

16. *DB,* October 27, November 24, 1965; *LAT,* November 6, 27, 1965.

17. Chapin and Prugh, *Wizard of Westwood,* 244 (see chap. 1, n. 1); *UCLA Basketball Media Guide,* 1965–66; *LAT,* November 27, 1965, February 23, 1967; Joe Jares, "The Hot Brubabes," *SI,* December 6, 1965, 46; Bob Hunter, "Alcindor Leads UCLA's Fabulous Frosh," *SN,* March 5, 1966, 35; *DB,* February 9, 1968; Lucius Allen interview in N. Johnson, *Wooden Pyramid of Success,* 312–13 (see chap. 1, n. 14).

18. "Christians in Sport," *Newsweek,* September 3, 1956, 58; *CSM,* August 20, 1956, February 23, 1965; "A Muscular Boost for Christian Doctrine," *Life,* September 17, 1956, 67; "Christian Athletes Flex Muscle," *Christianity Today,* August 22, 1969, 37–38; "Harnessing Hero Worship," *Christianity Today,* August 22, 1969, 25; "God's Muscle," *Time,* May 21, 1973, 66; Baker, *Playing with God,* 193–204 (see chap. 1, n. 15).

19. Allen Palmeri, "Character Coaching," *Sharing the Victory,* March 2004, 8–13; John Wooden, "My First Seven Points," *Sharing the Victory,* March–April 1983, 3–5; "Pride of Westwood Reigns on Hardwood," *Purdue Alumnus,* May 1965, 14; Becker, "Coach Who Arranges Chaos," 93 (see chap. 3, n. 28); John Wooden, "Shooting Is the Least Important Part of Basketball," *Look,* January 25, 1966, 66; Wooden and Carty, *Coach Wooden's Pyramid of Success,* 130 (see chap. 1, n. 7); *LAT,* May 3, 1964; Leonard E. Le Sourd, "John Wooden: The Elements of Victory," *Guideposts,* February 1971, 15.

20. *CSM,* November 1, 1965; *LAT,* December 1, 1965; Joe Jares, "The Two Faces of the Rubber Man," *SI,* January 6, 1969, 24–25; Hano, "Winning," 31; Chapin and Prugh, *Wizard of Westwood,* 8; Hunter, "Alcindor Leads UCLA's Fabulous Frosh," 35.

21. *LAT,* March 23, 1965; *CSM,* March 24, 1965; Jares, "The Hot Brubabes," 46; Joe Goldstein, "UCLA Can Do It, Says Expert—Third U.S. Cage Title in Row," *SN,* December 4, 1965, 46; Medley, *UCLA Basketball,* 69–71.

22. Hyman, "Press That Panics Them All," 77–80, 85, 86 (see chap. 3, n. 23); Jares, "The Hot Brubabes," 46–47; *LAT,* November 28, 29, 1965; *DB,* November 30, 1965; "Height of Temerity," *Newsweek,* December 13, 1965, 66.

23. Wooden with Tobin, *They Call Me Coach,* 137 (see chap. 1, n. 2); *LAT,* December 14, 22, 1965, January 31, February 4, 17, March 3, 1966; *LAHE,* February 5, 1966; *DB,* February 17, March 18, 1966.

24. George, *Elevating the Game,* 137 (see chap. 1, n. 44); Frank Fitzpatrick, *And the Walls Came Tumbling Down: The Basketball Game That Changed American Sports* (Lincoln: University of Nebraska Press, 1999), 25, 40, 225; Curry Kirkpatrick, "The Night They Drove Old Dixie Down," *SI,* April 1, 1991, 70–81; Charles H. Martin, "Jim Crow in the Gymnasium: The Integration of College Basketball in the American South," *International Journal of the History of Sport* 10 (April 1993): 80; *Glory Road,* DVD, directed by James Gartner (Burbank, Calif.: Walt Disney Home Entertainment, 2006). Nolan Richardson claims that Don Haskins started five blacks during the 1963 season, while Harry Flournoy maintains that Haskins first did it in 1965. The Texas Western coach cannot recall when he first started an all-black lineup. See Don Haskins with Dan Wetzel, *Glory Road: My Story of the 1966 NCAA Basketball Championship and How One Team Triumphed against the Odds and Changed America Forever* (New York: Hyperion, 2006), 8–10, 113–17.

25. Fitzpatrick, *And the Walls Came Tumbling Down,* 25, 225.

26. Barry Jacobs, *Across the Line: Profiles in Basketball Courage—Tales of the First Black Basketball Players in the ACC and SEC* (Guilford, Conn.: Lyons Press, 2008), xiv, 183, 333; Joan Paul et al., "The Arrival and Ascendence of Black Athletes in the

Southeastern Conference, 1966–1980," *Phylon* 45 (December 1984): 284–97; "When Are All the SEC Colleges Going to Recruit Negro Athletes?," *Sport,* July 1967, 94; Frank Deford, "The Negro Athlete Is Invited Home," *SI,* June 14, 1965, 26–27; "Deadline in Dixie," *SI,* June 6, 1966, 11; "Desegregating College Sports Creates Scheduling Problems," *Southern School News,* May 1962, 15; Fitzpatrick, *And the Walls Came Tumbling Down,* 37–38; Harry Lancaster as told to Cawood Ledford, *Adolph Rupp as I Knew Him* (Lexington, Ky.: Lexington Productions, 1977), 88.

27. Haskins and Wetzel, *Glory Road,* 180; Kirkpatrick, "Night They Drove Old Dixie Down," 74; Fitzpatrick, *And the Walls Came Tumbling Down,* 205–14; Frank Deford, "Go-Go with Bobby Joe," *SI,* March 28, 1966, 26–29.

28. Deford, "Go-Go with Bobby Joe," 26–29; Ronald A. Smith, *Play-by-Play: Radio, Television, and Big-Time College Sport* (Baltimore: Johns Hopkins University Press, 2001), 183; Fitzpatrick, *And the Walls Came Tumbling Down,* 40; *Pittsburgh Courier,* April 2, 1966; *NYT,* March 21, 1966; *WP,* March 20, 1966; *CT,* March 20, 1966; *Lexington (Ky.) Leader,* March 20, 1966.

29. *LH,* March 21, 23, 1966; Jacobs, *Across the Line,* 181; Randy Roberts and James Olson, *Winning Is the Only Thing: Sports in America since 1945* (Baltimore: Johns Hopkins University Press, 1989), 45; Fitzpatrick, *And the Walls Came Tumbling Down,* 220; Martin Kane, "An Assessment of Black Is Best," *SI,* January 18, 1971, 72–76, 79–83.

30. *LH,* March 21, 1966; *NYT,* March 21, November 27, 1966; *LAT,* October 27, November 30, December 16, 1966; *DB,* November 23, 1966; *LAHE,* December 1, 1966; *CD,* December 15, 1966; Joe Goldstein, "Alcindor Big Word in Bruin Cage Boom," *SN,* December 3, 1966, 21; "AAWU," *SI,* December 5, 1966, 47; Deford, "'Lewie Is a Minority of One,'" 42 (see chap. 3, n. 41).

31. Joe Jares, "The Biggest Bruin Had Friends," *SI,* December 19, 1966, 44.

32. *LAT,* December 3, 4, 1966; *LAHE,* December 3, 1966; *NYT,* December 5, 1966; Jares, "Biggest Bruin Had Friends," 44; "Lew-CLA," *Newsweek,* December 19, 1966, 63; Lardner, "Can Basketball Survive Lew Alcindor?," 71; *Orange County Register,* October 11, 2000.

33. *LAT,* December 11, 1966; Jares, "Biggest Bruin Had Friends," 44.

34. Ibid.

35. *NYT,* December 5, 1966; *LAT,* December 23, 1966, February 5, 6, 1967; *LAHE,* February 8, 1967; Lardner, "Can Basketball Survive Lew Alcindor?," 70–71; "What to Do about Lew," *Time,* December 16, 1966, 58; Mervin Hyman, "The Case for the 12-Foot Basket," *SI,* December 4, 1967, 78–83; "Who's No. 2?," *Time,* January 6, 1967, 73.

36. *LAT,* December 13, 23, 1966, January 14, 1967; *LAHE,* December 23, 27, 1966, January 14, 1967; *NYT,* January 15, 1967; *DB,* January 20, 1967.

37. *LAT,* January 4, 9, February 3, 1967; *LAHE,* December 31, 1966, January 7, March 3, 1967.

38. *CT,* January 26, 27, 1967; *CDN,* January 25, 1967.

39. *CDN,* January 26, 27, 28, 1967; *CST,* January 27, 28, 1967.

40. *CST,* January 26, 1967; *LAT,* January 27, February 3, 1967; *LAHE,* January 27, 1967; Lynn Shackelford, phone interview with the author, April 13, 2011; Ken Heitz, phone interview with the author, April 20, 2011.

41. *CDN,* January 27, 1967; *CST,* January 28, 29, 1967; *CT,* January 39, 1967; *LAHE,* January 28, 1967; *LAT,* January 28, 29, 1967; Medley, *UCLA Basketball,* 98–99.

42. *CST,* January 29, 30, 1967; *CT,* January 29, 1967; *CDN,* January 30, 1967; *LAT,* March 20, 1967.

43. *LAHE,* February 1, 1967; *LAT,* February 1, 1967; *CT,* January 31, 1967; Pepe, *Stand Tall,* 89 (see chap. 3, n. 33).

44. Hano, "Heart of Lew Alcindor," 73; *LAHE,* March 25, November 30, 1967.

45. Ibid.; Abdul-Jabbar and Knobler, *Giant Steps,* 157–58 (see chap. 3, n. 38).

46. *LAT,* February 3, 1967; Hano, "Heart of Lew Alcindor," 76–78; Riley, "Big Lew Measures His Lonely World," 105–6; "Alcindor the Awesome," 96; Lake, "Making of a Legend," 61–62; Alcindor with Olsen, "UCLA Was a Mistake," 36.

47. Van Deburg, *New Day in Babylon,* 2–6; Joseph, *Waiting 'til the Midnight Hour,* 8, 89–92 (for both, see chap. 3, n. 46).

48. Alcindor with Olsen, "UCLA Was a Mistake," 36; Abdul-Jabbar with McCarthy, *Kareem,* 155–56 (see chap. 3, n. 46); Abdul-Jabbar and Knobler, *Giant Steps,* 140–41; Jack Scott, *Bill Walton: On the Road with the Portland Trail Blazers* (New York: Crowell, 1978), 187. On the myth of the American "melting pot," see Gary Gerstle, *American Crucible: Race and Nation in the Twentieth Century* (Princeton, N.J.: Princeton University Press, 2001), 3–4.

49. *DB,* February 22, 1967; "Alcindor the Awesome," 96–97; Riley, "Big Lew Measures His Lonely World," 106; "Lew Alcindor: Alone in a Crowd"; Lake, "Making of a Legend," 62.

50. Chapin and Prugh, *Wizard of Westwood,* 259–62; Alcindor with Olsen, "UCLA Was a Mistake," 39; Pepe, "Lew Alcindor Sounds Off!," 37–38.

51. *LAT,* June 9, 1971.

52. Chapin and Prugh, *Wizard of Westwood,* 299; Scott, *Bill Walton,* 212–14; "A Patron Called Papa Sam," *Time,* February 25, 1974, 77; *DB,* May 10, 1965; Abdul-Jabbar and Knobler, *Giant Steps,* 156.

53. *CDN,* January 25, 1967; *DB,* January 27, February 24, March 3, 1967; *LAT,* February 24, 1967; Bob Hunter, "Unheralded Heroes—Alcindor's 4 Helpers," *SN,* March 4, 1967, 35–36; Shackelford, phone interview.

54. *LAT,* February 26, March 1, 4, 25, 1967; *NYT,* March 4, 1967; *LAHE,* February 13, 22, 1967.

55. Frank Deford, "Two to Go for Lew," *SI,* March 27, 1967, 14–17; Frank Deford, "Terror in the Air," *SI,* April 3, 1967, 19; *LAT,* March 23, 1967; John Papanek, "The Big E Wants an MVP," *SI,* October 16, 1978, 49–50; Wells Twombly, "Happy Accident Sent Hayes to Cougar Lair," *SN,* December 16, 1967, 19; Katherine Lopez, *Cougars of Any Color: The Integration of University of Houston Athletics, 1964–1968* (Jefferson, N.C.: McFarland, 2008), 31–42, 55. Houston football coach Bill Yeoman started recruiting

black athletes at the same time as Guy Lewis. Warren McVea became Houston's first black varsity football player in 1965. Lewis had tried to recruit black players earlier, including David Lattin, but the administration resisted his efforts.

56. Elvin Hayes and Bill Gilbert, *They Call Me Big E: The Elvin Hayes Story* (Englewood Cliffs, N.J.: Prentice-Hall, 1978), 5–38; Papanek, "Big E Wants an MVP," 49.

57. Lopez, *Cougars of Any Color,* 57–61; David Llorens, "No Back Seat for Elvin," *Ebony,* March 1968, 125–30; Jack Olsen, "The Cruel Deception," *SI,* July 1, 1968, 20–23.

58. Lopez, *Cougars of Any Color,* 143; Olsen, "The Cruel Deception," 20.

59. Llorens, "No Back Seat for Elvin," 126–29; Lopez, *Cougars of Any Color,* 155.

60. *LAT,* March 24, 1967; *LAHE,* March 25, 1967; *NYT,* March 25, 1967; Deford, "Terror in the Air," 16, 19, 21.

61. Deford, "Terror in the Air," 21; *NYT,* March 27, 1967; *CT,* March 26, 1967; *LAT,* March 26, 1967; "UCLA Wraps It Up," *Newsweek,* April 3, 1967, 56.

62. Ibid.

63. *LAT,* March 29, 1967; "Knocking the Stuffing Out," *SI,* April 10, 1967, 24; Pepe, "Lew Alcindor Sounds Off!," 36; *CT,* April 6, 1967.

64. On black manhood in the civil rights era, see Steve Estes, *I Am a Man! Race, Manhood, and the Civil Rights Movement* (Chapel Hill: University of North Carolina Press, 2005).

65. *LAT,* March 29, 1967; George, *Elevating the Game,* xv; Abdul-Jabbar and Knobler, *Giant Steps,* 160.

Chapter 5. Everybody's All-American

1. Wooden with Tobin, *They Call Me Coach,* 144 (see chap. 1, n. 2); Wooden with Jamison, *My Personal Best,* 154–55 (see chap. 1, n. 3).

2. *LAT,* February 3, 23, 1967; *WP,* March 25, 1967; Chapin and Prugh, *Wizard of Westwood,* 143 (see chap. 1, n. 1); *NYT,* December 28, 1968.

3. Gary Smith, "Now, More than Ever, a Winner," *SI,* December 23, 1985, 81; W. E. B. DuBois, *The Souls of Black Folk* (1903; reprint, New York: Dover, 1994), 2. For a discussion on black athletes and double-consciousness, see David K. Wiggins, *Glory Bound: Black Athletes in a White America* (Syracuse, N.Y.: Syracuse University Press, 1997).

4. Francis Rogers, "Lew Alcindor: First Million Dollar Baby?," *Sports Review's Basketball* (1968–69): 23; Ans Dilley, "Lew Alcindor: Is He That Great—or Greater?," *Sports Review's Basketball* (1967–68): 33.

5. *NYT,* July 23, 1968; *CD,* July 29, 1968. For works that deal with sports and television, see Benjamin G. Rader, *In Its Own Image: How Television Has Transformed Sports* (New York: Free Press, 1984); and Roberts and Olson, *Winning Is the Only Thing* (see chap. 4, n. 29).

6. *NYT,* April 29, 1967; Edwin Shrake, "Taps for the Champ," *SI,* May 8, 1967, 19–24; Herman Graham III, *The Brothers' Vietnam War: Black Power, Manhood, and*

the Military Experience (Gainesville: University Press of Florida, 2003), 78; Thomas Hauser, *Muhammad Ali: His Life and Times* (New York: Simon & Schuster, 1991), 168–70; Jeffrey T. Sammons, *Beyond the Ring: The Role of Boxing in American Society* (Urbana: University of Illinois Press, 1988), 203.

7. Ibid. Some sources claim that there were only twenty-five other men who were inducted with Ali, but Robert Lipsyte reported in the *New York Times* that there were forty-five other inductees. See *NYT,* April 29, 1967.

8. Graham, *Brothers' Vietnam War,* 72–76; Hauser, *Muhammad Ali,* 144–45, 167; *NYT,* April 30, May 2, 1967; Jeffrey T. Sammons, "Rebel with a Cause: Muhammad Ali as Sixties Protest Symbol," in *Muhammad Ali: The People's Champ,* edited by Elliot Gorn (Urbana: University of Illinois Press, 1995), 165–66; Shrake, "Taps for the Champ," 22.

9. Graham, *Brothers' Vietnam War,* 79–86; *Eyes on the Prize: Ain't Gonna Shuffle No More,* produced by Henry Hampton (Boston: Blackside, 1986); *CD,* May 11, 1967; *Michigan Chronicle,* May 6, June 17, 1967; Bill Russell with Tex Maule, "I'm Not Worried about Ali," *SI,* June 19, 1967, 18–21; *CT,* June 3, 5, 1967; *LAT,* June 3, 1967; *Cleveland Plain Dealer,* June 5, 1967; *Muhammad Speaks,* June 16, 1967. No newspaper quoted Alcindor at the press conference. The other athletes present were the Cleveland Browns' Walter Beach, Sid Williams, and John Wooten; the Washington Redskins' Bobby Mitchell and Jim Shorter; the Kansas City Chiefs' Curtis McClinton; and the Green Bay Packers' Willie Davis.

10. Abdul-Jabbar with McCarthy, *Kareem,* 21 (see chap. 3, n. 46); Hauser, *Muhammad Ali,* 178; "Kareem Abdul-Jabbar: Best Man in His Game," *Sepia,* March 1978, 50; Edwards, *Revolt of the Black Athlete,* 89–90 (see chap. 2, n. 25).

11. Lew Alcindor as told to Dick Kaplan, "Why I Turned Down a Million Dollars," *Sport,* November 1968, 27, 76; Pepe, "Lew Alcindor Sounds Off!," 91–92 (see chap. 4, n. 2); *NYAN,* July 22, 29, 1967, August 31, 1968.

12. *CT,* September 11, 1967; *NYAN,* September 16, 1967; "Playboy Interview: Kareem Abdul-Jabbar," *Playboy,* June 1986, 62; Hauser, *Muhammad Ali,* 185–90.

13. Harry Edwards to "Brothers," October 16, 1967, Box 41, NCAA 1975 Folder, Athletic Department Administrative Files, UCLA Archives; *SFC,* November 16, 1967; Harry Edwards, "Why Negroes Should Boycott Whitey's Olympics," *SEP,* March 9, 1968, 6, 10; Arnold Hano, "The Black Rebel Who 'Whitelists' the Olympics," *New York Times Magazine,* March 12, 1968, 32–50; Edwards, *Revolt of the Black Athlete,* 49–52; Harry Edwards, *The Struggle That Must Be: An Autobiography* (New York: Macmillan, 1980), 168–69; Jack Olsen, "The Cruel Deception," *SI,* July 1, 1968, 15; Axthelm, "The Angry Black Athlete," 56, 59 (see chap. 4, n. 12); Dick Schaap, "The Revolt of the Black Athletes," *Look,* August 6, 1968, 72; Douglas Hartmann, *Race, Culture, and the Revolt of the Black Athlete: The 1968 Olympic Protests and Their Aftermath* (Chicago: University of Chicago Press, 2003), 85–8; Amy Bass, *Not the Triumph but the Struggle: The 1968 Olympics and the Making of the Black Athlete* (Minneapolis: University of Minnesota Press, 2002), 89–92; Michael E. Lomax, "Revisiting *The Revolt of the Black Athlete:* Harry Edwards and the Making of the New African

American Sport Studies," *Journal of Sport History* 29 (Fall 2002): 470–74; *The Journey of the African American Athlete*, VHS, produced by Leslie D. Farrell (HBO Home Video, 1996).

14. *NYT,* December 16, 1967.

15. Edwards, *Revolt of the Black Athlete,* 53; Johnathan Rodgers, "A Step to an Olympic Boycott," *SI,* December 4, 1967, 30–31.

16. Edwards, *Revolt of the Black Athlete,* 53–54; Rodgers, "Step to an Olympic Boycott," 31; Hartmann, *Race, Culture, and the Revolt of the Black Athlete,* 56–57.

17. *SJMN,* November 24, 1967; *LAT,* November 24, 1967; Rodgers, "Step to an Olympic Boycott," 31.

18. *LAT,* November 25, 1967. In January 1968, Alcindor told the *Daily Bruin* that he was the only UCLA athlete who attended the OPHR. See *DB,* January 5, 1968.

19. *LAT,* December 1, 1967; *WP,* December 17, 1967; Lew Alcindor with Jack Olsen, "A Year of Turmoil and Decision," *SI,* November 10, 1969, 35.

20. "Olympics Boycott Is Off Target," *Life,* December 8, 1967, 4; *LAHE,* November 26, December 10, 1967; *NYT,* November 28, 1967; *SJMN,* November 26, 1967.

21. Dick Gregory with Robert Lipsyte, *Nigger: An Autobiography* (New York: Dutton, 1964); Lipsyte, *SportsWorld,* 74–91 (see chap. 3, n. 15); David Remnick, *King of the World: Muhammad Ali and the Rise of an American Hero* (New York: Vintage Books, 1998), 156; *NYT,* November 25, 1967.

22. *SFC,* November 26, 1967; *LAT,* November 25, 1967; *SJMN,* November 25, 1967.

23. Alcindor with Olsen, "Year of Turmoil and Decision," 35; *LAT,* December 1, 1967; Axthelm, "The Angry Black Athlete," 56; *LAS,* December 28, 1967.

24. John Wooden, "Organizational Plans," in *"Instant Replay" Notebook,* Seven-Up National Coaches Clinic, 1968, Goodwin Goldfaden Collection, University of Notre Dame Archives, South Bend, Ind.; N. Johnson, *Wooden Pyramid of Success,* 167 (see chap. 1, n. 14); *LAT,* February 23, 1967; Heitz, phone interview (see chap. 4, n. 40); Abdul-Jabbar and Knobler, *Giant Steps,* 147–48 (see chap. 3, n. 38).

25. Jill Jonnes, *Hep-Cats, Narcs, and Pipe Dreams: A History of America's Romance with Illegal Drugs* (New York: Scribner, 1996), 227–39; Perlstein, *Nixonland,* 75–78, 92–95 (see chap. 4, n. 5). See also Richard Goldstein's two-part series, "Drugs on the Campus," *SEP,* May 21, 1966, 40–62, and June 4, 1966, 34–44; *LAT,* January 30, April 6, 1966; Gerard J. De Groot, "Ronald Reagan and Student Unrest in California, 1966–1970," *Pacific Historical Review* 65 (February 1996): 107–13; and Dallek, *Right Moment,* 185–96 (see chap. 4, n. 5).

26. Chapin and Prugh, *Wizard of Westwood,* 256–58; *LAT,* May 24, June 24, 1967; *LAS,* May 25, 1967.

27. "Playboy Interview: Kareem Abdul-Jabbar," 58; Abdul-Jabbar and Knobler, *Giant Steps,* 137–39, 143. The literature on college athletes and drugs in the 1960s is almost nonexistent. See Scott, *The Athletic Revolution,* 143–51 (see preface, n. 8); and Bill Gilbert, "Problems in a Turned-On World," *SI,* June 23, 1969, 64–72.

28. "Welcome to Year Two in the Reign of King Lew," *SI,* December 4, 1967,

34–35; Jim Scott, "UCLA Powerhouse Five Is Back Intact," *SN,* December 9, 1967, 3, 6; *DB,* October 27, 1967; *LAT,* October 27, November 8, 1967; *LAS,* December 28, 1967.

29. *LAT,* September 22, 1965, November 10, 28, 1967, March 22, 2007; *DB,* February 12, 1973; Medley, *UCLA Basketball,* 83–88 (see chap. 1, n. 3); Dick Enberg with Jim Perry, *Dick Enberg: Oh My!* (Champaign, Ill.: Sports Publishing, 2004), 73–74; Robert A. Fischer, "The Right Man at the Right Time: J .D. Morgan," interview by David Rose, 1982, transcript 1984, UCLA OHC, 58–59.

30. R. Smith, *Play-by-Play,* 182–85 (see chap. 4, n. 28); Charles M. Neinas to Walter Byers, memorandum, March 27, 1962, Byers Papers, Folder "Basketball, University Division, March 1965–June 1965"; Charles M. Neinas to NCAA Basketball Managers, March 1, 1963, Byers Papers, Folder "Basketball, University Division, March 1965–June 1965"; *1963–1964 Yearbook of the National Collegiate Athletic Association,* Convention Proceedings, January 6–8, 1964, 180; Gwilym S. Brown, "The Maitre D' of Sports TV," *SI,* November 8, 1965, 52–54; *DB,* January 6, 1967, January 21, 1971; Jim Scott, "TV Sports Net Growing Fast," *SN,* June 17, 1967, 46; "TVS Station Clearances and Contracts Signed as of November 27, 1967," Byers Papers, Folder "Television, General, October 1967–November 1967"; Einhorn with Rapoport, *How March Became Madness,* vii–ix (see chap. 3, n. 38). In 1968 Howard Hughes purchased SNI and renamed the company the Hughes Sports Network. See "New Interest," *SI,* September 16, 1968, 17.

31. *LAT,* December 4, 1966, March 14, 1974, January 20, 2008; William Leggett, "NBC and the New College Try," *SI,* June 2, 1975, 52; Enberg with Perry, *Dick Enberg: Oh My!,* 76; Einhorn with Rapoport, *How March Became Madness,* 37–39, 55–56; Wells Twombly, "UCLA-Houston Game Excites Texas Fans," *SN,* January 20, 1968, 7; *HC,* January 20, 1988; Eddie Einhorn, phone interview with the author, May 10, 2011.

32. Roy Terrell, "Fast Man with a .45," *SI,* March 26, 1962, 32–36, 41–42; Roger Angell, "The Cool Bubble," *New Yorker,* May 14, 1966, 132, 135; Liz Smith, "Giltfinger's Golden Dome," *SI,* April 12, 1965, 44–46, 51–52, 54, 56, 58, 63; Gary Cartwright, "A Barnum Named Hofheinz, a Big Top Called Astrodome," *New York Times Magazine,* July 21, 1968, 10, 13, 16; Tex Maule, "The Greatest Showman on Earth, and He's the First to Admit It," *SI,* April 21, 1969, 36–38, 41, 44, 49.

33. "The Man in Huckster House," *Time,* August 15, 1955, 10; "Here Comes the Judge—Again," *Newsweek,* 74–75; Terrell, "Fast Man with a .45," 34–36; Maule, "Greatest Showman on Earth," 38, 41; Cartwright, "Barnum Named Hofheinz," 18.

34. Houston Sports Association, Inc., to H. B. "Bebe" Lee, July 9, 1968, Byers Papers, Folder "Basketball, Tournament Committee, 1968"; Terrell, "Fast Man with a .45," 36; L. Smith, "Giltfinger's Golden Dome," 51–52; Frank X. Tolbert, "The Incredible Houston Dome," *Look,* April 20, 1965, 96, 98; Angell, "Cool Bubble," 130–31; *DB,* January 22, 1968.

35. Cartwright, "Barnum Named Hofheinz," 10; Einhorn with Rapoport, *How March Became Madness,* 38; *LAT,* November 10, 1967; *HC,* January 20, 1988.

36. Dick Moore, "52,000 Crowd at Cage Game? It May Happen!," *SN*, December 9, 1967, 10; *WP*, January 5, 1968; *NYT*, January 6, 1968; *HC*, January 17, 19, 20, 21, 1968; *LAT*, January 6, 20, 1968; *The Houston-U.C.L.A. Basketball Classic: A TVS Sports Special*, promotional brochure, Byers Papers, Folder "Television, General, October 1967–December 1967"; *DB*, January 19, 1968; Joe Jares, "A Dandy in the Dome," *SI*, January 29, 1968, 16; Einhorn with Rapoport, *How March Became Madness*, 57; *HC*, January 21, 1968.

37. Einhorn with Rapoport, *How March Became Madness*, ix–x; *LAT*, January 20, 1968, March 14, 1974; Jares, "Dandy in the Dome," 16; *Houston-U.C.L.A. Basketball Classic; HC*, January 22, 1968; William Leggett, "Midsummer's Night Kickoff," *SI*, May 6, 1974, 57; Einhorn, phone interview. *Sports Illustrated* reported that TVS profited fifty thousand dollars from the UCLA-Houston game in the Astrodome.

38. *WP*, January 18, 1968; *LAT*, January 21, 1968; Jares, "Dandy in the Dome," 19; *HC*, January 21, 1968; Shackelford, phone interview (see chap. 4, n. 40); Bill Sweek, phone interview with the author, March 24, 2011.

39. *DB*, January 16, 1968; *WP*, January 17, 1968; Medley, *UCLA Basketball*, 120–21; *LAT*, January 19, 1968; *HC*, January 22, 1968; Alcindor with Olsen, "UCLA Was a Mistake," 40 (see chap. 3, n. 53).

40. *LAT*, January 21, 1968; Jares, "Dandy in the Dome," 16; "Alcindor vs. Hayes," *Sport*, April 1968, 48; Medley, *UCLA Basketball*, 122, 128.

41. Medley, *UCLA Basketball*, 123; Einhorn with Rapoport, *How March Became Madness*, 51, 73; *HC*, January 21, 1968.

42. *LAT*, January 21, 1968; *HC*, January 21, 22, 1968; Medley, *UCLA Basketball*, 123–24; *The Game That Changed College Basketball*, accompanying DVD (game footage) in Einhorn with Rapoport, *When March Became Madness*.

43. Ibid.

44. R. Smith, *Play-by-Play*, 187; Rader, *In Its Own Image*, 67; Roberts and Olson, *Winning Is the Only Thing*, 02; Carl Lindeman Jr., vice president of NBC Sports, to NCAA Basketball Television Committee, April 9, 1968, and Walter Byers to Lindeman, April 15, 1968, Byers Papers, Folder "Television, Basketball Championships, 1969"; William Hyland to Walter Byers, May 27, 1968, Byers Papers, Folder "Television, General, May 1968–August 1968"; Leggett, "NBC and the New College Try," 52; Hazel Hardy, "The Many Slices of the Sports TV Pie," *Broadcasting*, December 1, 1969, 50. In 1968 SNI paid two hundred thousand dollars to show the NCAA Championship.

45. *LAS*, January 25, 1968; Lopez, *Cougars of Any Color*, 143, 155–56 (see chap. 4, n. 55); Martin, "Jim Crow in the Gymnasium," 81–82 (see chap. 4, n. 24); Jacobs, *Across the Line*, 333 (see chap. 4, n. 26).

46. Chapin and Prugh, *Wizard of Westwood*, 167; *LAT*, January 25, 1968; Medley, *UCLA Basketball*, 115–17; Alcindor with Olsen, "Year of Turmoil and Decision," 38.

47. *LAT*, January 25, 1968; Medley, *UCLA Basketball*, 125–26.

48. Chapin and Prugh, *Wizard of Westwood*, 263–65; *LAT*, January 29, 1968.

49. Chapin and Prugh, *Wizard of Westwood,* 262; Alcindor with Olsen, "Year of Turmoil and Decision," 38.

50. Alcindor with Olsen, "Year of Turmoil and Decision," 38; *DB,* January 12, 1968; *LAT,* January 30, 1968; Sweek, phone interview.

51. Bass, *Not the Triumph but the Struggle,* 194–95; Wiggins, *Glory Bound,* 114–15, 126–30; Axthelm, "The Angry Black Athlete," 58; "The Olympic Jolt: 'Hell No, Don't Go!,'" *Life,* March 15, 1968, 26; William Johnson, "Collision on the New Underground Railroad," *SI,* February 12, 1968, 52–53; *LAT,* January 24, 1968; David Llorens, "Natural Hair: New Symbol of Race Pride," *Ebony,* December 1967, 140–41; Van Deburg, *New Day in Babylon,* 195–201 (see chap. 3, n. 46). For more on the career of Bob Presley, see Herb Michelson, *Almost a Famous Person* (New York: Harcourt, 1980).

52. Edwards, *Revolt of the Black Athlete,* 88; Wiggins, *Glory Bound,* 124; *NYT,* May 19, 1968, November 16, 1969; Scott, *The Athletic Revolution,* 80 (see preface, n. 8).

53. *LAT,* January 30, 1968; *LAS,* February 1, 1968.

54. Olsen, "Pride and Prejudice," 27–28, 31 (see chap. 4, n. 11); *LAT,* April 1, 1969; *CSM,* March 26, 1968; Axthelm, "The Angry Black Athlete," 56; Chapin and Prugh, *Wizard of Westwood,* 161–62.

55. "Olympic Jolt," 27; Kirkpatrick, "UCLA: Simple, Awesomely Simple," 43 (see chap. 4, n. 11); Chapin and Prugh, *Wizard of Westwood,* 304.

56. Kirkpatrick, "UCLA: Simple, Awesomely Simple," 43; Wooden, *Practical Modern Basketball,* 58 (see chap. 1, n. 26); Wooden with Jamison, *Wooden: A Lifetime of Observations,* 123 (see chap. 1, n. 28); Bill Libby, *The Walton Gang* (New York: Coward, McCann & Geoghegan, 1974), 170.

57. Wooden with Tobin, *They Call Me Coach,* 144; Wooden with Jamison, *My Personal Best,* 154–55; Wooden with Jamison, *Wooden,* 156–57; *LAT,* February 7, 1969.

58. *LAT,* February 28, 1968; *DB,* February 28, 1968; "Olympic Jolt," 28; *WP,* March 6, 1968.

59. *SI,* January 29, 1968; Abdul-Jabbar and Knobler, *Giant Steps,* 162; Joe Jares, "Rematch for Elvin and Big Lew," *SI,* March 18, 1968, 26–29; Joe Jares, "A Sleeper Sneaks into the NCAA Cast," *SI,* March 25, 1968, 26–29.

60. *LAT,* March 23, 1968; Joe Jares, "Two Routs to a Title," *SI,* April 1, 1968, 12; Einhorn with Rapoport, *How March Became Madness,* 47, 84.

61. *LAT,* March 23, 1968; Jares, "Two Routs to a Title," 14.

62. Ibid.

63. *LAT,* March 24, 1968; Jares, "Two Routs to a Title."

64. Ibid.; *CT,* March 24, 1968; Bob Oates, "Three in Row? Bruins 'Have It in Mind,'" *SN,* April 6, 1968, 41–42.

65. *NYT,* July 23, 1968; *CD,* August 3, 1968; Alcindor as told to Kaplan, "Why I Turned Down a Million Dollars," 76.

66. Hartmann, *Race, Culture, and the Revolt of the Black Athlete,* 128–29; *CD,* April 3, 1968; *LAT,* July 30, August 23, 1968. In 1968 Charles Maher wrote a five-part series on black athletes for the *Los Angeles Times.*

Chapter 6. Woman Chasers and Hopheads

1. Abdul-Jabbar and Knobler, *Giant Steps*, 165–69 (see chap. 3, n. 38); Alcindor with Olsen, "Year of Turmoil and Decision," 36–37 (see chap. 5, n. 19); Alcindor with Olsen, "UCLA Was a Mistake," 36–37, 45 (see chap. 3, n. 53). On Malcolm X, see Manning Marable, *Malcolm X: A Life of Reinvention* (New York: Viking, 2011).

2. Alcindor with Olsen, "Year of Turmoil and Decision," 37; Abdul-Jabbar and Knobler, *Giant Steps*, 168–73.

3. Abdul-Jabbar and Knobler, *Giant Steps*, 172–81.

4. "Playboy Interview: Kareem Abdul-Jabbar," 62, 66 (see chap. 5, n. 12); Langlais, "Exclusive: Kareem Abdul-Jabbar," 12 (see chap. 4, n. 1); *LAT,* March 3, 1977; Abdul-Jabbar with Obstfeld, *On the Shoulders of Giants*, 123, 126 (see chap. 3, n. 46); Richard Brent Turner, *Islam in the African American Experience* (Bloomington: Indiana University Press, 1997), 1–4; *NYT,* October 13, 1996; Abdul-Jabbar and Knobler, *Giant Steps*, 60–61. In the late 1960s and 1970s, many African American basketball players accepted Muslim names, including UCLA stars Walt Hazzard (Mahdi Abdul-Rahmad) and Keith Wilkes (Jamaal Abdul-Lateef). See Bill Rhoden, "Athletes Search for Inner Peace through Religions and Mind Science," *Ebony,* July 1975, 94–99; George, *Elevating the Game*, 162–64 (see chap. 1, n. 44).

5. Alcindor with Olsen, "Year of Turmoil and Decision," 37–38; Abdul-Jabbar with Obstfeld, *On the Shoulders of Giants*, 123. In 1971, before the State Department sponsored his trip to Africa, Kareem Abdul-Jabbar asked the press and the public to use his Muslim name. See *NYT,* June 4, 1971. Since the public still called him Lew Alcindor in 1969, I will continue to use that name.

6. *LAT,* May 25, 1968; *DB,* May 27, 1968.

7. Libby, *The Walton Gang*, 160 (see chap. 5, n. 56); Hano, "Winning," 138 (see chap. 3, n. 37); Chapin and Prugh, *Wizard of Westwood*, 7, 9 (see chap. 1, n. 1).

8. *LAT,* May 28, 1968, February 20, 1969, March 4, 1984, March 19, 2007; Medley, *UCLA Basketball*, 11, 138; Dwight Chapin, phone interview with the author, March 25, 2011.

9. *LAT,* March 19, 2007; Bisheff, *John Wooden*, 238 (see chap. 1, n. 33); Jerry Norman interview in N. Johnson, *Wooden Pyramid of Success*, 403–4 (see chap. 1, n. 14).

10. *LAT,* December 26, 1967; *DB,* May 29, 1968; *LAHE,* January 9, 1969; Bill Bruns, "The UCLA Dynasty: Behind the Scenes with Lew Alcindor and Company," *Sport,* April 1969, 90; Einhorn with Rapoport, *How March Became Madness,* 75 (see chap. 3, n. 38). In an HBO documentary, Lucius Allen said, "We weren't the closest team off the court. We'd go on the road and the black guys hang together [and] the white guys hang together." See *The UCLA Dynasty,* DVD (Home Box Office, 2008).

11. *DB,* October 15, 1968; *LAT,* October 15, December 23, 1968; *LAHE,* January 7, 1969; Joe Goldstein, "It's UCLA All the Way," *SN,* December 7, 1968, 3; Shackelford, phone interview (see chap. 4, n. 40).

12. *LAT,* November 29, December 8, 24, 1968, January 13, 1969; Jeff Prugh, "Triple-

Threat Soph Phalanx Is Aiding Lew," *SN*, March 8, 1969, 17; *NYT*, December 28, 1968; *NYDN*, December 27, 29, 1968.

13. Pepe, *Stand Tall*, 113 (see chap. 3, n. 33); Bruns, "UCLA Dynasty," 90.

14. Sweek, phone interview (see chap. 5, n. 38); Heitz, phone interview (see chap. 4, n. 40); Abdul-Jabbar and Knobler, *Giant Steps*, 176.

15. *NYDN*, December 28, 1968; *New York Post*, December 28, 1968; *DB*, February 23, 1968, February 21, 1969; Bruns, "UCLA Dynasty," 89; Heitz, phone interview.

16. Bruns, "UCLA Dynasty," 90; *Meriden (Conn.) Journal*, January 16, 1969.

17. Bruns, "UCLA Dynasty," 90; Heitz, phone interview.

18. James Tuite, "No Knock on Wooden," *Basketball Extra* (1970–71): 76; Le Sourd, "John Wooden," 12 (see chap. 4, n. 19); Bruns, "UCLA Dynasty," 90; *Meriden (Conn.) Journal*, January 16, 1969.

19. *LAT*, January 12, 1969; Heitz, phone interview.

20. *LAT*, January 19, 1969; *DB*, January 20, 1969; Heitz, phone interview.

21. Libby, *The Walton Gang*, 80–81; Chapin and Prugh, *Wizard of Westwood*, 306.

22. "Racial Conflict: Black against Black," *Newsweek*, January 27, 1969, 30; *DB*, November 20, 1967; "California: University on Trial," *Newsweek*, November 23, 1970, 85.

23. Kemper, "Reformers in the Marketplace of Ideas," 219–20 (see chap. 1, n. 22). *Nommo* (UCLA's black student newsmagazine), December 4, 1968. On black student organizations and institutions, see Van Deburg, *New Day in Babylon*, 64–82 (see chap. 3, n. 46). UCLA conducted its first ethnic student survey in 1968. See *DB*, January 19, 1968.

24. "Racial Conflict," 30; *LAT*, February 16, 1969; Ray Rogers, "Black Guns on Campus," *Nation*, May 5, 1969, 558–59; Kemper, "Reformers in the Marketplace of Ideas," 214–34. For a history of US, see Scott Brown, *Fighting for US: Mualana Karenga, the US Organization, and Black Cultural Nationalism* (New York: New York University Press, 2003).

25. R. Rogers, "Black Guns on Campus," 559; *DB*, January 20, 21, 1969; Bisheff, *John Wooden*, 154–55.

26. *LAHE*, March 9, 12, 17, 1969.

27. *LAT*, March 18, 20, 21, 1969; Joe Jares, "Reprieve—and an Electroluminescent Finale," *SI*, March 31, 1969, 17; Medley, *UCLA Basketball*, 154–55.

28. Medley, *UCLA Basketball*, 154–55; *LAT*, March 21, 1969; Chapin and Prugh, *Wizard of Westwood*, 177–78; Wooden with Tobin, *They Call Me Coach*, 156 (see chap. 1, n. 2); Sweek, phone interview.

29. Alcindor with Olsen, "Year of Decision and Turmoil," 38, 43; Medley, *UCLA Basketball*, 154; Sweek, phone interview.

30. Sweek, phone interview; Alcindor with Olsen, "Year of Decision and Turmoil," 43; Libby, *The Walton Gang*, 58; Curry Kirkpatrick, "The Week He Finally Got Rid of the Yoke," *SI*, March 31, 1969, 18.

31. *LAT*, March 22, 23, 1969; *LAHE*, March 23, 1969.

32. Kirkpatrick, "Week He Finally Got Rid of the Yoke," 18; *LAT,* March 23, 1969; *DB,* February 14, 1969; "UCLA Coach Says Alcindor Has Had Migraines," *Jet,* February 27, 1969, 54.

33. *CT,* March 24, 1969.

Chapter 7. The Desperate Coach

1. UCLA Basketball Awards Banquet Program, May 4, 1970; *LAT,* May 11, 1970; Hill, phone interview (see preface, n. 6).

2. *DB,* April 6, May 15, 1970; *LAT,* May 11, 1970; *Pasadena Star-News,* May 6, 1970; Andrew Hill with John Wooden, *Be Quick—but Don't Hurry: Finding Success in the Teachings of a Lifetime* (New York: Simon & Schuster, 2001), 32–33.

3. *LAT,* May 11, 1970; *DB,* April 6, 1970.

4. *DB,* April 2, 4, May 29, 1968; *Santa Monica Evening Outlook,* February 27, 1968; Kemper, "Reformers in the Marketplace of Ideas," 185 (see chap. 1, n. 22). On political conservatism in Southern California, see McGirr, *Suburban Warriors* (see chap. 1, n. 21).

5. Anderson, *Movement and the Sixties,* 326–27 (see chap. 2, n. 17); Rorabaugh, *Berkeley at War,* 145–66 (see chap. 3, n. 11); De Groot, "Ronald Reagan and Student Unrest," 107–29 (see chap. 5, n. 25); Todd Gitlin, *The Sixties: Years of Hope, Days of Rage* (New York: Bantam Books, 1993), 414–15.

6. *DB,* May 19, 20, 22, 26, 1969; Kemper, "Reformers in the Marketplace of Ideas," 185–88; *LAT,* June 15, 1969. The *Daily Bruin* estimated that 30 percent of UCLA students boycotted classes during the strike.

7. *LAT,* June 15, 1969; *DB,* May 20, 22, 1969.

8. *DB,* October 15, 16, 1969; *LAT,* June 15, 1969; Perlstein, *Nixonland,* 423–24 (see chap. 4, n. 5); Tom Wells, *The War Within: America's Battle over Vietnam* (Berkeley and Los Angeles: University of California Press, 1994), 371; "Over the Threshold of Dissent," *Life,* October 24, 1969, 35; Charles DeBenedetti with Charles Chatfield, *An American Ordeal: The American Antiwar Movement* (Syracuse, N.Y.: Syracuse University Press, 1990), 255–57.

9. Hill with Wooden, *Be Quick—but Don't Hurry,* 24–27; Hill, phone interview.

10. Hill with Wooden, *Be Quick—but Don't Hurry,* 24–27; Farber, *Age of Great Dreams,* 167–68 (see chap. 3, n. 7). One interviewer later quoted Walt Hazzard who said that he did not think that Wooden "was really in favor of the demonstrations back in the early sixties when there was civil disobedience. I believe he felt they should obey the law." See Hazzard interview in N. Johnson, *Wooden Pyramid of Success,* 364 (see chap. 1, n. 14). In 1990 Wooden said that during the Vietnam War, he criticized draft dodgers. He believed that if a young man was drafted, he had a duty to serve. See *San Diego Evening-Tribune,* November 16, 1990.

11. Perlstein, *Nixonland,* 304–5; Robert Mason, *Richard Nixon and the Quest for a New Majority* (Chapel Hill: University of North Carolina Press, 2004), 28–32, 43–45; "Man and Woman of the Year: The Middle Americans," *Time,* January 1970, 10–17.

12. Wind, "West of the Wabash," 101 (see chap. 1, n. 36); Tuite, "No Knock on Wooden," 6 (see chap. 6, n. 18).

13. *LAHE,* December 4, 1968; Wooden with Tobin, *They Call Me Coach,* 158 (see chap. 1, n. 2); *St. Petersburg Evening Independent,* July 21, 1970; Medley, *UCLA Basketball,* 179–80; *LAT,* February 6, 1971; Zang, *SportsWars,* 15 (see preface, n. 8); John Ecker, phone interview with the author, March 29, 2011. In 1971 Wooden explained, "If a boy comes to me and wants to wear long hair or a beard, I ask him to prove to me that it is part of his ethnic culture. If he can do it, he can wear it." See Edwards, *The Sociology of Sport,* 106 (see chap. 3, n. 19).

14. Steve Murdock, "The Dissident Varsity," *Nation,* March 16, 1970, 305–7; Anderson, *Movement and the Sixties,* 258–61; Michael Oriard, *Bowled Over: Big-Time Football from the Sixties to the BCS Era* (Chapel Hill: University of North Carolina Press, 2009), 15–17, 41, 48; Zang, *SportsWars,* 13–17; Edwards, *The Sociology of Sport,* 105–6; John Underwood, "The Desperate Coach," *SI,* August 25, 1969, 66–76; John Underwood, "Shave Off That Thing!," *SI,* September 1, 1969, 21–27.

15. Underwood, "Shave Off That Thing!," 22; Zang, *SportsWars,* 5, 13–17, 78; Oriard, *Bowled Over,* 15–21; "From Hair to Eternity!," *Scholastic Coach,* September 1970, 5, 106–9; *CT,* May 25, 1968; *NYT,* November 16, 1969; Lipsyte, *SportsWorld,* 126–27 (see chap. 3, n. 15); Jack Scott, "Jocks—1, War—0," *Ramparts,* August 1970, 15; Underwood, "The Desperate Coach," 71.

16. *LAT,* January 8, 1969; Underwood, "The Desperate Coach," 70–71; Oriard, *Bowled Over,* 48.

17. *Program of the 63rd Annual Convention of the National Collegiate Athletic Association,* January 6–8, 1969, 29, NCAA Archives, Indianapolis; "Out of Right Field," *Newsweek,* January 5, 1970, 35; *NYT,* January 9, November 6, 1969, January 24, 1970; Scott, *The Athletic Revolution,* 188–90 (see preface, n. 8); "A Special *NEWS* Feature . . . Militant Groups," *NCAA News,* December 1969, 2–3. It is unclear why only 246 votes were cast in regards to legislation that affected 610 NCAA member schools. I am uncertain whether John Wooden or J. D. Morgan attended the convention, though it is highly possible that they did, considering that it took place in Los Angeles.

18. *NYT,* January 20, 1969; Frank J. Remington to Walter Byers, February 14, 1969, Byers Papers, Folder "Constitutions, Bylaws, and Amendments, 1969"; "Hogwash," *SI,* January 20, 1969, 7.

19. *LAT,* October 15, November 30, 1969; *DB,* October 17, 1969; *LAHE,* December 1, 1969; Bruns, "UCLA Dynasty," 90 (see chap. 6, n. 10).

20. Heitz, phone interview (see chap. 4, n. 40); Rich Buchea, "Keeper of the Flame," *UCLA Alumni Magazine,* Winter 1970, 32–34; *LAT,* January 30, 1969; *DB,* January 22, 1971; Chapin and Prugh, *Wizard of Westwood,* 205 (see chap. 1, n. 1).

21. *LAT,* March 12, 1974; *DB,* January 22, 1971; Alexander Wolff, "The Coach and His Champion," *SI,* April 3, 1989, 98; Ecker, phone interview.

22. *LAT,* January 8, 1970; *DB,* January 23, 1970; *Orange County Register,* February 22, 1996.

23. *LAHE,* February 10, 1967; Dwight Chapin, "King Lew Is Gone, but Bruin

Reign Rolls On," *SN*, March 7, 1970, 31; *LAT*, January 16, 1969, February 27, 1970; *DB*, January 31, 1969, February 2, 1970; Dwight Chapin, "Super Sidney Wicks—College Player of Year," *SN*, March 13, 1971, 3; Steve Bisheff, "When Sidney Turns On, Opponents Flip Out," *Sport*, March 1971, 44–45.

24. Chapin and Prugh, *Wizard of Westwood*, 192–93; *LAT*, February 27, 1970, March 10, 1971; *LAHE*, February 22, 1971; Mark Ribowsky, "I Don't Really Care Who Likes Me," *Black Sports*, January 1978, 19.

25. *LAHE*, December 1, 1969, January 5, 1970; *LAT*, December 13, 1969, January 4, 1970.

26. Curry Kirkpatrick, "It's More Fun without Lew," *SI*, February 2, 1970, 9–11; Chapin, "King Is Long Gone," 31; *LAT*, February 22, 1970; *LAHE*, February 23, 1970.

27. John Vallely, phone interview, April 20, 2011; Hill with Wooden, *Be Quick—but Don't Hurry*, 35; Medley, *UCLA Basketball*, 166–67, 173.

28. *LAT*, March 7, 1970; Joe Jares, "Time for the Mighty Scramble," *SI*, March 16, 1970, 22, 24, 27.

29. National Enterprise Association writer Mark Ribowsky reported the altercation between Wooden and Wicks and the subsequent confrontation between Wooden and a sportswriter. See his wire story in the *Waterloo Daily Courier*, March 29, 1970; and *WP*, March 19, 1970.

30. Ibid.

31. Medley, *UCLA Basketball*, 171; *NYT*, July 28, December 6, 1969; Jerry Izenburg, *How Many Miles to Camelot? The All American Sports Myth* (New York: Holt, Rinehart, and Winston, 1972), 40–45; "Eli Harvard," *SI*, March 23, 1970, 16. Andy Hill asked J. D. Morgan if he could compete in the Maccabiah Games. Morgan told Hill that if he played in the Games, the NCAA would not allow him to play for UCLA when he returned. See *DB*, November 6, 1970.

32. Joe Jares, "Up, Up, and Away Go Artis and New J.U.," *SI*, January 5, 1970, 18–21; *WP*, March 21, 1970; *LAHE*, March 21, 1970; *LAT*, March 21, 1970; *CT*, March 21, 1970; *Albuquerque Journal*, March 21, 1970; Steve Guback, "Bruins' Fast Break Sends Dolphins Off the Deep End," *SN*, April 4, 1970, 39.

33. *LAT*, March 21, 1970.

34. On expressions of black "soul," see Van Deburg, *New Day in Babylon*, 194–204 (see chap. 3, n. 46); and Jares, "Up, Up, and Away," 18–20.

35. *WP*, March 21, 1970; Jares, "Up, Up, and Away," 18.

36. Joe Jares, "Victory by Mystique," *SI*, March 30, 1970, 16–19; *The UCLA Dynasty* (see chap. 6, n. 10); *LAT*, March 22, 1970.

37. *WP*, March 23, 1970; Jares, "Victory by Mystique," 19; *LAHE*, March 22, 1970.

38. *LAT*, March 24, 1970; *LAHE*, March 24, 1970.

39. Wooden never publicly discussed his political views and did not explain why he voted for Nixon. Previously, he considered himself a Democrat because his father voted Democrat. Wooden voted for Nixon in 1968 and again in 1972. He also voted for Republican Ronald Reagan twice. See N. Johnson, *Wooden Pyramid of Success,*

217; Seth Davis, "Checking in on John Wooden," SI.com, August 24, 2009, http://sportsillustrated.cnn.com/2009/writers/seth_davis/08/24/john.wooden/index.html; and Perlstein, *Nixonland,* 476–79.

40. Hill, phone interview; Heineman, *Put Your Bodies upon the Wheels,* 174–76 (see chap. 3, n. 7); Anderson, *Movement and the Sixties,* 349–51; Kemper, "Reformers in the Marketplace of Ideas," 189–90; Perlstein, *Nixonland,* 488.

41. *LAT,* May 11, 1970; Medley, *UCLA Basketball,* 175–76.

42. Medley, *UCLA Basketball,* 175–79.

43. *DB,* May 5, 6, 1970; *Violence at UCLA: May 5, 1970,* a report by the Chancellor's Commission on the events of May 5, 1970, 9–10, 12–17. Scholars disagree about the number of protests and strikes that occurred in the week after Kent State. See Anderson, *Movement and the Sixties,* 350; Wells, *War Within,* 425; Perlstein, *Nixonland,* 490; and *The Report of the President's Commission on Campus Unrest* (Washington, D.C.: U.S. Government Printing Office, 1970), 17–18.

44. *Violence at UCLA,* 20, 22, 24–27, 35; *DB,* May 6, 1970; *A Preliminary Report on the Conduct of Police on Campus, May 12, 1970,* Record Series 260, Records Pertaining to Campus Unrest, 1966–71, Folder 8, Petitions and Resolutions—1970, Box 1, Moratorium History Committee, UCLA Archives.

45. *LAHE,* May 7, 1970; *LAT,* May 7, 1970; Medley, *UCLA Basketball,* 176–77; Libby, *The Walton Gang,* 68 (see chap. 5, n. 56).

46. Libby, *The Walton Gang,* 68; *LAT,* June 9, 1971, March 20, 1974, January 31, February 1, 1982; John Akers, untitled article, *Basketball Times,* April 2005, n.p.

47. Ecker, phone interview; Medley, *UCLA Basketball,* 177.

48. Supposedly, the *Los Angeles Times* agreed to print the entire team letter, but the conservative newspaper reported only that the team wrote a letter in protest against the war. See *LAT,* May 8, 1970, February 1, 1982; Medley, *UCLA Basketball,* 177; Hill with Wooden, *Be Quick—but Don't Hurry,* 36–37; UCLA 1970 NCAA Basketball Champions [thirteen names] to President Richard Nixon, c/o H. R. Haldeman, May 7, 1970, English Undergraduate Association, 1970 Folder, Box 1, Moratorium History Committee, UCLA Archives.

49. *NYT,* May 7, 1970; *LAT,* May 20, 1970; *DC,* May 12, 13, 1970; Scott, "Jocks—1, War—0," 17–18.

50. *DC,* May 22, 1970.

51. Anderson, *Movement and the Sixties,* xiii; *DB,* March 30, 2010.

52. Medley, *UCLA Basketball,* 177–78.

53. Kirkpatrick, "UCLA: Simple, Awesomely Simple," 43 (see chap. 4, n. 11); Hill with Wooden, *Be Quick—but Don't Hurry,* 34; Medley, *UCLA Basketball,* 177; Libby, *The Walton Gang,* 69.

Chapter 8. The Red Menace

1. *NYT,* December 24, 1972; Jeff Prugh, "UCLA's Rebel with a Cause," *Popular Sports Basketball,* 1972, 8; Dwight Chapin, "College Player of the Year—UCLA Soph

Walton," *SN,* March 18, 1972, 5. This description is drawn from a photo taken by George Long on October 14, 1971. See Getty Images, http://www.gettyimages.com/detail/81393465/Sports-Illustrated.

2. Libby, *The Walton Gang,* 20–21, 35 (see chap. 5, n. 56).

3. *DB,* January 14, 1972; Chapin and Prugh, *Wizard of Westwood,* 275–76 (see chap. 1, n. 1); Bortstein, *UCLA's Fabulous Bruins,* 92 (see chap. 2, n. 32); Libby, *The Walton Gang,* 29; *LAT,* December 29, 1971; William F. Reed, "Big Bill Loves to Eat 'Em Up," *SI,* March 6, 1972, 24–26; Prugh, "UCLA's Rebel with a Cause," 10.

4. Libby, *The Walton Gang,* 149.

5. Ibid., 254; Hill with Wooden, *Be Quick—but Don't Hurry,* 116–17 (see chap. 7, n. 2); "The Wooden Style," *Time,* February 12, 1973, 66; Wooden with Jamison, *Wooden: A Lifetime of Observations,* 99–100 (see chap. 1, n. 28); Wooden and Jamison, *Wooden on Leadership,* 238–39 (see chap. 1, n. 15).

6. *LAT,* October 16, 1971, January 14, 1972; Bill Walton with Gene Wojciechowski, *Nothing but Net: Just Give Me the Ball and Get Out of the Way* (New York: Hyperion, 1994), 17.

7. Nater and Gallimore, *You Haven't Taught until They Have Learned,* 4–5, 18, 79 (see chap. 1, n. 26); *LAT,* January 14, 1972; Walton with Wojciechowski, *Nothing but Net,* 18.

8. "The Wooden Style," 66; Walton with Wojciechowski, *Nothing but Net,* 18; Dan Berger, "Wooden's Way," *College Basketball Guide,* 1972, 50, 52; *WP,* February 17, 1971; Chapin and Prugh, *Wizard of Westwood,* 228–29. On Vince Lombardi's coaching philosophy, see David Maraniss, *When Pride Still Mattered: A Life of Vince Lombardi* (New York: Simon & Schuster, 2000), 213–26, 255.

9. *LAHF,* February 4, 22, 1971; Joe Jares, "Camille Goes under Again," *SI,* February 15, 1971; Medley, *UCLA Basketball,* 186–87, 197 (see chap. 1, n. 3); *DB,* January 6, March 5, 1971.

10. Larry Farmer, phone interview with the author, April 27, 2011.

11. Ibid.

12. Chapin, phone interview (see chap. 6, n. 8).

13. *LAT,* October 16, 1971; William F. Reed, "Court Trial for UCLA's New Gang," *SI,* January 10, 1972, 20.

14. Reed, "Court Trial for UCLA's New Gang," 20; Reed, "Big Bill Loves to Eat 'Em Up," 25–26; *LAT,* November 28, 1971.

15. *LAHE,* December 2, 1971; Chapin and Prugh, *Wizard of Westwood,* 253; Reed, "Court Trial for UCLA's New Gang," 20.

16. Richard "Digger" Phelps and Larry Keith, *A Coach's World* (New York: Warner Books, 1975), 17; *LAHE,* December 22, 23, 1971; *LAT,* December 23, 1971; Digger Phelps with Tim Bourret, *Digger Phelps's Tales from the Notre Dame Hardwood* (Champaign, Ill.: Sports Publishing, 2004), 20–21. Phelps cleaned up the quote for his book.

17. *LAHE,* December 23, 1971; Phelps with Bourret, *Digger Phelps's Tales,* 20–21.

18. Reed, "Court Trial for UCLA's New Gang," 19; Ray Marquette, "'Walton Key

to UCLA Bid for 7 in a Row'—Wooden," *SN,* February 26, 1972, 26; Reed, "Big Bill Loves to Eat 'Em Up," 26; *LAHE,* December 1, 1971, February 28, 1972.

19. *LAT,* February 11, December 29, 1971; David Halberstam, *The Breaks of the Game* (New York: Ballantine Books, 1981), 147–52; John Papanek, "Climbing to the Top Again," *SI,* October 15, 1979, 113; "Bill Walton: Basketball's Vegetarian Tiger," *Time,* February 25, 1974, 76.

20. Reed, "Big Bill Loves to Eat 'Em Up," 24; *DB,* January 24, 1972.

21. Reed, "Big Bill Loves to Eat 'Em Up," 24; Papanek, "Climbing to the Top Again," 104; Ralph Barbieri, "A Visit with Bill Walton . . . & from the FBI," *Sport,* August 1975, 81; Halberstam, *Breaks of the Game,* 148; Michael Jay Kauffman, "At Home with Bill Walton," *Crawdaddy,* May 1975, 40; Libby, *The Walton Gang,* 98; Einhorn with Rapoport, *How March Became Madness,* 25–28 (see chap. 3, n. 38).

22. Einhorn with Rapoport, *How March Became Madness,* 25; Walton with Wojciechowski, *Nothing but Net,* 13; Bisheff, *John Wooden,* 136–37 (see chap. 1, n. 33); "He Just May Be the Baddest Ever," *SI,* November 26, 1973, 66.

23. Reed, "Big Bill Loves to Eat 'Em Up," 26; Walton with Wojciechowski, *Nothing but Net,* 14; Halberstam, *Breaks of the Game,* 147–53; Libby, *The Walton Gang,* 97.

24. *LAT,* December 29, 1971, March 3, 1981; Walton with Wojciechowski, *Nothing but Net,* 14–16; Halberstam, *Breaks of the Game,* 148–49; Reed, "Big Bill Loves to Eat 'Em Up," 26.

25. Reed, "Big Bill Loves to Eat 'Em Up," 26; Prugh, "UCLA's Rebel with a Cause," 8; *Seattle Times,* February 20, 1972; Todd Boyd, *Young, Black, Rich, & Famous: The Rise of the NBA, the Hip Hop Invasion, and the Transformation of American Culture* (New York: Doubleday, 2003), 25; Frank T. Bannister, "Search for 'White Hopes' Threatens Black Athletes," *Ebony,* February 1980; "The Black Dominance," *Time,* May 9, 1977, 57; Libby, *The Walton Gang,* 100; Leonard Shecter, *The Jocks* (New York: Paperback Library, 1970), 258. On Jack Johnson and the search for a Great White Hope, see Randy Roberts, *Papa Jack: Jack Johnson and the Era of White Hopes* (New York: Free Press, 1983).

26. Reed, "Big Bill Loves to Eat 'Em Up," 26; Prugh, "UCLA's Rebel with a Cause," 10; Libby, *The Walton Gang,* 141; *Boston Herald,* May 27, 1999; Walton with Wojciechowski, *Nothing but Net,* 206–07; Bill Russell as told to William McSweeny, *Go Up for Glory* (New York: Berkley-Medallion Books, 1966).

27. Reed, "Big Bill Loves to Eat 'Em Up," 26; *LAHE,* March 6, 1972; *Long Beach Press-Telegram,* March 27, 2005, March 9, 2008.

28. Libby, *The Walton Gang,* 36–8; *LAT,* December 29, 1971; Reed, "Big Bill Loves to Eat 'Em Up," 29.

29. *LAT,* March 2, 1972; *LAHE,* March 16, 17, 19, 1972; Chapin and Prugh, *Wizard of Westwood,* 210.

30. William F. Reed, "Welcome to the Ball," March 27, 1972, 12–14; *LAHE,* March 19, 1972; Brondfield, *UCLA Story,* 135 (see chap. 2, n. 12); Chapin and Prugh, *Wizard of Westwood,* 215–17.

31. *LAT,* March 24, 1972.

32. *LAT,* December 29, 1971, March 11, 1972; Curry Kirkpatrick, "Oh, Johnny, Oh, Johnny, Oh!," *SI,* April 3, 1972, 31–32.

33. *LAT,* March 22, 25, 1972; *LAHE,* March 24, 1972; Curry Kirkpatrick, "Odds On for the Pro Bowl," *SI,* February 9, 1970, 47.

34. Ibid.

35. Kirkpatrick, "Oh, Johnny, Oh, Johnny, Oh!," 32, 37; Brondfield, *UCLA Story,* 5–6, 9–10; *LAHE,* March 26, 1972; *WP,* March 22, 1972.

36. Kirkpatrick, "Oh, Johnny, Oh, Johnny, Oh!," 32; *LAT,* March 26, 1972.

37. Kirkpatrick, "Oh, Johnny, Oh, Johnny, Oh!," 32; Dwight Chapin, "Bruins Do It Again . . . Will Dynasty Ever End?," *SN,* April 8, 1972, 56.

38. Kirkpatrick, "Oh, Johnny, Oh, Johnny, Oh!," 37; Chapin and Prugh, *Wizard of Westwood,* 221–22.

39. *DB,* April 5, 1972; Walton with Wojciechowski, *Nothing but Net,* 22.

40. Brondfield, *UCLA Story,* 13; *LAT,* May 23, 1969, July 27, 1980; "California: University on Trial," 83, 85 (see chap. 6, n. 22).

41. Charles Berst, "Building for the Future," *UCLA Magazine,* Fall 1994, 35, 37; UCLA Foundation annual fund donor advertisement, reprinted in *The Hoop* (program), January 14, 1972, Alumni, 1977–1982 Folder, Box 2, Administration Files of Robert Fischer and J. D. Morgan, UCLA Archives; Young, phone interview (see chap. 1, n. 55).

42. Anderson, *Movement and the Sixties,* 378–80 (see chap. 2, n. 17); DeBenedetti with Chatfield, *American Ordeal,* 314–17 (see chap. 7, n. 8); Perlstein, *Nixonland,* 574–75 (see chap. 4, n. 5); *DB,* May 5, 6, 1971, April 21, 1972.

43. *DB,* January 20, April 17, 28, 1972; Libby, *The Walton Gang,* 147–48.

44. *LAFP,* November 24, 1972; Perlstein, *Nixonland,* 656–57; Wells, *War Within,* 542–43 (see chap. 7, n. 8); DeBenedetti with Chatfield, *American Ordeal,* 330; *DB,* May 10, 1972; *LAT,* May 10, 1972.

45. *DB,* May 10, 1972; *LAT,* May 10, 1972; Chapin and Prugh, *Wizard of Westwood,* 277; Farmer, phone interview.

46. *LAHE,* May 11, 1972; *DB,* May 11, 1972; *LAFP,* November 24, 1972.

47. *LAFP,* November 24, 1972; *DB,* May 12, 1972; *LAHE,* May 12, 1972; Chapin and Prugh, *Wizard of Westwood,* 278; *LAT,* May 12, 1972; Kemper, "Reformers in the Marketplace of Ideas," 209 (see chap. 1, n. 22); Einhorn with Rapoport, *How March Became Madness,* 28; Young, phone interview.

48. *Van Nuys (Calif.) News,* May 12, 1972; Chapin and Prugh, *Wizard of Westwood,* 278; "Tall Stories," *SI,* May 22, 1972, 11. In 1974 sportswriter Bill Libby reported that Gilbert paid for Walton's bail. See Libby, *The Walton Gang,* 150. Two years later, Walton's close friend, sociologist, and leftist political activist Jack Scott wrote that Bruce bailed Bill out of jail. Considering that he lived with Walton at the time, Scott's version reads credibly. See Scott, *Bill Walton,* 12 (see chap. 4, n. 48). For Walton's version of Wooden bailing him out of jail, see Einhorn with Rapoport, *How March Became Madness,* 28; *The UCLA Dynasty;* Bisheff, *John Wooden,* 138–39.

In an interview with the *Los Angeles Free Press,* Walton said, "It's really hard to say what [Wooden's] reaction was." See *LAFP,* November 24, 1972.

49. *Van Nuys (Calif.) News,* May 12, 1972; *LAHE,* May 12, 1972; *Orange County Register,* May 14, 1972; *LAFP,* November 24, 1972; "Basketball's Vegetarian Tiger," 76. On Sam Yorty and anticommunism, see Dallek, *Right Moment,* 160–61, 169 (see chap. 4, n. 5). See also William Nichols, "The Right Man at the Right Time: J. D. Morgan," interview by David Rose, 1982, transcript 1984, UCLA OHC, 540; Ernest D. Greci to Honorable Ronald Reagan, November 23, 1972, CEY, Box 45, Intramural Relations–Student Disruptions and Discipline, May 10–11, 1972, Folder 2; Gerald W. Briggs to Dr. Charles E. Young, May 15, 1972, CEY, Box 45, Folder 2; David L. Springmann to Honorable Charles Young, May 16, 1972, CEY, Box 45, Folder 2.

50. *DB,* July 7, 1972; *LAFP,* November 24, 1972; Libby, *The Walton Gang,* 150; "Tall Stories," 11; *LAT,* June 9, 1972; Roger Rapoport, "Walton & Ratleff: Any Resemblance Is Purely Coincidental," *Sport,* January 1973, 58.

51. *LAFP,* November 24, 1972.

Chapter 9. *The Rebel and the Saint*

1. Einhorn with Rapoport, *How March Became Madness,* 27–28 (see chap. 3, n. 38); Walton with Wojciechowski, *Nothing but Net,* 21, 24–25 (see chap. 8, n. 6); *LAT,* October 16, 17, 1973. The quote from Wooden's letter is taken from Hano, "Winning," 31 (see chap. 3, n. 37).

2. I am using Terry Anderson's broad definition of the counterculture as a "counter to the dominant cold war culture" and "as a counter to the political establishment." Anderson, *Movement and the Sixties,* 241 (see chap. 2, n. 17).

3. Mike Morrow, "Wooden and Walton . . . They Are Different," *Basketball News,* 1973–74 college yearbook, 6; Libby, *The Walton Gang,* 146–47 (see chap. 5, n. 56).

4. Walton with Wojciechowski, *Nothing but Net,* 24–25.

5. *The UCLA Dynasty* (see chap. 6, n. 10); Walton interview in N. Johnson, *Wooden Pyramid of Success,* 434 (see chap. 1, n. 14).

6. On the Athletic Revolution, see Scott, *The Athletic Revolution* (see preface, n. 8); Leila B. Gemme, *The New Breed of Athlete* (New York: Washington Square Press, 1975); Glenn Dickey, *The Jock Empire: Its Rise and Deserved Fall* (Radnor, Pa.: Chilton Book, 1975); Edwards, *The Sociology of Sport* (see chap. 3, n. 19); Shecter, *The Jocks,* (see chap. 8, n. 25); Lipsyte, *SportsWorld* (see chap. 3, n. 15); Zang, *SportsWars* (see preface, n. 8).

7. Hano, "Winning," 143–46; Chapin and Prugh, *Wizard of Westwood,* 231 (see chap. 1, n. 1).

8. Libby, *The Walton Gang,* 170; Brondfield, *UCLA Story,* 17 (see chap. 2, n. 12); *LAHE,* January 29, 1973; Melvin Durslag, "The Surest Thing," *SN,* December 15, 1973, 32.

9. Libby, *The Walton Gang,* 168.

10. Ibid.; "Basketball's Vegetarian Tiger," 75 (see chap. 8, n. 19).

11. Rapoport, "Walton & Ratleff," 58 (see chap. 8, n. 51); Rick Telander, "Bill Walton, Won't You Please Play Ball?," *SI,* January 27, 1975, 13; Bruce J. Schulman, *The Seventies: The Great Shift in American Culture, Society, and Politics* (New York: Free Press, 2001), 146–48.

12. Walton quotes combined from Bill Libby's article and book. See Libby, "Reluctant All-American," *Los Angeles Times WEST Magazine,* October 1, 1972, 23; and Libby, *The Walton Gang,* 139.

13. Peter Braunstein and Michael William Doyle, "Historicizing the American Counterculture of the 1960s and '70s," introduction to *Imagine Nation: The American Counterculture of the 1960s and '70s,* edited by Peter Braunstein and Michael William Doyle (New York: Routledge, 2002), 10; Prugh, "UCLA's Rebel with a Cause," 8 (see chap. 8, n. 1); Dave Klein, "Just the Best Ever," *College Basketball Guide,* 1974, 15; Ali quoted in *NYT,* February 27, 1964.

14. Tom Brokaw, *The Greatest Generation* (New York: Random House, 1998); Anderson, *Movement and the Sixties,* 246–58.

15. Libby, *The Walton Gang,* 141, 145–46; Libby, "Reluctant All-American," 23, 26.

16. Libby, *The Walton Gang,* 137–38.

17. Ibid., 143–44.

18. Zang, *Sports Wars,* 64–65; Shecter, *The Jocks,* 9–10; Maraniss, *When Pride Still Mattered,* 365–70 (see chap. 8, n. 8).

19. Zang, *Sports Wars,* 65–66; Libby, *The Walton Gang,* 148.

20. Halberstam, *Breaks of the Game,* 143–45 (see chap. 8, n. 19); *DB,* April 5, May 11, 1972; Zang, *Sports Wars,* 66, 80.

21. Roberts and Olson, *Winning Is the Only Thing,* 5–7, 13–14 (see chap. 4, n. 29); *LAT,* May 4, 1972; *Orange County Register,* May 14, 1972; Rapoport, "Walton & Ratleff," 77; Prugh, "UCLA's Rebel with a Cause," 10; Larry Bortstein, "Bill Walton: Strong in His Ways," *Annual Basketball,* 1972–73, 17. On the politics of sports in the Cold War, see Stephen Wagg and David L. Andrews, eds., *East Plays West: Sport and the Cold War* (New York: Routledge, 2007).

22. Carson Cunningham, *American Hoops: U.S. Men's Olympic Basketball from Berlin to Beijing* (Lincoln: University of Nebraska Press, 2009), 206–9, 212, 215.

23. *WP,* July 22, 1972; *LAT,* July 21, 1972.

24. *LAT,* May 4, July 21, August 11, 1972; *DB,* July 25, 1972.

25. *CSM,* May 11, 1972.

26. For an excellent summary of the 1972 gold-medal game between the United States and the Soviet Union, see Cunningham, *American Hoops,* 220–26; Walton with Wojciechowski, *Nothing but Net,* 51; Rapoport, "Walton & Ratleff," 77; "Ill-Equipped IBA," *SN,* October 14, 1972, 6; Libby, *The Walton Gang,* 151.

27. *LAT,* February 11, 1970; *Oakland Tribune,* March 23, 1971; Hano, "Winning"; "Letters," *New York Times Magazine,* December 23, 1973, 136.

28. Hano, "Winning," 138–43; "Letters," 136.

29. *NYT,* November 19, 1972; *LAT,* November 22, 1972; *LAHE,* January 20, 1973.

30. "Scouting Reports: #1 UCLA," *SI,* November 27, 1972, 45.

31. *LAT,* December 12, 14, 25, 1972; *LAHE,* December 14, 18, 19, 1972; Wooden with Tobin, *They Call Me Coach,* 179 (see chap. 1, n. 2); Libby, *The Walton Gang,* 187.

32. Wooden with Tobin, *They Call Me Coach,* 179.

33. *LAT,* December 21, 22, 1972.

34. *LAT,* December 23, 1972; *LAHE,* December 23, 1972; Curry Kirkpatrick, "The Ball in Two Different Courts," *SI,* December 25, 1972. For more on the career of Billie Jean King, see Susan Ware, *Game, Set, Match: Billie Jean King and the Revolution in Women's Sports* (Chapel Hill: University of North Carolina Press, 2011).

35. Kirkpatrick, "Ball in Two Different Courts," 30, 33.

36. Hano, "Winning," 154; *LAT,* January 25, 1973; Curry Kirkpatrick, "Who Are These Guys?," *SI,* February 5, 1973, 74.

37. Kirkpatrick, "Who Are These Guys?," 74; Libby, *The Walton Gang,* 21–22, 226; *LAHE,* January 27, 1973; *SBT,* January 26, 1973.

38. *LAHE,* January 26, 28, 1973; *LAT,* January 28, 1973; Kirkpatrick, "Who Are These Guys?," 80; *DB,* January 29, 1973; Libby, *The Walton Gang,* 25.

39. *LAT,* January 28, 1973; *NYT,* January 28, 1973; Libby, *The Walton Gang,* 24; *LAHE,* January 3, 1974.

40. *PI,* January 29, 1973; *LAHE,* January 28, 1973; *LAT,* January 28, 1973; Hano, "Winning," 145.

41. *PI,* January 29, 1973.

42. *LAHE,* March 4, 1973.

43. *LAHE,* February 15, 1973; Kirkpatrick, "Who Are These Guys?," 74; *LAT,* March 25, 1972, February 7, 1973; *WP,* March 13, 1973.

44. *DB,* January 29, 1973; Kirkpatrick, "Who Are These Guys?," 74.

45. Libby, *The Walton Gang,* 16–17, 228, 232; *LAHE,* March 19, 1973.

46. Kirkpatrick, "Who Are These Guys?," 77–78.

47. Kirkpatrick, "Who Are These Guys?," 76; Libby, *The Walton Gang,* 14, 229–30.

48. *LAT,* May 21, 1972.

49. "New TV Contract, Bracket Expanded in Cage Tourney," *NCAA News,* May 15, 1972, 9; Stern, *They Were Number One,* 332, 356 (see chap. 2, n. 31); *WP,* March 4, 25, 1973.

50. *LAT,* March 21, 1972, May 3, 1973; *WP,* April 10, 1973; "1974 Tournament Already Sold Out," *NCAA News,* April 15, 1973, 1. The 1973 championship game drew a 20.5 Nielsen rating, a 30 percent increase over the 1972 championship rating of 16.0. For a list of television markets, see James Michener, *Sports in America* (New York: Random House, 1976), 381.

51. *SPD,* March 26, 1973; *MCA,* March 26, 1973.

52. *LAT,* March 27, 1973; *LAHE,* March 27, 1973; Wooden with Tobin, *They Call Me Coach,* 181.

53. *SPD*, March 26, 27, 1973; Libby, *The Walton Gang*, 212–15; *CST*, March 27, 1973.

54. *PI*, March 27, 1973.

55. Walton with Wojciechowski, *Nothing but Net*, 35–36.

56. *LAHE*, March 26, 1973; *LAT*, March 26, 1973; *PI*, March 26, 1973; *SPD*, March 27, 1973; *Newsday*, March 27, 1973.

57. "NCAA Files Suit against Porter, ABA," *NCAA News*, March 1, 1972, 1; "Enough Is Enough!," *NCAA News*, March 1, 1972, 2; "Second Lawsuit Seeks Disclosure of Early Cage Signings," *NCAA News*, April 27, 1972, 1; Melvin Durslag, "Pro Raids Continuous Problem for Colleges," *NCAA News*, October 1, 1972, 2.

58. *SFC*, March 29, 1973; *Newsday*, March 29, 1973.

59. *LAHE*, March 27, 1973; *LAT*, March 27, 1973; Curry Kirkpatrick, "A Slight Case of Being Superhuman," *SI*, April 2, 1973, 18; *LAT*, March 27, 1973; Matt Fulks, ed., *CBS Presents: Stories from the Final Four* (Lenexa, Kans.: Addax, 2000), 60.

60. Fulks, *CBS Presents*, 60; *SPD*, March 27, 1973.

61. *LAT*, March 27, 1973; Gary Mueller, "W Is for Walton, Wooden, and WOW," *SN*, April 7, 1973, 19; *SFC*, March 27, 1973; Walton with Wojciechowski, *Nothing but Net*, 37. In 1965 Gail Goodrich scored forty-two points against Michigan in UCLA's 91–80 national championship victory.

62. *LAHE*, March 27, 1973; Libby, *The Walton Gang*, 271–72; *LAT*, March 28, 1973.

63. *SFC*, March 27, 1973; *SPD*, March 27, 1973; *Newsday*, March 28, 1973; *MCA*, March 29, 1973; *LAHE*, March 27, 1973.

64. Kirkpatrick, "Slight Case of Being Superhuman," 20; *MCA*, March 26, 1973.

65. "Two Leaders Who Lead," *SN*, May 13, 1972, 14; *LAT*, January 18, 1973; Chapin and Prugh, *Wizard of Westwood*, 310.

66. Chapin and Prugh, *Wizard of Westwood*, 320; *SPD*, March 26, 1973; *LAT*, March 25, 1973; Joe Pollack, "Man behind the Wizard: Fascinating and Complex," *SN*, March 31, 1974, 54.

67. Chapin, phone interview (see chap. 6, n. 8); Medley, *UCLA Basketball* (see chap. 1, n. 3); Bortstein, *UCLA's Fabulous Bruins* (see chap. 2, n. 32); Libby, *The Walton Gang*, 185; *DB*, February 16, 1973; *Newsday* commentary quoted in *LAT*, April 24, 1973.

68. Libby, *The Walton Gang*, 81; *WP*, April 1, 1973; *SPD*, March 27, 1973; *Centralia (Wash.) Daily Chronicle*, August 14, 1973; *LAT*, January 18, 1973.

69. Chapin, phone interview.

70. *WP*, April 1, 1973; *PI*, March 28, 1973.

71. Libby, *The Walton Gang*, 82, 253, 267; *PI*, March 27, 1973; Myers and Gregory quoted in *LAT*, April 24, 1973.

72. *PI*, March 27, 1973.

Chapter 10. Cracks in the Pyramid

1. Schulman, *Seventies,* xv, 48–49 (see chap. 9, n. 11); Peter Carroll, *It Seemed Like Nothing Happened: The Tragedy and Promise of America in the 1970s* (New York: Holt, Rinehart, and Winston, 1982), 116, 134–35; James T. Patterson, *Restless Giant: The United States from Watergate to Bush v. Gore* (New York: Oxford University Press, 2005), 8–10; Art Spander, "UCLA Still Hale, Hearty," *SN,* March 23, 1974, 26.

2. *LAT,* November 1973, January 9, 1974; "The Top Twenty: #1 UCLA," *SI,* November 26, 1973, 70.

3. Curry Kirkpatrick, "Po-tential Almost Stole It," *SI,* December 10, 1973, 22–25; *LAT,* December 2, 1973.

4. *LAHE,* December 8, 11, 1973; *WP,* December 14, 1973; Curry Kirkpatrick, "Half of Big Red Is Too Much," *SI,* December 24, 1973, 30.

5. Bill Beezely, *The Wolfpack: Intercollegiate Athletics at North Carolina State University* (Raleigh: University Graphics, North Carolina State University, 1976), 306–14.

6. Kirkpatrick, "Half of Big Red Is Too Much," 30–31; *LAT,* December 15, 19, 1973; *WP,* December 15, 1973; *NYT,* December 13, 1973; *SPD,* December 13, 14, 1973.

7. *SPD,* December 13, 1973; "The Top Twenty: #2 North Carolina State," *SI,* November 26, 1973, 70; Curry Kirkpatrick, "David Goes after Goliath," *SI,* November 26, 1973, 60–61; *NYT,* December 11, 1973; Bob Whitley, "David Thompson Would Like to Introduce Himself to UCLA . . . Again," *Sport,* March 1974," 89; editors of ESPN, *ESPN College Basketball Encyclopedia* (New York: Ballantine Books, 2009), 325; David Thompson with Sean Stormes and Marshall Terrill, *David Thompson: Skywalker* (Champaign, Ill.: Sports Publishing, 2003), xi.

8. Whitley, "Thompson Would Like to Introduce Himself," 89; Kirkpatrick, "David Goes after Goliath," 61; *SPD,* December 13, 14, 1973; *RNO,* December 11, 1973.

9. *LAT,* December 16, 19, 1973; *LAHE,* December 16, 1973; *SPD,* December 16, 1973.

10. Ibid.

11. *LAT,* December 16, 1973.

12. *LAT,* January 17, 1974.

13. *LAHE,* January 8, 12, 14, 1974; *DB,* January 8, 11, 14, 1974; Barry McDermott, "Sore Back and a Hot Hand," *SI,* January 21, 1974, 48; Walton with Wojciechowski, *Nothing but Net,* 30 (see chap. 8, n. 6); Nick Canepa, "Back Pain Nearly Drove Bill Walton to End It All," *San Diego Tribune,* April 17, 2010.

14. *LAHE,* January 18, 1974; Barry McDermott, "After 88 Comes Zero," *SI,* January 28, 1974, 21.

15. *LAHE,* January 16, 1974; Phelps and Keith, *A Coach's World,* 75, 99, 106–7, 127 (see chap. 8, n. 16); Phelps with Bourret, *Digger Phelps's Tales,* 25 (see chap. 8, n. 16); Larry Keith, "The End of a Week That Never Was," *SI,* February 4, 1974, 26; McDermott, "After 88 Comes Zero," 18, 20. Phelps read Medley's *UCLA Basketball* (see chap. 1, n. 3).

16. *LAT,* January 20, 1974; Phelps with Bourret, *Digger Phelps's Tales,* 27; McDermott, "After 88 Comes Zero," 18.

17. *LAHE,* January 20, 1974; *SBT,* January 20, 1974; *LAT,* January 20, 1974.

18. McDermott, "After 88 Comes Zero," 21; *LAT,* January 20, 1974; *DB,* January 22, 1974.

19. *SBT,* January 20, 1974; *LAT,* January 20, 1974.

20. Ibid.

21. Phelps with Bourret, *Digger Phelps's Tales,* 34–35.

22. *SBT,* January 20, 1974; *CT,* January 20, 1974.

23. *LAHE,* January 25, March 21, 1974; *LAT,* January 26, March 14, 1974; David W. Gould, "How to Succeed in Business," *Beyond Winning: John Wooden (DB* special issue), June 6, 1975, 16.

24. Einhorn, phone interview (see chap. 5, n. 31); *LAHE,* January 24, 1974; *NYT,* May 14, 1974; Leggett, "NBC and the New College Try," 52 (see chap. 5, n. 31). The terms of NBC's agreement with TVS were not disclosed.

25. Gould, "How to Succeed in Business," 15; George H. Hanford, *An Inquiry into the Need for and Feasibility of a National Study of Intercollegiate Athletics* (Washington, D.C.: American Council on Education, 1974), 9; *LAT,* November 13, 1974.

26. *LAHE,* January 23, 1974; Keith, "End of a Week That Never Was," 24.

27. *LAHE,* February 11, 1974; *LAT,* February 14, 1974; *NYT,* February 24, 1975; "John Wooden's Simple Strategy," *Time,* February 25, 1974, 75; Einhorn with Rapoport, *How March Became Madness,* 30 (see chap. 3, n. 38).

28. *Portland Oregonian,* February 17, 1974; *LAT,* February 18, 1974; Kenny Moore, "Ambushed on the Oregon Trail," *SI,* February 25, 1974, 18–19.

29. *LAHE,* February 21, February 22, 1974; *WP,* February 26, 1974; Moore, "Ambushed on the Oregon Trail," 18; *LAT,* February 14, 1974.

30. *LAHE,* February 18, 20, 1974; *DB,* February 15, 20, 1974; *LAT,* February 20, 1974.

31. *DB,* February 20, 1974; *LAT,* February 20, 1974; *LAHE,* February 18, 21, 1974; *WP,* February 26, 1974.

32. Patterson, *Restless Giant,* 10–11; "In Quest of Leadership," *Time,* July 15, 1974, 22–23.

33. *WP,* March 23, 1974.

34. Ibid.

35. *LAHE,* February 21, March 11, 17, 1974; Curry Kirkpatrick, "But UCLA Is Snarling," *SI,* March 18, 1974, 21; Schulman, *Seventies,* 145; Christopher Lasch, *The Culture of Narcissism* (New York: W. W. Norton, 1979), xv.

36. *WP,* March 23, 1974; *LAT,* March 27, 1974.

37. Papanek, "Climbing to the Top Again," 113 (see chap. 8, n. 19); "Basketball's Vegetarian Tiger," 72 (see chap. 8, n. 19); *LAT,* February 11, 1974.

38. Halberstam, *Breaks of the Game,* 319 (see chap. 8, n. 19). In 2001 Walton's first wife, Susie, who attended UCLA with him, said, "Wooden let Bill smoke pot but

not the other players." See Pat Jordan, "Bill Walton's Inside Game," *New York Times Magazine,* October 28, 2001, 56.

39. Halberstam, *Breaks of the Game,* 319. Sportswriter Mike Morrow quoted "one UCLA student" in a story on Walton. The UCLA student claimed to be friends with Walton. He said, "But Bill's smart. He knows they're not going to kick him off the team. He's showing what a double standard they have for athletes. I know one guy who was caught with weed and they bounced him. But, are they going to bounce Walton? I doubt it." See Morrow, "Wooden and Walton," 5 (see chap. 9, n. 3).

40. "Basketball's Vegetarian Tiger," 72, 76; "Patron Called Papa Sam," 77 (see chap. 4, n. 52); Chapin and Prugh, *Wizard of Westwood,* 261 (see chap. 1, n. 1); *LAT,* January 31, 1982.

41. *DB,* March 1, 1974; *LAT,* March 20, 1974; Douglas Hobbs, "The Right Man at the Right Time: J. D. Morgan," interview by David Rose, 1982, transcript 1984, UCLA OHC, 274–75.

42. *Long Beach Press-Telegram,* April 1, 1974; Medley, *UCLA Basketball,* 209 (see chap. 1, n. 3); *LAT,* December 10, 1981, January 31, 1982; Byron Atkinson, "The Right Man at the Right Time: J. D. Morgan," interview by David Rose, 1982, transcript 1984, UCLA OHC, 212, 221.

43. James Bush, "The Right Man at the Right Time: J. D. Morgan," interview by David Rose, 1982, transcript 1984, UCLA OHC, 384; Hobbs, "Right Man at Right Time," 272–75; Wiles Hallock, "The Right Man at the Right Time: J. D. Morgan," interview by Rick Harmon, 1982, transcript 1984, UCLA OHC, 596; *LAT,* January 31, 1982.

44. *LAT,* June 9, 1971, March 20, 1974, December 27, 1981; *NYT,* February 4, 1982; John Wooden interview in N. Johnson, *Wooden Pyramid of Success,* 93 (see chap. 1, n. 14); Chapin and Prugh, *Wizard of Westwood,* 281–82.

45. *LAHE,* February 25, 26, 1974.

46. *DB,* March 11, 1974; *LAHE,* March 11, 1974.

47. Kirkpatrick, "But UCLA Is Snarling," 23; *LAT,* March 15, 1974.

48. *LAHE,* March 17, 1974; Barry McDermott, "Down and Out, Back Up and Ready," *SI,* March 25, 1974, 25.

49. McDermott, "Down and Out," 25; Walton with Wojciechowski, *Nothing but Net,* 31; *RNO,* March 17, 1974.

50. Norm Sloan with Larry Guest, *Confessions of a Coach* (Nashville, Tenn.: Rutledge Hill, Press, 1991), 94–96; McDermott, "Down and Out," 25; *RNO,* March 17, 22, 1974; *LAT,* March 23, 1974.

51. *RNO,* March 22, 23, 1974; *LAT,* March 23, 1974; *LAHE,* March 21, 22, 1974.

52. *LAT,* March 24, 1974; *RNO,* March 24, 1974; Curry Kirkpatrick, "Nothing Could Be Finer," *SI,* April 1, 1974, 24–25.

53. *LAT,* March 24, 1974; Kirkpatrick, "Nothing Could Be Finer," 25.

54. Ibid.; *RNO,* March 24, 1974; *LAHE,* March 24, 1974.

55. *LAT,* March 24, 1974; Kirkpatrick, "Nothing Could Be Finer," 25.

56. *Greensboro (N.C.) Daily News,* March 24, 1974; *LAT,* March 24, 1974.

57. *LAT,* March 24, 1974; *RNO,* March 24, 1974; *Greensboro (N.C.) Daily News,* March 24, 1974; *LAHE,* March 24, 1974.

58. *LAHE,* March 24, 1974; *RNO,* March 24, 1974; *LAT,* March 24, 1974; Kirkpatrick, "Nothing Could Be Finer," 23.

Chapter 11. The Godfather

1. *LAT,* March 30, 1975; *CT,* March 30, 1975.

2. *LAT,* October 14, 1975; *LAHE,* December 1, 1974; "Scouting Reports: #4 UCLA," *SI,* December 2, 1974, 52.

3. *LAHE,* February 26, 1975; *WP,* December 20, 1974; *LAT,* January 30, 1975.

4. Wooden with Tobin, *They Call Me Coach,* 226 (see chap. 1, n. 2); *LAT,* January 31, 1975; *LAHE,* February 25, 1975.

5. On the significance of the NCAA's 1973 scholarship rule change, see Oriard, *Bowled Over,* 127–41 (see chap. 7, n. 14).

6. *WP,* March 28, 1975; Dwight Chapin, "Wooden's Swan Song . . . UCLA Victory March," *SN,* April 19, 1975, 45.

7. *WP,* March 9, 1975; *LAHE,* March 19, 1975; *LAT,* March 29, 31, 1975; Curry Kirkpatrick, "What a Wiz of a Win It Was," *SI,* April 7, 1975, 21. At the time, Nell Wooden confirmed to the *Los Angeles Times* that her husband had decided as early as December 1974 that he would retire at the end of the season. Years later, Wooden consistently claimed that he did not actually make the decision until right after UCLA defeated Louisville in the 1975 semifinals. See N. Johnson, *Wooden Pyramid of Success,* 117 (see chap. 1, n. 14).

8. Wooden and Jamison, *Wooden on Leadership,* xiii–xv (see chap. 1, n. 15).

9. Wooden with Jamison, *My Personal Best,* 191–92 (see chap. 1, n. 3); Wooden with Tobin, *They Call Me Coach,* 195–96; Kirkpatrick, "What a Whiz of a Win It Was," 21.

10. *LAT,* March 30, 1975; Chapin, "Wooden's Swan Song," 45.

11. *LCJ,* April 1, 1975; Kirkpatrick, "What a Wiz of a Win It Was," 18.

12. "The Quiet Man," *Newsweek,* April 14, 1975, 93; *LAT,* April 1, 1975; *LAHE,* April 1, 1975; Kirkpatrick, "What a Wiz of a Win It Was," 18.

13. *LCJ,* April 1, 1975.

14. *LAHE,* April 1, 1975; *LAT,* April 1, 1975.

15. *LAHE,* April 3, 1975; *LAT,* March 31, April 1, 1975; Curry Kirkpatrick, "Wise in the Ways of the Wizard," *SI,* November 30, 1981, 107.

16. *LAT,* April 3, 4, 1975; *LAHE,* April 3, 1975.

17. Sam Moses, "Pursued by a Very Long Shadow," *SI,* November 17, 1975, 33.

18. Barry McDermott, "Grim, but They're Bearing It," *SI,* February 16, 1976, 16; Kirkpatrick, "Wise in the Ways of the Wizard," 110.

19. Kirkpatrick, "Wise in the Ways of the Wizard," 110–11; *LAT,* June 11, 14, 1977; Gene Bartow interview in N. Johnson, *Wooden Pyramid of Success,* 322–23.

20. *LAT,* February 1, 1982; Mario Puzo, *The Godfather* (New York: G. P. Putnam and Sons, 1969).

21. *LAT,* January 31, February 1, 1982, August 4, 1993; Scott Heisler, *They Shoot Coaches, Don't They? UCLA and the NCAA since John Wooden* (New York: Macmillan, 1996), 69, 93.

22. Heisler, *They Shoot Coaches Don't They?,* 79; Don Yaeger, *Undue Process: The NCAA's Injustice for All* (Champaign, Ill.: Sagamore, 1991), 42–43; *LAT,* February 1, 1982. On the ABA-NBA merger, see Terry Pluto, *Loose Balls: The Short, Wild Life of the American Basketball Association* (New York: Simon & Schuster, 2007), 421–33.

23. *LAT,* January 31, 1982; Clark Testimony, *NCAA Hearings,* 11.

24. John Underwood, "It Was a Trial but Worth It," *SI,* October 9, 1978; *NYT,* February 26, 28, 1978; *LAT,* February 28, 1978; *WP,* February 28, 1978; Clark Testimony, *NCAA Hearings,* 3–69.

25. Clark Testimony, *NCAA Hearings,* 11.

26. *LAT,* January 31, 1982.

27. Scott, *Bill Walton* (see chap. 4, n. 48); *NYT,* January 19, 1975; Kauffman, "At Home with Bill Walton," 35–37 (see chap. 8, n. 21); Barbieri, "Visit with Bill Walton," 75–76 (see chap. 8, n. 21); Telander, "Bill Walton, Won't You Please Play Ball?," 14 (see chap. 9, n. 11).

28. Robert Lipsyte, "Radical Jocks," *New York Times Magazine,* September 21, 1975, 71; Kauffman, "At Home with Bill Walton," 37; Ray Kennedy, "The Man Who Stood Sport on Its Head," *SI,* April 28, 1975, 29; "The Patty Hearst Trail Heats Up," *Time,* March 24, 1975, 27–28; "Fugitives: The Best Defense . . .," *Newsweek,* April 21, 1975, 46–47; *NYT,* April 15, 1975. On Scott's involvement with Patty Hearst, see William Graebner, *Patty's Got a Gun: Patricia Hearst in 1970s America* (Chicago: University of Chicago Press, 2008), 44.

29. Pete Axthelm, "Who Is Jack Scott?," *Newsweek,* October 6, 1975, 39; Roger Kahn, "Jack Scott: How Radical Is Radical, Anyhow?," *Esquire,* October 1975, 48, 52, 54; Halberstam, *Breaks of the Game,* 320–21 (see chap. 8, n. 19); Kennedy, "Man Who Stood Sport on Its Head," 23; Lipsyte, "Radical Jocks," 79.

30. Scott, *The Athletic Revolution,* 160–69, 187–88 (see preface, n. 8); Scott, *Bill Walton,* 215 (see chap. 4, n. 48).

31. Scott, *Bill Walton,* 212.

32. Ibid., 213–14.

33. *LAT,* June 28, 1978; *Portland Oregonian,* June 27, 28, 1978.

34. *LAT,* February 11, 1974, June 28, 29, 30, 1978; Scott, *Bill Walton,* 215.

35. Heisler, *They Shoot Coaches, Don't They?,* 89–90, 93–100; Joe Jares, "The Wizard's Disciple," *SI,* December 5, 1977, 110; *LAT,* July 10, November 24, March 23, 1977; Kirkpatrick, "Wise in the Ways of the Wizard," 111.

36. Heisler, *They Shoot Coaches, Don't They?,* 110–15; *LAT,* January 31, 1982; Alexander Wolff, "Call Him Irreplaceable," *SI,* April 11, 1989, 27; Kirkpatrick, "Wise in the Ways of the Wizard," 112.

37. *LAT,* March 13, 1981, February 29, 1980, March 17, 1981.

38. *LAT,* October 30, 1979, December 17, 1980.

39. *LAT,* July 23, 1972; Ken Rappoport, *The Classic: The History of the NCAA Basketball Championship* (Mission, Kans.: National Collegiate Athletics Association, 1979), 235; Chapin and Prugh, *Wizard of Westwood,* 249 (see chap. 1, n. 1).

40. *LAT,* March 18, 1981; Kirkpatrick, "Wise in the Ways of the Wizard," 101–2, 104; Heisler, *They Shoot Coaches, Don't They?,* 130–32.

41. *LAT,* February 2, 1982; Heisler, *They Shoot Coaches, Don't They?,* 135; Farmer, phone interview (see chap. 8, n. 10).

42. Kirkpatrick, "Wise in the Ways of the Wizard," 113; *LAT,* December 9, 1981, January 31, February 2, 1982; NCAA Public Infraction Report, "University of California, Los Angeles, Placed on NCAA Probation," released December 8, 1981.

43. *LAT,* December 9, 1981.

44. *LAT,* December 10, 15, 1981.

45. *LAT,* December 27, 1981. Wooden later said of the NCAA's investigation, "You may remember when the NCAA checked very carefully but there was nothing [improper] in my years. [Gilbert] worried me but they found no irregularity in my years. They found some after it but I had retired. But not in my time." See Heisler, *They Shoot Coaches, Don't They?,* 56.

46. *LAT,* January 31, 1982.

47. *LAT,* January 31, February 2, 1982.

48. *NYT,* March 21, 22, 1982; *LAT,* October 15, 1980; "The Shame of College Sports," *Newsweek,* September 22, 1980, 54–59; Alvin P. Sanoff, "Behind the Scandals in College Sports," *U.S. News and World Report,* February 11, 1980, 61–63; George Will, "Our Schools for Scandal," *Newsweek,* September 15, 1986, 84; John Underwood, "Special Report—Student Athletes: The Sham, the Shame," *SI,* May 19, 1980, 36–74. For a history of reforms in college athletics, see Thelin, *Games Colleges Play* (see chap. 1, n. 51); and Ronald A. Smith, *Pay for Play: A History of Big-Time College Athletic Reform* (Urbana: University of Illinois Press, 2011).

49. *NYT,* February 7, 1982.

50. *LAT,* February 2, 1982; Young, phone interview (see chap. 1, n. 55).

51. *LAT,* September 15, November 23, 26, 1987; *Orange County Register,* December 6, 1987.

52. *CSM,* May 31, 1977; *WP,* June 5, 2010; Wolff, "Coach and His Champion," 95–96 (see chap. 7, n. 21).

53. Curry Kirkpatrick, "Same as He Ever Was," *Sport,* January 1998, 74–75; Wolff, "Coach and His Champion," 104–5; Wolff, "Remembering the Wizard," 32–34 (see preface, n. 1); Wooden with Jamison, *My Personal Best,* 197–204.

54. Halberstam, *Breaks of the Game,* 286.

55. Dave Dorr, "High Drama: 'Greatest Single College Sports Event,'" *SN,* March 29, 1980, 3; Curry Kirkpatrick, "Memories," *SI,* March 31, 1986, 63.

56. R. Smith, *Play-by-Play,* 190–91 (see chap. 4, n. 28); Dorr, "High Drama," 3; Seth Davis, *When March Went Mad: The Game That Transformed Basketball* (New York: Times Books, 2009), 8; Benjamin G. Rader, *American Sports: From the Age of*

Folk Games to the Age of Televised Sports, 4th ed. (Upper Saddle River, N.J.: Prentice-Hall, 1999), 273.

57. Halberstam, *Breaks of the Game,* 286–87.

58. John Wooden, "What It Takes to Win the Championship," *TV Guide,* March 31–April 6, 1984, n.p.; *NYT,* April 3, 1988; Wooden with Tobin, *They Call Me Coach,* 208–12; *San Diego Evening Tribune,* November 16, 1990.

59. For Wooden's economic plan for the NCAA Tournament, see Wooden with Tobin, *They Call Me Coach,* 212–14.

60. Einhorn with Rapoport, *How March Became Madness,* 17 (see chap. 3, n. 38); *HC,* January 20, 1988.

61. Bisheff, *John Wooden,* xv–xviii (see chap. 1, n. 33); Pat Williams with David Wimbish, *How to Be Like Coach Wooden: Life Lessons from Basketball's Greatest Leader* (Deerfield Beach, Fla.: Health Communications, 2006); Hano, "Winning," 141 (see chap. 3, n. 37); Libby, *The Walton Gang,* 17–18 (see chap. 5, n. 56). In 2009 the *Sporting News* surveyed 118 coaches, former athletes, and sportswriters to determine who was the greatest coach of all time. John Wooden was ranked at the very top. See "Sports 50 Greatest Coaches," *SN,* August 3, 2009, 32–34.

62. Rick Reilly, "A Paragon Rising above the Madness," *SI,* March 20, 2000, n.p.; Rick Reilly, "Wooden Set the Bar High," ESPN.com, June 7, 2010.

63. *NYT,* February 4, 1982; John Akers, untitled article, *Basketball Times,* April 2005, n.p.

64. *Seattle Times,* June 10, 2010.

Index

Abdul-Jabbar, Kareem, x, xi, 138, 243. *See also* Alcindor, Lew

Abdul-Khaalis, Hammas, 138

Ackerman, William, 16

Alcindor, Lew: and Black Power, 76, 84, 98–99, 108; college basketball career, 88–89, 92–98, 100–101, 104–8, 124–26, 148–51; drug use of, 118; and hate mail, 97, 116, 136; high school basketball career, 67–68; and Malcolm X, 98–99, 137; name change of, 138–39; and Olympic boycott movement, 108–9, 112–17, 132, 135–36; political views of, 80–81, 84, 108–9, 111–12, 114–15, 135–36; and racism at UCLA, 83, 99; recruitment by UCLA, 67, 69–71, 77; relationship with Muhammad Ali, 110–13; relationship with Jack Donohue, 73–74; relationship with Sam Gilbert, 99–100, 243, 268; relationship with the press, 71, 76–77, 79–80, 97–98, 114–15; relationship with John Wooden, x, 77, 94, 97, 116, 132; religious views of, 98, 137–38; as

a television attraction, 108, 119, 123, 219, 272–73; views of the civil rights movement, 72–73, 98

"Alcindor Rule," 105–6, 273

Ali, Muhammad, 109–13, 139, 205

Allen, Lucius, 86, 88, 93, 99–101, 112, 125–26, 127, 132, 142; arrest of, 117–18, 139; and marijuana use, 117–18, 139; relationship with Sam Gilbert, 268

Allen, Raymond B., 23

American Basketball Association (ABA), 207, 221–22, 258

American Broadcast Company (ABC), 120

Arnold, Frank, 246

Ashe, Arthur, 69

Athletic Association of Western Universities (AAWU), 24

"Athletic Revolution," xiii, 154, 159–60, 166–67, 173–75, 188, 198–99, 202, 243, 252–53, 261. *See also* Scott, Jack

Atkinson, Byron, 199

Atlantic Coast Conference (ACC), 120, 127

JOHN MATTHEW SMITH is an assistant professor of history at Georgia Tech.

Sport and Society

The University of Illinois Press
is a founding member of the
Association of American University Presses.

———————————————————

Composed in 10.5/15 Adobe Garamond Pro
with Bauhaus Std display
by Celia Shapland
at the University of Illinois Press
Manufactured by Thomson-Shore, Inc.

University of Illinois Press
1325 South Oak Street
Champaign, IL 61820-6903
www.press.uillinois.edu